AF784599

Se...
Bookmarks;
pg: 92-93
pg 126-127
pg 150-151

THE WIL
ESTATE PLA
AND
TRUSTS
LEGAL KIT

Your Complete Legal Guide to Planning for the Future

Douglas E. Godbe
Attorney at Law

SPHINX® PUBLISHING
AN IMPRINT OF SOURCEBOOKS, INC.®
NAPERVILLE, ILLINOIS
www.SphinxLegal.com

Copyright © 2003 by Douglas E. Godbe
Cover and internal design © 2003 by Sourcebooks, Inc®

All rights reserved. No part of this book may be reproduced in any form or by any electronic or mechanical means including information storage and retrieval systems—except in the case of brief quotations embodied in critical articles or reviews—without permission in writing from its publisher, Sourcebooks, Inc.® Purchasers of the book are granted a license to use the forms contained herein for their own personal use. No claim of copyright is made to any official government forms reproduced herein.

First Edition, 2003

Published by: **Sphinx® Publishing, An Imprint of Sourcebooks, Inc.®**

Naperville Office
P.O. Box 4410
Naperville, Illinois 60567-4410
630-961-3900
Fax: 630-961-2168
www.sourcebooks.com
www.SphinxLegal.com

This publication is designed to provide accurate and authoritative information in regard to the subject matter covered. It is sold with the understanding that the publisher is not engaged in rendering legal, accounting, or other professional service. If legal advice or other expert assistance is required, the services of a competent professional person should be sought.

From a Declaration of Principles Jointly Adopted by a Committee of the American Bar Association and a Committee of Publishers and Associations

This product is not a substitute for legal advice.

Disclaimer required by Texas statutes.

Library of Congress Cataloging-in-Publication Data

Godbe, Douglas, 1951-
The wills, estate planning, and trusts legal kit : your complete legal guide to planning for the future / by Douglas E. Godbe.-- 1st ed.
p. cm.
ISBN 1-57248-330-X (pbk.)
1. Estate planning--United States--Popular works. 2. Wills--United States--Popular works. 3. Trusts and trustees--United States--Popular works. I. Title.

KF750.Z9 G63 2003
346.7305'2--dc21

2003014581

Printed and bound in the United States of America.

VHG Paperback — 10 9 8 7 6 5 4 3 2 1

CONTENTS

Using Self-Help Law Books

Before using a self-help law book, you should realize the advantages and disadvantages of doing your own legal work and understand the challenges and diligence that this requires.

The Growing Trend

Rest assured that you won't be the first or only person handling your own legal matter. For example, in some states, more than seventy-five percent of the people in divorces and other cases represent themselves. Because of the high cost of legal services, this is a major trend and many courts are struggling to make it easier for people to represent themselves. However, some courts are not happy with people who do not use attorneys and refuse to help them in any way. For some, the attitude is, "Go to the law library and figure it out for yourself."

We write and publish self-help law books to give people an alternative to the often complicated and confusing legal books found in most law libraries. We have made the explanations of the law as simple and easy to understand as possible. Of course, unlike an attorney advising an individual client, we cannot cover every conceivable possibility.

Cost/Value Analysis

Whenever you shop for a product or service, you are faced with various levels of quality and price. In deciding what product or service to buy, you make a cost/value analysis on the basis of your willingness to pay and the quality you desire.

When buying a car, you decide whether you want transportation, comfort, status, or sex appeal. Accordingly, you decide among such choices as a Neon, a Lincoln, a Rolls Royce, or a Porsche. Before making a decision, you usually weigh the merits of each option against the cost.

When you get a headache, you can take a pain reliever (such as aspirin) or visit a medical specialist for a neurological examination. Given this choice, most people, of course, take a pain reliever, since it costs only pennies; whereas a medical examination costs hundreds of dollars and takes a lot of time. This is usually a logical choice because it is rare to need anything more than a pain reliever for a headache. But in some cases, a headache may indicate a brain tumor and failing to see a specialist right away can result in complications. Should everyone with a headache go to a specialist? Of course not, but people treating their own illnesses must realize that they are betting on the basis of their cost/value analysis of the situation. They are taking the most logical option.

The same cost/value analysis must be made when deciding to do one's own legal work. Many legal situations are very straight forward, requiring a simple form and no complicated analysis. Anyone with a little intelligence and a book of instructions can handle the matter without outside help.

But there is always the chance that complications are involved that only an attorney would notice. To simplify the law into a book like this, several legal cases often must be condensed into a single sentence or paragraph. Otherwise, the book would be several hundred pages long and too complicated for most people. However, this simplification necessarily leaves out many details and nuances that would apply to special or unusual situations. Also, there are many ways to interpret most legal questions. Your case may come before a judge who disagrees with the analysis of our authors.

Therefore, in deciding to use a self-help law book and to do your own legal work, you must realize that you are making a cost/value analysis. You have decided that the money you will save in doing it yourself outweighs the chance that your case will not turn out to your satisfaction. Most people handling their own simple legal matters never have a problem, but occasionally people find that it ended up costing them more to have an attorney straighten out the situation than it would have if they had hired an attorney in the beginning. Keep this in mind while handling your case, and be sure to consult an attorney if you feel you might need further guidance.

Local Rules

The next thing to remember is that a book which covers the law for the entire nation, or even for an entire state, cannot possibly include every procedural difference of every jurisdiction. Whenever possible, we provide the exact form needed; however, in some areas, each county, or even each judge, may require unique forms and procedures. In our state books, our forms usually cover the majority of counties in the state, or provide examples of the type of form which will be required. In our national books, our forms are sometimes even more general in nature but are designed to give a good idea of the type of form that will be needed in most locations. Nonetheless, keep in mind that your state, county, or judge may have a requirement, or use a form, that is not included in this book.

You should not necessarily expect to be able to get all of the information and resources you need solely from within the pages of this book. This book will serve as your guide, giving you specific information whenever possible and helping you to find out what else you will need to know. This is just like if you decided to build your own backyard deck. You might purchase a book on how to build decks. However, such a book would not include the building codes and permit requirements of every city, town, county, and township in the nation; nor would it include the lumber, nails, saws, hammers, and other materials and tools you would need to actually build the deck. You would use the book as your guide, and then do some work and research involving such matters as whether you need a permit of some kind, what type and grade of wood are available in your area, whether to use hand tools or power tools, and how to use those tools.

Before using the forms in a book like this, you should check with your court clerk to see if there are any local rules of which you should be aware, or local forms you will need to use. Often, such forms will require the same information as the forms in the book but are merely laid out differently or use slightly different language. They will sometimes require additional information.

Changes in the Law

Besides being subject to local rules and practices, the law is subject to change at any time. The courts and the legislatures of all fifty states are constantly revising the laws. It is possible that while you are reading this book, some aspect of the law is being changed.

In most cases, the change will be of minimal significance. A form will be redesigned, additional information will be required, or a waiting period will be extended. As a result, you might need to revise a form, file an extra form, or wait out a longer time period; these types of changes will not usually affect the outcome of your case. On the other hand, sometimes a major part of the law is changed, the entire law in a particular area is rewritten, or a case that was the basis of a central legal point is overruled. In such instances, your entire ability to pursue your case may be impaired.

Again, you should weigh the value of your case against the cost of an attorney and make a decision as to what you believe is in your best interest.

Introduction

Estate planning is an essential activity for every individual and couple. It can protect your assets, provide for minor children, and save potentially millions of dollars in taxes. Careful planning can provide peace of mind and ensure maximum wealth transfer at your death. This book can serve as a guide to begin your estate planning, as it contains basic forms that most people can use to accomplish their goals.

The purpose of this book is:

- to describe basic law regarding the disposition of assets by will, by a living trust (called an *inter-vivos trust*), by joint tenancy, and by transfer on death methods (T.O.D.) such as Totten trusts, pension plan beneficiary designations, and life insurance beneficiary designations;

- to guide you through the preparation and execution of a will, a codicil to a will, an inter-vivos trust (and the funding of the inter-vivos trust), an amendment to an inter-vivos trust, and nomination of guardian without a lawyer;

- to advise when you need a lawyer;

- to describe the types of property that pass at death, without a will or inter-vivos trust; and,

- to provide over fifty different blank forms for wills, inter-vivos trusts, codicils, amendments to inter-vivos trust, nomination of guardians etc., and samples of completed forms for wills, inter-vivos trust and nomination of guardian to fit most family situations and estate disposition objectives.

Reading the book and following the instructions will enable you to prepare, (using the fill-in-the-blank included forms) and execute a will, an inter-vivos trust, and a nomination of guardian. This book also warns you of situations when you need to hire an attorney. After reviewing this book you might decide to consult with an attorney either to draft your estate plan or to review the will or inter-vivos trust you have prepared from the forms included in this book. In that event, this book will assist you in determining what your estate planning objectives are and to better under the process when guided by an attorney.

Some estate planners call a will the *wastebasket* of estate planning because, contrary to popular belief, very few assets are disposed of at death under a will. This book will identify what types of property ownership avoids both disposition under a will and *probate* through the court.

This book will explain why the inter-vivos trust has become so popular in the last twenty years. It will give you the information you need to determine if it is appropriate for your situation and estate.

The differences between making outright bequests, leaving someone a *life estate* in an asset, using custodianships for minors, and when to use trusts for the purpose of managing and distributing assets for a beneficiary will be explained. This legal kit will discuss federal estate taxes, state inheritance taxes, and how to plan your estate to minimize or even completely avoid those death taxes.

Twenty-four different wills, two nomination of guardians, ten inter-vivos trusts and more than fifteen other forms are provided for your use. Sample *filled-in* forms and step-by-step forms with instructions will assist you in completing the forms. The will and inter-vivos trust forms included with this book cover four basic family situations: married with children, married without children, unmarried with children, and unmarried without children. Separate forms are provided for the nomination of guardians for minor children.

An asset roadmap form is also provided. It will help you identify assets—both for your own estate planning decisions and to assist the person you appoint to manage your estate after your death. You can use the forms directly from the book, photocopy them or even scan them into your computer.

(The author's experience as an estate planning attorney for over twenty-five years is reflected in both the forms and the text of this book. However, this book does not cover the subjects of generation skipping transfers limitations, qualified charitable unitrusts, or remainder trusts.)

Chapter 1 is a general section that will familiarize you with various terms and concepts in planning your will or inter-vivos trust. It also generally covers estate and inheritance taxes.

Chapter 2 explains the types of assets that are subject to disposition under a will and which assets can be distributed at death without a will.

Chapter 3 discusses some of the differences in estate planning choices. It covers the advantages and disadvantages to assist you in coordinating your estate plan.

Chapter 4 discusses who can be listed as beneficiaries and, as such, who can inherit. Issues related to adult beneficiaries versus beneficiaries who are still minors and persons who are *disqualified* to inherit due to relationship to the testator are also discussed.

Chapter 5 discusses the various types of bequests that can be made. It discusses the advantages and disadvantages of outright bequests, bequests for the lifetime use of the beneficiary (life estates), bequests to minors (custodianships and trusts instead of guardianships), and bequests in trust for a beneficiary's lifetime.

Chapter 6 discusses how to select an executor to probate your will. It also explains how to select an administrator for your estate, a trustee to administer your inter-vivos trust, or a trust created under your will or inter-vivos trust after your death for the benefit of the trust's beneficiaries when a outright bequest is not appropriate, and a guardian to care for your orphaned children.

Chapter 7 discusses the formalities necessary to properly execute your will or inter-vivos trust, discusses how to be sure your will or inter-vivos trust is preserved during your lifetime and not destroyed after your death, and explains the formalities necessary to revoke your will or inter-vivos trust.

Chapter 8 discusses the legal requirements necessary to properly execute an amendment to your will or inter-vivos trust.

Chapter 9 details the various paragraphs of the will, including the introductory paragraph, the declaration of family status, the disposition of assets, and the nomination of executors, as well as the *boilerplate* provisions.

It also details the various paragraphs of the inter-vivos trust including the rights reserved to the settlors (right to amend and revoke the inter-vivos trust and to receive, during their lifetime, the benefits from the inter-vivos trust), the disposition of assets after the death of the settlor of one of the settlors (including the creation of exemption and marital deduction trusts), and the nomination of trustees as well as the *boilerplate* provisions.

At the end of this book you will find a Glossary of the terms used in this book. Appendix A discusses the issue of *forced share* statutes throughout the states that require that a surviving spouse be entitled to a specified portion of a decedent's estate. Included in Appendix A is an abbreviated statement as to the laws of each state and a listing of each state's applicable statutes covering that issue. Appendix B provides an asset roadmap form to list your property for your executor and family. Appendix C provides step-by-step instructions to complete and execute all of the blank forms as well as several sample complete forms. Appendix D provides over fifty fill-in-the-blank forms, including forms for wills, a codicil, inter-vivos trusts, amendments to trust, and revocation of trust.

I AN OVERVIEW

Before preparing your will or drafting your trust, it is helpful to review some of the fundamentals of estate planning, and to ask yourself a couple of questions. This chapter will explore the basics of what the key documents are and assist you in determining which is best for you.

What is a Will?

A *will* is a written document that disposes of a person's property effective at the death of that person. To be valid, a will must be signed by the person, called the *testator*, whose property it affects.

What is a Trust?

The term *trust* refers to an arrangement where one person holds legal title to property for the benefit of another person. For example, Bob holds title to 1,000 shares of IBM stock, as "Trustee" for Mary. The written trust document provides that trust income is paid to Mary. Bob would pay the IBM stock dividends to Mary. There are many kinds of trusts for many different reasons. However, the trust which is oftentimes used as a will substitute is generally called a *grantor trust*, a *revocable trust*, a *living trust*, or an *inter-vivos trust*. This book will refer to such a trust as an *inter-vivos trust*. An inter-vivos trust permits property to be distributed at death without the requirement of *probate*.

What is Probate?

Assets that Must be Probated

Probate is the court supervision of the distribution of the *assets* of a deceased person to his or her *beneficiaries* or *heirs*. Probate exists because there is no other way to change the *title* to assets from the deceased person's name to the persons entitled under his or her will. If there is no will, his or her heirs by *interstate succession*.

Assets Not Probated

As a simple guideline, all assets of the decedent must go through probate unless the law specifically provides otherwise. However, most property that belonged to a deceased person does not go through probate because the exceptions to probate are numerous.

Most property never goes through the probate process due to the many exceptions to probate. Assets that do not pass through probate include:

- assets where the title lists the decedent and at least one living person as joint tenants;
- (in some states) assets passing outright to a surviving spouse (does not include property passing to a trust for the benefit of a surviving spouse);
- bank accounts where the title is in the decedent's name "As Trustee For" or "In Trust For" a living person (a Totten trust);
- brokerage accounts where the title is in the decedent's name with the designation "Transfer on Death" to a living person;
- bank accounts or savings bonds where the title is in the name of the decedent with the instruction to pay on death to a living person;

- assets where the title is in the name of the decedent as the trustee of an inter-vivos trust;
- assets belonging to the decedent wherein the decedent, by contract, designated a *beneficiary* or payee in the event of death such as a pension plan, an IRA, a 401(k) plan, or life insurance and the beneficiary survived the decedent; and,
- assets where the title is in the name of the decedent, but have a small gross value (the actual amount varies from state to state).

NOTE: *A decedent often leaves both assets that can be transferred at his or her death without probate and assets that must be transferred via a probate process.*

Finding the Law

The law, itself, is found primarily in the *Probate Code* for each state. Each state's Probate Code can be purchased in most law bookstores for about $25 and are generally available at several Internet websites. A good way to find the statutes in your state is to use a search engine and type in name of your state's code as found in Appendix A (i.e., the Arizona Revised Statutes Annotated + probate.)

Community Property

In Arizona, California, Idaho, Louisiana, New Mexico, Nevada, Oregon, Texas, Washington, Wisconsin, and Wyoming, property is either *separate property* or *community property*. *Separate property* are the assets of a single, divorced, or widowed person. The assets of a married person that were acquired before marriage or after marriage by gift or inheritance are also described as separate property.

Although the laws differ from state to state, *community property* is generally defined as property acquired during marriage by a married person, unless acquired by gift or inheritance.

In most community property states, the income from separate property is also separate property, but this can be modified depending on the time and efforts expended by one or both of the spouse's in maintaining the property.

Example: The wife, at the time of marriage, owns a successful retail store. During the marriage, she expends considerable time and expertise on the business; takes a very small salary; puts most of the profits back into the business; and, expands to a chain of one hundred retail stores. At her death, her business might be considered to be partly community property as her community property *efforts* were put back into the business.

Further, in community property states, the separate property of one spouse can be commingled with community property to the extent that the separate property is no longer traceable and becomes community property.

NOTE: *In some community property states, community property may be held in the name of only* one *of the spouses.*

Another aspect of community property is that each spouse may generally transfer, at his or her death, his or her one-half interest in any community property asset to someone other than the *surviving spouse*. The surviving spouse's one-half interest in the community property, regardless of the disposition made by the predeceased spouse, is not affected by the predeceasing spouse's disposition of his or her one-half interest in the community property.

Community property can only exist during the marriage. At the moment of the death of either spouse, the property then becomes separate property—one-half owned by the deceased spouse and one-half owned by the surviving spouse. Any property inherited from the deceased spouse by the surviving spouse becomes the separate property of the surviving spouse.

Marital Property

In noncommunity property states, property acquired during the marriage is generally referred to as *marital property*. While the distinction between community property and separate property is important, community property and marital property is essentially the same thing. (This book will use the term community property throughout when referring to property acquired during the marriage with each spouse owning a one-half interest.)

Quasi-Community Property

Quasi-community property is recognized in a few community property states such as California. It is property acquired by a married person who dies a resident of the community property state, while owning property acquired while he or she was living outside of the community property state. Further, at the time of death, that property would have to have been community property, if the person had been living in the community property state at the time the property was acquired. In such a situation, the quasi-community property is treated like community property.

Estate and Inheritance Taxes

There can be federal estate taxes regardless of how a decedent's assets are passed (i.e., under will, living trust/inter-vivos trust, joint tenancy, pensions, life insurance proceeds, etc.) or whether or not a decedent's assets pass through a probate.

A federal estate tax can apply in all situations where a decedent's assets have a net value of over $1,000,000, for assets passing to someone other than a surviving spouse or a qualified charity. There are also certain requirements on how the assets are left to the surviving spouse if he or she is not a U.S. citizen. Accordingly, if a decedent has an estate worth $9,000,000 and he or she leaves $6,000,000 to his or her spouse, $2,000,000 to a qualified charity, and $1,000,000 to his or her best friend, there would be no federal estate tax as the bequests to the spouse and qualified charity would be exempt from taxation. The $1,000,000 to the friend would be equal to the $1,000,000 exemption.

However, if the same decedent instead left $5,000,000 to his or her spouse, $2,000,000 to a qualified charity, and $2,000,000 to the friend, then the taxable estate, after the $1,000,000 exemption amount, would be $1,000,000. The federal estate tax would be about $420,000. (The federal estate tax, after the $1,000,000 exemption amount, starts at 39% and goes up.)

NOTE: *The federal estate tax exemption amount increases from $1,000,000 to $1,500,000 for decedent's dying in 2004 with scheduled increases through the year 2009. In 2010, the federal estate tax will be abolished for that year. In 2011, the federal estate tax will return with a new exemption amount of $1,000,0000.*

(The federal estate tax has been a political football for the last few years. Depending on the health of the economy and who controls Congress over the next few years, the federal estate tax laws may change substantially.)

State Death Taxes

Only a few years ago, nearly all states imposed their own *death taxes*, generally called *inheritance taxes*. In some states, the death tax is based upon the amount passing to each beneficiary or heir. In other states, the death tax, like the federal estate tax, is based on the size of the estate of the deceased person rather than who receives the estate assets. However, now, only sixteen states impose a death tax. They are: Connecticut, Indiana, Iowa, Kentucky, Louisiana, Maryland, Mississippi, Montana, Nebraska, New Hampshire, New Jersey, New York, Ohio, Pennsylvania, South Dakota, and Tennessee.

Do You Need a Lawyer?

You can, of course, hire a lawyer to provide estate tax planning advice and prepare the estate planning documents such as a will or inter-vivos trust. If this is your preference, this book will help you follow what the lawyer is doing and intelligently communicate your desires.

Beware of solicitations from non-lawyers who wish to sell a product, such as an *annuity*, in conjunction with estate planning services, such as an inter-vivos trust. Usually their main goal is the sales commission that goes with the product sale, not the achievement of an appropriate estate plan for you.

It is strongly recommended that you hire a lawyer in the following circumstances.

- The will or inter-vivos trust is likely to be contested; i.e., if you believe that someone may attack the will or any of its provisions after the death of the testator or *settlor*.

- The estate of the testator's or settlor's exceeds one million dollars ($1,000,000). (Although the forms contained in this book are appropriate for an estate of that size or larger, it makes good sense to consult with an attorney to review other estate planning options that are beyond the scope of this book.)

- The testator's or settlor's assets are complicated, such as a sole proprietorship or partnership business interest. (Again, although the forms contained in this book are appropriate for persons who own business interests, it simply makes sense to discuss those issues with an attorney to review estate planning options that are outside the scope of this book.)

- The testator or settlor wishes to leave property to a *disqualified person* such as a caregiver or other person who has a *fiduciary relationship* with the *testator* or *settlor*. (See Chapter 4 for a discussion of disqualified persons.)

- There are questions about the mental capacity of the testator to sign his or her will or the capacity of the settlor to execute his or her inter-vivos trust.

Finding a Lawyer

Many states certify lawyers as specialists in estate planning. Your State Bar Association or local County Bar Association can give you a list of the certified specialists in your area. A lawyer becomes a certified specialist by proof of experience in the area of certification and passing a test. It is no secret that lawyers who are knowledgeable in one area of the law may not know much about another area. It makes good sense to get a specialist.

If your state does not certify a specialist, the organizations listed above can still be of assistance in finding appropriate counsel. As with the choice of anyone you hire, a personal interview, references, costs, and a general feeling of being comfortable with the person are your guidelines.

2 ASSETS

Not all property that a person owns is actually subject to disposition at their death by a will. This chapter discusses which assets are disposed of at death via a will and which assets are disposed of at death outside of the will—regardless of the terms of the will. There is a common misperception that all of a person's assets are disposed of by his or her will. In fact, most property passes title at death without a will—regardless of the provisions of a will.

Assets Subject to Disposition by a Will

Assets that can be disposed of by a will include:

- property held in the name of the *decedent only* without any designation on the title of the asset such as *T.O.D.* (transfer on death), *P.O.D.* (payable on death), or "as Trustee" (trust);

> ***Warning:*** If the decedent is married and the property in his or her name only is community property, then the decedent can only dispose of his or her one-half interest in that property. Simply because only one spouse is listed on the title does not necessarily mean that asset is separate property.

Example: Property with the written title of "Bob" or "Bob, a single man," are examples of property held in the name of one person only.

- property held by one person, another without any designation on the title, or as *tenants in common;*

Example 1: Property has the written title of "Bob and Mary." In that event, as no type of title is indicated, the law presumes that Bob and Mary are tenants in common, meaning that each owns a separate property interest in the property.

Example 2: Property has the written title of "Bob and Mary, as tenants-in-common." Bob and Mary are tenants-in-common, meaning that each owns a separate property interest in the property.

NOTE: *If the separate property interest is not identified (i.e., such as a 25% interest), the law presumes they own the property as equal tenants-in-common—50% each.*

- property held by a person and his or her spouse as "husband and wife," or as "community property." (In this situation, each spouse can dispose of only his or her one-half community property interest by will); and,
- one-half of property held in the name of the person's spouse if that property is community property.

Example: Property has the written title of "Mary." The property is community property of Mary and her spouse, Bob. Bob can, by his will, dispose of his one-half community property interest.

Property *Subject* to Disposition in a Will, but Passing without Probate to a Surviving Spouse

In some states, any property left *outright* to a surviving spouse either by will or by interstate succession, passes *without* a probate. The estate could be $10,000,000, and if the deceased spouse's will says "all to my spouse," there is no probate in those states. However, if there are any restrictions on the use of the property passing to the surviving spouse, i.e., a bequest to a spouse "in trust," or to a "spouse for her lifetime use," then the property is not passing *outright* to the surviving spouse, and the property is subject to probate

NOTE: *Remember, the community property interest of a surviving spouse does not pass to the surviving spouse as a result of the death of the predeceasing spouse as the surviving spouse owned it all along.*

Small Estate Distribution

Many states permit *small estates* (definition differs from state to state) to distribute without formal probate. For example, in California, a small estate is under $100,000 after you subtract all joint tenancies, tenancies by the entirety, property passing by contract, P.O.D.'s, T.O.D.'s, Totten trusts, and property passing without probate to a surviving spouse that otherwise would go through probate, but may pass and be distributed to the beneficiary or heir without a formal probate in court.

Small estate distribution procedures are designed to be much simpler and quicker than a complete probate. They are also intended to be a less costly way to change title to assets and pass the property of a decedent to the intended recipients.

Assets *Not Subject* to Disposition by a Will and Passing without Probate

Most property passes title at death without a will (or, regardless of the provisions of a will) and without a probate. Even when there is a probate proceeding, much of the decedent's estate will pass outside of the probate process. The reason the property described in this chapter passes without a will is due to the type of *title vesting* that the property was held before the death of a person or due to a contract covering the distribution of the property on the death of the decendent.

Example: Property has the written title of "Bob and Mary, as joint tenants." That property title is vested in Bob and Mary as joint tenants.

Joint Tenancy

Joint tenancy may be the most common way that title to property passes at death without the need of a will and without the need of probate. Property can be held in the names of two or more persons as joint tenants.

Most states require that title to joint tenancy property be in writing. Sometimes the initials "JTWROS," *joint tenants with right of survivorship,* is used to designate joint tenancy property.

Example: Property with a written title "Bob and Mary, as joint tenants" or "Bob and Mary, husband and wife, JTWROS" is joint tenancy property. Property with a written title "Bob and Mary as husband and wife" or "Bob and Mary as tenants in common" is not joint tenancy property.

Title to joint tenancy property at the death of one of the joint tenant passes to the surviving joint tenants. Accordingly, all the surviving joint tenant has to do to acquire the decedent joint tenant's interest is to survive the deceased joint tenant.

Warning: Community property held in joint tenancy between a deceased spouse and someone other than the surviving spouse is, at the death of the deceased spouse, subject to the community property interest claim of the surviving spouse. The deceased spouse did not have the right to dispose of the surviving spouse's community property interest in the joint tenancy property. In this event contact a lawyer.

NOTE: *Property held in joint tenancy is equally owned by each joint tenant. If a parent deeds his residence to himself and his child as joint tenants, the child becomes a one-half owner of the property. Even if the parent is still living, the creditors of that child could attach the residence or the child could demand the residence be sold and the proceeds equally divided. In addition, most transfers into joint tenancy are considered gifts for federal gift tax purposes, except when the asset is a bank account or the joint tenants are spouses.*

Tenancy by the Entirety

Tenancy by the entirety is a title used in some states as a method of holding title between *spouses*. Tenancy by the entirety is like joint tenancy in that title to property passes at death without the need of a will and without the need of a probate.

Example: Property with a written title "Bob and Mary, by tenancy by the entirety" passes at death without the need of a will and probate.

The title to tenancy by the entirety property passes at the death of one of the spouses to the surviving spouse. Accordingly, all the surviving spouse has to do to acquire the decedent spouse's interest, is survive the predeceasing spouse.

P.O.D. and T.O.D. Accounts

Most states permit *Payable on Death (P.O.D.)* and *Transfer on Death (T.O.D.)* bank and/or brokerage accounts that transfer title at death of the owner of the account without a will (and regardless of the provisions of the will). Of course, the account must be held in the name of the owner with the designation "payable on death" or "transfer on death." The difference between joint tenancy and a P.O.D. or T.O.D. account is that the beneficiary of the P.O.D. or T.O.D. account has no rights to the property until the death of the owner. Whereas, a joint tenant is, legally, an equal co-owner of the property before the death of the other joint tenant.

> ***Warning:*** If someone other than the surviving spouse is the named beneficiary of a P.O.D. or T.O.D. account, the surviving spouse has a claim for his or her community property interest in the account, if the account was community property. In this event, contact a lawyer.

Contractual Accounts

Life insurance, annuities, pensions, individual retirement accounts (IRAs), and private retirement accounts are all examples of property that passes at death based upon a contract, and not pursuant to the provisions in a will. The owner of the contract (the insured, the annuitant, the owner, or the employee in essence *contracts* with the insurer, employer, or plan administrator, to pay the benefits, property, or proceeds to a beneficiary designated as the recipient in the event of his or her death.

In the event the insured, annuitant, employee, or owner of the property fails to designate a beneficiary, some contracts will designate a *default* beneficiary, such as the spouse, children, etc. At the death of the insured, annuitant, owner, or employee, the beneficiary need only execute the appropriate claim forms, and submit a certified copy of decedent's death certificate to claim the benefits, property, or proceeds.

> ***Warning:*** Where the contractual property benefits are community property, or the premiums that paid for the benefits were community property, and someone other than the surviving spouse is the named beneficiary of the benefits or property, then the surviving spouse has a claim for his or her community property interest in the benefits or property. In that event, contact a lawyer.

Totten Trust Accounts

In many states, a financial institution account can be held in the name of an individual "as trustee for,"or "in trust for" a named beneficiary. In this situation, the *trustee* (who is legally the owner of the account) has created a *mini* revocable trust for the account commonly called a *Totten Trust.* In the event of the death of the account owner, the named beneficiary becomes the owner of the account without the need of a probate.

If the account is held in the name of two persons as joint tenants "as trustees for" or "in trust for" a named beneficiary and one of the account owners dies, the surviving account owner, as the surviving joint tenant, owns all of the account and can revoke the account and/or change the named beneficiary.

> ***Warning:*** Where the Totten trust account contains community property and someone other than the surviving spouse of the account holder is the named beneficiary, the surviving spouse of the account holder has a claim for his or her community property interest in the account. In this event, contact a lawyer.

Property titled in the name of an inter-vivos trust or property in a living trust with the settlor (the person that created and transferred the property to the trust) and the trustee (the one who administers and manages the trust property) being the same person, is not subject to probate. The title to property in a living trust might read something like: "John Smith, Trustee of the Smith Family Trust dated 4/2/03."

One of the main purposes of creating a living trust is to avoid probate. Upon the death of the settlor, the trustee (often a successor trustee as the settlor is usually the trustee until he or she dies) administers and distributes the living trust estate pursuant to the written instructions in the living trust document. The will of the settlor cannot dispose of the property held by the trust, as title to the property in the trust is held by the trust.

Inter-Vivos Trust

In some states, if the settlor declares in his or her inter-vivos trust that certain property is part of the inter-vivos trust, but fails to actually change the title of the property to the name of the inter-vivos trust, a simple action can be brought in the probate court to have such property declared to be part of the inter-vivos trust. In this event, a lawyer should be consulted.

3 Deciding Which Plan Best Meets Your Goals

There is no *one size fits all* in planning your estate. A blanket statement that an inter-vivos trust is the answer to all situation is just as ridiculous as a statement that a will is the best solution in all cases. You need to weigh many different factors in deciding how to structure your estate plan. In addition, you need to realize that nearly all estates are passed at death in several different ways, for example, by joint tenancy, by will, by contract, and so on. It is important to understand and coordinate your *total* estate plan.

Coordinating Your Estate Plan

Before preparing a will or inter-vivos trust, it is a good idea, using the Asset Roadmap in Appendix B of this book, to list your assets and the manner that you hold title to the assets. Remembering that assets held in joint tenancy, tenancy by the entirety, T.O.D., P.O.D., Totten trusts, inter-vivos trusts, pension plans, IRAs, 401(k)'s, life insurance and annuities will pass to your intended beneficiary at death without a will, and without a probate. Knowing what your assets are, and how they are titled, might affect your decision to create a will or inter-vivos trust, or the terms of it. Further, you may also decide to change the title to assets you own in your name alone to some other method to permit transfer at your death without a will and without probate.

Example: Rather than holding your brokerage account in the name of "Bob," have the brokerage firm change the title to "Bob, Transfer on Death to Mary." That way Mary would receive the assets at your death without probate and regardless of any contrary provisions in your Will.

> ***Warning:*** Creating a *joint tenancy* title is not recommended for property that you own in your name only as the other joint tenant becomes a one-half owner of the property during your lifetime.

In fact, if your assets are relatively simple you might be able to develop a plan that passes ALL of your estate at your death without the need of will or inter-vivos trust.

Example: Bob's estate consists of a stock brokerage account, his 401(k) pension plan and $200,000 in life insurance. Bob wants to leave all of his estate to his two adult daughters, Ellen and Sue. Bob could avoid probate, and the necessity of a will or inter-vivos trust, simply by changing the title to his brokerage account to "Bob, T.O.D. (transfer on death) to Ellen and Sue," and naming Ellen and Sue as the beneficiaries on his 401k pension plan and life insurance.

You may, after considering all of your assets, conclude that you are going to utilize joint tenancy, contractual beneficiary designations *along* with an inter-vivos trust and/or a will to have what is referred to as a *blended estate plan*.

A will allows you to direct the disposition of property you own that does not pass by joint tenancy, contract, or inter-vivos trust. The advantage of a will, instead of an inter-vivos trust, is that a will is a relatively simple document that can be signed and put into a safe place until your death.Unlike the inter-vivos trust there is no need to *fund* a will. The disadvantage of the will is that it must be probated. However, in many cases the will is the best alternative because of its simplicity and the fact that the court supervises the disposition of assets through the probate process.

Inter-Vivos Trusts

The primary purpose for the inter-vivos trust is to avoid a court supervised probate. The inter-vivos trust can act as a will substitute by holding title to your assets during your lifetime. Accordingly, upon your death, because the inter-vivos trust holds title to your property (instead of you), a probate court need not become involved to issue court orders changing title to your assets from your name, to the names of your estate beneficiaries. During your lifetime, your inter-vivos trust can be *amendable*, *revocable* and entirely for your benefit. Upon your death, your inter-vivos trust may terminate, or may continue, in trust, for the benefit of your beneficiaries.

Since the assets held by the inter-vivos trust are managed by the trustee (usually yourself), if you become incapacitated during your lifetime, the assets in your inter-vivos trust can then be managed for your benefit by the successor trustee you have selected. This avoids the need of setting a court supervised *conservatorship* or *guardianship* proceeding.

Although inter-vivos trust have been available and used for generations, they have only become commonplace in the past twenty-five years for several reasons.

- Before the late 1980's, preparation of the inter-vivos trust, by typewriter, was prohibitively expensive. An inter-vivos trust is a lengthy document and most people were not inclined to pay for the labor intensive costs associated with it.

- Attorneys began to advertise about 25 years ago. The inter-vivos trust, as a *product*, lends itself well to legal advertising.

- In the early 1980's the IRS stopped the requirement that inter-vivos trusts, during the lifetime of the settlors use a tax identification number, and file a separate income tax return (form 1041).

- In 1981, Congress passed extensive legislation in the federal estate tax law that made the use of an inter-vivos trust more attractive.

Advantages

Some of the advantages of an inter-vivos trust include:

- avoids probate;

- less expensive to administer at death than an estate passing through probate;

NOTE: *However, the trustee often still needs the assistance of a lawyer to assist and advise in the distribution of the inter-vivos trust assets. Generally speaking, there should be a savings in administration costs at death if the inter-vivos trust estate is over $300,000, the assets are relatively uncomplicated, the trustee is relatively sophisticated, and the beneficiaries are reasonable.*

- a private document, whereas probate records are open to the public. In most states, however, the inter-vivos trust terms must be disclosed to the beneficiaries and heirs of the settlor. In other states, the trustee need not disclose the terms of the inter-vivos trust unless ordered to do so by the court;

- convenient for some planning. For example, if you have an estate in excess of $1,000,000 (after 2003 the threshold amount will be $1,500,000), and you want to utilize the concepts of a *decedent's trust* (see discussion following regarding decedent's trust) at your death, then the inter-vivos trust is a convenient method to implement your plan; and,

- avoids probate in multiple states. While all of your *personal property* is probated in the state of your residence (regardless of where it is located), real property must be probated in the state in which it is located. An inter-vivos trust avoids the need for probate in each state where the settler owned real property.

Disadvantages

Some of the disadvantages of an inter-vivos trust include:

- adds a layer of complexity. After you execute your will, you can simply place it in a safe place and forget about it. With an inter-vivos trust, the execution is only the first step. After you execute your inter-vivos trust you have to *fund* the inter-vivos trust with your assets. Assets not funded in your inter-vivos trust may not avoid probate. Furthermore, every time you acquire a new asset you must be careful to take title in the name of your inter-vivos trust. The more your assets change, (i.e., the more you buy and sell assets) the more complicated this becomes;

- funding involves executing new deeds to all of your real property and arranging for the change of the title to personal property from your name to the name as *trustee* of your inter-vivos trust;

Example: Instead of owning your house as "Bob Jones, a single man" the new deed might read "Bob Jones, Trustee of the Bob Jones Trust dated 4/30/03."

- not court-supervised, and thus a trustee's dishonesty or mistakes are less likely to be discovered;
- not filed with the court and may, therefore, be misplaced and unavailable in the future; and,
- may be more expensive than a probate if the assets are complicated and/or the trustees and beneficiaries do not get along well.

In sum, if you have five children, two of whom are minors, who all hate each other, and your estate contains a myriad of assets with a total value of under $300,000, forget the inter-vivos trust. On the other hand, if you have $1,000,000, all of which is in your personal residence, and have two adult children who get along well, use the inter-vivos trust.

Funding Your Inter-Vivos Trust

Funding your inter-vivos trust is essential. *Funding* means to transfer the title of your assets to your name or names as trustees of your inter-vivos trust. For example: "Bob Jones and Mary Jones, Trustees of the Bob Jones and Mary Jones Trust dated April 2, 2003." Assets *not* funded in the inter-vivos trust do *not* avoid probate.

Not all assets need to be transferred. You do not transfer:

- pension and retirement plans;
- stock options;
- life insurance;

- annuities; or,

- T.O.D. accounts (joint tenancies) if you are comfortable with their disposal at death.

As to pension and retirement plans, life insurance, annuities and T.O.D. accounts you merely need to designate your inter-vivos trust as a beneficiary.

NOTE: *If you are married you generally, for income tax deferral purposes, want to name your spouse as the primary beneficiary on all retirement accounts or pensions. However, your inter-vivos trust can be the alternate beneficiary of those assets.*

When naming your inter-vivos trust as such a beneficiary the designation should read, as an example: "The Trustee of the Bob Jones Trust dated 2 April 2003, to hold, administer and distribute as to the terms of said trust."

Real Estate

Transferring real estate is very tricky. Each state has its own particular rules. You need to hire someone who is a professional to prepare the deeds to transfer your real estate to your inter-vivos trust. If you decide to do it yourself, contact your local county recorder to find out what deed forms are used in your county and if any additional forms need to be filed with the deed. For example, in California you are required to file a *Preliminary Change of Ownership Report* with any deed to be recorded.

You must list the *grantors* on the deed to transfer your real property to your inter-vivos trust exactly as they are listed on the current deed as *grantees*. For example: The deed to your house lists you as "Bob Jones, a single man." On the new deed do not list the grantor as "Robert Jones, a married man" but rather as "Bob Jones, a married man who took title as a single man." Also, be sure to take the current title vesting and legal description from the actual current deed, not from a mortgage, deed of trust, or property tax bill, as they can differ from the current deed.

Some lenders in some states consider your transfer of real estate to your inter-vivos trust to be a *transfer* that accelerates the *due on sale* provision of your mortgage. To determine your options and avoid problems, check with your lender or use an experienced attorney in your area to handle this chore.

Personal Property With personal property that has a written title, you need to change title to the name of your inter-vivos trust.

With stocks and bonds you need to contact the transfer agent for the security and follow their instructions for re-titling the securities (it is much easier to first place the securities into a brokerage account street account first, and then simply change the entire account).

For bank and brokerage accounts you simply give the brokerage a written instruction to transfer the account to your inter-vivos trust and provide them with either a copy of your inter-vivos trust (not a good idea) or a notarized *Trust Certification* (a summary of your inter-vivos trust minus a description of who gets what when you die). Many brokerage houses and banks now require that you use their *Trust Certification form.* Included with this book are two forms of a **TRUST CERTIFICATION.** (see form 48, p.358 and form 49, p.359.)

For *limited partnership interests* you need to contact the general partner and request what information he or she will need to transfer your interest to your inter-vivos trust. Unless you have very expensive cars or boats, do not bother with transferring them to your inter-vivos trust.

Do not place your checking account in your inter-vivos trust unless you carry a very large balance in the account. If you do transfer your checking account to your inter-vivos trust do not have the name of your inter-vivos trust imprinted on the face of your checks. Identify fraud is easier with a trust than with a person.

Promissory Notes Execute an **ASSIGNMENT** of the note from your name to the name of your inter-vivos trust. (see form 53, p.363.)

Tangible Personal Property Some lawyers have their clients sign assignments wherein all of their personal, tangible property is assigned to their inter-vivos trust. However, such an assignment is likely not effective to tangible, personal property acquired after the date of the assignment. It might be better to simply dispose of that type of property via your *pourover will.*

Using a Will to Create a Trust at Your Death

The following material describes situations when a will is used to *create* a trust, and provides some useful information regarding these situations.

Testamentary Trust

A *testamentary trust* is a trust created by a will. By definition, it has no effect until the death of the testator of the will. Testamentary trusts are used for several reasons such as protecting assets from creditors, maximizing estate tax savings, and controlling how your estate is distributed.

Couples with Young Children

Often couples with young children select an estate plan like the will forms in this book (each spouse leaves all of his or her estate to the other spouse), but if there is no surviving spouse then everything goes into a *testamentary trust* for the benefit of their minor children. In that event, the spouses name the surviving spouse as the beneficiary of T.O.D., P.O.D. assets or contractual assets such as annuities, retirement plans or life insurance, by name, as an example, "The Trustee of the Trust created under my Will dated 2 April 1999, to be held, administered and distributed per the terms of said Trust" as the alternate beneficiary. By naming the testamentary trust created for their children in their wills as the alternate beneficiary there will be no probate of those life insurance or pension proceeds on the death of the surviving spouse even though the proceeds pass to the trustee of the testamentary trust.

Tax Planning

Decedent's Trust

As mentioned in Chapter 1, the federal estate tax law exempts the first $1,000,000 of your estate from the federal estate tax when you die. Your estate includes all assets in which you have an ownership interest, including such things as life insurance, pensions, joint tenancy properties, and all gifts you made since 1976 that exceeded the federal annual gift tax exemption amount ($10,000-$11,000 per year per gift recipient).

If you own, at your death in 2003, assets worth $2,000,000 for federal estate tax purposes and you want to leave everything to your children, then the first $1,000,000 will pass federal estate tax free, and the remaining $1,000,000 will have a federal estate tax of about $440,000 taken. However, if you are married you have options to avoid paying this tax. For purposes of illustration we will assume that your spouse has no assets.

Option 1. Leave everything to your spouse. Anything left to a surviving spouse is federal estate tax free. The problem is that upon your spouse's subsequent death he or she now owns the $2,000,000 in assets and your children pay $440,000 in federal estate taxes.

Option 2. Leave $1,000,000 of your estate to your spouse and $1,000,000 directly to your children. The $1,000,000 you leave your children passes federal estate tax free, and the $1,000,000 your spouse receives is also federal estate tax free. At your spouse's subsequent death your children can then receive his or her $1,000,000 estate free from federal estate taxes also.

Option 3. However, you may not wish to leave the $1,000,000 to your children before the death of your surviving spouse as you might wish to provide for your surviving spouse first. Leave $1,000,000 to a Decedent's Trust (there is no magic to the name *Decedent's Trust*—sometimes it is called the *Tax Credit Trust* or the *Credit Shelter Trust* or the *By-Pass Trust*). Although you can have any terms you want as to the distribution to beneficiaries from the decedent's trust, the inter-vivos trust forms in this book provide for the decedent's trust to pay all of its income to your surviving spouse as well as pay principal from the decedent's trust necessary for the support of your surviving spouse in his or her accustomed manner of living. Because your surviving spouse is not, for federal estate tax purposes, the owner of the decedent's trust, the decedent's trust will not be part of his or her estate when he or she later dies and can pass, federal estate tax free, to your children.

In this option you leave the other $1,000,000 of your estate to your surviving spouse. At his or her subsequent death that $1,000,000 can also pass to your children federal estate tax free. By using this option, your surviving spouse has the use of *all* of your estate when you die and your children save $440,000 in federal estate taxes. What you essentially did was not *waste* the federal estate tax exemption available at the death of the predeceasing spouse. This third option permitted each spouse to *fully* utilize his or her federal estate tax exemption.

Marital Trust

In each of the three options above the predeceasing spouse left at least $1,000,000 to the surviving spouse *outright* (outright means without any strings attached). Sometimes it is not prudent to leave assets to a surviving spouse outright. For example, the surviving spouse is not the parent of your children and you are concerned that he or she will bequeath whatever you leave that spouse to his or her relatives and exclude your children or other relatives. Or it may be that your surviving spouse is a *spendthrift* (loose with money) or has significant money judgments or the potential of significant creditors who could claim the money. If your estate is in excess of the federal tax law exemption amount, you can leave a portion, or all of that excess into a marital trust.

A marital trust, sometimes called a *QTIP* trust, must:

- be for the benefit of a surviving spouse;
- pay all of its income to the surviving spouse; and,
- give the surviving spouse the right to require the trustee to convert any non-income producing assets in the marital trust to income producing assets.

The federal estate tax on the marital trust assets is deferred until the death of your surviving spouse. The marital trust assets are added to the estate of your surviving spouse, and if he or she does not have other assets that fully use up his or her federal estate tax exemption, the marital trust assets use the remainder of the federal estate tax exemption.

Example: Husband leaves estate of $1,800,000 with $1,000,000 in a decedent's trust and $800,000 in a marital trust. At wife's death in 2004 (federal estate tax exemption in year 2004 is $1,500,000), the marital trust is worth $800,000 and the wife leaves $700,000 of her own assets at death. As the wife's estate of $700,000 leaves $800,000 of her federal estate tax exemption remaining, the marital trust assets of $800,000 are then passed, federal estate tax free, to the persons directed by the predeceasing husband.

Non-Tax Advantages of Decedent's Trusts and Marital Trusts

There are non-tax advantages that sometimes are significant enough to employ the decedent's trust or marital trust even if the estate under the federal estate tax exemption. First, as discussed above, use of a decedent's trust or a marital trust, like any trust you create for the lifetime benefit of another, permits you to direct the eventual distributions of assets you left for the benefit of your spouse, after his or her death. This prevents the surviving spouse from lavishing the assets upon his or her new boyfriend, girlfriend, or new spouse.

Second, the assets in trust are protected from the creditors of your spouse if you utilize, a spendthrift clause in the trust, as is provided in all forms in this book that create trusts. Third, for larger estates, there is usually a probate cost savings by using an inter-vivos trust.

Inter-vivos Trusts and the Pourover Will

If you decide to use an inter-vivos trust, you still need to also execute a *pour-over will* to dispose of your tangible, personal property, and any assets that you have not effectively transferred to your inter-vivos trust by time of death.

Example: You believe you have effectively transferred title/ownership of everything you own to your inter-vivos trust. You buy a winning lottery ticket and suffer a fatal heart attack upon learning of your new found riches. The lottery proceeds were not, before your death, transferred to your inter-vivos trust. There will likely be a probate of those lottery proceeds. Your pourover will (forms 21–24) provide that the lottery proceeds would be distributed, after probate, to your inter-vivos trust.

Final Caution

When preparing your will or inter-vivos trust consider the total inheritance of each beneficiary based both upon what that beneficiary receives under your will and/or inter-vivos trust, and what that beneficiary receives outside of the will and inter-vivos trust.

Example: Assume your total estate consists of $400,000 of life insurance, a $500,000 house in your name and a $100,000 bank account in the name of your inter-vivos trust. You want Mary Jones to receive 100% of your estate. However, if Mary Jones is the sole beneficiary under your will, Bob Smith is the sole beneficiary in your life insurance contract, and Billy Jones is the sole beneficiary in your inter-vivos trust, Mary will only get the house which accounts for

50% of your estate, Bob will get the life insurance proceeds (40% of the estate), and Billy will get the bank account from the inter-vivos trust (10% of estate). In this case, Mary Jones is actually entitled to only 50% of your estate.

4 Beneficiaries

This chapter discusses who or what *can* inherit from your will or inter-vivos trust and who or what *cannot* inherit from them. For example, you cannot leave money to your dog, Fido, but you could leave money to a friend for the purpose of taking care of Fido. This chapter also discusses the problems in leaving property to minors, persons who are considered disqualified to inherit, and your rights to disinherit persons.

Who and What *can* Inherit?

Three types of *entities* can inherit from your estate. They are:

- persons;
- government; and,
- non-profit organizations.

Persons You can leave your property to any person regardless of age, location, or status.

Example 1: You can leave your property to a cousin in North Korea. However, North Korea may or may not allow the beneficiary to receive the bequest or may take the bequest from the beneficiary.

Example 2: You can leave property to a friend in state prison.

There are some limitations on this category. In some states, notably California, there are certain persons who are considered to be disqualified to inherit your property unless you take certain prescribed steps to qualify the bequest to them. There are also special considerations to make if the person is a minor.

You do *not* have to leave your one-half interest in *community property* or any of your *separate property* to your spouse or your children. On the other hand, you *cannot* leave your spouse's one-half interest in community property to someone else, as your spouse owns that property. However, nearly every state permits a surviving spouse, regardless of the terms of a decedent's will or inter-vivos trust, to take a *forced share* of his or her predeceasing spouse's estate. Accordingly, although you do not have to *leave* a surviving spouse any portion of your estate, the state of your residence may permit your surviving spouse to *take* a portion of your estate. Appendix A summarizes the *forced share* rights of surviving spouses in the different states.

Government

You can leave your property to any governmental entity in the United States.

Example: A bequest to the city of Atlanta is legal.

Non-Profit Organizations

You can leave your property to a non-profit organization, such as a charity.

Example: A bequest to the American Red Cross is legal.

Who and What *cannot* Inherit?

You cannot take it with you, but you cannot leave your property to certain types of organizations or to animals.

Partnerships

You cannot leave your property to a *partnership*; however, you can leave your property to the *individuals* of a partnership.

Corporations You cannot leave your property to a corporation.

Animals You cannot leave your property to an animal. However, you can leave your property to a person or non-profit organization *in trust* to care for an animal.

Special Limitations on Bequests to Minors

If you leave your property to a minor, the court appoints a *guardian* of the minor's estate to manage the *bequest* (and any other asset of the minor) until the minor attains the age of majority (usually 18 years of age; 21 in some states). At that time, the property is delivered, outright, to the former minor. Guardianships are safe in that the court appointed guardian must post a *surety bond* to insure the minor's estate against any dishonesty of the guardian. The guardian must periodically file an account of the minor's assets with the court.

On the other hand, it costs money to create the guardianship through the court, to obtain a surety bond, and to file the required accountings to the court. However, the biggest problem to guardianships is that they end when the minor attains age of majority. Most eighteen-year-olds are too young to manage their assets. Fortunately, there are several alternatives to court supervised guardianships of a minor's estate.

Uniform Transfer to Minor's Act Under the *Uniform Transfer to Minors Act*, sometimes called the *Uniform Gift to Minors Act*, you can bequeath property to an adult person as *custodian* to hold for the benefit of the minor. This is an *informal trust arrangement*. The custodian, who is not under automatic court supervision, is required by law to hold and manage the property for the minor's benefit only. The custodian delivers the property to the minor at an age directed by you—up to age 25.

Example: "I bequeath $10,000 to Bob Smith, as custodian under the Uniform Transfer to Minor's Act for the benefit of Terry Smith until Terry Smith attains 25 years of age."

Forms are provided for bequests to a custodian for a minor's benefit in Appendix D. Leaving property to a custodian avoids the court costs and court supervision involved in guardianships. Also, the custodians can hold the property for the minor past his or her 18th birthday, if you direct. However, if you fail to specify an age for distribution, the custodian must distribute the property to the former minor when he or she turns 18 years old (or 21 years depending on your state. Check your state's law.).

The disadvantage of custodianships is the lack of mandatory court filed accountings and bonds. Accordingly, you must be very careful in the selection of the custodian. You should consider requiring that the custodian post a surety bond as a condition of his or her appointment.

IRC 529 College Plans

Congress has enacted legislation that permits states to create and administer college education investment plans. Most investment plans are essentially mutual stock and/or bond funds. Most states offer different investment options within their plans. Some of the benefits of these plans are:

- the assets in the plans earn income *tax deferred* (federal and state) until the monies are withdrawn and
- the income earned is not taxed (federal) upon withdrawal if the withdrawn funds are used for a *qualified higher educational expense* in college. A qualified higher educational expense includes books, tuition, school room/board, and even many off-campus living expenses.

In an *IRC 529 College Plan*, the *plan contributor* names someone to *control* the plan, i.e., to determine when and what expenses to pay. That person is called the *plan participant*. The beneficiary of the plan is called the *plan beneficiary*. Forms in Appendix D permit a custodian or a trustee for a beneficiary to distribute property they manage into a 529 College Plan. Neither the plan contributor, the plan participant, or the plan beneficiaries need to be a resident of the state where the college plan is opened.

NOTE: *The IRC 529 College Plans can be created by contributions during lifetime as well.*

Trusts

At your death, you can leave property to a trustee to hold in trust for the benefit of the minor until the minor reaches a more mature age for distribution. In many ways, a *trust* is like custodianship. A trust avoids automatic court involvement and supervision like custodianship. However, unlike a custodianship, a trust can be created for a beneficiary who is not a minor, can delay final distribution beyond age 25, and permits you to place greater conditions and restrictions on the use of the property. For example, you can direct the trustee to pay educational expenses of the beneficiary and/or permit the trustee to withhold a distribution if the beneficiary fails a reasonable drug and/or alcohol abuse test. (See the forms in Appendix D for trusts for minors.)

Disqualified Beneficiaries

In what appears to be the wave of the future, California, by statute, disqualifies bequests to certain individuals based upon their involvement in the making of the will, relationship to the person making the will, or their occupation. California Probate Code Section 21350 disqualifies bequests to:

- the person who *drafted* the will or inter-vivos trust (and the employees, law partners, cohabitants, and certain relatives of said person);
- any person who has a *fiduciary* relationship with the testator or settlor, who transcribes the will or inter-vivos trust or causes the will or inter-vivos trust to be transcribed (and employees, cohabitants, and certain relatives of said persons); and,
- any *care custodian* of a *dependent adult.*

The disqualified bequest becomes *qualified* if:

- the disqualified person is related by blood to the testator or settlor within five degrees. (Your parents and children are related to you within one degree. Your siblings are related to you within two degrees, a niece or nephew is related to you within three degrees, etc.);
- the disqualified person cohabitates with the testator or settlor (as husband, wife, or gay partner);
- the testator or settlor receives a written *certificate of independent review* of the document from a lawyer after the lawyer reviews the otherwise disqualified transfer with the testator or settlor; or,

- the disqualified person can prove in court by clear and convincing evidence that the bequest was not the product of undue influence, fraud, or duress.

Generally, the disqualified person is involved in the preparation of the will or inter-vivos trust in question or is related to the person involved in the preparation of the will. However, the *care custodian* of a *dependent adult* category is a trap for the unwary. The term *care custodian* essentially means anyone who has ever helped an adult. The term dependent adult means any person whose mental or physical capacities have diminished at all during their lifetime. The care custodian does not have to be involved in the preparation of the will or inter-vivos trust in which he or she is left a bequest. Nor does the care custodian have to ever give assistance to the testator. In sum, every adult person is a care custodian of a dependent adult. Accordingly, by statute in California, every beneficiary of a will or inter-vivos trust is arguably a disqualified person as a care custodian of a dependent adult unless one of the qualifying exceptions mentioned earlier is met.

Example: "I leave $1,000.00 to my gardener, Bob Smith." This bequest violates the statute and is disqualified unless the gardener cohabitates with you (as husband, wife, or gay partner), is related to you within five degrees, or you receive a written certificate of independent review as to said bequest from a lawyer.

Furthermore, the statute is not limited to bequests under a will or inter-vivos trust. It also applies to lifetime gift transfers and transfers by trusts, joint tenancies, life insurance, etc.

> ***Warning:*** An attorney's written *Certificate of Independent Review* is essential if you want to leave a bequest to a potentially disqualified person.

Although California is the only state to currently have a *disqualified persons* statute, you should be aware of such laws as they can, if enacted, apply retroactively. Accordingly, if bequests you are considering fall within the California *disqualified persons* statute you should consider safeguards such as the *qualifying* procedures discussed earlier.

Family Changes after Execution of the Will

In many states, a spouse or child *acquired* after the date of the execution of a will are considered to be *forgotten* by the testator and, therefore, entitled to their intestate succession share of the testator's estate.

Example: Bob, a single man with one child, executes a will leaving everything to his one child. Bob then marries Sue. Bob dies on his honeymoon with Sue, without amending or executing a new will. In many states, Sue is now entitled to that share of Bob's estate that she would have received if Bob had no will regardless of the fact that Bob's will leaves everything to his one child.

Who can You Disinherit?

You do not have to leave your estate to someone you do not want to even, if that person is your spouse or your child. You have the right to *disinherit* anyone. However, nearly every state has a *forced share* statute that provides for a share of your estate to pass to a surviving spouse. (see Appendix A.)

Disinheritance Clause

Paragraph THIRD of the will forms and Paragraph 6.12 of the inter-vivos trust forms in this book use a comprehensive disinheritance clause that disinherits all persons other than those specifically named as beneficiaries in the will. Accordingly, if someone shows up after your death claiming to be your long lost brother, he is still subject to the disinheritance clause and would receive no part of your estate.

Who can Contest Your Will or Your Inter-Vivos Trust?

Although you have the right to disinherit anyone, certain persons can contest your will or inter-vivos trust claiming:

- that the will or inter-vivos trust was improperly executed;
- that you lacked mental competency to execute a will or inter-vivos trust;
- that the will or inter-vivos trust was the result of fraud; or,
- that the will or inter-vivos trust was the result of undue influence.

Only certain persons have the right to contest your will or inter-vivos trust. The persons are:

- those persons who would take your estate if there were no will or inter-vivos trust (your heirs) and
- those persons who received a bequest from you under a prior will or inter-vivos trust.

Example: You are single with one adult child. Your child has two children. Your first and only will leaves everything to your brother. Your child, the person who would take you property if there were no will, has the legal right to contest your will. Your grandchildren do not have the right to contest your will as they would not inherit your property if your will was declared to be invalid.

Anti-Contest Clause

In the second part to paragraph THIRD of the wills, or paragraph 6.12 of the inter-vivos trusts, is an *anti-contest clause* that disinherits not only anyone who contests, but also disinherits anyone who contests transfers such as joint tenancies, T.O.D. securities accounts, or life insurance. It even disinherits persons who make claims against your estate for services rendered or agreements to share property.

Therefore, the only persons truly affected by the anti-contest clause are the persons who have something to lose under your will or inter-vivos trust if they contest it and lose, i.e., the beneficiaries.

Example: A beneficiary who receives 10% of your estate under your will or inter-vivos trust but who would be entitled to 25% of your estate if you died without a will is affected by the anti-contest clause. A decision then must be made as to whether to *not* contest the will or inter-vivos trust and take the 10% *or* to contest the will or inter-vivos trust and possibly lose the 10%.

The anti-contest clause does not prohibit anyone from contesting the will; it simply states that anybody who *contests* your will is disinherited. If a person is not a beneficiary of your estate, they have nothing to lose under the anti-contest clause.

Bequest Incentives to Avoid Contests

Will or inter-vivos trust contests are messy and expensive legal matters. Yet, as discussed above, the anti-contest clause only helps to prevent will contests by persons who have something to lose. Accordingly, if you want to disinherit an *heir* (a person who would take a portion or all of your estate if there was no will), consider leaving that heir a small bequest as an incentive not to contest the will or inter-vivos trust.

Example: You dislike your son, one of the two heirs to your estate, and want to leave all of your property to your other heir. However, you know that the disinherited son will contest your will simply to exact an emotional and financial toll on the beneficiary of your property. You could decide to leave the son you dislike $10,000 in your will with the anti-contest clause. At your death, the son you dislike now has a dilemma. If he contests the will and loses, he also loses the $10,000 bequest.

Obviously, the amount of the bequest incentive will differ depending on the value of your estate and the potential anger of the person.

5 Bequests

Each time you dispose of property in your will or inter-vivos trust, you are said to be making a *bequest*. The act of making a bequest is to *bequeath*. Historically, a bequest was a gift in a will of personal property and a *devise* was a gift in a will or inter-vivos trust of real estate. Certain states may call all gifts in a will or inter-vivos trust either devises or bequests. However, because of the common usage of the word bequest, that term is used exclusively in this book.

This chapter discusses three separate and often intermingled topics about bequests. First it discusses the difference between a *specific bequest* and a *residual bequest*. As part of that topic, we will discuss the difference between *tangible personal property*, *intangible personal property*, and *real property*.

Finally, this chapter will discuss various ways property can be left to beneficiaries. Those ways include:

- outright (no strings attached);
- with conditions;
- in a *life estate*; or,
- in trust (including custodianships).

Specific and Residual Bequests

Regardless of other categorizations, bequests are either *specific* or *residual.*

Specific Bequests

Specific bequests are where the property bequeathed is specifically identified by item (i.e., my 1974 Ford Pinto), by type (i.e., all of my household furnishings), or by amount (i.e., $100,000). Specific bequests can be further described by the type of property.

Tangible personal property. Personal property you can touch, move, or hold such as cars, clothes, or household items are called *tangible, personal property.* Specifically bequeathing identified items of tangible, personal property such as "my pink couch in my living room" is discouraged for several reasons.

- First, said items may be sold, discarded, or gifted before your death, which then raises the question whether the beneficiary is to get the new "green couch" in your living room.
- Second, if the specifically identified property cannot be found after your death, your executor must either explain to the court if he or she knows what happened to the property or make diligent efforts to locate the specifically identified property and describe those efforts to the court.
- Finally, if you do own the specifically identified property at the time of your death, your executor will have to have it separately appraised and separately inventoried on any federal estate tax returns filed with the IRS. Any probate inventories filed with the probate court may result in an increased value (bad for tax purposes) as well as an additional cost of appraisal. Sometimes the cost of appraisal can exceed the value of the item.

On the other hand, a beneficiary of your highly valued Van Gogh painting may want it to be specifically devised, appraised, and inventoried for income tax basis purposes, insurance purposes, and to later be able to prove how he or she acquired title to the painting.

In paragraph SECOND of the will forms, you have the opportunity to make a specific bequest of tangible, personal property. Therefore, you *can* bequeath your Van Gogh painting or "green couch in your living room" if you wish.

After the listing of any specific bequests of tangible, personal property, paragraph SECOND permits you to bequeath the remaining (or all, if you made no specific bequests) of the tangible, personal property to one or more persons or entities, in equal shares.

Occasionally, the division of the tangible, personal property among the family members can be the most troublesome part of the distribution of your estate. Although the dollar amount may be small, sentimental attachment or long-term resentments are often involved. In those situations, you may wish to prepare an informal note advising the beneficiaries of how you want certain items of tangible, personal property to be distributed. Keep that note with your will. Although the note may not be legally enforceable, it could guide reasonable beneficiaries.

Intangible personal property. This property includes cash, securities accounts, securities, partnership interests, promissory notes, and business interests that are merely representative of value. Paragraph SECOND in the will forms permits the bequeathing of intangible personal property.

Bequests of specific, non-cash, intangible personal property such as "my 500 shares of IBM stock" is discouraged as the stock could, before your death, be sold, have a 3 for 1 stock split, or changed substantially in value. Remember the maxim, "A will speaks as of the date of death." On the other hand, cash bequests, assuming the cash will be available at your death, are not a problem.

Example: "I bequeath ten thousand dollars ($10,000.00) to Bob Smith."

Real property. Improved and unimproved real estate, including mineral interests and condo stock co-ops, are all *real property*. The bequeathing of specific parcels of real property is also discouraged as it may be sold or exchanged before your death or its value or mortgage encumbrances may materially change from time to time.

However, paragraph SECOND permits bequeathing specific real property. If such a bequest is made, you must decide whether the real property is to be distributed to the beneficiary subject to all mortgages on the real property or whether your estate is to pay-off the mortgages for the beneficiary.

Residual Bequests

Residual bequests dispose of the *residue* of your estate. The residue is *what is left* in the estate after payment of all costs of the administration of your estate, all of your debts, and all of your specific bequests in your will. In many wills or inter-vivos trusts, the residue is the largest portion of the estate and sometimes, in those cases where there are no specific bequests, the residue is the *entire* estate. Because the residue includes *what is left*, it includes both real property and all types of personal property.

If there is more than one residual beneficiary, you need to determine what portion of the residue each beneficiary is to receive. The interest of each beneficiary need not be the same as another.

Example: "I leave Bob 10% of the residue and Mary 90% of the residue."

Instead of listing the interest of each beneficiary in terms of a percentage of the residue, using *shares* is recommended. The reason to use shares is because one or more of the residual beneficiaries might die before you. If each share represents a fraction of the residue, then regardless of whether any shares lapse, it is easy to determine what each beneficiary receives. You might find this concept easier to conceptualize if you start with 100 shares—each share then equals 1%. If a bequest of 5 shares, for example, lapses due to the death of the beneficiary before you, then there are 95 shares and each share is worth 1/95, slightly more than 1%.

Example: "I devise all of the rest of my estate as follows:

A. 25 shares to Bob Smith;

B. 10 shares to Mary Jones; and,

C. 65 shares to John Doe.

If any of the above persons die before my death their devise shall lapse."

In the example, if all three beneficiaries survive you, Bob will get 25% of the residue, Mary will get 10% of the residue, and John will get 65% of the residue. If Bob and Mary survive the decedent, but John does not, then Bob will get 25/35 of the residue (about 78%) and Mary will get 10/35 (about 22%).

Conditional Outright Bequests

So far, we have been discussing unconditional outright bequests. However, outright bequests can have conditions attached. Generally, conditions are *conditions precedent*, that is, a condition that must be met before delivery of the bequest. For example, a condition that a bequest not be paid until the beneficiary graduates from a university is valid.

Conditions cannot be illegal or against public policy. For example, a condition that the beneficiary do an illegal act—such as murder someone—would be illegal and non-enforceable. A condition that the beneficiary not marry anyone of Hungarian heritage would also be a violation of anti-discrimination laws and thus unenforceable. However, a condition that a beneficiary not marry a specific individual *is* enforceable. This author recommends *against* imposing any conditions to bequests, however, if you wish to do so, you should seek the expertise of a lawyer.

The most common condition to a bequest is that of surviving the testator by a certain period of time. (Where applicable, the will forms in this book have used a 30-day *survivorship* requirement.)

Life Estates

Sometimes you want the beneficiary to have only the right to use the property for his or her lifetime, and then have the property distributed to a second beneficiary after the death of the first beneficiary. The beneficiary using the property for his or her lifetime is called the *life tenant*. The beneficiary who takes the property after the death of the life tenant is called the *remainderman*.

Although any type of property can be subject to a life estate, the most common situation involves the use of real property.

Example: You bequeath your daughter a life estate in your residence. Your daughter has the right to use your residence after your death, for the remainder of her lifetime. Your daughter could live in the residence, rent the residence to others (however, she could not rent the

> residence for a period of time beyond her lifetime), or even sell her life estate (the buyer of a life estate buys only the right to use the property during the lifetime of the selling life tenant).
>
> During her life estate your daughter, as the life tenant, would pay all interest (but not principal) on any encumbrance on the property, association dues, normal repairs, insurance, and property taxes.

After the death of the life tenant, the remainderman becomes the absolute owner of the property. Sometimes, in a second marriage situation, the predeceasing spouse leaves the surviving spouse a life estate in the predeceasing spouse's residence with the remaindermen being the children of the predeceasing spouse's prior marriage.

Testamentary Trusts

Many different *testamentary trusts* (trusts created at your death by will or inter-vivos trust) exist, and are used to hold your assets at death for the benefit of others. The testamentary trusts utilized in the will and inter-vivos forms in this book are used to manage assets for the benefit of one beneficiary until he or she either receives the trust assets upon attaining a designated age or he or she dies and the trust estate is delivered to a second beneficiary, or, in the case of a surviving spouse, to save federal estate taxes.

In many ways, the trusts used in the will and inter-vivos trust forms contained in this book work like the life estate discussed above, with some exceptions.

- First, a trust is a more convenient method of handling a group of assets, especially a residual interest in an estate, rather than multiple life estates—one for each property.
- Second, a trust places the legal title to property in the hands of a trustee to manage for the beneficiary rather than relying on the beneficiary to properly manage the property. (In many cases, the beneficiary is too financially unsophisticated to manage the property.)

- Third, the trust provides flexibility in distributions during the life of the trust (i.e., more than simply use of property can be distributed to the beneficiary) and can provide for distributions to the beneficiary upon the beneficiary attaining a specified age.

The will or inter-vivos trust forms in Appendix D provide for trusts of residual shares of the estate for a spouse, child, or friend. Some of the will forms provide for the beneficiary to receive discretionary payment of principal for illnesses as well as the *income* of the trust. If you want greater flexibility as to distributions from the trust to the beneficiaries, you need to consult with a lawyer to draft your will or inter-vivos trust. Of course, as with any bequest in your will or inter-vivos trust, the funding and administration of the trust created by your will or inter-vivos trust does not occur until after your death.

6 FIDUCIARY POSITIONS

A *fiduciary* is someone who owes a duty of loyalty and fairness to another. It is a position of trust, wherein the fiduciary cannot take a financial or personal advantage. This chapter discusses three types of fiduciaries: the guardian, the executor, and the trustee or custodian.

Guardian

You have the right to nominate a *guardian* to care for your minor children after your death. There are two types of guardians. First, there is the guardian of the *person*. The guardian of the person is responsible for the minor's housing, food, clothing, etc. Then there is the guardian of the *estate*. The guardian of the minor's estate manages any assets of the minor that are not managed by a custodian or a trustee.

Only *persons* can be appointed by the court to be a guardian of a minor's person. However, *trust companies,* as well as persons, can be appointed by the court to be a guardian of a minor's estate. The guardian of the person and the guardian of the estate do not have to be the same person. Although a *guardianship estate* of a minor can be substantial, many times the assets of the minor are in the hands of the *custodians* or *trustees* (discussed later in this chapter). Guardianships of person and estate both end when the minor attains the age of majority in their state of residence (usually eighteen years of age).

You have the right to nominate a guardian for your children only if there is no natural parent of the minor living (unless the natural parent is legally determined to be unfit). Simply because you are the divorced, custodial parent of your child does not mean that you have the sole right to nominate a guardian for your minor children in the event of your demise.

In most states, minors aged 14 years and older, have the right to express a preference for the guardian of their person. You, the parent of the minor, have only the right to *nominate* a guardian. Only the court can *appoint* a guardian. Although the court will consider your written nomination of a guardian, the court's appointment of the guardian will be based upon what the court determines to be *in the best interest of the minor.* In short, your nomination of a guardian is not legally binding on the court.

Selection of the Guardian of the Person

Obviously, it is wise to verify with a prospective guardian that he or she is willing to act. In addition, you must be comfortable with the lifestyle choices of the prospective guardian. Sometimes your best friends would make the worst guardians. In selecting a guardian of the person for a minor child consider the following questions.

- *Does the guardian live near the minor's family members?* It might be wiser to select your cousin who lives near the minor's family members than a sister who lives on the other side of the nation.
- *Is there religious compatibility between the guardian and your child?*
- *If the child is older, is the proximity of the guardian's residence to the friends and school of the child important?*
- *What is the age of the prospective guardians?* Your mother may be too old to handle your minor child.
- *What is the family situation of the guardian?* Your friends with the 2-year-old quintuplets might be too busy with their children to act as guardians for your 13-year-old twins.

- *Is the issue of divorce a consideration on your selection?* If you choose Mary Smith who is married at the time of the nomination, do you still want her to act if, at the time of your death, she is divorced or married to someone new?

- *Is there a problem of nominating a husband and wife as co-guardians? Which one might or should continue as guardian if they divorce after your death?* Consider nominating only the husband or the wife as guardian to avoid confusion over your intent in the event that person and his or her spouse later divorce.

Instructions to the Nominated Guardian

As the court acts in the *best interest of the child*, the nominated guardian should be aware beforehand of the nomination and should have at least one copy of your **NOMINATION OF GUARDIAN** for their use if necessary. (see form 1, p.133.) You need to tell the proposed guardian that, in the event of your death, no one is automatically going to hand him or her your children; nor is the court going to appoint him or her without the proposed guardian petitioning the court to do so. In the event of your death, the nominated guardian needs to immediately take physical possession of the minor(s), and petition the court for temporary guardianship of each minors' *person* pending the court hearing on the appointment of the permanent guardian.

Persons you might *not* want to act as guardians for your children, often become the guardians simply because they acted more quickly than the deceased parent's nominated guardian. Many judges refuse to move a minor child from the custody of the first person to take possession of the child after the death of the child's parent to avoid a further disruption of the minor child's life.

Use of the Nomination of Guardian Forms

The two **NOMINATION OF GUARDIAN** forms (form 1, p.133 and form 2, p.134) in this book are designed to be used independent of the will. Using a separate **NOMINATION OF GUARDIAN** form does not give the proposed guardian a copy of your will.

The first form is your basic guardianship nomination form when you do not expect any conflict over the nomination. The second form should be used when you suspect there may be a conflict over the appointment of the guardian, and the appointment of a particular guardian is of the utmost importance to you. Both forms provide that the same person is nominated to act as guardian of your minor child's person *and* estate.

Executor

An *executor* is the person or *corporate fiduciary* (trust company) that is appointed under your will to manage your estate after you die. The executor will:

- offer your will to the court for probate;
- marshal your assets;
- file an inventory of your assets with the court;
- pay all debts, expenses of administration, and taxes; and,
- sell any property that must be sold to put the estate in a position to be closed.

The executor will petition the court to make an order to distribute your estate. During the probate of your estate, the executor has the duties to account for the financial transactions of the estate and to keep the court and the beneficiaries informed as to the progress of the estate administration. After the court issues the order for distribution, the executor will distribute your estate pursuant to the terms of that order that incorporates the asset disposition provisions of your will.

The term *executor* means that the person or trust company was appointed under a will. If the person or trust company is not named under a will, then that person or trust company is called an *administrator.* Years ago the above terms referred only to men or trust companies. Women were referred to as an *executrix* or an *administratrix.* In recent years, there has been a tendency to refer to executors, executrixes, administrators, and administratrices simply as *personal representatives.*

A will does not have to nominate an executor to be valid. However, nomination in your will of the executor permits you to select the executor and permits you to determine whether the executor should be bonded or not.

Selecting Your Executor

Carefully select your executor. Too many people feel that the job is merely honorary and that competence is a secondary consideration. Nothing could be further from the truth. A good executor will make the difference between an estate that is handled efficiently and expeditiously versus an estate that will bog down into eventual litigation and losses. A good executor is one who keeps detailed financial records, is not a procrastinator, and can make difficult decisions. Although the executor will most likely hire a lawyer for assistance, the responsibility begins with and ends with the executor.

If you do not have someone you trust and who fits the above description to select as your executor, consider naming a trust company to act as the executor. Many banks have trust companies as part of their operations. The primary objections to trust companies are that they are impersonal and they charge the maximum statutory fee permitted. However, being impersonal can be a good thing. Many family or friends who act as executor also take the statutory fee, as being an executor is work and the fee is earned.

Trust companies are professionals. They have created systems to keep track of all transactions and progress of estate. They do not wait until the end of the month to make income deposits; they keep records of financial transactions; and, they do not steal the estate assets. However, if your estate is under $200,000, most trust companies will decline to act, as the statutory fee is too small. If you select a trust company as your executor, you may wish to discuss the matter with them beforehand; contract a fee agreement with them; and, even give them a copy of your will. However, you do not have to contact the trust company before your death.

Surety Bonds

Many lawyers will tell you that if you cannot trust a person enough to waive the requirement of posting a *surety bond* as the executor, then you should not appoint that person as the executor. However, bonds often help keep an executor honest and no honest executor should object to posting a surety bond.

The surety bond posted by the executor is in an amount equal to the value of the personal property of estate (real property does not have to be bonded as it cannot be sold without consent of the beneficiaries or the court). It is an inexpensive form of insurance to guarantee that the executor will act honestly. The cost of such a bond is relatively modest, (i.e., $500.00 per year for a $200,000 bond), but adds financial protection to the estate and the benefit of the concern of the bonding company.

The bonding company does not want to lose money. Accordingly, the bonding company checks the credit rating of the executor and sometimes require the executor to give the bonding company joint control over major estate assets to lessen the bonding company's liability exposure. Bonds are especially important when minors are beneficiaries of the estate, as they usually are unable to ascertain if the estate is being mishandled or not.

Waiver of Publication

In the will forms in this book, paragraph FOURTH is the nomination of executor paragraph. In that paragraph, you waive the requirement of publishing a legal notice in a newspaper each time the executor wishes to sell estate property. Publication requirements differ from state to state. However, where required, publication is a formality that costs money and time, but does not protect the estate or assist in obtaining the highest price for the property sold. In most states, the waiving of the publication requirement *does not* give the executor the right to sell property without either the permission of all affected beneficiaries under the will or the court.

Trustee

As described above, the executor manages the estate after your death and during the probate process. On the other hand, the *trustee* of a trust created in a will (a *testamentary trust*) receives, from the executor of your will, property at the end of the probate of your estate and then manages that property.

A trustee of an inter-vivos trust (one created by you during your lifetime), administers the property in that inter-vivos trust for the benefit of the trust's beneficiaries that are named in it. This trustee might be acting during your lifetime (i.e., you could be incapacitated or simply not wish to be bothered with the management of your estate) and/or after your death.

we need permission from beneficiary to buy, sell if a trust is set up.

The trustee has legal title to the property under his or her control and can buy or sell assets without permission from the court or the beneficiaries (unless, under the terms of the trust, permission from the court or beneficiaries is required). Unlike an executor, the trustee is not automatically under the jurisdiction of the court. Like an executor, the trustee must render accountings to the beneficiaries and must keep the beneficiaries informed. The trustee is entitled to reasonable compensation for his or her services, but may make no other profit at the expense of the trust (i.e., a trustee may not receive a commission on trust property he or she sells).

Unlike the short tenure of an executor (it takes about one year to probate an estate), a trustee might act for a substantial number of years. In addition, unlike an executor, a trustee generally does not rely upon an attorney for the day-to-day management of the trust.

You should take even greater concerns about the appointment of your trustee, as he or she holds the assets for a greater period of time and the court does not supervise trustees. Only consider persons who are financially sophisticated, extremely conscientious, and keep excellent financial records. Being a trustee is a job, so be sure the person you nominate has the time.

It is advisable to nominate multiple trustees (usually two) called *co-trustees* and/or requiring the trustees to post a surety bond. If you do not have someone you trust who fits the above description to select as your trustee, then consider naming a trust company (many banks have trust companies as part of their operations).

Like with using a trust company to act as your executor, a trust company as trustee will charge a fee. The fee is usually about 1% annually of the value of the trust assets. To avoid this fee, some people name family members or friends as trustees. However, family members or friends may decide to take a fee larger than what a trust company would and they do not have the financial systems or expertise that the trust company has. If you are considering the appointment of a trust company to handle your trust interview several trust companies to learn more about their employees (trust officers), their methods of doing business (i.e., financial management viewpoint), and their fee schedule. Sometimes the fee schedule can be negotiated in advance and can protect your estate from unhappy surprises.

Custodian

Custodians are like trustees except that custodians are limited to handling assets of persons under the age of 25 years (the maximum age can differ from state to state). Custodians hold assets transferred to a minor under the *Uniform Transfer to Minors Act*. Custodians are not automatically under court supervision.

Conclusion

Be careful. The appointment of your fiduciaries is not to be taken lightly. The best planned will or trust will disintegrate in the hands of an incompetent or dishonest fiduciary. Selecting the best guardian, executor, trustee, or custodian is more important than being concerned over hurting the feelings of a friend or family member. Additional care must be exercised when the trustee you are considering might have to act during your lifetime due to your incapability as you could then personally feel the pain of an unqualified or dishonest trustee.

7 Execution, Safekeeping, and Revocation of Wills and Inter-Vivos Trusts

This chapter will explain the formalities required to properly execute your will or inter-vivos trust; give suggestions for the safekeeping of your will or inter-vivos trust; and, will discuss the steps needed to revoke your will or inter-vivos trust.

Will Execution

The actual requirements differ from state to state. However, the following instructions are legal in each state except Louisiana. The requirements for Louisiana are explained throughout the discussion of the execution of wills.

Self-Proving Wills

Nearly all states permit the admission to probate of uncontested wills without testimony of a witness to the will if the will is *self-proving* under the law of that state. A will that is not self-proving is not inadmissible or invalid. Such wills simply need the testimony of a witness (or evidence that a witness cannot be found and then other evidence such as the testimony of a person familiar with the decedent's handwriting that the signature of the decedent on the will is in the handwriting of the decedent). However, because self-proving wills are easier to have admitted to probate by the court you should, whenever possible, take the necessary steps to have your will be self-proving.

In California, a will is self-proving if the witnesses attest, under penalty of perjury, that the will was properly executed. (Each of the will forms and the codicil form in this book comply with California's self-proving statute.)

Alabama, Alaska, Arizona, Arkansas, Colorado, Hawaii, Idaho, Illinois, Indiana, Maine, Minnesota, Mississippi, Montana, Nebraska, Nevada, New Mexico, New York, North Dakota, Oregon, South Carolina, South Dakota, Tennessee, Utah, Washington, and West Virginia all use the **SELF-PROVING AFFIDAVIT.** (form 25, p.205.)

Delaware, Florida, Georgia, Kansas, Kentucky, Massachusetts, Michigan, Missouri, New Jersey, North Carolina, Oklahoma, Pennsylvania, Rhode Island, Virginia, and Wyoming use the **SELF-PROVING AFFIDAVIT.** (form 26, p.206.)

Texas uses the **SELF-PROVING AFFIDAVIT.** (form 27, p.207.) New Hampshire uses the **SELF-PROVING AFFIDAVIT.** (form 28, p.208.) Louisiana uses the **SELF-PROVING AFFIDAVIT.** (form 29, p.209.) Iowa uses the **SELF-PROVING AFFIDAVIT.** (form 30, p.210.)

As states tend to change their self-proving affidavits from time to time, contact a *notary* in your state to obtain the most recent self-proving affidavit for your state.

In the District of Columbia, Maryland, Ohio, Vermont, and Wisconsin self-proving wills are either unnecessary or not recognized.

To execute your will, do the following.

- Step One: Optional—Have a notary present. (The notary cannot be one of your witnesses.) *In Louisiana, this Step One is mandatory.*

- Step Two: The *testator* announces, in the presence of two (in Vermont, there must be three) adult, competent witnesses (who are not beneficiaries or relatives of beneficiaries of the will), that:

    - the testator has read the will;

- the testator understands the provisions of the will; and,
- the will disposes of the testator's property in the manner that the testator wants.

Example: This is my will. I have read it. I understand it. It disposes of my property in a manner that I want it to be disposed of at my death.

NOTE: *This announcement should also be made in front of the notary if one is present. And remember—the notary cannot be one of the witnesses.*

- Step Three: In the presence of the witnesses, the testator signs the will at the end of the signature paragraph (but before the witnesses' signatures) and dates the will. The signature paragraph is very short, it simply reads

  "In Witness hereof I set my hand hereto on this___day of___, 200___" and then has a place for the signature of the testator.

- Step Four: In the presence of the witnesses, the testator initials the bottom of each page of the will. *In Louisiana the testator must sign each page.*

- Step Five: The witnesses each read the *attestation clause* in the will and then date and sign in the presence of the testator, and then in the presence of each other. The witnesses should print their names under their signed names if their handwriting is difficult to read. They should also include their addresses. *In Louisiana the will must be notarized as well as witnesses.*

- Step Six: All witnesses initial each page.

- Step Seven: The testator and witnesses complete the *self-proving affidavit* (where necessary) under the supervision of the notary.

Duplicate Originals

You may execute more than one original will. Execute the duplicates at the same time with the same witnesses present.

Execution of Inter-Vivos Trust

The settlors has his and/or her signature at the end of the inter-vivos trust acknowledged by a notary. As an extra precaution, the settlors may wish to initial each page of the inter-vivos trust. Witnesses are not necessary to execute an inter-vivos trust.

You may execute more than one original inter-vivos trust. Execute the duplicates at the same time as the original

Safekeeping Your Will

Do not place the original will in a location where a person who would benefit if the will was *not* found after your death has access to it. Generally, a safe deposit box is a good location for the original will, so long as any co-renter of the box has no interest in the will being destroyed. Having the safe deposit box in your name only does not cause a delay in obtaining the original will. In most states, in the event of the death of the safe deposit box renter, his or her safe deposit box may be opened for the purpose of the will search. The box opening is done in the presence of a bank officer who will make a copy of the will for their file and give the original to the named executor in the will.

Some states permit you to file your original will with the clerk of the probate court before death. If this option appeals to you, call your local probate court clerk to see if your state permits such safekeeping and if your local probate court will be the custodian. Be sure to keep the *receipt* for the safekeeping of your will in a safe place like your safe deposit box.

Safekeeping Your Inter-Vivos Trust

Loss of your inter-vivos trust during your lifetime could be a substantial problem as you will likely transfer ownership of your estate to the name of the trust. If you do lose your inter-vivos trust during your lifetime, it is imperative that you then *restate* the terms of your inter-vivos trust with a *trust amendment.*

Generally, a safe deposit box is a good location for the original inter-vivos trust. It is a good idea that the safe deposit box be held in the name of the inter-vivos trust so that *successor trustees* can remove assets in the safe deposit box in the event of your death or incapacity. If your state law will not permit a safe deposit box to be in the name of the inter-vivos trust, consider placing a successor trustee or a co-trustee on the safe deposit box as a co-renter of the box.

If you decide to keep the safe deposit box in your name only then, at your death (but not incapacity) the successor trustee should be able to obtain the original inter-vivos trust. In most states, in the event of the death of a safe deposit box renter, his or her safe deposit box may be opened for the purpose of an inter-vivos trust search. The box opening is done in presence of a bank officer who will make a copy of the inter-vivos trust for their file and give the original to the named trustee in the inter-vivos trust.

Revocation

You can revoke a will or inter-vivos trust in two basic ways. First, you can revoke the will or inter-vivos trust by physically destroying it or by crossing out all of the provisions of the will or inter-vivos trust. However, revocation by destruction is not suggested as a court might later determine that your physically destroyed or crossed-out will or inter-vivos trust was merely lost and permit the use of a copy of it.

The best way to revoke a will is by a executing a new will that states on its face that all prior wills are revoked. All of the forms in this book have the standard revocation of prior wills language in the introductory paragraph.

Unless the inter-vivos trust provides otherwise, only the person (the settlor) who creates the inter-vivos trust can revoke it. As in a will, often the best way to revoke an inter-vivos trust is to amend it by a complete *restatement* of the terms of the inter-vivos trust. If you wish to revoke you inter-vivos trust, it is recommended that you physically destroy the original inter-vivos trust and execute a separate **REVOCATION OF TRUST**. (see form 50, p.358 and form 51, p.359.) Before you revoke your trust, make certain that you transfer all property in the trust to be revoked to either your name or to the name of the new trust.

8 Changing Your Will or Inter-Vivos Trust

This chapter will explain how you can make changes to your will or inter-vivos trust both before you execute it, or by preparing a separate amendment to your executed inter-vivos trust or an amendment (called a *codicil*) to your executed will.

Changes *before* Execution

While reviewing your will or inter-vivos trust, you may find a small error or change you wish to make before you sign it. For example, the specific cash bequest to your sister is listed as $1,000 and you want to leave her $2,000. The simplest way of correcting or changing your un-executed will may be to simply make a handwritten correction by crossing out the "$1,000" and handwriting in "$2,000" next to the crossed-out amount. This is called an *inter-lineation.*

There is always a danger in making a change to your will or inter-vivos trust before you execute it. How is the court supposed to know if you made the change before or after you signed the will or inter-vivos trust? Handwritten or typed changes *before* you sign the will or inter-vivos trust are valid. Such changes *after* you sign are invalid.

Before executing your will or inter-vivos trust, date and initial each change as well as have each witness initial the changes *before* you execute the will or inter-vivos trust. If the written inter-vivos trust is challenged, the likelihood of the court determining your handwritten changes to be valid, are increased.

Changes *after* Execution

Often, you want to make changes to your will or inter-vivos trust *after* it has been executed. Do *not* make such changes by crossing out certain parts of the document and/or by inter-lineations. This method is *not* valid even if you date and initial the changes.

Changes to your Will

After your will is executed, you have two choices if you want to make changes. First, execute a new will. This is the preferred method if the changes are substantial or if the change may later hurt someone's feelings if they find out.

Example: You want to leave $100 instead of $100,000 to your niece. Consider a new will rather than amending your existing will so that your niece will not know about the prior, larger bequest.

Second, you can execute a separate document amending your will. This might be appropriate if the change is relatively small.

Example: You want to leave $1,000 to your niece who does not receive anything under your will. Consider an amendment to your will.

Amendments to your will are called *codicils.* A codicil adds to your will, subtracts from your will, or simply replaces portions of your existing will. However, a codicil leaves those portions of your will not removed or replaced, intact.

Example: Your will names your sister as executor. You execute a codicil naming your brother as alternative executor. Your sister, pursuant to the will, is still your first appointed executor.

Codicils are executed in the same manner as wills. A **CODICIL** is located in Appendix D as form 31, p.211.

Changes to your Inter-Vivos Trust

After your inter-vivos trust is executed, you have two choices if you want to make changes. First, you can execute a separate document, called an *amendment*, to insert the changes to your inter-vivos trust. This is especially appropriate if the change is relatively small.

Example: You want to leave the $1,000 to your niece who does not receive anything under your inter-vivos trust. Consider an amendment to your inter-vivos trust.

Second, you can amend your entire inter-vivos trust by a new inter-vivos trust called a *restatement*. Trust amendments by a restatement are done for several reasons.

- The changes are substantial. The change may later hurt someone's feelings if they find out.

Example: You want to leave $100 instead of $100,000 to your niece. Consider an amendment by a complete *restatement* of your inter-vivos trust rather than amending your existing inter-vivos trust so that your niece will not know about the prior, larger bequest.

- You have made several changes over the years. The various amendments to your inter-vivos trust have made review of the inter-vivos trust difficult.

Example: You are amending your inter-vivos trust for the tenth time. You have a twenty page inter-vivos trust plus ten, five page amendments, a total of seventy pages. To understand your inter-vivos trust, one must read the inter-vivos trust and then read each amendment to determine the current provisions of your inter-vivos trust. At this point, it would be easier to restate all of the terms of the inter-vivos trust in a single, eleventh amendment by a restatement of the entire inter-vivos trust.

An amendment to your inter-vivos trust subtracts or simply replaces portions of your existing inter-vivos trust. But an amendment leaves those portions of your inter-vivos trust not removed or replaced, intact.

Trust amendments are executed in the same matter as trusts. Forms 44 and 45, p.352 and p.353 are two types of **TRUST AMENDMENTS**.

9 Anatomy of Your Will or Inter-Vivos Trust

This chapter explains the format of the will and inter-vivos trust forms in this book. Refer to these instructions/explanations as you complete your desired forms. Additional paragraphs not discussed either contain necessary legal information to make your will or inter-vivos trust valid, or are specific to the form you are using. Review each paragraph of the form you are using. Complete any necessary requirements it may have.

Will

Title. The "Last Will and Testament" identifies the document as a will.

Introductory Clause/Revocation of Prior Wills. This paragraph:

- identifies you as the testator of the will;
- declares your county and state of residence to assure the county court that it is the proper county of jurisdiction in the event your will needs to be probated after your death; and,

- revokes any and all of your prior wills and codicils. (All prior wills and codicils are expressly revoked because if your new will does not automatically revoke prior wills and codicils, each would have to be read together with your new will.)

Paragraph FIRST. This is a declaration of your marital status and names any predeceased spouse to assist your executor who must advise the court of the same in the event of the probate of your will. The names and birth dates of your children advises the court if you have any children, as well as identifies if any children are minors is listed. Also listed are the names of any predeceased children as wells as the names and birth dates of any descendants of predeceased children. These statements assist the executor in giving the required written legal notice to all heirs if the will is filed with the court for probate after your death. The statement "I have no other children or issue of a predeceased child" advises the executor and the court that you have no other issue.

NOTE: Directive to Pay Debts: *A directive to the executor to pay all of your debts adds nothing to the validity or effect of the will. By law, debts must be paid after your death before the bequests are paid. Accordingly, this paragraph is NOT used in the forms included with this book.*

Paragraph SECOND. This paragraph directs the disposition of your property subject to your will. Most will forms in this book provide separately for bequests of personal property (both tangible and intangible), cash, real property, and the residue of your estate.

Paragraph THIRD. This paragraph provides a comprehensive disinheritance and anti-contest clauses. The *disinheritance clause* states that all persons other than your specifically named beneficiaries are disinherited. If someone shows up after your death claiming to be your long lost brother, they are still subject to the disinheritance clause and receive no part of your estate.

The *anti-contest clause* disinherits anyone who *contests* the will. It also disinherits any persons who attempt to contest non-will transfers such as joint tenancies, T.O.D. securities accounts or life insurance, or make claims against your estate for services rendered or under alleged oral agreements to share property.

Paragraph FOURTH. This paragraph nominates the executor of the will and permits the executor to sell property without publishing a written notice of his or her intent to sell the property.

After Paragraph FOURTH is the subscription statement where you date and sign your will.

Attestation Clause. After your signature is the *attestation clause* where the witnesses declare under penalty of perjury that they witnessed your will. By making their statement *under penalty of perjury,* some states do not require their testimony to prove the validity of your will if its execution is not contested after you die. The will is considered *self-proving.* For a will to be considered self-proving in other states, you and your witnesses need to execute, in the presence of a notary, the **SELF-PROVING AFFIDAVITS** appropriate for your state found in Appendix D. At the end of the attestation clause, the witnesses will each sign his or her name and someone will affix the date.

Guardianship Nomination

If you have minor children and you wish to nominate a guardian to raise them (or manage their estates if no custodian or trustee is named), you need to execute one of the two separate forms provided. (see form 1, p.133 and form 2, p.134.)

Inter-Vivos Trust

Title. INTER-VIVOS TRUST identifies the document as a revocable, amendable, living trust.

Article I

Paragraph 1.01. Introductory clause identifies you as the settlor or settlors and identifies the persons who will act as your trustees (probably you) of your inter-vivos trust. It also establishes the trust by your declaration and refers to the assets that you declare to be part of your inter-vivos trust as Exhibit "A." It is attached to the end of your inter-vivos trust.

Paragraph 1.02. Identifies the name and date of your inter-vivos trust. Although you can give your inter-vivos trust any name you want, it is recommended that you use your own names for the inter-vivos trust.

Paragraph 1.03. Defines certain terms used in your inter-vivos trust.

Paragraph 1:04 (married couple's inter-vivos trust). Confirms that separate property of either spouse or community property contributed to your inter-vivos trust remains the separate property of the contributing spouse or their community property.

Article II

Paragraphs 2.01 and 2.02. Provide that during your lifetime (if your inter-vivos trust is created by only you) or during the joint lifetime of you and your spouse, all of the trust income and that principal are requested to be paid to you or both of you.

Paragraph 2.03. Provides that in the event of your incapacity or your spouse's incapacity (if your inter-vivos trust was created by you and your spouse), the trustee shall make appropriate payments from the trust income and/or principal for your support. If you have a single person inter-vivos trust, then the trustee is instructed to make payments during your incapacity at a level that would permit you to remain in your home even if it requires 24-hour care and exhausts the principal of the trust. (This instruction is not given in the married couple's inter-vivos trust form as the non-incapacitated spouse should have greater flexibility in determining how the total estate is expended for the benefit of the incapacitated spouse.)

Paragraphs 2.04 and 2.05. Provide that you, as a single settlor, may revoke or amend your inter-vivos trust at any time. It also provides that you and your spouse, as married settlors of a joint inter-vivos trust, may only revoke or amend as to community property jointly, but that each of you may amend or revoke the inter-vivos trust as to your separate property.

Article III

Paragraph 3.01. Directs the trustee to pay the debts of the deceased settlor. If you have a married couple's inter-vivos trust form, this paragraph also gives the surviving spouse all of the inter-vivos trust estate.

Paragraph 3.02. If you have a single person inter-vivos trust, this paragraph directs the disposition of your assets that are subject to your inter-vivos trust at your death. If you have a married couple's inter-vivos trust, this paragraph directs the disposition of your assets that are subject to your inter-vivos trust at the death of the surviving spouse. The inter-vivos trust forms in this book provide for bequests of intangible personal property, cash, real property and the residue of your inter-vivos trust estate. Tangible personal property as it is bequeathed in the *pour-over* will that you will execute in addition to the your inter-vivos trust

If you have a married couple's inter-vivos trust, this paragraph either creates a *Decedent's Trust* and *Survivor's Trust* out of your inter-vivos trust on the death of the predeceasing spouse, or a *Decedent's Trust*, a *Marital Trust* and a *Survivor's Trust* out of your inter-vivos trust on the death of the predeceasing spouse.

In form 38, p.276 and form 43, p.341 the *Survivor's Trust* consists of the surviving spouse's one-half interest in any community property in the inter-vivos trust *plus* the surviving spouse's separate property in the inter-vivos trust *plus* whatever the predeceasing spouse did not leave to the *Decedent's Trust.* In form 39, p.289 and form 40, p.302, the *Survivor's Trust* consists of the surviving spouse's one-half interest in any community property in the inter-vivos trust *plus* the surviving spouse's separate property in the inter-vivos trust.

In those forms, the *Decedent's Trust* is funded with assets from the predeceasing spouse's separate property in the inter-vivos trust or the predeceasing spouse's one-half interest in community property in the inter-vivos trust having a value equal to the federal estate tax exemption available in the predeceasing spouse's year of death (for year 2002 that amount is $1,000,000. In years 2003 and 2004, that amount is $1,500,000, etc.).

In form 42, p.329, the *Marital Trust* is funded with assets from the predeceasing spouse's separate property in the inter-vivos trust or the predeceasing spouse's one-half interest in community property in the inter-vivos trust that were not funded into the *Decedent's Trust* (i.e., that amount of the predeceasing spouse's estate in excess of the federal estate tax exemption amount).

After the death of the predeceasing spouse, the *Decedent's Trust* and *Marital Trust* become irrevocable and non-amendable. However, the surviving spouse continues to have the power to amend or revoke the *Survivor's Trust.*

Further, the surviving spouse is entitled to any part of the principal of the *Survivor's Trust* plus 5% of the principal, annually (if he or she wants), from the *Marital Trust.* Finally, the surviving spouse is entitled to principal from the *Decedent's Trust* or *Marital Trust* if necessary for his or her care or support, in his or her accustomed manner of living.

Paragraph 3.03 (only in married couple's inter-vivos trust forms). Directs the trustee to pay the debts of the surviving spouse upon his or her death.

Paragraph 3.04 (only in married couple's inter-vivos trust forms). This paragraph permits the surviving spouse to direct the distribution of the *Survivor's Trust* by a written document called a *testamentary power of appointment* to whomever he or she wishes. However, absent such a written directive the *Survivor's Trust* shall be distributed in the same manner as the *Decedent's Trust* and *Marital Trust* as directed in Paragraph 3.05.

Paragraph 3.05 (only in married couple's inter-vivos trust forms). This paragraph directs the disposition of the *Decedent's Trust* and *Marital Trust.* This disposition plan became irrevocable at the death of the predeceasing spouse. The inter-vivos trust forms in this book provide for bequests of intangible (but not tangible, personal property as it is bequeathed in the *pourover will* that you will execute in addition to the your inter-vivos trust), personal property, cash, real property, and the residue of your inter-vivos trust estate.

Article IV

Paragraph 4.01. Confirms who is the original trustee and provides for succession of successor trustees. The forms provide that the settlors will be the original trustees. However, those *defaults* can be changed by you. If a settlor who is acting as a trustee becomes incapacitated, his or her restoration to capacity shall restore him or her as a trustee. In married couple inter-vivos trust forms, a *special* trustee shall be appointed to hold any life insurance policy on the life of the surviving spouse that is held as an asset of the *Decedent's Trust.*

Paragraph 4.02. In the single person inter-vivos trusts, you may change the order of trustee succession at any time. In the married persons' trusts, the change of trustee succession must be done jointly if both spouses are living, or by the surviving spouse alone.

Paragraph 4.06. Lists the expansive powers of the trustees in terms of management and investment of the trust estate. The range of powers that can be granted or withheld from a trustee is too vast to completely discuss here. The powers given are designed to permit a trustee to act within the general statutory guidelines permitted by most states.

Paragraph 4.06K. This paragraph is for married couples' inter-vivos trusts only. It is designed to avoid the problem of needing the trustees (i.e., husband and wife) to act jointly to transact bank and stock brokerage transactions of check writing and securities trading.

Paragraph 5.01. Prohibits a beneficiary of an irrevocable portion of the inter-vivos trust (i.e., the beneficiaries after the death of the original settlor or settlors or the surviving spouse as to a Decedent's Trust or Marital Trust) from assigning his or her share to another and further prohibits the creditor's of such beneficiary from attaching the beneficiaries interest in the trust.

Article V

Paragraph 5.02. Provides for the trustee to use the *Uniform Principal and Income Act* to allocate expenses and income between principal and income. For example, under trust law, a capital gain on a sale or disposition is considered a principal receipt and not distributed to an ordinary *income* beneficiary.

Paragraph 5.03. Provides that the trust will have to end in about 90 years so it does not violate the common law doctrine of *rule against perpetuities* (i.e., that a trust cannot last forever). Approximately eleven states have abolished the *rule against perpetuities* and thus, in those states, a trust can last forever.

Paragraph 5.04. This paragraph permits the trustee to make payments to a beneficiary or the beneficiary's guardian or even to make payments for the benefit of a beneficiary directly (i.e., pay the beneficiary's house payment directly).

Paragraph 5.08. Provides for the ultimate disposition of the trust if all named beneficiaries are deceased. If you have a single person trust, then it all goes to your heirs. If you have a married couple's trust, then one half to the heirs of each spouse.

Paragraph 5.16. Provides for which state law is to be used in construing the trust. Normally you list your home state.

Paragraph 5.17. Provides a comprehensive disinheritance and anti-contest clauses. The *disinheritance clause* states that all persons other than your specifically named beneficiaries are disinherited. If someone shows up after your death claiming to be your long lost brother, he is still subject to the disinheritance clause and receives no part of your estate.

The *anti-contest clause* disinherits anyone who *contests* your inter-vivos trust or will, as well as persons who attempt to contest other date of death transfers such as joint tenancies, T.O.D. securities accounts or life insurance, or make claims against your estate for services rendered or under alleged oral agreements to share property.

Paragraph 5.18. Provides that a beneficiary must survive you or your spouse (as the case may be) by thirty days to be entitled to his or her bequest under the trust.

Paragraph 5.19. Provides that all typed and handwritten *fill-ins* where directed in your inter-vivos trust were made before the execution of your trust and are not initialed by you. All crossed through words and inter-lineations were made before the execution of your trust and are initialed by you.

After Paragraph 5.19 is the *Certification* where you date and sign your inter-vivos trust in the presence of a notary who acknowledges your signatures.

Exhibit "A" is a list of the assets you declare to be part of your inter-vivos trust. In most situations, a simple declaration, even if in writing, is insufficient to actually transfer the asset to your inter-vivos trust. You must physically change the title of the assets that you want to transfer to your inter-vivos trust. (see Chapter 8.)

Conclusion

As stated in the Introduction, estate planning is an essential activity for every individual or couple. By reading this book and using the forms provided, you are now ready to put into action a plan that will protect your assets, provide for your minor children, and avoid paying exorbitant federal estate taxes. With some thoughtful analysis, careful drafting and execution, and the all important follow-through of funding, you can have peace of mind and know that you will be transferring maximum wealth at your death. By reviewing the samples and selecting the most appropriate form for your your situation you can accomplish your goals.

GLOSSARY

A

administrator. A personal representative who is not named in the decedent's will. In earlier times, a female administrator was called an administratrix. See also *executor* and *personal representative.*

anti-contest clause. A clause that disinherits anyone who *contests* the will. It also disinherits any persons who attempt to contest non-will transfers such as joint tenancies, T.O.D. securities accounts or life insurance, or make claims against your estate for services rendered or under alleged oral agreements to share property.

attestation clause. This clause comes after your signature and is where the witnesses declare under penalty of perjury that they witnessed your will.

B

beneficiary. The named recipient of an asset belonging to a decedent, as distinguished from an *heir.*

bequest. A gift effective at time of death.

bond. An insurance policy issued to provide financial protection to an estate, a trust, or a custodianship from the dishonest acts of a fiduciary (i.e., an executor, trustee, or custodian).

C

certification. The certification is where you date and sign your inter-vivos trust in the presence of a notary who acknowledges your signatures.

codicil. An amendment to a will.

community property. Property acquired during marriage from the efforts of one or more of the spouses. Term applies in Arizona, California, Idaho, Louisiana, Nevada, New Mexico, Texas, Washington, and Wisconsin. See also *separate property.*

custodian. A person appointed under the *Uniform Gift to Minors Act* (sometimes called *Uniform Transfers to Minors Act*), who has a fiduciary position over assets which are for the benefit of a minor or person under the age of 25 years. In essence, a trustee without formal trust documents.

D

decedent. The person who has died.

decedent trust. A trust created at the decedent's death to take advantage of decedent's federal estate tax exemption.

descendant. A living person born into the family line (a child, grandchild, etc.)

devise. Generally a bequest of real property. In many states, used interchangeably with bequest.

devisee. The person who is left real property in a will.

disinheritance clause. This clause states that all persons other than your specifically named beneficiaries are disinherited.

disqualified person. California is the only state to currently have a *disqualified persons* statute. If bequests you are considering fall within the California *disqualified persons* statute you should consider safeguards such as the *qualifying* procedures discussed earlier. It is important to be aware of such laws as they can, if enacted, apply retroactively.

E

elective share. *See forced share.*

executor. A personal representative who is named in the decedent's will. In earlier times, a female executor was called an executrix. See also *administrator* and *personal representative.*

execution. The act of signing a will by the testator and the witnesses.

exemption trust. See *decedent's trust.*

F

family allowance. An amount allowed by Statute to go to the spouse and children of decedent.

fiduciary. A term describing a duty to act on behalf of or for another in a fair and trustworthy manner. Also used to describe a person who holds such a duty.

forced share. Rights granted by state law to the surviving spouse to take a portion of the decedent's estate regardless of what the will may allow.

G

grantor. See *settlor.*

guardian. Person appointed to care for the person and/or the estate of a minor.

H

heir. The relative entitled to an asset belonging to a decedent when no person is named as the beneficiary. See also *beneficiary.*

holographic will. A will wherein the essential terms are all in the handwriting of the testator. Although the will must be signed by the testator, the signature need not be at the end of the document, and the will need not be witnessed by any other persons. This type of will is valid in most states.

I

inter-lineations. When one or more words are inserted between the lines or on the margin of a document such as a will.

inter-vivos trust. A trust created during lifetime (instead of created at someone's death via their will). Generally the trust is for the benefit of the person who creates the trust, but it becomes irrevocable upon the death of the person who creates the trust. The term means the same as *living trust.*

intestate. When a person dies without a will.

I/T/F. Abbreviation that stands for "in trust for." A way to designate that certain assets are being held in trust for another person.

intestate succession. The distribution of a decedent's property to the decedent's heirs when there is either no will, or the will fails to dispose of the property.

IRC 529 college plan. State-run college education programs permitted by the Internal Revenue Code wherein accounts can be funded by persons for the higher educational benefit of others they select. These programs have substantial federal income tax advantages when the account assets are used for higher educational expenses.

issue. Legal term to describe the lineal descendants of a person. Your issue would be your children, your grandchildren, your great-grandchildren, etc.

J

joint tenancy. A written title naming one or more persons as joint tenants, which means they have equal ownership and, in the event the death of a joint tenant, the remaining joint tenants take the share of the deceased joint tenant "by right of survivorship," regardless of contrary provisions in a will.

L

legacy. A gift of personal property in a will.

life estate. The right to use property during your lifetime, but not the right to dispose of the entire property during your life or any of the property at your death. See *inter-vivos trust.*

living trust. A trust created during lifetime (instead of created at someone's death via their will). Generally the trust is for the benefit of the person who creates the trust, but it becomes irrevocable upon the death of the person who creates the trust. The term means the same as *inter-vivos trust.*

M

marital property. Property acquired during marriage from the efforts of one or more of the spouses. See also *separate property*.

marital trust. A trust created at death for the benefit of the decedent's spouse that takes advantage of federal estate tax exemptions, but is not able to be changed by the surviving spouse.

minor. In most states, someone under the age of 18 years.

N

notary. A person authorized to administrator oaths.

P

payable on death (POD). An account that passes directly to a designated beneficiary upon the owner's death.

personal property. Anything that is not real property. For example: cash, securities, partnership interests, rights in a lawsuit, household furniture and furnishings and personal effects.

personal representative. The generic term for the court appointed person or corporation who manages a decedent's probate estate.

probate. The court supervision of the changing of title to assets from a decedent's name to the name of the beneficiaries under the decedent's will or the decedent's heirs if the decedent died with no will.

probate code. Statutes enacted in virtually every state that governs wills, trust, and probate.

Q

quasi-community property. Property acquired by a married person who dies a resident of the community property state, while owning property acquired while he or she was living outside of the community property state. Further, at the time of death, that property would have to have been community property, if the person had been living in the community property state at the time the property was acquired. In such a situation, the quasi-community property is treated like community property.

R

real property. Land, buildings on land, long-term leases, mineral rights, condominiums and co-op buildings (condos where the ownership is indicated by a certificate rather than a deed).

remainder. Balance of an estate after all specific gifts have been distributed.

remainderman. Person who takes the property after the life usage of the property by another. For example, if the testator bequeaths a life estate in his residence to Bob, and then at Bob's death the residence passes to Mary, then Mary is the *remainderman*.

residue. Those assets of an estate or a will that are left over after the distribution of all specific bequests.

restatement. This involves restating the terms of the inter-vivos trust and acts as an amendment as a way to revoke the trust.

right of representation. To take the place, for inheritance purposes, of a deceased ancestor. For example, if a will leaves a testator's estate to "my issue by right of representation" and the testator leaves two living children and one deceased child who left two children of his or her own, then the estate would go one-third to each of the living children of the testator and one-sixth to each of the children of the deceased child of the testator.

S

self-proving affidavit. A document used in most states so that a witness will not be needed to testify in court to prove a will offered for probate is the last will of testament of the decedent.

self-proving will. If a will is self-proving under the law of a particular state, nearly all states will permit the admission to probate of uncontested wills without testimony of a witness to the will. In California, a will is self-proving if the witnesses attest, under penalty of perjury, that the will was properly executed.

separate property. Property that belongs entirely to one person.

settlor. The person creating a trust.

subscribed will. A will that is signed by the testator at the end of the document and then signed by at least two witnesses.

successor trustee. A person or entity (e.g. bank trust department) that serves as trustee of a trust document upon the resignation, removal or death of a trustee. For most inter-vivos trust, the person or entity you name to act as trustee once you are no longer able to do so.

surety bond. A surety bond posted by the executor is in an amount equal to the value of the personal property of estate (real property does not have to be bonded as it cannot be sold without consent of the beneficiaries or the court). It is an inexpensive form of insurance to guarantee that the executor will act honestly.

survivor's trust. A trust created at death for the benefit of the decedent's spouse that takes advantage of federal estate tax exemptions, and the surviving spouse has the power to make changes to it.

T

tax credit trust. See *decedent's trust.*

testamentary capacity. The legal and mental capacity to execute a will. Generally defined as being 18 years of age or older and aware of one's assets, one's relatives, and knowledge that document takes effect at time of death.

testamentary trust. A trust created by a person's will.

testate. When a person dies with a will.

testator. The person whose will we are referring to.

Totten trust. Assets designated "in trust for" another person.

transfer on death (TOD). An account that passes directly to a designated beneficiary upon the owner's death.

trust. A legal entity and relationship wherein one person or entity holds legal title and responsibility to property for the financial benefit of another person or entity.

trustee. Person who holds *title* to the trust assets for the benefit of the beneficiary of the trust. A trustee is responsible for managing the trust assets and has a fiduciary relationship to the beneficiaries of the trust.

trustor. See *settlor.*

W

will. A document that, at someone's death, directs the distribution of his or her assets. A will generally cannot affect the distribution of assets held in joint tenancy, distributed pursuant to a contract (life insurance, pensions, retirement plans, annuities, etc.), or property subject to a "payable on death" or "transfer on death" designation.

witness. A person who sees a testator sign his or her will and signs the will after the testator. A witness must be eighteen years or older, aware that the document he or she is signing is a will, and not a beneficiary under the will who takes any more than he or she would have under intestate succession.

Appendix A
Forced Shares Statutes

Virtually every state permits a surviving spouse, regardless of the terms of the decedent's will, to claim a certain portion of the decedent's estate. Some states call this a *forced share* or *elective share* as the decedent's estate is forced to leave a certain portion to the surviving spouse or the surviving spouse can elect to take a certain portion.

The *forced share* is sometimes independent of a surviving spouse's right to other probate protections such as *family allowance* (often called a *widow's allowance*). A family allowance is the right for a surviving spouse and minor children to receive a monthly stipend from the estate during probate administration. The right often includes the ability to stay in the family residence and retain certain personal property such as household furniture. Other items may be specifically included by statute in the family allowance, regardless of the terms of the will.

In some states, the *forced share* only affects property that is disposed of by will or intestate succession. This means that property passing by joint tenancy, inter-vivos trust, or contract (i.e., pensions and life insurance) are not affected. Some states look at the assets of the surviving spouse and the length of the marriage in determining the amount of the forced share for the surviving spouse. Nearly all states permit the surviving spouse to waive his or her right to the *forced share* either before or after the death of the decedent.

Following is a very brief summary of each state's forced share rules. As many factors particular to each state affect the application of the rules, it is wise to review the state's *actual* statute.

Summary of Forced Share Rules

Alabama: The surviving spouse is entitled to the lesser of one-third of the decedent's spouse's estate or all of the decedent's spouse's estate reduced by the value of the surviving spouse's separate property.
(Ala. Code Sec. 43-8-70 through 43-8-76.)

Alaska: The surviving spouse is entitled to one-third of the estate after payment of funeral expenses, family allowances, administration expenses, and certain claims.
(Alaska Stat. Sec. 13.12.070 through 13.12.100.)

Arizona: No *forced share* rights. However, as Arizona is a community property state, the surviving spouse owns one-half of the community property. Surviving spouse has rights to family allowances.
(Ariz. Rev. Stat. Ann. Sec. 14-2101 through 14-2114.)

Arkansas: No *forced share* rights. Surviving spouse has rights to family allowances and probate homestead.
(Ark. Code Ann. Sec. 28-39-201.)

California: No *forced share* rights. However, as California is a community property state, the surviving spouse owns one-half of the community property and one-half of quasi-community property. Surviving spouse has rights to family allowances, probate homestead and exempt property set-asides. California also provides that a spouse who is not named in the will is, in most cases, entitled the decedent spouse's one-half of the community property and quasi-community property and between one-third and one-half of the decedent's spouse's separate property.
(Cal. Probate Code Sec. 6401, 6560 and 6561.)

Colorado: The surviving spouse is entitled to up to one-half of the estate depending on the years of the marriage.
(Colo. Rev. Stat. Sec. 15-11-201 through 15-11-208.)

Connecticut: The surviving spouse is entitled to use one-third of the estate for his or her lifetime.
(Conn. Gen. Stat. Ann. Sec. 45a-436.)

Delaware: The surviving spouse is entitled to take one-third of the estate less what he or she received otherwise as a result of the decedent's death.
(Del. Code Ann. Title 12 Sec. 901-908.)

District of Columbia: No *forced share* rights. However, if the decedent spouse dies with a will and leaves nothing to the surviving spouse, then he or she will receive his or her intestate share, i.e., one-third to one-half.
(D.C. Stat. Ann. Sec. 19-113 and 19-302 through 19-304.)

Florida: The surviving spouse can take elect to take 30% of the estate (except for real property outside of Florida). The surviving spouse also has the right to certain household items, personal effects, and one car.
(Fla. State. Ann. Sec. 732.201 through 732.215.)

Georgia: The surviving spouse is entitled to one year's support.
(Ga. Code Ann. Sec. 53-3-5.)

Hawaii: If there are no surviving parents or children of the decedent, the surviving spouse can receive the whole estate. Otherwise, the surviving spouse can elect to take one-half or up to the first $50,000 of the estate, whichever amount is greater.
(Haw. Rev. Stat. Sec. 560:2-1-1 through 2-207.)

Idaho: As Idaho is a community property state, the surviving spouse owns one-half of the community property. The surviving spouse can elect to take one-half of quasi-community property.
(Idaho Code Sec. 15-2-210 through 15-2-213.)

Illinois: If there is no surviving issue of the decedent, the surviving spouse can elect to take one-half of the estate. If there are descendants of the decedent, the surviving spouse can elect to take one-third of the estate.
(755 ILCS 5/2-8.)

Indiana: If there are no surviving issue of the decedent, the surviving spouse can elect to take one-half of the estate. If there are descendants of the decedent, the

surviving spouse can elect to take one-third of the personal property and a one-third *life estate* in the real property.
(Ind. Code Ann. Sec. 29-1-3-1 through 29-1-3-3.)

Iowa: If the decedent has no other children than those with the surviving spouse, the surviving spouse can elect to take all of the decedent's estate. If there are issue of the decedent who are not issue of the surviving spouse, the surviving spouse can elect to take all of the personal property and one-half of the real property of the decedent.
(Iowa Code Ann. Title XV Subtitle 4, Sec. 632 through 638.)

Kansas: The surviving spouse is entitled to a homestead of 160 acres rural and 1 acre city and one-half estate if there are issue of the decedent; all of the estate if there are no issue of the decedent.
(Kan. Stat. Ann. Sec. 59-6A201 through 59-6A217.)

Kentucky: The surviving spouse can elect to take one-third of the estate.
(Ky. Rev. Stat. Ann. Sec. 392.080.)

Louisiana: As Louisiana is a community property state, the surviving spouse owns one-half of the community property. Further, the surviving spouse can claim a *legal usufruct for life* which is similar to a life estate (unless he or she remarries) over a portion of the decedent's estate.
(La. Civ. Code Ann. Art. 890.)

Maine: The surviving spouse can elect to take one-third of the augmented estate.
(Me. Rev. Stat. Ann. Tit. 18A, Sec. 2-201 through 2-207.)

Maryland: The surviving spouse can elect to take one-third of the estate if there are children or one-half of the estate if there are no children.
(Md. Code Ann. Est. & Trust, Sec. 3-203 through 3-208.)

Massachusetts: The surviving spouse can elect to take the first $25,000 plus one-third of the estate if there are children or the first $25,000 plus one-half of the estate if there are no children.
(Mass. Gen Laws Ann. Ch. 191 Sec. 15.)

Michigan: The surviving spouse can elect to take one-half of his or her *intestate* share reduced by one-half of the value of all other property passing to the surviving spouse by the decedent by means outside of the will. In intestate succession, the surviving spouse takes 100% if there are no issue or parents of the decedent and takes the first $150,000 plus one-half if there are issue of the decedent.
(Mich. Comp. Laws Ann. Sec. 700-2102 and 700-2202.)

Minnesota: The surviving spouse is entitled to take up to one-half of the estate depending on the years of the marriage or $50,000, whichever amount is greater.
(Minn. Stat. Ann. Sec. 524.2-201 through 524.2-214.)

Mississippi: The surviving spouse can *elect against the will* and take his or her intestate share which is no greater than one-half.
(Miss. Code Ann. Sec. 91-5-25.)

Missouri: The surviving spouse can elect to take one-third of the estate if there are children or one-half of the estate if there are no children.
(Mo. Ann. Stat. Sec. 474.160.)

Montana: The surviving spouse is entitled to take up to one-half of the estate depending on the years of the marriage.
(Mont. Code Ann. Sec. 72-2-221 through 72-2-230.)

Nebraska: The surviving spouse is entitled to take up to one-half of the estate.
(Neb. Rev. Stat. Sec. 30-2313 through 30-2319.)

Nevada: No *forced share* rights. However, as Nevada is a community property state, the surviving spouse owns one-half of the community property. Nevada also provides that a spouse who is not named in the will is, in most cases, entitled to between one-third and one-half of the decedent's spouse's estate.
(Nev. Rev. Stat. Sec. 134.040 through 134.050.)

New Hampshire: The surviving spouse is entitled to take between one-third and one-half of the estate.
(N.H. Rev. Stat. Ann. Sec. 560.10.)

New Jersey: The surviving spouse is entitled to take up to one-third of the estate.
(N.J. Stat. Ann. Sec. 3B:8-17.)

New Mexico: No *forced share* rights. However, as New Mexico is a community property state, the surviving spouse owns one-half of the community property. New Mexico also provides that a spouse who is not named in the will is, in most cases, entitled to between one-fourth and all of the decedent's estate.
(N.M. Stat. Ann. Sec. 45-2-301.)

New York: The surviving spouse may elect to take his or her intestate share, between one-third and one-half of the decedent's estate.
(N.Y. Probate Law Sec. 5-1.1.)

North Carolina: The surviving spouse is entitled to take between one-sixth and one-half of the estate depending on what issue survived the decedent.
(N.C. Gen Stat. Sec. 30.)

North Dakota: The surviving spouse is entitled to take up to one-half of the estate depending on the years of the marriage.
(N.D. Cent Code Sec. 30.1-05 through 30.1-08.)

Ohio: The surviving spouse may elect to take his or her intestate share up to $60,000 plus between one-third and one-half of the decedent's estate.
(Ohio Rev. Code Ann. Sec. 2106.01.)

Oklahoma: The surviving spouse may elect to take one-half of the property acquired during the marriage by the joint industry of the spouses during the marriage plus a conditional life estate in a homestead.
(Okla. Stat. Title. Sec. 84-44.)

Oregon: The surviving spouse can elect to take one-fourth reduced by the value of all other property passing to the surviving spouse by the decedent by means outside of the will.
(Or. Rev. Stat. Sec. 114.105.)

Pennsylvania: The surviving spouse is entitled to take one-third of the estate.
(Pa. Stat. Ann. Title 20, Sec. 2203-2211.)

Rhode Island: Besides the provisions by the decedent's will to a surviving spouse, the surviving spouse is also entitled to a life estate in all real property. (R.I. Gen. Laws Sec. 33-25-2 through 33-25-6.)

South Carolina: The surviving spouse is entitled to take one-third of the estate. (S.C. Code Ann. Sec. 62-2-201 through 62-2-207.)

South Dakota: The surviving spouse is entitled to take up to one-half of the estate depending on the years of the marriage.
(S.D. Codified Laws Ann. Sec. 29A-2-201 through 29A-2-214.)

Tennessee: The surviving spouse is entitled to take one-third of the estate. (Tenn. Code Ann. Sec. 31-4-101,102.)

Texas: No *forced share* rights. However, as Texas is a community property state, the surviving spouse owns one-half of the community property.
(Tex. Probate Code Ann. Sec. 38.)

Utah: The surviving spouse is entitled to take one-third of the estate.
(Utah Code Ann. Sec. 75-2-201 through 75-2-207.)

Vermont: The surviving spouse is entitled to take one-third of the estate.
(Vt. Stat. Ann. Title 14, Sec. 401.)

Virginia: The surviving spouse is entitled to take between one-third and one-half of the estate depending on what issue survived the decedent.
(Va. Code Ann. Sec. 64.1 through 64.13.)

Washington: The surviving spouse is entitled to take between one-third and all of the estate depending on what issue and other relatives survived the decedent. (Wash. Rev. Code Ann. Sec. 11.12.095.)

West Virginia. The surviving spouse is entitled to take up to one-half of the estate depending on the years of the marriage.
(W. Va. Code Sec. 42-3-1 through 42-3-7.)

Wisconsin. The surviving spouse is entitled to take one-half of the estate.
(Wis. Stat. Ann. Chapter 861.02.)

Wyoming: The surviving spouse is entitled to take between one-fourth and one-half of the estate depending on what issue survived the decedent.
(Wyo. Stat. Title 2, Chapter 5, SEC. 101.)

Appendix B
Asset Roadmap

Sometimes I am involved in a decedent's estate when no one, not even the decedent's family, has any idea as to what the assets or the estate are or where they should look for the decedent's will and other important papers. In those cases, we often find health care powers of attorney after the decedent has died or the decedent's burial instructions after the funeral—when it is too late. To avoid putting your family through such heartache, I suggest that you keep an *asset roadmap* detailing where your important papers are going to be found and listing both your assets as well as the tentative disposition of your assets that pass outside of your will and probate.

The following roadmap should be copied and used by you, from time to time, to update where your family can find your will, inter-vivos trust, powers of attorney for health care and estate management, location of your safe deposit box, as well as a listing of your life insurance, insurance for your health, your car, and your house. If you want, you can even list where you keep your tax returns and make a suggestion as to what attorney your family should hire to assist them in the event of your death. In addition, there is space to insert, right on the roadmap, a legally binding directive as to your burial or funeral instructions. Finally, the roadmap permits you to list your assets, i.e., your real property, your securities, your bank accounts, and any other assets you own.

Instructions:

Will. List the date of your will, where the original is kept, and who the nominated Executor is.

Trust. List the date of your inter-vivos trust, where the original is kept, and who the successor trustees are.

Codicil. List the date of your codicil and where the original is kept.

Power of Attorney. List the date, location of the original, and name of the nominated agent for both your Health Care Power of Attorney and your Power of Attorney for Estate Management. (Remember, by law, a copy of your Health Care Power of Attorney has the legal effect of an original.)

Safe Deposit Box. List the name and location of the bank, the location of the safe deposit box key, the number of the box, and the names of any *co-renters* of the box.

Life Insurance. List the name of each insurance company, the face amount of the policy, the policy number, the location of the original policy, and the name of the policy beneficiary.

Other Insurance. List the location of your original policies for auto, household, etc.

Burial/Funeral Instructions. You may leave written instructions as to the disposition of your remains. If you have made pre-arrangements or if you own a crypt or plot, include that information as well as the location of any pre-need contracts or cemetery deeds.

Assets. List all of your real property, securities, bank accounts, personal property such as cars and boats and other miscellaneous property.

> *Real Property.* List the location of the property and how you hold title. For example, 20 Maple St., Los Angeles, John Smith and Mary Smith, as joint tenants.
>
> *Securities.* List all stocks, bonds, and brokerage accounts. As to actual certificates for stocks and bonds, you should list the number of shares under the subheading "Account #." As to brokerage accounts, you do

not need to list the individual securities within the account. As with real property, list how the title is held as to each security or brokerage account. If you hold a brokerage account in your name with a "transfer on death" designation, list your name with TOD and the name of the beneficiary in the event of your death.

Bank Accounts. List the name and location of each financial institution, the account numbers, where the bank books or CD certificates are located, and the title vesting for each account. For Totten trust accounts list your name and then ATF ("as trustee for") and then the name of the beneficiary in the event of your death.

Autos/Boats/Etc. List the location of the certificate of title for each asset. The certificate of title itself will indicate any co-ownership rights.

Partnerships/Annuities/Royalties/Misc. Assets. List the names of assets, location of original documentation of ownership, a description of the assets with any account number, and the name of any beneficiary.

Tax Returns. List where your prior year tax returns can be found.

Lawyer. List the name of any lawyer that either has information concerning any of the above and/or that you would like your family/beneficiaries to contact regarding assistance in the handling of your estate.

ASSET ROADMAP

WILL

Date

Location

Executor

TRUST

Date

Location

Successor Trustee

CODICIL

Date

Location

POWER OF ATTORNEY

HEALTH

Date

Location

Agent

FINANCIAL

Date

Location

Agent

SAFE DEPOSIT BOX

Location

Location of Key

Box #

Co-Renter

LIFE INSURANCE

Company

Amount

Policy #

Location

Company

Amount

Policy #

Location

Company
Amount
Policy #
Location

Company
Amount
Policy #
Location

OTHER INSURANCE

Auto

Household

Other

BURIAL/FUNERAL INSTRUCTIONS

ASSETS

Real Property

Location
Title

Location
Title

Location
Title

Location
Title

Securities

Name Account #
Title
1.
2.
3.
4.
5.

Bank Accounts

Location Account #

Title

1.

2.

3.

4.

5.

Autos/Boats/Etc

Description of Auto/Boat/etc.

Location of Title Certificate

Description of Auto/Boat/etc.

Location of Title Certificate

Description of Auto/Boat/etc.

Location of Title Certificate

Partnerships/Annuities/Royalties/Misc. Investments

1.

2.

3.

TAX RETURNS

Location

LAWYER REFERRAL

Appendix C
Step-By-Step Instructions with Sample Completed Forms

Number Key

In the forms included in this book the *blanks* to be filled in by you are each numbered. Use the following as a reference guide as to how to complete each blank based upon its assigned number. (Three sample completed forms are located in this section. Use these as models to complete the blank forms in Appendix D.)

(1): *Your name* (not your signature).

(1a): *The name of your trust.* Generally your name or your family name. For example, "The Smith Family Trust."

(1b): *The signature of spouse.*

(2): *Name of the county where you live.*

(2a): *Name of the state in which you live.*

(3): *State whether you are a widow or unmarried.*

(4): *Name of your spouse if you are married or a widow.* If you are unmarried (never married or divorced) write "Not Applicable."

(5): *Name(s) of your child(ren) and their birthdates.* If a child is an adult, you can simply list his or her name, a comma, and the words "an adult."

Example: "Bob Smith, born 12/25/02" or "Mary Lee, an adult."

(6): *Name(s) of the descendants now living of any predeceased children you have.*

Example: If your son, Bob, is now deceased, but left two children and one grandchild now living, you would list all three of those descendants of Bob and their relationship to you (i.e., a grandchild, great-grandchild, etc.).

If you have no deceased child who left descendants now surviving, write "Not Applicable."

(7): *If you wrote* Not Applicable *for (6) above, insert* "Not Applicable," *here.*

If you have a predeceased child(ren) who left descendants now surviving and listed all of the descendants in (6) above, insert "no other."

(8): *List all bequests of personal, tangible property like furniture, cars, jewelry, etc.*

Example: "My green couch to my nephew, Bob Smith" for a will or "The Settlor's nephew, Bob Smith" or "Settlor's friends, Ned Jones and Mary Lee" for a trust.

If you are not making any specific bequests of personal, tangible property, simply write "Not Applicable."

(9): *List who will receive your personal, tangible property that is not specifically disposed of in (8).*

Example: "My nephew, Bob Smith" or "my friends, Ned Jones and Mary Lee" for a will or "The settlor's nephew, Bob Smith" or "Settlor's friends, Ned Jones and Mary Lee" for a trust.

If you want to leave your personal, tangible property to your residual beneficiaries listed in item (18) write "Not Applicable."

(10): *List any cash bequests to beneficiaries.*

Example: "My nephew, Bob Smith, the cash sum of Ten Thousand Dollars ($10,000.00)" or "The Settlor's nephew, Bob Smith, the cash sum of Ten Thousand Dollars ($10,000.00)" for a trust.

If you do not wish to make any cash bequests write "Not Applicable."

(11): *List any specific bequests of real estate to beneficiaries.*

Example: "My nephew, Bob Smith, the residential real property located at 12 Maple Ave., Los Angeles, CA."

If you do not wish to make any specific bequests of real estate, write "Not Applicable."

(12): *If you do not make any specific bequests of real estate in item (11) you can ignore item (12).* If you do make specific bequests of real estate in item (11) you need to either do nothing at item (12) if you want the beneficiary of the real estate to receive the property free of all mortgages and liens. If, however, you want to the bequest of real property to carry with it any mortgage or liens recorded against that property, you need to put a line through the sentence after item (12), and place your initials next to the end of the cross out BEFORE you sign your will or trust.

(13) *Name of the* life estate *beneficiary.* If you are not giving a life estate to anyone write "Not Applicable."

(14): *Location of property subject to the life estate.*

(15): *Name of person or entity that takes the life estate property after the death of the life estate beneficiary named in (13).*

(16) and (17): *You are bequeathing the residue of your estate under your will or inter-vivos trust, i.e., everything not already specifically bequeathed.* If you are leaving your residue in differing proportions, such as 40 shares to Bob and 60 shares (remember to use shares, when

possible, instead of percentages to avoid problems when a beneficiary predeceases you) to Mary (or "All" to a single beneficiary), then you will leave the words between items (16) and (17) intact, cross out the words "in equal shares" after item (16), and initial said cross out BEFORE you sign your will or trust.

If, instead, you want to leave the residue of your estate to more than one beneficiary, in equal shares, you will cross out the words between item (16) and (17) and initial said cross out BEFORE you sign your will or trust.

If in your will or trust, you are leaving everything to a trust under (19) then write "Not Applicable" at (18).

(18): *Names of only the beneficiaries of the residue of your estate under your will or inter-vivos trust* (if you crossed out the words between item (16) and (17)) or names of the beneficiaries of the residue of your estate and their proportions (if you crossed out the words "in equal shares" after item (17)).

Example: "To my nephew, Bob Smith, 20 shares and to my niece, Mary Lee, 80 shares" or " All to my nephew, Bob Smith" for a will or "The Settlor's nephew, Bob Smith, 20 shares and to the Settlor's niece, Mary Lee, 80 shares" or "All to the Settlor's nephew, Bob Smith" for a trust.

If, in your will or trust, you are leaving everything to a trust under (19) then write "Not Applicable" at (18).

(19): *The number of shares of the residue of your estate under your will or inter-vivos trust going to the trust created under your will or inter-vivos trust.* (If you are not leaving any portion of the residue of your estate to a trust created under your will, you should be using a different form.) If you are leaving everything to the trust created under your will insert "All" after (19).

(20): *Name of the beneficiary of the trust,* that is, the person who receives the income/principal of the trust.

(21): *The age at which time the beneficiary receives one-half of his/her trust principal.* If you want the beneficiary to receive all of his/her trust principal at one age, write in "N/A" for "Not Applicable" and proceed to item (22).

(22): *The age at which time the beneficiary receives the rest (or all) of his/her trust principal.* Typically you will separate the ages at which time the beneficiary receives his/her trust principal. For example, one half at age 25 and the remainder at age 30.

(23): *Name of the beneficiary who receives the trust estate after the death of the life beneficiary of the trust.*

(24): *Name of the beneficiary who receives the trust estate after the death of the life beneficiary, if the beneficiary in item (23) is then deceased.* If no such beneficiary is to be named in item (23) write "Not Applicable."

(25): *Name of the person or entity who acts as the trustee.* You can nominate two trustees.

(26): *Insert "co" before the word "trustee" and an "s" at the end of the word trustee if you nominate more than one trustee at item (25).* If you nominate one trustee at item (25), do nothing at item (26).

(27): *Do nothing if you want the trustee you nominated to act without posting a surety bond.* Cross out the words "without bond" and initial said cross out if you want your trustee to post a surety bond (recommended). (Remember that corporate trustees do not have to post bonds.)

(28): *Name of the person or entity who is to act as the back-up trustee.*

(29): *The age (anywhere from 18 years to 25 years) that the beneficiary will receive his or her custodial property.*

(30): *Name of the person or entity who is to act as guardian/custodian.*

(31): *Identify which codicil you are preparing. Is it the first codicil to your will or the second, etc., codicil?*

(32): *Do nothing if you want the custodian(s) you nominated to act without posting a surety bond.* Cross out the words "without bond" and initial said cross out if you want your Custodian to post a surety bond (recommended). (Remember that corporate custodians do not have to post bonds.)

(33): *Name of the person or entity who is to act as the back-up guardian/custodian.*

(34): *Name of the person or entity who is to act as your executor.* (Remember that you can nominate two executors.)

(35): *Insert "co" before the word "executor" and an "s" at the end of the word executor if you nominate more than one executor in item (34).* If you nominate one executor at item (34) do nothing at item (35).

(36): Do nothing if you want your executor to act without posting a surety bond. Cross out the words "without bond" and initial said cross out if you want your Executor to post a surety bond (recommended). (Remember that corporate executors do not have to post bonds.)

(37): *Name of the person or entity who is to act as the back-up executor.*

(38): *Insert the date.*

(39): *Insert the name of the city and state where your will or trust is being signed.*

(40): *Sign your name.*

(41): *First witness signs his or her name.*

(41a): *Name of first witness.*

(42): *First witness writes his or her address.*

(43): *Second witness signs his or her name.*

(43a): *Name of second witness.*

(44): *Second witness writes his or her address.*

(45): *Insert date of will you are amending.*

(46): *Insert amendment words.*

Example: "I married Sue Smith on August 1, 2003."

(47): *You must select either Option 1 or Option 2.* If you select Option 1, then you must cross through the words between (47—Option 2 Start) and (47—Option 2B End) AND place your initials in the margin near the crossed through words.

If you select Option 2, cross through the words between (47—Option 1 Start) and (47—Option 1 End) AND either cross through the words between (47—Option 2A End) and (47—Option 2B Start) OR cross through the words between (47—Option 2B Start) and (47—Option 2B End), depending on your selections. Place your initials on the margin next to the crossed through words.

(48): *Date that trust was executed (i.e., date trust was signed and notarized).*

(49): *Name of original trustee or trustees.*

(50): *Insert "co" before the word "trustee" and an "s" at the end of the word "trustee" if there are two or more currently acting trustees at (49).*

(51): *Name of trustee in (49) if there is only one currently acting trustee. If there are two trustees in (49) then the word "either should be inserted.*

(52): *Name of next successor trust (after currently acting trustee).* If there are two or more trustees at (49), insert the name of the remaining acting trustee if he or she is to then act alone. Insert the name of the remaining trustee plus a successor trustee if the remaining trustee is to then act with another.

(53): *Attach a copy of all pages of the trust which relate to the powers of the trustee.* (In the forms located in this book said trustee powers are always at Paragraph 4.6.)

(54): *Signature of currently acting trustee(s).*

(55): *Insert the street address and legal description (if possible) of all real property, account numbers of all brokerage and bank accounts and any other property that you intend to transfer to the trust.*

(56): *Name of original trustee (see (4a)).* Very likely the settlor.

(57): *If the trust has been previously amended cross out the following word "not."*

(58): *If the trust has been previously amended, cross out the following word "further."*

(59): *Cross out and initial the word "not" if you wish to include your adopted children as your descendants* (by law your adopted children are already considered your children). In this sentence, you are addressing the question of whether your children's or grandchildren's adopted children are to be considered your issue (i.e., your descendants).

(60): *Cross out the words "codicil to his/her" if attaching affidavit to the will.* If attaching affidavit to a codicil, leave in.

Sample Forms

LAST WILL AND TESTAMENT

I, (1) ROBERT SMITH, a resident of (2) LOS ANGELES County (2a), CALIFORNIA, being of sound and disposing mind and memory and not acting under duress, menace, fraud or undue influence of any person whomsoever, do make, publish and declare this to be my Last Will and Testament, and I hereby expressly revoke all other wills, codicils, and testamentary writings heretofore made by me.

FIRST. I declare that I am married. My spouse's name is (4) MARTHA SMITH. I have the following children:

(5) MARY SMITH, BORN 3/1/98; AND

TOM SMITH, BORN 7/2/00

I have a deceased child who left the following issue now surviving:

(6) NOT APPLICABLE

I have no other children and (7) NOT APPLICABLE deceased children who left issue now surviving.

SECOND. I devise all of estate to my spouse. In the event my spouse should predecease me then I leave all of my estate to my issue, by right of representation.

THIRD: I have intentionally and with full knowledge omitted to provide for my issue, ancestors, relatives and heirs living at the time of my demise, except for such provisions as are made specifically herein.

If any person who is or claims under or through a beneficiary of this Will, or if any person who would be entitled to share in my estate if I died intestate, should in any manner whatsoever, directly or indirectly, attack, contest or seek to impair or invalidate in court any provision of the following:

A. This Will or any Codicil to this Will;

B. Any revocable or irrevocable Trust established by me;

C. Any beneficiary designation executed by me with respect to any insurance policy, any "totten trust" account, any joint tenancy, any "transfer on death" account or any pension plan, or conspire or cooperate with anyone attempting to do any of the actions or things aforesaid, then I hereby specifically disinherit each such person and any devise, share or interest in my estate otherwise given to each such person under this Will or to which each such person might be entitled by law, is hereby revoked and shall pass and be distributed as though each such person had predeceased me leaving no issue or heirs whatsoever.

Any and every individual who asserts, or conspires or cooperates with any person who asserts, any claim against my Estate based on:

D. "Quantum meruit" theory;

E. Common law marriage, Marvin v. Marvin, 18 Cal. 3d 660 (1976) type of agreement or similar theory;

F. Constructive trust theory; or,

G. Oral agreement or written agreement which is to be proved by parole evidence, claiming that I agreed to gift or devise anything to such person or to pay such person or another for services rendered, regardless of whether a court may find that such agreement existed, then I hereby specifically disinherit each such person and any devise, share or interest in my estate otherwise given to each such person under this Will or to which each such person might be entitled by law, is hereby revoked and shall pass and be distributed as though each such person had predeceased me leaving no issue or heirs whatsoever.

FOURTH: I nominate and appoint my spouse as Executor hereunder without bond. In the event my spouse should decline, become unable or, for any reason, cease to serve as Executor then I nominate and appoint (37) BILL E. SMITH as Executor hereunder (36) without bond.

I authorize my Executor to sell, at either public or private sale, encumber or lease any property belonging to my estate, either with or without public notice, subject to such confirmation as may be required by law, and to hold, manage and operate any such property.

FIFTH. All typed and handwritten "fill-ins" where directed above were made before the execution of this Will and are not initialed by me. All crossed through words and inter-lineations were made before the execution of this Will and are initialed by me.

Except as provided otherwise herein, the masculine, feminine, and neuter gender and the singular or plural number, shall each be deemed to include the others whenever the context so indicates.

IN WITNESS WHEREOF, I have hereunto set my hand this (38)_JANUARY 31, 2003_____ at (39) GLENDALE____________, (2a) CA____.

(40)_*Robert Smith*__________

The foregoing instrument, consisting of four pages, including the page on which this attestation clause is completed and signed, was at the date hereof by (1)_ROBERT SMITH______ signed as and declared to be his/her Will, in the presence of us who, at his/her request and in his/her presence, and in the presence of each other, have subscribed our names as witnesses thereto. Each of us observed the signing of this Will by (1)_ROBERT SMITH_____ and by each other subscribing witness and knows that each signature is the true signature of the person whose name was signed.

Each of us is now an adult and a competent witness and resides at the address set forth after his or her name.

We are acquainted with (1)_ROBERT SMITH________. At this time, he/she is over the age of eighteen years, and to the best of our knowledge, he/she is of sound mind and is not acting under duress, menace, fraud, misrepresentation, or undue influence.

We declare under penalty of perjury that the foregoing is true and correct.

Executed on (38) JANUARY 31, 2003 at (39) GLENDALE, (2a) CA.

(41) *Mabel Jones*

Residing at (42) 555 MAIN ST.,

EAGLE ROCK, CA

(43) *Ralph Jones*

Residing at (44) 555 MAIN ST.

EAGLE ROCK, CA

LAST WILL AND TESTAMENT

I, (1) ROBERT SMITH, a resident of (2) LOS ANGELES County, (2a) CALIFORNIA, being of sound and disposing mind and memory and not acting under duress, menace, fraud or undue influence of any person whomsoever, do make, publish and declare this to be my Last Will and Testament, and I hereby expressly revoke all other wills, codicils, and testamentary writings heretofore made by me.

FIRST. I declare that I am married. My spouse's name is (4) MARTHA SMITH. I have the following children:

(5) ANDREW SMITH, BORN 10/03/88; AND,

ALISON SMITH, BORN 5/18/90

I have a deceased child who left the following issue now surviving:

(6) MIKE SMITH

I have no other children and (7) NOT APPLICABLE deceased children who left issue now surviving.

SECOND. I devise the following personal, tangible property:

(8) MY MORRIS MINOR CAR TO MY BROTHER, BILLY SMITH

I devise to (9) MARTHA SMITH AND ANDREW SMITH all of my remaining personal effects, household furniture and furnishings, trailers, boats, pictures, works of art and art objects, collections, jewelry, silverware, wearing apparel, collections, sporting goods, and all other articles of household or personal use or ornament at whatsoever time acquired by me and wheresoever situated.

I devise to the following persons the cash amount listed after their respective names:

(10) ALISON SMITH, TEN THOUSAND DOLLARS ($10,000.00)

I devise to the following persons the real property described after their respective names. (12) Said real property is given free of all encumbrances or liens thereon.

(11) MY RESIDENCE LOCATED AT 24 TINDAYA, GLENDALE, TO MY WIFE, MARTHA SMITH

In the event any of the above named persons should predecease me or fail to survive me then his or her share shall lapse unless I have specifically named a person to take said bequest in the event of the first beneficiary's death.

Any beneficiary above who fails to survive me by thirty days shall be deemed to have predeceased me.

I devise all of the rest, residue and remainder of my estate, real, personal and mixed, of whatsoever kind or character and wheresoever situated, of which I die possessed or to which I may in any manner be entitled, to the following persons or entities (16) in the pro-portions listed after their names (17) in equal shares.

(18) MARTHA SMITH, 80 SHARES; AND

MIKE SMITH, 1 SHARE

(19)_19___ shares to the Trustee hereinafter named, to have and to hold for the benefit of (20)ANDREW SMITH _________upon the uses, trusts, purposes and conditions hereinafter provided.

1. If the beneficiary, his or her spouse, or any of his children should at any time or from time to time be in need, in the discretion of the Trustee, of funds due to illness, infirmity or other physical or mental disability or any emergency, the Trustee may relieve or contribute toward the relief of any such need or needs of the beneficiary by paying to him or her or using and applying for his or her ben-

efit, such sum or sums out of the income and/or principal of his or her trust as the Trustee, in the Trustee's discretion, may deem necessary or advisable.

2. The Trustee shall pay the beneficiary all of the net income, in monthly or other convenient installments, from the trust.

3.a. (47 - Option 1 Start) Upon the beneficiary attaining the age of (21)_25__ years, the Trustee shall distribute and deliver to such beneficiary one-half of his trust estate. Upon each beneficiary attaining the age of (22)_30____ years, the Trustee shall distribute and deliver to such beneficiary all of the remainder of his or her trust estate.

3.b. If, upon the attaining of the above ages, the Trustee suspects that said beneficiary may be abusing drugs and/or alcohol, the Trustee may require the beneficiary to take a reasonable drug and/or alcohol test. If the beneficiary fails said test, the trustee shall defer said principal payment to the beneficiary until the beneficiary passes said test. After a failed test, subsequent drug tests shall be administered at the request of the beneficiary but not less than six months after a prior test. In the event a beneficiary fails a drug and/or alcohol test, the Trustee may use said beneficiary's trust estate to pay for a drug and/or alcohol abuse rehabilitation program and may require the beneficiary to enroll and to complete said program as a condition precedent to the taking of a subsequent drug and/or alcohol test.

3.c. In the event the beneficiary should die before complete distribution to him or her of his or her trust estate, his or her entire trust estate on hand at the time of his death shall thereupon be apportioned and distributed to his or her surviving issue, by right of representation. If such beneficiary should die before complete distribution to him or her of his or her trust estate and leave no surviving issue, then the balance of the trust estate then on hand shall go and be distributed to my heirs to be determined according to the laws of the State of California then in effect relating to the intestate succession of separate property not acquired from a predeceased spouse. (47 - Option 1 End)

~~OR~~

~~3.a. (47 - Option 2 Start) In addition to any other payments to the beneficiary hereunder, the Trustee shall, upon the written request of the beneficiary in December of each calendar year, pay to the beneficiary amounts from principal that the beneficiary requests, not exceeding in any single calendar year the~~

~~greater of the following amounts: $5,000.00 or 5 percent of the value of the principal of the beneficiary's trust estate; determined as of the end of the calendar year. This right of withdrawal is noncumulative, so that if the beneficiary does not withdraw the full amount permitted to be withdrawn during any calendar year, the right to withdraw the remaining amount will lapse at the end of the calendar year.~~

~~3.b. On the death of the beneficiary his or her entire trust estate on hand at the time of his death shall thereupon be apportioned and distributed to (23)____________________________. If (23)____________________________ is then deceased then the trust estate then on hand shall go to (24)____________________________, if he is then living. (47 - Option 2A End)~~

OR:

~~the beneficiary's surviving issue, by right of representation. If such beneficiary should die before complete distribution to him or her of his or her trust estate and leave no surviving issue, then the balance of the trust estate then on hand shall go and be distributed to my heirs to be determined according to the laws of the State of California then in effect relating to the intestate succession of separate property not acquired from a predeceased spouse. (47 - Option 2B End)~~
RS

4. Each beneficiary hereunder is hereby prohibited from anticipating, encumbering, assigning, or in any other manner alienating his or her interest in either income or principal, and is without power so to do, nor shall such interest be subject to his or her liabilities or obligations, nor to attachment, execution, or other legal processes, bankruptcy proceedings or claims of creditors or others. The Trustee may, however, deposit in any bank designated in writing by a beneficiary, to his or her credit, income or principal payable to such beneficiary.

5. If, at any time, a trust created hereunder shall, in the sole judgment of the Trustee, be of the aggregate principal value of Fifty Thousand Dollars ($50,000.00) or less, the Trustee may, but need not, terminate such trust and distribute the assets thereof in the Trustee's possession to the beneficiary or beneficiaries, at the time of the current income thereof, and if there is more than one beneficiary, in the proportion in which they are beneficiaries.

6. I nominate and appoint (25)__MARTHA SMITH__ as (26)__Not Applicable__ Trustee hereunder (27) without bond. In the event he/she or both of them should die, decline to act, or for any other reason, be unable to act as Trustee then I appoint (28) __BILLY SMITH__ as Trustee hereunder (27) without bond.

THIRD: I have intentionally and with full knowledge omitted to provide for my issue, ancestors, relatives and heirs living at the time of my demise, except for such provisions as are made specifically herein.

If any person who is or claims under or through a beneficiary of this Will, or if any person who would be entitled to share in my estate if I died intestate, should in any manner whatsoever, directly or indirectly, attack, contest or seek to impair or invalidate in court any provision of the following:

A. This Will or any Codicil to this Will;

B. Any revocable or irrevocable Trust established by me;

C. Any beneficiary designation executed by me with respect to any insurance policy, any "totten trust" account, any joint tenancy, any "transfer on death" account or any pension plan, or conspire or cooperate with anyone attempting to do any of the actions or things aforesaid, then I hereby specifically disinherit each such person and any devise, share or interest in my estate otherwise given to each such person under this Will or to which each such person might be entitled by law, is hereby revoked and shall pass and be distributed as though each such person had predeceased me leaving no issue or heirs whatsoever.

Any and every individual who asserts, or conspires or cooperates with any person who asserts, any claim against my Estate based on:

D. "Quantum meruit" theory;

E. Common law marriage, Marvin v. Marvin, 18 Cal. 3d 660 (1976) type of agreement or similar theory;

F. Constructive trust theory; or,

G. Oral agreement or written agreement which is to be proved by parole evidence, claiming that I agreed to gift or devise anything to such person or to pay such person or another for services rendered, regardless of whether a court may find that such agreement existed, then I hereby specifically disinherit each such person and any devise, share or interest in my estate otherwise given to each such person under this Will or to which each such person might be entitled by law, is hereby revoked and shall pass and be distributed as though each such person had predeceased me leaving no issue or heirs whatsoever.

FOURTH: I nominate and appoint (34) MARTHA SMITH AND BILLY SMITH as (35) CO-ExecutorS hereunder (36) without bond. In the event he/she or both of them should decline, become unable or, for any reason, cease to serve as Executor then I nominate and appoint (37) BRIAN HOPP as Executor hereunder (36) without bond.

I authorize my Executor to sell, at either public or private sale, encumber or lease any property belonging to my estate, either with or without public notice, subject to such confirmation as may be required by law, and to hold, manage and operate any such property.

FIFTH. All handwritten "fill-ins" where directed above were made before the execution of this Will and are not initialed by me. All inter-lineations were made before the execution of this Will and are initialed by me.

The masculine, feminine, and neuter gender and the singular or plural number, shall each be deemed to include the others whenever the context so indicates.

IN WITNESS WHEREOF, I have hereunto set my hand this

(38) JANUARY 31, 2003 at (39) GLENDALE, (2a) CA

(40) *Robert Smith*

The foregoing instrument, consisting of seven pages, including the page on which this attestation clause is completed and signed, was at the date hereof by (1)_ROBERT SMITH______ signed as and declared to be his/her Will, in the presence of us who, at his/her request and in his/her presence, and in the presence of each other, have subscribed our names as witnesses thereto. Each of us observed the signing of this Will by (1)_ROBERT SMITH______ and by each other subscribing witness and knows that each signature is the true signature of the person whose name was signed.

Each of us is now an adult and a competent witness and resides at the address set forth after his or her name.

We are acquainted with (1)_ROBERT SMITH________. At this time, he/she is over the age of eighteen years, and to the best of our knowledge, he/she is of sound mind and is not acting under duress, menace, fraud, misrepresentation, or undue influence.

We declare under penalty of perjury that the foregoing is true and correct.

Executed on (38)_JANUARY 31, 2003_____ at (39) _GLENDALE_____, (2a) CA____.

(41)_*Mabel Jones*___________

Residing at (42)_555 MAIN ST.______

_EAGLE ROCK, CA_______________

(43)_*Ralph Jones*__________

Residing at (44)_555 MAIN ST._______

_EAGLE ROCK, CA_______________

LAST WILL AND TESTAMENT

I, (1) ROBERT SMITH, a resident of (2) LOS ANGELES County, (2a) CALIFORNIA, being of sound and disposing mind and memory and not acting under duress, menace, fraud or undue influence of any person whomsoever, do make, publish and declare this to be my Last Will and Testament, and I hereby expressly revoke all other wills codicils, and testamentary writings heretofore made by me.

FIRST. I declare that I am (3) DIVORCED. My spouse's name was (4) MARTHA SMITH. I have the following children:

(5) ANDREW SMITH, BORN 10/03/70; AND,

ALISON SMITH, BORN 5/18/72

I have a deceased child who left the following issue now surviving:

(6) NOT APPLICABLE

I have no other children and (7) NOT APPLICABLE deceased children who left issue now surviving.

SECOND. I devise the following personal, tangible property to the follow persons:

(8) 1911 SILVER DOLLAR TO ANDREW SMITH

I devise to (9) ANDREW SMITH AND ALISON SMITH all of my remaining personal effects, household furniture and furnishings, trailers, boats, pictures, works of art and art objects, collections, jewelry, silverware, wearing apparel, collections, sporting goods, and all other articles of household or personal use or ornament at whatsoever time acquired by me and wheresoever situated.

I devise to the following persons the cash amount listed after their respective names:

(10) NOT APPLICABLE

I devise to the following persons the real property described after their respective names. (12) Said real property is given free of all encumbrances or liens thereon.

(11) NOT APPLICABLE

I devise to (13) TERRY HOPP a life estate in the following property located at:(14) 213 CLUB DR., LONG BEACH. After the death of (13) TERRY HOPP said property shall go, outright, to (15) ANDREW SMITH AND ALISON SMITH as the remainder person(s).

I devise all of the rest, residue and remainder of my estate, real, personal and mixed, of whatsoever kind or character and wheresoever situated, of which I die possessed or to which I may in any manner be entitled, to the following persons or entities (16) in the pro-portions listed after their names (17) in equal shares.

(18) ANDREW SMITH AND ALISON SMITH

In the event any of the above named persons should predecease me or fail to survive me then his or her share shall lapse unless I have specifically named a person to take said bequest in the event of the first beneficiary's death.

Any beneficiary above who fails to survive me by thirty days shall be deemed to have predeceased me.

THIRD: I have intentionally and with full knowledge omitted to provide for my issue, ancestors, relatives and heirs living at the time of my demise, except for such provisions as are made specifically herein.

If any person who is or claims under or through a beneficiary of this Will, or if any person who would be entitled to share in my estate if I died intestate, should in any manner whatsoever, directly or indirectly, attack, contest or seek to impair or invalidate in court any provision of the following:

A. This Will or any Codicil to this Will;

B. Any revocable or irrevocable Trust established by me;

C. Any beneficiary designation executed by me with respect to any insurance policy, any "totten trust" account, any joint tenancy, any "transfer on death" account or any pension plan, or conspire or cooperate with anyone attempting to do any of the actions or things aforesaid, then I hereby specifically disinherit each such person and any devise, share or interest in my estate otherwise given to each such person under this Will or to which each such person might be entitled by law, is hereby revoked and shall pass and be distributed as though each such person had predeceased me leaving no issue or heirs whatsoever.

Any and every individual who asserts, or conspires or cooperates with any person who asserts, any claim against my Estate based on:

D. "Quantum meruit" theory;

E. Common law marriage, Marvin v. Marvin, 18 Cal. 3d 660 (1976) type of agreement or similar theory;

F. Constructive trust theory; or,

G. Oral agreement or written agreement which is to be proved by parole evidence, claiming that I agreed to gift or devise anything to such person or to pay such person or another for services rendered, regardless of whether a court may find that such agreement existed, then I hereby specifically disinherit each such person and any devise, share or interest in my estate otherwise given to each such person under this Will or to which each such person might be entitled by law, is hereby revoked and shall pass and be distributed as though each such person had predeceased me leaving no issue or heirs whatsoever.

FOURTH: I nominate and appoint (34) ANDREW SMITH as (35) Executor hereunder (36) without bond. In the event he/she/they should decline, become unable or, for any reason, cease to serve as Executor then I nominate and appoint (37) ALISON SMITH as Executor hereunder (36) without bond.

I authorize my Executor to sell, at either public or private sale, encumber or lease any property belonging to my estate, either with or without public notice, subject to such confirmation as may be required by law, and to hold, manage and operate any such property.

FIFTH. All typed and handwritten "fill-ins" where directed above were made before the execution of this Will and are not initialed by me. All crossed through words and inter-lineations were made before the execution of this Will and are initialed by me.

Except as provided otherwise herein, the masculine, feminine, and neuter gender and the singular or plural number, shall each be deemed to include the others whenever the context so indicates.

IN WITNESS WHEREOF, I have hereunto set my hand this

(38) JANUARY 31, 2003 at (39) GLENDALE, (2a) CA.

(40) *Robert Smith*

The foregoing instrument, consisting of five pages, including the page on which this attestation clause is completed and signed, was at the date hereof by (1) ROBERT SMITH signed as and declared to be his/her Will, in the presence of us who, at his/her request and in his/her presence, and in the presence of each other, have subscribed our names as witnesses thereto. Each of us observed the signing of this Will by (1) ROBERT SMITH and by each other subscribing witness and knows that each signature is the true signature of the person whose name was signed.

Each of us is now an adult and a competent witness and resides at the address set forth after his or her name.

We are acquainted with (1) ROBERT SMITH. At this time, he/she is over the age of eighteen years, and to the best of our knowledge, he/she is of sound mind and is not acting under duress, menace, fraud, misrepresentation, or undue influence.

We declare under penalty of perjury that the foregoing is true and correct.

Executed on (38) JANUARY 31, 2003 at (39) GLENDALE, (2a) CA.

(41) *Mabel Jones*

Residing at (42) 555 MAIN ST.,

EAGLE ROCK, CA

(43) *Ralph Jones*

Residing at (44) 555 MAIN ST.

EAGLE ROCK, CA

Appendix D
Blank Forms

Choosing the correct form is very important. The **Nomination of Guardian**, forms 1 and 2, gives you two selections. Form 1 should be used when it is unlikely there will be a controversy over your choice. Form 2 should be used when you are concerned about the acceptance of others over your choice of the guardian of the person and/or the estate of your minor children.

The *will forms* are divided into four categories. You should first determine which category you are in and then pick only from the forms within that category. Forms 3 through form 9 are designed for persons who are married and have children. Forms 10 through form 12 are designed for persons who are married and have no children. Forms 13 through form 17 are designed for persons who are unmarried and have children, and forms 18 through form 20 are designed for persons who are unmarried and have no children.

The *inter-vivos trust forms* are divided into two categories. You should first determine which category you are in and then pick only from the forms within that category. Forms 31 through form 33 are designed for persons who are single or for married persons who wish to create their own inter-vivos trust instead of jointly creating an inter-vivos trust with their spouse. Forms 34 through form 42 are designed for persons who are married. In Forms 34 through 42, both spouses create the inter-vivos trust and the provisions of the inter-vivos trust are *reciprocal* in that they are the same regardless of which spouse dies first.

Each of the inter-vivos trust forms also gives the *option* of leaving some property in a *life estate* for a person's lifetime benefit. Use of the optional life estate provision would most likely be used when a spouse, child, relative, or friend needs the use or income from the property selected for the life tenancy and you are either worried he or she might lose the property or the life tenant would leave it at his or her death to someone other than who you would like to see receive the life tenancy property (e.g., a sister who lives with you might be a choice as a life tenant to your residence with your children being the remaindermen of the life tenancy).

Each of the inter-vivos trust forms also gives the *option* of leaving specific property or cash outright before disposing of the *residue* of the inter-vivos trust estate. If you do not wish to leave specific property or cash bequests simply write in *Not Applicable* where appropriate.

Caution: There are many forms that have very similar titles and wording in this appendix. You must carefully read the description of each form to find the one that best suits your needs. Often the slightest change in a form's wording can change the entire meaning of the form.

Table of Forms

receives all net income of the Decedent's Trust and could invade the principal of the Decedent's Trust as necessary for his or her support in his or her accustomed manner of living. Upon the surviving spouse's death, portions of the inter-vivos trust estate passes outright to your children and/or others but a portion of the inter-vivos trust estate passes to a child, and/or another in trust wherein the trust beneficiary receives income from the trust portion until he or she dies and then it is distributed to another. This form would be used when you want a portion of the estate held in trust for the benefit of a beneficiary who is unable to manage assets, to minimize federal estate taxes your children might have to pay by creation of the Decedent's Trust, and/or to either control the eventual distribution of the Decedent's Trust portion of the predeceasing spouse's estate and/or to protect the surviving spouse from creditors by the use of the asset protection attributes of the Decedent's Trust.

Use this form if you want to create a Decedent's Trust and after funding of the Decedent's Trust, a Marital Trust. The Decedent's Trust and Marital Trust will consist of all of the predeceasing spouse's inter-vivos trust estate. The Decedent's Trust and Marital Trust are irrevocable at the death of the predeceasing spouse. The surviving spouse's assets in the inter-vivos trust will go into the Survivor's Trust over which he or she will have complete control. The surviving spouse receives all of the net income of the Decedent's Trust and Marital Trust, can take 5% of the principal of the marital trust, and could invade the principal of the Decedent's Trust and/or Marital Trust as necessary for his or her support in his or her accustomed manner of living. Upon the surviving spouse's death, the inter-vivos trust estate passes outright to children and/or others. This form would be used when you want a portion of the estate held in trust for the benefit of a beneficiary who is unable to manage assets, to minimize federal estate taxes your children might have to pay by creation of the Decedent's Trust, and/or to either control the eventual distribution of the Decedent's Trust and Marital Trust (i.e., the predeceasing spouse's inter-vivos trust estate) and/or to protect the surviving spouse from creditors by the use of the asset protection attributes of the Decedent's Trust and Marital Trust.

Use this form if you want to create a Decedent's Trust and after funding of the Decedent's Trust, a Marital Trust. The Decedent's Trust and Marital Trust will consist of all of the predeceasing spouse's inter-vivos trust estate. The Decedent's Trust and Marital Trust are irrevocable at the death of the predeceasing spouse. The surviving spouse's assets in the inter-vivos trust will go into the Survivor's Trust over which he or she will have complete control. The surviving spouse receives all of the net income of the Decedent's Trust and Marital Trust, can take 5% of the principal of the marital trust, and could invade the principal of the Decedent's Trust and/or Marital Trust as necessary for his or her sup-

port in his or her accustomed manner of living. Upon the surviving spouse's death, portions of the inter-vivos trust estate can pass outright to children and/or others but the residue of your estate stays in trust for your children, in equal shares. You select the ages for distribution of the principal of each child's share of the trust to that child. This form would be selected to minimize federal estate taxes your children might have to pay by creation of the Decedent's Trust and/or to either control the eventual distribution of the Decedent's Trust and Marital Trust (i.e., the predeceasing spouse's inter-vivos trust estate), and/or to protect the surviving spouse from creditors by the use of the asset protection attributes of the Decedent's Trust and Marital Trust, and, if your children were minors or you wanted to delay distribution to your adult children to a later age.

form 41: Inter-Vivos Trust—Married couple, creation of tax-savings trust for life benefit of surviving spouse, then to trust for minor children; remainder of trust estate outright to surviving spouse 316

Use this form if you want to create a Decedent's Trust out of the estate of the predeceasing spouse with all of the rest of the inter-vivos trust estate passing outright to the surviving spouse in his or her Survivor's Trust over which the surviving spouse has complete control, including the right to revoke or amend. The Decedent's Trust is funded with that amount from the predeceasing spouse's estate equal to the federal estate tax exemption available in the predeceasing spouse's year of death. If the value of the predeceasing spouse's estate is less than the federal estate tax exemption then the Decedent's Trust is funded with all of the predeceasing spouse's inter-vivos trust estate. The surviving spouse receives all net income of the Decedent's Trust and could invade the principal of the Decedent's Trust as necessary for his or her support in his or her accustomed manner of living. Upon the surviving spouse's death, portions of the inter-vivos trust estate can pass outright to children and/or others but the residue of your estate stays in trust for your children, in equal shares. You select the ages for distribution of the principal of each child's share of the trust to that child. This form would be selected to minimize federal estate taxes your children might have to pay by creation of the Decedent's Trust, and/or to either control the eventual distribution of the Decedent's Trust portion of the predeceasing spouse's estate, and/or to protect the surviving spouse from creditors by the use of the asset protection attributes of the Decedent's Trust, and if your children were minors or you wanted to delay distribution to your adult children to a later age.

form 42: Inter-Vivos Trust—Married couple, creation of tax-savings trust and marital trust for life benefit of surviving spouse; after death of surviving spouse outright bequests to children/others with portion remaining in trust for child/other 329

Use this form if you want to create a Decedent's Trust and after funding of the Decedent's Trust, a Marital Trust. The Decedent's Trust and Marital Trust will consist of all of the predeceasing spouse's inter-vivos trust estate. The Decedent's Trust and Marital Trust are irrevocable at the death of the predeceasing spouse. The surviving spouse's assets in the inter-vivos trust will go into the Survivor's Trust over which he or she will have complete control. The surviving spouse receives all of the net income

of the Decedent's Trust and Marital Trust and could invade the principal of the Decedent's Trust and/or Marital Trust as necessary for his or her support in his or her accustomed manner of living. Upon the surviving spouse's death, portions of the inter-vivos trust estate passes outright to your children and/or others but a portion of the inter-vivos trust estate passes to a child and/or another in trust wherein the trust beneficiary receives income from the trust portion until he or she dies and then it is distributed to another. This form would be used when you want a portion of the estate held in trust for the benefit of a beneficiary who is unable to manage assets, to minimize federal estate taxes your children might have to pay by creation of the Decedent's Trust, and to either control the eventual distribution of the Decedent's Trust and Marital Trust portion of the predeceasing spouse's estate and/or to protect the surviving spouse from creditors by the use of the asset protection attributes of the Decedent's Trust and Marital Trust.

Use this form if you want to create a Decedent's Trust out of the estate of the predeceasing spouse with all of the rest of the inter-vivos trust estate passing outright to the surviving spouse in his or her Survivor's Trust over which the surviving spouse has complete control, including the right to revoke or amend. The Decedent's Trust is funded with that amount from the predeceasing spouse's estate equal to the federal estate tax exemption, available in the predeceasing spouse's year of death. If the value of the predeceasing spouse's estate is less than the federal estate tax exemption then the Decedent's Trust is funded with all of the predeceasing spouse's inter-vivos trust estate. The rest of the trust estate belongs to the surviving spouse in the survivor's trust. The surviving spouse receives all net income of the Decedent's Trust and could invade the principal of the Decedent's Trust as necessary for his or her support in his or her accustomed manner of living. Upon the surviving spouse's death the inter-vivos trust estate passes outright to your children and/or others. This form would be used when you want to minimize federal estate taxes your children might have to pay by creation of the Decedent's Trust, and to either control the eventual distribution of the Decedent's Trust portion of the predeceasing spouse's estate and/or to protect the surviving spouse from creditors by the use of the asset protection attributes of the Decedent's Trust.

Use this form if you are making a minor amendment/change to your inter-vivos trust.

Sometimes it is easier or better to simply restate your inter-vivos trust rather than simply make the appropriate changes. For example, if you have amended your inter-vivos trust twenty times, it likely is difficult to read without constant interruptions to determine if each portion has been amended or not. In other situations you may not wish a beneficiary to know that his or her share has been reduced. If you do not amend via a complete restatement of your inter-vivos trust, the disinherited beneficiary would likely find out that their share had been changed. Accordingly, use this form if you are making substantial changes to your inter-vivos trust, if your inter-vivos trust has several prior amendments, or if you do not want the prior inter-vivos trust or prior amendments to be viewed after your death. The restated inter-vivos trust is attached as "Attachment A" and should be executed with the same formalities as the Trust Amendment.

Use this form if you are making a minor amendment/change to your inter-vivos trust.

Sometimes it is easier or better to simply restate your inter-vivos trust rather than simply make the appropriate changes. For example, if you have amended your inter-vivos trust twenty times, it likely is difficult to read your inter-vivos trust without constant interruptions to determine if each portion has been amended or not. In other situations you may not wish a beneficiary to know that his or her share has been reduced. If you do not amend via a complete restatement of your inter-vivos trust, the disinherited beneficiary would likely find out that their share had been changed. Accordingly, use this form if you are making substantial changes to your inter-vivos trust, if your inter-vivos trust has several prior amendments or if you do not want the prior inter-vivos trust or prior amendments to be viewed after your death. The restated inter-vivos trust is attached as "Attachment A" and should be executed with the same formalities as the Trust Amendment.

Use this form when a third party (i.e., a bank) asks for a copy of your trust. A Trust Certification can be used, in most states, in lieu of a copy of the trust. Many financial institutions will use their own trust certification form.

Use this form when a third party (i.e., a bank) asks for a copy of your trust. A Trust Certification can be used, in most states, in lieu of a copy of the trust. Many financial institutions will use their own trust certification form.

Use this form to revoke your inter-vivos trust. Revocation does not automatically unfund assets previously transferred to your revoked inter-vivos trust.

NOMINATION OF GUARDIAN

I (1)________________________, resident of (2)_____________ County, (2a)________________ declare as follows:

1. I am the parent of (5)

2. In the event I am deceased I wish that (30)__________________ be appointed as guardian of the person and estate of each of my minor children, to serve without bond. I understand that said nominated guardian may live in another State at the time of his/her appointment. I expressly consent to the removal of my children to said State if it will facilitate his or her guardianship appointment;

3. I further instruct my Trustee/Executor to permit (30)_______________ to reside in my home during the pendency of his/her appointment as guardian for a period not to exceed 90 days. I further instruct that any reasonable expenses they may incur in his/her quest to be appointed guardian be paid whether or not he/she is actually appointed guardian;

The appointment of (30)________________________ is extremely important to me as said nominated guardian shares the same philosophy of child raising as do I and the placement of my children in his or her care would result in the least trauma to their life.

4. In the event he/she declines or is unable, for any reason, to so act, I then appoint (33)________________________ as said guardian the age of majority at the time of my death to serve without bond.

5. I further permit the guardian of our children to use the estates of my children in the compliance of our request that our children have liberal and appropriate visitation with their family.

Executed on (38)________________, at (39)___________, (2a)____________.

____

(40)

____

(41) Witness

NOMINATION OF GUARDIAN

I (1)______________________________, resident of (2)________________ County, (2a)__________________, declare as follows:

1. I am the parent of (5)

2. In the event I am deceased I wish that (30)_____________________ be appointed as guardian of the person and estate of my minor children, to serve without bond.

3. In the event he/she declines or is unable, for any reason, to so act, I then appoint (33)______________________________ as said guardian the age of majority at the time of my death to serve without bond.

Executed on (38)___________________, at (39)_____________, (2a)_____________.

____
(40)

____
(41) Witness

LAST WILL AND TESTAMENT

I, (1)______________________________, a resident of (2)_______________ County, (2a)________________, being of sound and disposing mind and memory and not acting under duress, menace, fraud or undue influence of any person whomsoever, do make, publish and declare this to be my Last Will and Testament, and I hereby expressly revoke all other wills, codicils, and testamentary writings heretofore made by me.

FIRST. I declare that I am married. My spouse's name is (4)______________________________. I have the following children:
(5)

I have a deceased child who left the following issue now surviving:
(6)

I have no other children and (7)______________ deceased children who left issue now surviving.

SECOND. I devise all of estate to my spouse. In the event my spouse should predecease me then I leave all of my estate to my issue, by right of representation.

THIRD. I have intentionally and with full knowledge omitted to provide for my issue, ancestors, relatives and heirs living at the time of my demise, except for such provisions as are made specifically herein.

If any person who is or claims under or through a beneficiary of this Will, or if any person who would be entitled to share in my estate if I died intestate, should in any manner whatsoever, directly or indirectly, attack, contest or seek to impair or invalidate in court any provision of the following:

A. This Will or any Codicil to this Will;

B. Any revocable or irrevocable Trust established by me;

C. Any beneficiary designation executed by me with respect to any insurance policy, any "Totten trust" account, any joint tenancy, any "transfer on death" account or any pension plan, or conspire or cooperate with anyone attempting to do any of the actions or things aforesaid, then I hereby specifically disinherit each such person and any devise, share or interest in my estate otherwise given to each such person under this Will or to which each such person might be entitled by law, is hereby revoked and shall pass and be distributed as though each such person had predeceased me leaving no issue or heirs whatsoever.

Any and every individual who asserts, or conspires or cooperates with any person who asserts, any claim against my Estate based on:

D. "Quantum meruit" theory;

E. Common law marriage, Marvin v. Marvin, 18 Cal. 3d 660 (1976) type of agreement or similar theory;

F. Constructive trust theory; or,

G. Oral agreement or written agreement which is to be proved by parole evidence, claiming that I agreed to gift or devise anything to such person or to pay such person or another for services rendered, regardless of whether a court may find that such agreement existed, then I hereby specifically disinherit each such person and any devise, share or interest in my estate otherwise given to each such person under this Will or to which each such person might be entitled by law, is hereby revoked and shall pass and be distributed as though each such person had predeceased me leaving no issue or heirs whatsoever.

FOURTH. I nominate and appoint my spouse as Executor hereunder without bond. In the event my spouse should decline, become unable or, for any reason, cease to serve as Executor then I nominate and appoint (37)____________________ as Executor hereunder (36) without bond.

I authorize my Executor to sell, at either public or private sale, encumber or lease any property belonging to my estate, either with or without public notice, subject to such confirmation as may be required by law, and to hold, manage and operate any such property.

FIFTH. All typed and handwritten "fill-ins" where directed above were made before the execution of this Will and are not initialed by me. All crossed through words and inter-lineations were made before the execution of this Will and are initialed by me.

Except as provided otherwise herein, the masculine, feminine, and neuter gender and the singular or plural number, shall each be deemed to include the others whenever the context so indicates.

IN WITNESS WHEREOF, I have hereunto set my hand this (38)__________________ at (39)____________________, (2a)________________.

(40)________________________________

The foregoing instrument, consisting of __ pages, including the page on which this attestation clause is completed and signed, was at the date hereof by (1)___________________________________ signed as and declared to be his/her Will, in the presence of us who, at his/her request and in his/her presence, and in the presence of each other, have subscribed our names as witnesses thereto. Each of us observed the signing of this Will by (1)___________________________ and by each other subscribing witness and knows that each signature is the true signature of the person whose name was signed.

Each of us is now an adult and a competent witness and resides at the address set forth after his or her name.

We are acquainted with (1)_____________________. At this time, he/she is over the age of eighteen years, and to the best of our knowledge, he/she is of sound mind and is not acting under duress, menace, fraud, misrepresentation, or undue influence.

We declare under penalty of perjury that the foregoing is true and correct.

Executed on (38)__________________ at (39)__________________, (2a)_______________.

(41)________________________ Residing at (42)__________________________

____

(43)________________________ Residing at (44)__________________________

____

LAST WILL AND TESTAMENT

I, (1)__________________________________, a resident of (2)_________________________ County, (2a)_________________, being of sound and disposing mind and memory and not acting under duress, menace, fraud or undue influence of any person whomsoever, do make, publish and declare this to be my Last Will and Testament, and I hereby expressly revoke all other wills, codicils, and testamentary writings heretofore made by me.

FIRST. I declare that I am married. My spouse's name is (4)________________________________. I have the following children:
(5)

I have a deceased child who left the following issue now surviving:
(6)

I have no other children and (7)_______________ deceased children who left issue now surviving.

SECOND. I devise all of estate to my spouse. In the event my spouse should predecease me then I devise all my aforesaid estate to the Custodian under the Uniform Gift to Minors Act hereinafter named, to have and to hold upon the purposes and conditions of said act. I am secure in the knowledge that said Custodian will retain those items of personal use or sentimental value for my child or children in a manner I have made known or will make known to said Custodian.

My Executor, in making distribution to the Custodian, shall allocate the estate properties into as many shares as I have children then living and children then deceased who left issue then living. One such equal share shall be set aside for each of my children then living and one such equal share shall be set aside for the issue then living, by right of representation, of each of my children who are then deceased but left issue then living.

The Custodian may deposit any portion of a child's share in an IRC 529 college savings plan for the benefit of said child.

Upon each minor attaining the age of (29)_________ years, the Custodian shall deliver to said child all of the remainder of his or her share.

In the event a child should die before distribution to him or her of his or her share, his or her share on hand at the time of his or her death shall thereupon be apportioned and distributed to his or her surviving issue, by right of representation. If such child should die before complete distribution to him or her of his or her share and leave no surviving issue, then the balance of the share then on hand shall go and be distributed to my heirs to be determined according to the laws of the State of (2a)________________ then in effect relating to the intestate succession of separate property not acquired from a predeceased spouse.

Each beneficiary hereunder is hereby prohibited from anticipating, encumbering, assigning, or in any other manner alienating his or her interest in either income or principal, and is without power so to do, nor shall such interest be subject to his or her liabilities or obligations, nor to attachment, execution, or other legal processes, bankruptcy proceedings or claims of creditors or others. The Trustee may, however, deposit in any bank designated in writing by a beneficiary, to his or her credit, income or principal payable to such beneficiary.

I nominate and appoint (30)_______________________ as Custodian hereunder (32) without bond. In the event he/she or both of them should decline to act, or for any other reason, be unable to act as Custodian then I appoint (33)___________________________________ as Custodian hereunder (32) without bond.

THIRD. I have intentionally and with full knowledge omitted to provide for my issue, ancestors, relatives and heirs living at the time of my demise, except for such provisions as are made specifically herein.

If any person who is or claims under or through a beneficiary of this Will, or if any person who would be entitled to share in my estate if I died intestate, should in any manner whatsoever, directly or indirectly, attack, contest or seek to impair or invalidate in court any provision of the following:

A. This Will or any Codicil to this Will;

B. Any revocable or irrevocable Trust established by me;

C. Any beneficiary designation executed by me with respect to any insurance policy, any "Totten trust" account, any joint tenancy, any "transfer on death" account or any pension plan, or conspire or cooperate with anyone attempting to do any of the actions or things aforesaid, then I hereby specifically disinherit each such person and any devise, share or interest in my estate otherwise given to each such person under this Will or to which each such person might be entitled by law, is hereby revoked and shall pass and be distributed as though each such person had predeceased me leaving no issue or heirs whatsoever.

Any and every individual who asserts, or conspires or cooperates with any person who asserts, any claim against my Estate based on:

D. "Quantum meruit" theory;

E. Common law marriage, Marvin v. Marvin, 18 Cal. 3d 660 (1976) type of agreement or similar theory;

F. Constructive trust theory; or,

G. Oral agreement or written agreement which is to be proved by parole evidence, claiming that I agreed to gift or devise anything to such person or to pay such person or another for services rendered, regardless of whether a court may find that such agreement existed, then I hereby specifically disinherit each such person and any devise, share or interest in my estate otherwise given to each such person under this Will or to which each such person might be entitled by law, is hereby revoked and shall pass and be distributed as though each such person had predeceased me leaving no issue or heirs whatsoever.

FOURTH. I nominate and appoint my spouse as Executor hereunder without bond. In the event my spouse should decline, become unable or, for any reason, cease to serve as Executor then I nominate and appoint (37)____________________ as Executor hereunder (36) without bond.

I authorize my Executor to sell, at either public or private sale, encumber or lease any property belonging to my estate, either with or without public notice, subject to such confirmation as may be required by law, and to hold, manage and operate any such property.

FIFTH. All typed and handwritten "fill-ins" where directed above were made before the execution of this Will and are not initialed by me. All crossed through words and inter-lineations were made before the execution of this Will and are initialed by me.

The masculine, feminine, and neuter gender and the singular or plural number, shall each be deemed to include the others whenever the context so indicates.

IN WITNESS WHEREOF, I have hereunto set my hand this (38)____________________ at (39)______________________, (2a)____________________.

(40)__________________________________

The foregoing instrument, consisting of __ pages, including the page on which this attestation clause is completed and signed, was at the date hereof by (1)__________________ signed as and declared to be his/her Will, in the presence of us who, at his/her request and in his/her presence, and in the presence of each other, have subscribed our names as witnesses thereto. Each of us observed the signing of this Will by (1)__________________ and by each other subscribing witness and knows that each signature is the true signature of the person whose name was signed.

Each of us is now an adult and a competent witness and resides at the address set forth after his or her name.

We are acquainted with (1)______________________. At this time, he/she is over the age of eighteen years, and to the best of our knowledge, he/she is of sound mind and is not acting under duress, menace, fraud, misrepresentation, or undue influence.

We declare under penalty of perjury that the foregoing is true and correct.

Executed on (38)__________________ at (39)__________________, (2a)_______________.

(41)_________________________ Residing at (42)_________________________

____

(43)_________________________ Residing at (44)_________________________

____

LAST WILL AND TESTAMENT

I, (1)____________________________, a resident of (2)____________________________ County, (2a)________________, being of sound and disposing mind and memory and not acting under duress, menace, fraud or undue influence of any person whomsoever, do make, publish and declare this to be my Last Will and Testament, and I hereby expressly revoke all other wills, codicils, and testamentary writings heretofore made by me.

FIRST. I declare that I am married. My spouse's name is (4)____________________________. I have the following children:
(5)

I have a deceased child who left the following issue now surviving:
(6)

I have no other children and (7)______________ deceased children who left issue now surviving.

SECOND. I devise all of estate to my spouse. In the event my spouse should predecease me then I devise all my aforesaid estate to the Trustee hereinafter named, to have and to hold upon the uses, trusts, purposes and conditions hereinafter provided. I am secure in the knowledge that my Trustee will retain those items of personal use or sentimental value for my child or children in a manner I have made known or will make known to my Trustee.

My Executor, in making distribution to the Trustee, shall allocate the trust properties into as many shares as I have children then living and children then deceased who left issue then living. One such equal share shall be set aside for each of my children then living and one such equal share shall be set aside for the issue then living, by right of representation, of each of my children who are then deceased but left issue then living. Said shares shall be held, administered, and distributed as provided in the following sections:

Each share set aside for a child of mine shall be held, administered and delivered for and to such beneficiary as follows:

1. The net income from the trust while said beneficiary is under 19 years of age and not a high school graduate shall be added to principal, from which the Trustee shall pay to or for the benefit of such beneficiary such sums as in the Trustee's discretion the Trustee shall deem necessary for such beneficiary's proper care, comfort, maintenance, support or education.

In making payments for the benefit of any beneficiary pursuant to this section 1, the Trustee shall construe his or her authority liberally to permit payments reasonably necessary to ease the financial burden on the guardian of the person of such beneficiary or other suitable individual with whom they reside, and on his or her family, resulting from such beneficiary's presence in his or her household.

2. Upon the beneficiary reaching 19 years of age or finishing high school(whichever occurs first), the Trustee shall pay to or apply for his or her benefit, from his or her trust, as much of the trust principal as the Trustee, in the Trustee's discretion, considers appropriate pursuant to sections 3 and 4 following.

3. After the beneficiary attains 19 years of age or finishes high school (whichever occurs first), the Trustee may, in the Trustee's discretion, pay to or apply from his or her trust, such amounts necessary for his or her education. For purposes hereof, education shall mean enrollment, attendance, and satisfactory progression towards a degree as a student at a recognized and accredited college, university, or similar institution of higher learning, including any graduate, professional school or college or trade school. Such educational payments and benefits shall include tuition, books, all direct educational costs and fees, and all reasonable living

and transportation expenses. Payments hereunder shall be made during vacation periods within the regular school term under which the beneficiary is attending school and during "summer vacation" or similar vacation period between the regular school terms.

The Trustee may invest any portion of a beneficiary's trust share in an IRC 529 college savings plan for the benefit of said beneficiary.

4. If the beneficiary, his or her spouse, or any of his children should at any time or from time to time be in need, in the discretion of the Trustee, of funds due to illness, infirmity or other physical or mental disability or any emergency, the Trustee may relieve or contribute toward the relief of any such need or needs of the beneficiary by paying to him or her or using and applying for his or her benefit, such sum or sums out of the income and/or principal of his or her trust as the Trustee, in the Trustee's discretion, may deem necessary or advisable.

5. Upon the beneficiary attaining the age of 21 years, the Trustee shall begin to pay the beneficiary all of the net income, in monthly or other convenient installments, from the trust.

6. Upon the beneficiary attaining the age of (21)_______ years, the Trustee shall distribute and deliver to such beneficiary one-half of his trust estate. Upon each beneficiary attaining the age of (22)_______ years, the Trustee shall distribute and deliver to such beneficiary all of the remainder of his or her trust estate.

7. If, upon the attaining of the above ages, the Trustee suspects that said beneficiary may be abusing drugs, the Trustee may require the beneficiary to take a reasonable drug test. If the beneficiary fails said drug test, the Trustee shall defer said principal payment to the beneficiary until the beneficiary passes said drug test. After a failed drug test, subsequent drug tests shall be administered at six month intervals. In the event a beneficiary fails a drug test, the Trustee may use said beneficiary's trust estate to pay for a drug abuse rehabilitation program and may require the beneficiary to enroll and to complete said program as a condition precedent to the taking of a subsequent drug test.

8. In the event the beneficiary should die before complete distribution to him or her of his or her trust estate, his or her entire trust estate on hand at the time of his or her death shall thereupon be apportioned and distributed to his or her surviving issue, by right of representation. If such beneficiary should die before complete distribution to him or her of his or her trust estate and leave no surviving issue, then the balance of the trust estate then on hand shall go and be distributed to my heirs to be determined according to the laws of the State of (2a)_______________ then in effect relating to the intestate succession of separate property not acquired from a predeceased spouse.

9. Each beneficiary hereunder is hereby prohibited from anticipating, encumbering, assigning, or in any other manner alienating his or her interest in either income or principal, and is without power so to do, nor shall such interest be subject to his or her liabilities or obligations, nor to attachment, execution, or other legal processes, bankruptcy proceedings or claims of creditors or others. The Trustee may, however, deposit in any bank designated in writing by a beneficiary, to his or her credit, income or principal payable to such beneficiary.

10. If, at any time, a trust created hereunder shall, in the sole judgment of the Trustee, be of the aggregate principal value of Fifty Thousand Dollars ($50,000.00) or less, the Trustee may, but need not, terminate such trust and distribute the assets thereof in the Trustee's possession to the beneficiary or beneficiaries, at the time of the current income thereof, and if there is more than one beneficiary, in the proportion in which they are beneficiaries.

11. I nominate and appoint (25)________________ as (26)_____ Trustee hereunder (27) without bond. If he/she/both of them should die, resign, decline to act, or for any other reason, is unable to act as Trustee then I appoint (28)________________________________ as Trustee hereunder (27) without bond.

THIRD. I have intentionally and with full knowledge omitted to provide for my issue, ancestors, relatives and heirs living at the time of my demise, except for such provisions as are made specifically herein.

If any person who is or claims under or through a beneficiary of this Will, or if any person who would be entitled to share in my estate if I died intestate, should in any manner whatsoever, directly or indirectly, attack, contest or seek to impair or invalidate in court any provision of the following:

A. This Will or any Codicil to this Will;

B. Any revocable or irrevocable Trust established by me;

C. Any beneficiary designation executed by me with respect to any insurance policy, any "Totten trust" account, any joint tenancy, any "transfer on death" account or any pension plan, or conspire or cooperate with anyone attempting to do any of the actions or things aforesaid, then I hereby specifically disinherit each such person and any devise, share or interest in my estate otherwise given to each such person under this Will or to which each such person might be entitled by law, is hereby revoked and shall pass and be distributed as though each such person had predeceased me leaving no issue or heirs whatsoever.

Any and every individual who asserts, or conspires or cooperates with any person who asserts, any claim against my Estate based on:

D. "Quantum meruit" theory;

E. Common law marriage, Marvin v. Marvin, 18 Cal. 3d 660 (1976) type of agreement or similar theory;

F. Constructive trust theory; or,

G. Oral agreement or written agreement which is to be proved by parole evidence, claiming that I agreed to gift or devise anything to such person or to pay such person or another for services rendered, regardless of whether a court may find that such agreement existed, then I hereby specifically disinherit each such person and any devise, share or interest in my estate otherwise given to each such person under this Will or to which each such person might be entitled by law, is hereby revoked and shall pass and be distributed as though each such person had predeceased me leaving no issue or heirs whatsoever.

FOURTH. I nominate and appoint my spouse as Executor hereunder without bond. In the event he/she should decline, become unable or, for any reason, cease to serve as Executor then I nominate and appoint (34)____________________ as (35)______ Executor hereunder (36) without bond.

I authorize my Executor to sell, at either public or private sale, encumber or lease any property belonging to my estate, either with or without public notice, subject to such confirmation as may be required by law, and to hold, manage and operate any such property.

FIFTH: All typed and handwritten "fill-ins" where directed above were made before the execution of this Will and are not initialed by me. All crossed through words and inter-lineations were made before the execution of this Will and are initialed by me.

Except as provided otherwise herein, the masculine, feminine, and neuter gender and the singular or plural number, shall each be deemed to include the others whenever the context so indicates.

IN WITNESS WHEREOF, I have hereunto set my hand this

(38)________________________ at (39)________________________, (2a)_______________________.

(40)______________________________

The foregoing instrument, consisting of __ pages, including the page on which this attestation clause is completed and signed, was at the date hereof by (1)________________ signed as and declared to be his/her Will, in the presence of us who, at his/her request and in his/her presence, and in the presence of each other, have subscribed our names as witnesses thereto. Each of us observed the signing of this Will by (1)________________ and by each other subscribing witness and knows that each signature is the true signature of the person whose name was signed.

Each of us is now an adult and a competent witness and resides at the address set forth after his or her name.

We are acquainted with (1)____________________. At this time, he/she is over the age of eighteen years, and to the best of our knowledge, he/she is of sound mind and is not acting under duress, menace, fraud, misrepresentation, or undue influence.

We declare under penalty of perjury that the foregoing is true and correct.

Executed on (38)________________ at (39)________________, (2a)______________.

(41)______________________Residing at (42)______________________________

____

(43)______________________Residing at (44)______________________________

____

LAST WILL AND TESTAMENT

I, (1)______________________________, a resident of (2)________________ County, (2a)_____________________, being of sound and disposing mind and memory and not acting under duress, menace, fraud or undue influence of any person whomsoever, do make, publish and declare this to be my Last Will and Testament, and I hereby expressly revoke all other wills, codicils, and testamentary writings heretofore made by me.

FIRST. I declare that I am married. My spouse's name is (4)______________________________. I have the following children:
(5)

I have a deceased child who left the following issue now surviving:
(6)

I have no other children and (7)______________ deceased children who left issue now surviving.

SECOND. I devise the following personal, tangible property:
(8)

I devise to (9)_______________________________________ all of my remaining personal effects, household furniture and furnishings, trailers, boats, pictures, works of art and art objects, collections, jewelry, silverware, wearing apparel, collections, sporting goods, and all other articles of household or personal use or ornament at whatsoever time acquired by me and wheresoever situated.

I devise to the following persons the cash amount listed after their respective names:
(10)

I devise to the following persons the real property described after their respective names. (12) Said real property is given free of all encumbrances or liens thereon.
(11)

I devise all of the rest, residue and remainder of my estate, real, personal and mixed, of whatsoever kind or character and wheresoever situated, of which I die possessed or to which I may in any manner be entitled, to the following persons or entities (16) in the proportions listed after their names (17) in equal shares.
(18)

In the event any of the above named persons should predecease me or fail to survive me then his or her share shall lapse unless I have specifically named a person to take said bequest in the event of the first beneficiary's death.

Any beneficiary above who fails to survive me by thirty days shall be deemed to have predeceased me.

THIRD. I have intentionally and with full knowledge omitted to provide for my issue, ancestors, relatives and heirs living at the time of my demise, except for such provisions as are made specifically herein.

If any person who is or claims under or through a beneficiary of this Will, or if any person who would be entitled to share in my estate if I died intestate, should in any manner whatsoever, directly or indirectly, attack, contest or seek to impair or invalidate in court any provision of the following:

A. This Will or any Codicil to this Will;

B. Any revocable or irrevocable Trust established by me;

C. Any beneficiary designation executed by me with respect to any insurance policy, any "Totten trust" account, any joint tenancy, any "transfer on death" account or any pension plan, or conspire or cooperate with anyone attempting to do any of the actions or things aforesaid, then I hereby specifically disinherit each such person and any devise, share or interest in my estate otherwise given to each such person under this Will or to which each such person might be entitled by law, is hereby revoked and shall pass and be distributed as though each such person had predeceased me leaving no issue or heirs whatsoever.

Any and every individual who asserts, or conspires or cooperates with any person who asserts, any claim against my Estate based on:

D. "Quantum meruit" theory;

E. Common law marriage, Marvin v. Marvin, 18 Cal. 3d 660 (1976) type of agreement or similar theory;

F. Constructive trust theory; or,

G. Oral agreement or written agreement which is to be proved by parole evidence, claiming that I agreed to gift or devise anything to such person or to pay such person or another for services rendered, regardless of whether a court may find that such agreement existed, then I hereby specifically disinherit each such person and any devise, share or interest in my estate otherwise given to each such person under this Will or to which each such person might be entitled by law, is hereby revoked and shall pass and be distributed as though each such person had predeceased me leaving no issue or heirs whatsoever.

FOURTH. I nominate and appoint (34)__________________________ as (35)_____________ Executor hereunder (36) without bond. In the event he/she or both of them should decline, become unable or, for any reason, cease to serve as Executor then I nominate and appoint (37)____________________ as Executor hereunder (36) without bond.

I authorize my Executor to sell, at either public or private sale, encumber or lease any property belonging to my estate, either with or without public notice, subject to such confirmation as may be required by law, and to hold, manage and operate any such property.

FIFTH. All typed and handwritten "fill-ins" where directed above were made before the execution of this Will and are not initialed by me. All crossed through words and inter-lineations were made before the execution of this Will and are initialed by me.

The masculine, feminine, and neuter gender and the singular or plural number, shall each be deemed to include the others whenever the context so indicates.

IN WITNESS WHEREOF, I have hereunto set my hand this (38)__________________ at (39)______________________, (2a)_________________.

(40)__________________________________

The foregoing instrument, consisting of __ pages, including the page on which this attestation clause is completed and signed, was at the date hereof by (1)__________________ signed as and declared to be his/her Will, in the presence of us who, at his/her request and in his/her presence, and in the presence of each other, have subscribed our names as witnesses thereto. Each of us observed the signing of this Will by (1)__________________ and by each other subscribing witness and knows that each signature is the true signature of the person whose name was signed.

Each of us is now an adult and a competent witness and resides at the address set forth after his or her name.

We are acquainted with (1)______________________. At this time, he/she is over the age of eighteen years, and to the best of our knowledge, he/she is of sound mind and is not acting under duress, menace, fraud, misrepresentation, or undue influence.

We declare under penalty of perjury that the foregoing is true and correct.

Executed on (38)__________________ at (39)__________________, (2a)________________.

(41)__________________________ Residing at (42)__________________________

____

(43)__________________________ Residing at (44)__________________________

____

LAST WILL AND TESTAMENT

I, (1)______________________________, a resident of (2)______________ County, (2a)________________, being of sound and disposing mind and memory and not acting under duress, menace, fraud or undue influence of any person whomsoever, do make, publish and declare this to be my Last Will and Testament, and I hereby expressly revoke all other wills, codicils, and testamentary writings heretofore made by me.

FIRST. I declare that I am married. My spouse's name is (4)____________________________. I have the following children:
(5)

I have a deceased child who left the following issue now surviving:
(6)

I have no other children and (7)__________________ deceased children who left issue now surviving.

SECOND. I devise the following personal, tangible property to the follow persons:
(8)

I devise to (9)____________________________________ all of my remaining personal effects, household furniture and furnishings, trailers, boats, pictures, works of art and art objects, collections, jewelry, silverware, wearing apparel, collections, sporting goods, and all other articles of household or personal use or ornament at whatsoever time acquired by me and wheresoever situated.

I devise to the following persons the cash amount listed after their respective names:
(10)

I devise to the following persons the real property described after their respective names. (12) Said real property is given free of all encumbrances or liens thereon.
(11)

I devise to (13)__________________ a life estate in the following property located at: (14)_________________________. After the death of (13)____________________ said property shall go to (15)____________________________ as the remainder person(s).

I devise all of the rest, residue and remainder of my estate, real, personal and mixed, of whatsoever kind or character and wheresoever situated, of which I die possessed or to which I may in any manner be entitled, to (16) in the proportions listed after their names (17) or in equal shares.
(18)

In the event any of the above named persons should predecease me or fail to survive me then his or her share shall lapse unless I have specifically named a person to take said bequest in the event of the first beneficiary's death.

Any beneficiary above who fails to survive me by thirty days shall be deemed to have predeceased me.

THIRD. I have intentionally and with full knowledge omitted to provide for my issue, ancestors, relatives and heirs living at the time of my demise, except for such provisions as are made specifically herein.

If any person who is or claims under or through a beneficiary of this Will, or if any person who would be entitled to share in my estate if I died intestate, should in any manner whatsoever, directly or indirectly, attack, contest or seek to impair or invalidate in court any provision of the following:

A. This Will or any Codicil to this Will;

B. Any revocable or irrevocable Trust established by me;

C. Any beneficiary designation executed by me with respect to any insurance policy, any "Totten trust" account, any joint tenancy, any "transfer on death" account or any pension plan, or conspire or cooperate with anyone attempting to do any of the actions or things aforesaid, then I hereby specifically disinherit each such person and any devise, share or interest in my estate otherwise given to each such person under this Will or to which each such person might be entitled by law, is hereby revoked and shall pass and be distributed as though each such person had predeceased me leaving no issue or heirs whatsoever.

Any and every individual who asserts, or conspires or cooperates with any person who asserts, any claim against my Estate based on:

D. "Quantum meruit" theory;

E. Common law marriage, Marvin v. Marvin, 18 Cal. 3d 660 (1976) type of agreement or similar theory;

F. Constructive trust theory; or,

G. Oral agreement or written agreement which is to be proved by parole evidence, claiming that I agreed to gift or devise anything to such person or to pay such person or another for services rendered, regardless of whether a court may find that such agreement existed, then I hereby specifically disinherit each such person and any devise, share or interest in my estate otherwise given to each such person under this Will or to which each such person might be entitled by law, is hereby revoked and shall pass and be distributed as though each such person had predeceased me leaving no issue or heirs whatsoever.

FOURTH. I nominate and appoint (34)__________________________ as (35)_____________ Executor hereunder (36) without bond. In the event he/she/they should decline, become unable or, for any reason, cease to serve as Executor then I nominate and appoint (37)_____________________ as Executor hereunder (36) without bond.

I authorize my Executor to sell, at either public or private sale, encumber or lease any property belonging to my estate, either with or without public notice, subject to such confirmation as may be required by law, and to hold, manage and operate any such property.

FIFTH. All typed or handwritten "fill-ins" where directed above were made before the execution of this Will and are not initialed by me. All cross through words and inter-lineations were made before the execution of this Will and are initialed by me.

Except as provided otherwise herein, the masculine, feminine, and neuter gender and the singular or plural number, shall each be deemed to include the others whenever the context so indicates.

IN WITNESS WHEREOF, I have hereunto set my hand this (38)___________________ at (39)______________________, (2a)_________________.

(40)__________________________________

The foregoing instrument, consisting of __ pages, including the page on which this attestation clause is completed and signed, was at the date hereof by (1)________________ signed as and declared to be his/her Will, in the presence of us who, at his/her request and in his/her presence, and in the presence of each other, have subscribed our names as witnesses thereto. Each of us observed the signing of this Will by (1)________________ and by each other subscribing witness and knows that each signature is the true signature of the person whose name was signed.

Each of us is now an adult and a competent witness and resides at the address set forth after his or her name.

We are acquainted with (1)________________. At this time, he/she is over the age of eighteen years, and to the best of our knowledge, he/she is of sound mind and is not acting under duress, menace, fraud, misrepresentation, or undue influence.

We declare under penalty of perjury that the foregoing is true and correct.

Executed on (38)________________ at (39)________________, (2a)________________.

(41)________________ Residing at (42)________________

____

(43)________________ Residing at (44)________________

____

LAST WILL AND TESTAMENT

I, (1)____________________________, a resident of (2)______________ County, (2a)______________, being of sound and disposing mind and memory and not acting under duress, menace, fraud or undue influence of any person whomsoever, do make, publish and declare this to be my Last Will and Testament, and I hereby expressly revoke all other wills, codicils, and testamentary writings heretofore made by me.

FIRST. I declare that I am married. My spouse's name is (4)____________________________. I have the following children:
(5)

I have a deceased child who left the following issue now surviving:
(6)

I have no other children and (7)____________ deceased children who left issue now surviving.

SECOND. I devise the following personal, tangible property:
(8)

I devise to (9)_________________________________ all of my remaining personal effects, household furniture and furnishings, trailers, boats, pictures, works of art and art objects, collections, jewelry, silverware, wearing apparel, collections, sporting goods, and all other articles of household or personal use or ornament at whatsoever time acquired by me and wheresoever situated.

I devise to the following persons the cash amount listed after their respective names:
(10)

I devise to the following persons the real property described after their respective names. (12) Said real property is given free of all encumbrances or liens thereon.
(11)

In the event any of the above named persons should predecease me or fail to survive me then his or her share shall lapse unless I have specifically named a person to take said bequest in the event of the first beneficiary's death.

Any beneficiary above who fails to survive me by thirty days shall be deemed to have predeceased me.

I devise all of the rest, residue and remainder of my estate, real, personal and mixed, of whatsoever kind or character and wheresoever situated, of which I die possessed or to which I may in any manner be entitled, to the following persons or entities (16) in the proportions listed after their names (17) in equal shares. (18)______ and (19)______ shares to the Trustee hereinafter named, to have and to hold for the benefit of (20)____________________upon the uses, trusts, purposes and conditions hereinafter provided. 1. If the beneficiary, his or her spouse, or any of his or her children should at any time or from time to time be in need, in the discretion of the Trustee, of funds due to illness, infirmity or other physical or mental disability or any emergency, the Trustee may relieve or contribute toward the relief of any such need or needs of the beneficiary by paying to him or her or using and applying for his or her benefit, such sum or sums out of the income and/or principal of his or her trust as the Trustee, in the Trustee's discretion, may deem necessary or advisable.

2. The Trustee shall pay the beneficiary all of the net income, in monthly or other convenient installments, from the trust.

3.a. (47—Option 1 Start) Upon the beneficiary attaining the age of (21)________ years, the Trustee shall distribute and deliver to such beneficiary one-half of his or her trust estate. Upon each beneficiary attaining the age of (22)________ years, the Trustee shall distribute and deliver to such beneficiary all of the remainder of his or her trust estate.

3.b. If, upon the attaining of the above ages, the Trustee suspects that said beneficiary may be abusing drugs and/or alcohol, the Trustee may require the beneficiary to take a reasonable drug and/or alcohol test. If the beneficiary fails said test, the trustee shall defer said principal payment to the beneficiary until the beneficiary passes said test. After a failed test, subsequent drug tests shall be administered at the request of the beneficiary but not less than six months after a prior test. In the event a beneficiary fails a drug and/or alcohol test, the Trustee may use said beneficiary's trust estate to pay for a drug and/or alcohol abuse rehabilitation program and may require the beneficiary to enroll and to complete said program as a condition precedent to the taking of a subsequent drug and/or alcohol test.

3.c. In the event the beneficiary should die before complete distribution to him or her of his or her trust estate, his or her entire trust estate on hand at the time of his or her death shall thereupon be apportioned and distributed to his or her surviving issue, by right of representation. If such beneficiary should die before complete distribution to him or her of his or her trust estate and leave no surviving issue, then the balance of the trust estate then on hand shall go and be distributed to my heirs to be determined according to the laws of the State of California then in effect relating to the intestate succession of separate property not acquired from a predeceased spouse. (47—Option 1 End)

OR

3.a. (47—Option 2 Start) In addition to any other payments to the beneficiary hereunder, the Trustee shall, upon the written request of the beneficiary in December of each calendar year, pay to the beneficiary amounts from principal that the beneficiary requests, not exceeding in any single calendar year the greater of the following amounts: $5,000.00 or 5 percent of the value of the principal of the beneficiary's trust estate; determined as of the end of the calendar year. This right of withdrawal is noncumulative, so that if the beneficiary does not withdraw the full amount permitted to be withdrawn during any calendar year, the right to withdraw the remaining amount will lapse at the end of the calendar year.

3.b.On the death of the beneficiary his or her entire trust estate on hand at the time of his or her death shall thereupon be apportioned and distributed to (23)____________________________. If (23)______ ____________________ is then deceased then the trust estate then on hand shall go to (24)______________________________, if he/she is then living. (47—Option 2A End)

OR

the beneficiary's surviving issue, by right of representation. If such beneficiary should die before complete distribution to him or her of his or her trust estate and leave no surviving issue, then the balance of the trust estate then on hand shall go and be distributed to my heirs to be determined according to the laws of the State of (2a)_____________ then in effect relating to the intestate succession of separate property not acquired from a predeceased spouse. (47—Option 2B End)

4. Each beneficiary hereunder is hereby prohibited from anticipating, encumbering, assigning, or in any other manner alienating his or her interest in either income or principal, and is without power so to do, nor shall such interest be subject to his or her liabilities or obligations, nor to attachment, execution, or other legal processes, bankruptcy proceedings or claims of creditors or others. The Trustee may, however, deposit in

any bank designated in writing by a beneficiary, to his or her credit, income or principal payable to such beneficiary.

5. If, at any time, a trust created hereunder shall, in the sole judgment of the Trustee, be of the aggregate principal value of Fifty Thousand Dollars ($50,000.00) or less, the Trustee may, but need not, terminate such trust and distribute the assets thereof in the Trustee's possession to the beneficiary or beneficiaries, at the time of the current income thereof, and if there is more than one beneficiary, in the proportion in which they are beneficiaries.

6. I nominate and appoint (25)________________ as (26)________ Trustee hereunder (27) without bond. In the event he/she or both of them should die, decline to act, or for any other reason, be unable to act as Trustee then I appoint (28)____________________________ as Trustee hereunder (27) without bond.

THIRD. I have intentionally and with full knowledge omitted to provide for my issue, ancestors, relatives and heirs living at the time of my demise, except for such provisions as are made specifically herein.

If any person who is or claims under or through a beneficiary of this Will, or if any person who would be entitled to share in my estate if I died intestate, should in any manner whatsoever, directly or indirectly, attack, contest or seek to impair or invalidate in court any provision of the following:

A. This Will or any Codicil to this Will;

B. Any revocable or irrevocable Trust established by me;

C. Any beneficiary designation executed by me with respect to any insurance policy, any "Totten trust" account, any joint tenancy, any "transfer on death" account or any pension plan, or conspire or cooperate with anyone attempting to do any of the actions or things aforesaid, then I hereby specifically disinherit each such person and any devise, share or interest in my estate otherwise given to each such person under this Will or to which each such person might be entitled by law, is hereby revoked and shall pass and be distributed as though each such person had predeceased me leaving no issue or heirs whatsoever.

Any and every individual who asserts, or conspires or cooperates with any person who asserts, any claim against my Estate based on:

D. "Quantum meruit" theory;

E. Common law marriage, Marvin v. Marvin, 18 Cal. 3d 660 (1976) type of agreement or similar theory;

F. Constructive trust theory; or,

G. Oral agreement or written agreement which is to be proved by parole evidence, claiming that I agreed to gift or devise anything to such person or to pay such person or another for services rendered, regardless of whether a court may find that such agreement existed, then I hereby specifically disinherit each such person and any devise, share or interest in my estate otherwise given to each such person under this Will or to which each such person might be entitled by law, is hereby revoked and shall pass and be distributed as though each such person had predeceased me leaving no issue or heirs whatsoever.

FOURTH. I nominate and appoint (34)__________________________ as (35)______________ Executor hereunder (36) without bond. In the event he/she or both of them should decline, become unable or, for any reason, cease to serve as Executor then I nominate and appoint (37)______________________ as Executor hereunder (36) without bond.

I authorize my Executor to sell, at either public or private sale, encumber or lease any property belonging to my estate, either with or without public notice, subject to such confirmation as may be required by law, and to hold, manage and operate any such property.

FIFTH. All typed and handwritten "fill-ins" where directed above were made before the execution of this Will and are not initialed by me. All crossed through words and inter-lineations were made before the execution of this Will and are initialed by me.

The masculine, feminine, and neuter gender and the singular or plural number, shall each be deemed to include the others whenever the context so indicates.

IN WITNESS WHEREOF, I have hereunto set my hand this (38)________________ at (39)____________________, (2a)________________.

(40)______________________________

The foregoing instrument, consisting of __ pages, including the page on which this attestation clause is completed and signed, was at the date hereof by (1)________________ signed as and declared to be his/her Will, in the presence of us who, at his/her request and in his/her presence, and in the presence of each other, have subscribed our names as witnesses thereto. Each of us observed the signing of this Will by (1)________________ and by each other subscribing witness and knows that each signature is the true signature of the person whose name was signed.

Each of us is now an adult and a competent witness and resides at the address set forth after his or her name.

We are acquainted with (1)____________________. At this time, he/she is over the age of eighteen years, and to the best of our knowledge, he/she is of sound mind and is not acting under duress, menace, fraud, misrepresentation, or undue influence.

We declare under penalty of perjury that the foregoing is true and correct.

Executed on (38)__________________ at (39)________________, (2a)______________.

(41)________________________ Residing at (42)________________________

____

(43)________________________ Residing at (44)________________________

____

LAST WILL AND TESTAMENT

I, (1)____________________________, a resident of (2)_______________ County, (2a)________________, being of sound and disposing mind and memory and not acting under duress, menace, fraud or undue influence of any person whomsoever, do make, publish and declare this to be my Last Will and Testament, and I hereby expressly revoke all other wills, codicils, and testamentary writings heretofore made by me.

FIRST. I declare that I am married. My spouse's name (4)______________________________. I have the following children:
(5)

I have a deceased child who left the following issue now surviving:
(6)

I have no other children and (7)___________________ deceased children who left issue now surviving.

SECOND. I devise the following personal, tangible property:
(8)

I devise to (9)____________________________________ all of my remaining personal effects, household furniture and furnishings, trailers, boats, pictures, works of art and art objects, collections, jewelry, silverware, wearing apparel, collections, sporting goods, and all other articles of household or personal use or ornament at whatsoever time acquired by me and wheresoever situated.

I devise to the following persons the cash amount listed after their respective names:
(10)

I devise to the following persons the real property described after their respective names. (12) Said real property is given free of all encumbrances or liens thereon.
(11)

In the event any of the above named persons should predecease me or fail to survive me then his or her share shall lapse unless I have specifically named a person to take said bequest in the event of the first beneficiary's death.

Any beneficiary above who fails to survive me by thirty days shall be deemed to have predeceased me.

I devise all of the rest, residue and remainder of my estate, real, personal and mixed, of whatsoever kind or character and wheresoever situated, of which I die possessed or to which I may in any manner be entitled, to the following persons or entities (16) in the pro-portions listed after their names (17) in equal shares.
(18)

and
(19)______ shares to the Trustee hereinafter named, to have and to hold for the benefit of my spouse upon the uses, trusts, purposes and conditions hereinafter provided.

1. If my spouse or any of his or her children should at any time or from time to time be in need, in the discretion of the Trustee, of funds due to illness, infirmity or other physical or mental disability or any

emergency, the Trustee may relieve or contribute toward the relief of any such need or needs of my spouse by paying to him or her or using and applying for his or her benefit, such sum or sums out of the income and/or principal of his or her trust as the Trustee, in the Trustee's discretion, may deem necessary or advisable.

2. The Trustee shall pay my spouse all of the net income, in monthly or other convenient installments, from the trust.

3. My spouse shall have the right to require the Trustee to convert any non-income producing asset into an income producing asset.

4. Upon the death of my spouse the Trustee shall distribute any accrued but undistributed income to my spouse's estate. The Trustee shall distribute, free of trust, the remaining trust properties to: (23)________________________________.

5. My spouse is prohibited from anticipating, encumbering, assigning, or in any other manner alienating his or her interest in either income or principal, and is without power so to do, nor shall such interest be subject to his or her liabilities or obligations, nor to attachment, execution, or other legal processes, bankruptcy proceedings or claims of creditors or others. The Trustee may, however, deposit in any bank designated in writing by my spouse, to his or her credit, income or principal payable to my spouse.

6. I nominate and appoint (25)____________________ as (26)___________ Trustee hereunder (27) without bond. In the event he/she or both of them reason, be unable to act as Trustee then I appoint (28)__________________________ as Trustee hereunder (27) without bond.

THIRD. I have intentionally and with full knowledge omitted to provide for my issue, ancestors, relatives and heirs living at the time of my demise, except for such provisions as are made specifically herein.

If any person who is or claims under or through a beneficiary of this Will, or if any person who would be entitled to share in my estate if I died intestate, should in any manner whatsoever, directly or indirectly, attack, contest or seek to impair or invalidate in court any provision of the following:

A. This Will or any Codicil to this Will;

B. Any revocable or irrevocable Trust established by me;

C. Any beneficiary designation executed by me with respect to any insurance policy, any "Totten trust" account, any joint tenancy, any "transfer on death" account or any pension plan, or conspire or cooperate with anyone attempting to do any of the actions or things aforesaid, then I hereby specifically disinherit each such person and any devise, share or interest in my estate otherwise given to each such person under this Will or to which each such person might be entitled by law, is hereby revoked and shall pass and be distributed as though each such person had predeceased me leaving no issue or heirs whatsoever.

Any and every individual who asserts, or conspires or cooperates with any person who asserts, any claim against my Estate based on:

D. "Quantum meruit" theory;

E. Common law marriage, Marvin v. Marvin, 18 Cal. 3d 660 (1976) type of agreement or similar theory;

F. Constructive trust theory; or,

G. Oral agreement or written agreement which is to be proved by parole evidence, claiming that I agreed to gift or devise anything to such person or to pay such person or another for services rendered, regardless of whether a court may find that such agreement existed, then I hereby specifically disinherit each such person and any devise, share or interest in my estate otherwise given to each such person under this Will or to which each such person might be entitled by law, is hereby revoked and shall pass and be distributed as though each such person had predeceased me leaving no issue or heirs whatsoever.

FOURTH. I nominate and appoint (34)__________________________ as (35)____________ Executor hereunder (36) without bond. In the event he/she or both of them should decline, become unable or, for any reason, cease to serve as Executor then I nominate and appoint (37)______________________ as Executor hereunder (36) without bond.

I authorize my Executor to sell, at either public or private sale, encumber or lease any property belonging to my estate, either with or without public notice, subject to such confirmation as may be required by law, and to hold, manage and operate any such property.

FIFTH. All typed and handwritten "fill-ins" where directed above were made before the execution of this Will and are not initialed by me. All crossed through words and inter-lineations were made before the execution of this Will and are initialed by me.

The masculine, feminine, and neuter gender and the singular or plural number, shall each be deemed to include the others whenever the context so indicates.

IN WITNESS WHEREOF, I have hereunto set my hand this (38)______________________ at (39)______________________, (2a)__________________.

(40)___________________________________

The foregoing instrument, consisting of __ pages, including the page on which this attestation clause is completed and signed, was at the date hereof by (1)___________________ signed as and declared to be his/her Will, in the presence of us who, at his/her request and in his/her presence, and in the presence of each other, have subscribed our names as witnesses thereto. Each of us observed the signing of this Will by (1)___________________ and by each other subscribing witness and knows that each signature is the true signature of the person whose name was signed.

Each of us is now an adult and a competent witness and resides at the address set forth after his or her name.

We are acquainted with (1)______________________. At this time, he/she is over the age of eighteen years, and to the best of our knowledge, he/she is of sound mind and is not acting under duress, menace, fraud, misrepresentation, or undue influence.

We declare under penalty of perjury that the foregoing is true and correct.

Executed on (38)____________________ at (39)____________________, (2a)_________________.

(41)___________________________ Residing at (42)____________________________

____

(43)___________________________ Residing at (44)____________________________

____

LAST WILL AND TESTAMENT

I, (1)______________________________, a resident of (2)_______________ County, (2a)________________, being of sound and disposing mind and memory and not acting under duress, menace, fraud or undue influence of any person whomsoever, do make, publish and declare this to be my Last Will and Testament, and I hereby expressly revoke all other wills, codicils, and testamentary writings heretofore made by me.

FIRST. I declare that I am married. My spouse's name is (4)__________________________________. I have no children and no issue now living of a deceased child.

SECOND. I devise all of my estate, real, personal and mixed, of whatsoever kind or character and wheresoever situated, of which I die possessed or to which I may in any manner be entitled, to my spouse.
If my spouse fails to survive me then I devise the following personal, tangible property to the follow persons:
(8)

I devise to (9)___________________________________ all of my remaining personal effects, household furniture and furnishings, trailers, boats, pictures, works of art and art objects, collections, jewelry, silverware, wearing apparel, collections, sporting goods, and all other articles of household or personal use or ornament at whatsoever time acquired by me and wheresoever situated.

I devise to the following persons the cash amount listed after their respective names:
(10)

I devise to the following persons the real property described after their respective names. (12) Said real property is given free of all encumbrances or liens thereon.
(11)

I devise all of the rest, residue and remainder of my estate, real, personal and mixed, of whatsoever kind or character and wheresoever situated, of which I die possessed or to which I may in any manner be entitled, to (16) in the pro-portions listed after their names (17) in equal shares.
(18)

In the event any of the above named persons should predecease me or fail to survive me then his or her share shall lapse unless I have specifically named a person to take said bequest in the event of the first beneficiary's death.

Any beneficiary above who fails to survive me by thirty days shall be deemed to have predeceased me.

THIRD. I have intentionally and with full knowledge omitted to provide for my issue, ancestors, relatives and heirs living at the time of my demise, except for such provisions as are made specifically herein.

If any person who is or claims under or through a beneficiary of this Will, or if any person who would be entitled to share in my estate if I died intestate, should in any manner whatsoever, directly or indirectly, attack, contest or seek to impair or invalidate in court any provision of the following:

A. This Will or any Codicil to this Will;

B. Any revocable or irrevocable Trust established by me;

C. Any beneficiary designation executed by me with respect to any insurance policy, any "Totten trust" account, any joint tenancy, any "transfer on death" account or any pension plan, or conspire or cooperate with anyone attempting to do any of the actions or things aforesaid, then I hereby specifically disinherit each such person and any devise, share or interest in my estate otherwise given to each such person under this Will or to which each such person might be entitled by law, is hereby revoked and shall pass and be distributed as though each such person had predeceased me leaving no issue or heirs whatsoever.

Any and every individual who asserts, or conspires or cooperates with any person who asserts, any claim against my Estate based on:

D. "Quantum meruit" theory;

E. Common law marriage, Marvin v. Marvin, 18 Cal. 3d 660 (1976) type of agreement or similar theory;

F. Constructive trust theory; or,

G. Oral agreement or written agreement which is to be proved by parole evidence, claiming that I agreed to gift or devise anything to such person or to pay such person or another for services rendered, regardless of whether a court may find that such agreement existed, then I hereby specifically disinherit each such person and any devise, share or interest in my estate otherwise given to each such person under this Will or to which each such person might be entitled by law, is hereby revoked and shall pass and be distributed as though each such person had predeceased me leaving no issue or heirs whatsoever.

FOURTH. I nominate and appoint my spouse as Executor hereunder without bond. In the event my spouse should decline, become unable or, for any reason, cease to serve as Executor then I nominate and appoint (37)______________________ as (34)_____________ Executor hereunder (36) without bond.

I authorize my Executor to sell, at either public or private sale, encumber or lease any property belonging to my estate, either with or without public notice, subject to such confirmation as may be required by law, and to hold, manage and operate any such property.

FIFTH. All typed and handwritten "fill-ins" where directed above were made before the execution of this Will and are not initialed by me. All crossed through words and inter-lineations were made before the execution of this Will and are initialed by me.

Except as provided otherwise herein, the masculine, feminine, and neuter gender and the singular or plural number, shall each be deemed to include the others whenever the context so indicates.

IN WITNESS WHEREOF, I have hereunto set my hand this (38)_________________ at (39)____________________, (2a)_______________.

(40)______________________________

The foregoing instrument, consisting of __ pages, including the page on which this attestation clause is completed and signed, was at the date hereof by (1)________________ signed as and declared to be his/her Will, in the presence of us who, at his/her request and in his/her presence, and in the presence of each other, have subscribed our names as witnesses thereto. Each of us observed the signing of this Will by (1)________________ and by each other subscribing witness and knows that each signature is the true signature of the person whose name was signed.

Each of us is now an adult and a competent witness and resides at the address set forth after his or her name.

We are acquainted with (1)______________________. At this time, he/she is over the age of eighteen years, and to the best of our knowledge, he/she is of sound mind and is not acting under duress, menace, fraud, misrepresentation, or undue influence.

We declare under penalty of perjury that the foregoing is true and correct.

Executed on (38)____________________ at (39)____________________, (2a)__________________.

(41)__________________________ Residing at (42)__________________________

____

(43)__________________________ Residing at (44)__________________________

____

LAST WILL AND TESTAMENT

I, (1)______________________________, a resident of (2)______________ County, (2a)______________, being of sound and disposing mind and memory and not acting under duress, menace, fraud or undue influence of any person whomsoever, do make, publish and declare this to be my Last Will and Testament, and I hereby expressly revoke all other wills, codicils, and testamentary writings heretofore made by me.

FIRST. I declare that I am married. My spouse's name (4)______________________________. I have no children and no deceased children who left issue now surviving.

SECOND. I devise the following personal, tangible property:
(8)

I devise to (9)______________________________ all of my remaining personal effects, household furniture and furnishings, trailers, boats, pictures, works of art and art objects, collections, jewelry, silverware, wearing apparel, collections, sporting goods, and all other articles of household or personal use or ornament at whatsoever time acquired by me and wheresoever situated.

I devise to the following persons the cash amount listed after their respective names:
(10)

I devise to the following persons the real property described after their respective names. (12) Said real property is given free of all encumbrances or liens thereon.
(11)

In the event any of the above named persons should predecease me or fail to survive me then his or her share shall lapse unless I have specifically named a person to take said bequest in the event of the first beneficiary's death.

Any beneficiary above who fails to survive me by thirty days shall be deemed to have predeceased me.

I devise all of the rest, residue and remainder of my estate, real, personal and mixed, of whatsoever kind or character and wheresoever situated, of which I die possessed or to which I may in any manner be entitled, to the following persons or entities (16) in the pro-portions listed after their names (17) in equal shares.
(18)

and
(19)______ shares to the Trustee hereinafter named, to have and to hold for the benefit of my spouse upon the uses, trusts, purposes and conditions hereinafter provided.

1. If my spouse or any of his or her children should at any time or from time to time be in need, in the discretion of the Trustee, of funds due to illness, infirmity or other physical or mental disability or any emergency, the Trustee may relieve or contribute toward the relief of any such need or needs of my spouse by paying to him or her or using and applying for his or her benefit, such sum or sums out of the income and/or principal of his or her trust as the Trustee, in the Trustee's discretion, may deem necessary or advisable.

2. The Trustee shall pay my spouse all of the net income, in monthly or other convenient installments, from the trust.

3. My spouse shall have the right to require the Trustee to convert any non-income producing asset into an income producing asset.

4. Upon the death of my spouse the Trustee shall distribute any accrued but undistributed income to my spouse's estate. The Trustee shall distribute, free of trust, the remaining trust properties to: (23)________________________________.

5. My spouse is prohibited from anticipating, encumbering, assigning, or in any other manner alienating his or her interest in either income or principal, and is without power so to do, nor shall such interest be subject to his or her liabilities or obligations, nor to attachment, execution, or other legal processes, bankruptcy proceedings or claims of creditors or others. The Trustee may, however, deposit in any bank designated in writing by my spouse, to his or her credit, income or principal payable to my spouse.

6. I nominate and appoint (25)____________________________ as (26)__________ Trustee hereunder (27) without bond. In the event he/she/they should die, decline to act, or for any other reason, be unable to act as Trustee then I appoint (28)________________________ as Trustee hereunder (27) without bond.

THIRD. I have intentionally and with full knowledge omitted to provide for my issue, ancestors, relatives and heirs living at the time of my demise, except for such provisions as are made specifically herein.

If any person who is or claims under or through a beneficiary of this Will, or if any person who would be entitled to share in my estate if I died intestate, should in any manner whatsoever, directly or indirectly, attack, contest or seek to impair or invalidate in court any provision of the following:

A. This Will or any Codicil to this Will;

B. Any revocable or irrevocable Trust established by me;

C. Any beneficiary designation executed by me with respect to any insurance policy, any "Totten trust" account, any joint tenancy, any "transfer on death" account or any pension plan, or conspire or cooperate with anyone attempting to do any of the actions or things aforesaid, then I hereby specifically disinherit each such person and any devise, share or interest in my estate otherwise given to each such person under this Will or to which each such person might be entitled by law, is hereby revoked and shall pass and be distributed as though each such person had predeceased me leaving no issue or heirs whatsoever.

Any and every individual who asserts, or conspires or cooperates with any person who asserts, any claim against my Estate based on:

D. "Quantum meruit" theory;

E. Common law marriage, Marvin v. Marvin, 18 Cal. 3d 660 (1976) type of agreement or similar theory;

F. Constructive trust theory; or,

G. Oral agreement or written agreement which is to be proved by parole evidence, claiming that I agreed to gift or devise anything to such person or to pay such person or another for services rendered, regardless of whether a court may find that such agreement existed, then I hereby specifically disinherit each such person and any devise, share or interest in my estate otherwise given to each such person under this Will or to which each such person might be entitled by law, is hereby revoked and shall pass and be distributed as though each such person had predeceased me leaving no issue or heirs whatsoever.

FOURTH. I nominate and appoint (34)________________________ as (35)____________ Executor hereunder (36) without bond. In the event he/she/they should decline, become unable or, for any reason, cease to serve as Executor then I nominate and appoint (37)____________________ as Executor hereunder (36) without bond.

I authorize my Executor to sell, at either public or private sale, encumber or lease any property belonging to my estate, either with or without public notice, subject to such confirmation as may be required by law, and to hold, manage and operate any such property.

FIFTH. All typed and handwritten "fill-ins" where directed above were made before the execution of this Will and are not initialed by me. All crossed through words and inter-lineations were made before the execution of this Will and are initialed by me.

The masculine, feminine, and neuter gender and the singular or plural number, shall each be deemed to include the others whenever the context so indicates.

IN WITNESS WHEREOF, I have hereunto set my hand this (38)____________________ at (39)____________________, (2a)______________.

(40)______________________________

The foregoing instrument, consisting of __ pages, including the page on which this attestation clause is completed and signed, was at the date hereof by (1)________________ signed as and declared to be his/her Will, in the presence of us who, at his/her request and in his/her presence, and in the presence of each other, have subscribed our names as witnesses thereto. Each of us observed the signing of this Will by (1)________________ and by each other subscribing witness and knows that each signature is the true signature of the person whose name was signed.

Each of us is now an adult and a competent witness and resides at the address set forth after his or her name.

We are acquainted with (1)____________________. At this time, he/she is over the age of eighteen years, and to the best of our knowledge, he/she is of sound mind and is not acting under duress, menace, fraud, misrepresentation, or undue influence.

We declare under penalty of perjury that the foregoing is true and correct.

Executed on (38)__________________ at (39)__________________, (2a)______________.

(41)________________________ Residing at (42)________________________

____

(43)________________________ Residing at (44)________________________

____

LAST WILL AND TESTAMENT

I, (1)______________________________, a resident of (2)________________ County, (2a)____________________, being of sound and disposing mind and memory and not acting under duress, menace, fraud or undue influence of any person whomsoever, do make, publish and declare this to be my Last Will and Testament, and I hereby expressly revoke all other wills, codicils, and testamentary writings heretofore made by me.

FIRST. I declare that I am married. My spouse's name is (4)________________________________. I have no children and no issue now living of a deceased child.

SECOND. I devise the following personal, tangible property to the follow persons:
(8)

I devise to (9)_______________________________________ all of my remaining personal effects, household furniture and furnishings, trailers, boats, pictures, works of art and art objects, collections, jewelry, silverware, wearing apparel, collections, sporting goods, and all other articles of household or personal use or ornament at whatsoever time acquired by me and wheresoever situated.

I devise to the following persons the cash amount listed after their respective names:
(10)

I devise to the following persons the real property described after their respective names. (12) Said real property is given free of all encumbrances or liens thereon.
(11)

I devise all of the rest, residue and remainder of my estate, real, personal and mixed, of whatsoever kind or character and wheresoever situated, of which I die possessed or to which I may in any manner be entitled, to (16) in the pro-portions listed after their names (17) in equal shares.
(18)

In the event any of the above named persons should predecease me or fail to survive me then his or her share shall lapse unless I have specifically named a person to take said bequest in the event of the first beneficiary's death.

Any beneficiary above who fails to survive me by thirty days shall be deemed to have predeceased me.

THIRD. I have intentionally and with full knowledge omitted to provide for my issue, ancestors, relatives and heirs living at the time of my demise, except for such provisions as are made specifically herein.

If any person who is or claims under or through a beneficiary of this Will, or if any person who would be entitled to share in my estate if I died intestate, should in any manner whatsoever, directly or indirectly, attack, contest or seek to impair or invalidate in court any provision of the following:

A. This Will or any Codicil to this Will;

B. Any revocable or irrevocable Trust established by me;

C. Any beneficiary designation executed by me with respect to any insurance policy, any "Totten trust" account, any joint tenancy, any "transfer on death" account or any pension plan, or conspire or cooperate with anyone attempting to do any of the actions or things aforesaid, then I hereby specifically disinherit each such person and any devise, share or interest in my estate otherwise given to each such person under this Will or to which each such person might be entitled by law, is hereby revoked and shall pass and be distributed as though each such person had predeceased me leaving no issue or heirs whatsoever.

Any and every individual who asserts, or conspires or cooperates with any person who asserts, any claim against my Estate based on:

D. "Quantum meruit" theory;

E. Common law marriage, Marvin v. Marvin, 18 Cal. 3d 660 (1976) type of agreement or similar theory;

F. Constructive trust theory; or,

G. Oral agreement or written agreement which is to be proved by parole evidence, claiming that I agreed to gift or devise anything to such person or to pay such person or another for services rendered, regardless of whether a court may find that such agreement existed, then I hereby specifically disinherit each such person and any devise, share or interest in my estate otherwise given to each such person under this Will or to which each such person might be entitled by law, is hereby revoked and shall pass and be distributed as though each such person had predeceased me leaving no issue or heirs whatsoever.

FOURTH. I nominate and appoint (34)______________________ as (35)________________ Executor hereunder (36) without bond. In the event he/she or both of them should decline, become unable or, for any reason, cease to serve as Executor then I nominate and appoint (37)____________________ as Executor hereunder (36) without bond.

I authorize my Executor to sell, at either public or private sale, encumber or lease any property belonging to my estate, either with or without public notice, subject to such confirmation as may be required by law, and to hold, manage and operate any such property.

FIFTH. All handwritten "fill-ins" where directed above were made before the execution of this Will and are not initialed by me. All inter-lineations were made before the execution of this Will and are initialed by me.

The masculine, feminine, and neuter gender and the singular or plural number, shall each be deemed to include the others whenever the context so indicates.

IN WITNESS WHEREOF, I have hereunto set my hand this (38)_________________________ at (39)_____________________, (2a)___________________.

(40)_________________________________

The foregoing instrument, consisting of __ pages, including the page on which this attestation clause is completed and signed, was at the date hereof by (1)__________________ signed as and declared to be his/her Will, in the presence of us who, at his/her request and in his/her presence, and in the presence of each other, have subscribed our names as witnesses thereto. Each of us observed the signing of this Will by (1)__________________ and by each other subscribing witness and knows that each signature is the true signature of the person whose name was signed.

Each of us is now an adult and a competent witness and resides at the address set forth after his or her name.

We are acquainted with (1)_____________________. At this time, he/she is over the age of eighteen years, and to the best of our knowledge, he/she is of sound mind and is not acting under duress, menace, fraud, misrepresentation, or undue influence.

We declare under penalty of perjury that the foregoing is true and correct.

Executed on (38)__________________ at (39)__________________, (2a)________________.

(41)________________________ Residing at (42)________________________

____

(43)________________________ Residing at (44)________________________

____

LAST WILL AND TESTAMENT

I, (1)______________________________, a resident of (2)___________________________ County, (2a)____________________, being of sound and disposing mind and memory and not acting under duress, menace, fraud or undue influence of any person whomsoever, do make, publish and declare this to be my Last Will and Testament, and I hereby expressly revoke all other wills, codicils, and testamentary writings heretofore made by me.

FIRST. I declare that I am (3)______________________________________. My spouse's name was (4)____. I have the following children:
(5)

I have a deceased child who left the following issue now surviving:
(6)

I have no other children and (7)______________ deceased children who left issue now surviving.

SECOND. I devise the following personal, tangible property to the follow persons:
(8)

I devise to (9)____________________________________ all of my remaining personal effects, household furniture and furnishings, trailers, boats, pictures, works of art and art objects, collections, jewelry, silverware, wearing apparel, collections, sporting goods, and all other articles of household or personal use or ornament at whatsoever time acquired by me and wheresoever situated.

I devise to the following persons the cash amount listed after their respective names:
(10)

I devise to the following persons the real property described after their respective names. (12) Said real property is given free of all encumbrances or liens thereon.
(11)

I devise all of the rest, residue and remainder of my estate, real, personal and mixed, of whatsoever kind or character and wheresoever situated, of which I die possessed or to which I may in any manner be entitled, to (16) in the pro-portions listed after their names (17) or in equal shares.
(18)

In the event any of the above named persons should predecease me or fail to survive me then his or her share shall lapse unless I have specifically named a person to take said bequest in the event of the first beneficiary's death.

Any beneficiary above who fails to survive me by thirty days shall be deemed to have predeceased me.

THIRD. I have intentionally and with full knowledge omitted to provide for my issue, ancestors, relatives and heirs living at the time of my demise, except for such provisions as are made specifically herein.

If any person who is or claims under or through a beneficiary of this Will, or if any person who would be entitled to share in my estate if I died intestate, should in any manner whatsoever, directly or indirectly, attack, contest or seek to impair or invalidate in court any provision of the following:

A. This Will or any Codicil to this Will;

B. Any revocable or irrevocable Trust established by me;

C. Any beneficiary designation executed by me with respect to any insurance policy, any "Totten trust" account, any joint tenancy, any "transfer on death" account or any pension plan, or conspire or cooperate with anyone attempting to do any of the actions or things aforesaid, then I hereby specifically disinherit each such person and any devise, share or interest in my estate otherwise given to each such person under this Will or to which each such person might be entitled by law, is hereby revoked and shall pass and be distributed as though each such person had predeceased me leaving no issue or heirs whatsoever.

Any and every individual who asserts, or conspires or cooperates with any person who asserts, any claim against my Estate based on:

D. "Quantum meruit" theory;

E. Common law marriage, Marvin v. Marvin, 18 Cal. 3d 660 (1976) type of agreement or similar theory;

F. Constructive trust theory; or,

G. Oral agreement or written agreement which is to be proved by parole evidence, claiming that I agreed to gift or devise anything to such person or to pay such person or another for services rendered, regardless of whether a court may find that such agreement existed, then I hereby specifically disinherit each such person and any devise, share or interest in my estate otherwise given to each such person under this Will or to which each such person might be entitled by law, is hereby revoked and shall pass and be distributed as though each such person had predeceased me leaving no issue or heirs whatsoever.

FOURTH. I nominate and appoint (34)________________________ as (35)____________ Executor hereunder (36) without bond. In the event he/she/they should decline, become unable or, for any reason, cease to serve as Executor then I nominate and appoint (37)__________________ as Executor hereunder (36) without bond.

I authorize my Executor to sell, at either public or private sale, encumber or lease any property belonging to my estate, either with or without public notice, subject to such confirmation as may be required by law, and to hold, manage and operate any such property.

FIFTH. All handwritten "fill-ins" where directed above were made before the execution of this Will and are not initialed by me. All inter-lineations were made before the execution of this Will and are initialed by me.

The masculine, feminine, and neuter gender and the singular or plural number, shall each be deemed to include the others whenever the context so indicates.

IN WITNESS WHEREOF, I have hereunto set my hand this (38)_________________ at (39)____________________, (2a)_______________.

(40)______________________________

The foregoing instrument, consisting of __ pages, including the page on which this attestation clause is completed and signed, was at the date hereof by (1)__________________ signed as and declared to be his/her Will, in the presence of us who, at his/her request and in his/her presence, and in the presence of each other, have subscribed our names as witnesses thereto. Each of us observed the signing of this Will by

(1)__________________ and by each other subscribing witness and knows that each signature is the true signature of the person whose name was signed.

Each of us is now an adult and a competent witness and resides at the address set forth after his or her name.

We are acquainted with (1)______________________. At this time, he/she is over the age of eighteen years, and to the best of our knowledge, he/she is of sound mind and is not acting under duress, menace, fraud, misrepresentation, or undue influence.

We declare under penalty of perjury that the foregoing is true and correct.

Executed on (38)___________________ at (39)___________________, (2a)________________.

(41)_________________________ Residing at (42)___________________________

____

(43)_________________________ Residing at (44)___________________________

____

LAST WILL AND TESTAMENT

I, (1)____________________________, a resident of (2)______________ County, (2a)________________, being of sound and disposing mind and memory and not acting under duress, menace, fraud or undue influence of any person whomsoever, do make, publish and declare this to be my Last Will and Testament, and I hereby expressly revoke all other wills, codicils, and testamentary writings heretofore made by me.

FIRST. I declare that I am (3)____________________________________. My spouse's name was (4)____________________________. I have the following children:
(5)

I have a deceased child who left the following issue now surviving:
(6)

I have no other children and (7)____________________ deceased children who left issue now surviving.

SECOND. I devise all of estate to the Custodian under the Uniform Gift to Minors Act hereinafter named, to have and to hold upon the purposes and conditions of said act. I am secure in the knowledge that said Custodian will retain those items of personal use or sentimental value for my child or children in a manner I have made known or will make known to said Custodian.

My Executor, in making distribution to the Custodian, shall allocate the estate properties into as many shares as I have children then living and children then deceased who left issue then living. One such equal share shall be set aside for each of my children then living and one such equal share shall be set aside for the issue then living, by right of representation, of each of my children who are then deceased but left issue then living.

The Custodian may deposit any portion of a child's share in an IRC 529 college savings plan for the benefit of said child.

Upon each child attaining the age of (29)________ years, the Custodian shall deliver to said minor all of the remainder of his or her share.

In the event a child should die before distribution to him or her of his or her share, his or her share on hand at the time of his or her death shall thereupon be apportioned and distributed to his or her surviving issue, by right of representation. If such child should die before complete distribution to him or her of his or her share and leave no surviving issue, then the balance of the share then on hand shall go and be distributed to my heirs to be determined according to the laws of the State of (2a)_______________ then in effect relating to the intestate succession of separate property not acquired from a predeceased spouse.

Each beneficiary hereunder is hereby prohibited from anticipating, encumbering, assigning, or in any other manner alienating his or her interest in either income or principal, and is without power so to do, nor shall such interest be subject to his or her liabilities or obligations, nor to attachment, execution, or other legal processes, bankruptcy proceedings or claims of creditors or others. The Trustee may, however, deposit in any bank designated in writing by a beneficiary, to his or her credit, income or principal payable to such beneficiary.

I nominate and appoint (30)________________ as Custodian hereunder (32) without bond. In the event he/she/they should decline to act, or for any other reason, is unable to act as Custodian then I appoint (33)____________________________ as Custodian hereunder without bond.

THIRD. I have intentionally and with full knowledge omitted to provide for my issue, ancestors, relatives and heirs living at the time of my demise, except for such provisions as are made specifically herein.

If any person who is or claims under or through a beneficiary of this Will, or if any person who would be entitled to share in my estate if I died intestate, should in any manner whatsoever, directly or indirectly, attack, contest or seek to impair or invalidate in court any provision of the following:

A. This Will or any Codicil to this Will;

B. Any revocable or irrevocable Trust established by me;

C. Any beneficiary designation executed by me with respect to any insurance policy, any "Totten trust" account, any joint tenancy, any "transfer on death" account or any pension plan, or conspire or cooperate with anyone attempting to do any of the actions or things aforesaid, then I hereby specifically disinherit each such person and any devise, share or interest in my estate otherwise given to each such person under this Will or to which each such person might be entitled by law, is hereby revoked and shall pass and be distributed as though each such person had predeceased me leaving no issue or heirs whatsoever.

Any and every individual who asserts, or conspires or cooperates with any person who asserts, any claim against my Estate based on:

D. "Quantum meruit" theory;

E. Common law marriage, Marvin v. Marvin, 18 Cal. 3d 660 (1976) type of agreement or similar theory;

F. Constructive trust theory; or,

G. Oral agreement or written agreement which is to be proved by parole evidence, claiming that I agreed to gift or devise anything to such person or to pay such person or another for services rendered, regardless of whether a court may find that such agreement existed, then I hereby specifically disinherit each such person and any devise, share or interest in my estate otherwise given to each such person under this Will or to which each such person might be entitled by law, is hereby revoked and shall pass and be distributed as though each such person had predeceased me leaving no issue or heirs whatsoever.

FOURTH. I nominate and appoint (34)_________________________ as (35)____________ Executor hereunder (36) without bond. In the event he/she/they should decline, become unable or, for any reason, cease to serve as Executor then I nominate and appoint (37)_____________________ as Executor hereunder (36) without bond.

I authorize my Executor to sell, at either public or private sale, encumber or lease any property belonging to my estate, either with or without public notice, subject to such confirmation as may be required by law, and to hold, manage and operate any such property.

FIFTH. All typed and handwritten "fill-ins" where directed above were made before the execution of this Will and are not initialed by me. All crossed through words and inter-lineations were made before the execution of this Will and are initialed by me.

The masculine, feminine, and neuter gender and the singular or plural number, shall each be deemed to include the others whenever the context so indicates.

IN WITNESS WHEREOF, I have hereunto set my hand this (38)____________________ at (39)______________________, (2a)__________________.

(40)__________________________________

The foregoing instrument, consisting of __ pages, including the page on which this attestation clause is completed and signed, was at the date hereof by (1)____________________ signed as and declared to be his/her Will, in the presence of us who, at his/her request and in his/her presence, and in the presence of each other, have subscribed our names as witnesses thereto. Each of us observed the signing of this Will by (1)__________________ and by each other subscribing witness and knows that each signature is the true signature of the person whose name was signed.

Each of us is now an adult and a competent witness and resides at the address set forth after his or her name.

We are acquainted with (1)______________________. At this time, he/she is over the age of eighteen years, and to the best of our knowledge, he/she is of sound mind and is not acting under duress, menace, fraud, misrepresentation, or undue influence.

We declare under penalty of perjury that the foregoing is true and correct.

Executed on (38)___________________ at (39)___________________, (2a)_______________.

(41)_________________________ Residing at (42)__________________________

____

(43)_________________________ Residing at (44)__________________________

____

LAST WILL AND TESTAMENT

I, (1)____________________________, a resident of (2)______________ County, (2a)________________, being of sound and disposing mind and memory and not acting under duress, menace, fraud or undue influence of any person whomsoever, do make, publish and declare this to be my Last Will and Testament, and I hereby expressly revoke all other wills, codicils, and testamentary writings heretofore made by me.

FIRST. I declare that I am (3)____________________________________. My spouse's name was (4)______________________________. I have the following children:
(5)

I have a deceased child who left the following issue now surviving:
(6)

I have no other children and (7)_____________ deceased children who left issue now surviving.

SECOND. I devise the following personal, tangible property to the follow persons:
(8)

I devise to (9)___________________________________ all of my remaining personal effects, household furniture and furnishings, trailers, boats, pictures, works of art and art objects, collections, jewelry, silverware, wearing apparel, collections, sporting goods, and all other articles of household or personal use or ornament at whatsoever time acquired by me and wheresoever situated.

I devise to the following persons the cash amount listed after their respective names:
(10)

I devise to the following persons the real property described after their respective names. (12) Said real property is given free of all encumbrances or liens thereon.
(11)

I devise to (13)____________________ a life estate in the following property located at: (14)_________________________. After the death of (13)____________________ said property shall go, outright, to (15)____________________________ as the remainder person(s).

I devise all of the rest, residue and remainder of my estate, real, personal and mixed, of whatsoever kind or character and wheresoever situated, of which I die possessed or to which I may in any manner be entitled, to the following persons or entities (16) in the pro-portions listed after their names (17) in equal shares.
(18)

In the event any of the above named persons should predecease me or fail to survive me then his or her share shall lapse unless I have specifically named a person to take said bequest in the event of the first beneficiary's death.

Any beneficiary above who fails to survive me by thirty days shall be deemed to have predeceased me.

THIRD. I have intentionally and with full knowledge omitted to provide for my issue, ancestors, relatives and heirs living at the time of my demise, except for such provisions as are made specifically herein.

If any person who is or claims under or through a beneficiary of this Will, or if any person who would be entitled to share in my estate if I died intestate, should in any manner whatsoever, directly or indirectly, attack, contest or seek to impair or invalidate in court any provision of the following:

A. This Will or any Codicil to this Will;

B. Any revocable or irrevocable Trust established by me;

C. Any beneficiary designation executed by me with respect to any insurance policy, any "Totten trust" account, any joint tenancy, any "transfer on death" account or any pension plan, or conspire or cooperate with anyone attempting to do any of the actions or things aforesaid, then I hereby specifically disinherit each such person and any devise, share or interest in my estate otherwise given to each such person under this Will or to which each such person might be entitled by law, is hereby revoked and shall pass and be distributed as though each such person had predeceased me leaving no issue or heirs whatsoever.

Any and every individual who asserts, or conspires or cooperates with any person who asserts, any claim against my Estate based on:

D. "Quantum meruit" theory;

E. Common law marriage, Marvin v. Marvin, 18 Cal. 3d 660 (1976) type of agreement or similar theory;

F. Constructive trust theory; or,

G. Oral agreement or written agreement which is to be proved by parole evidence, claiming that I agreed to gift or devise anything to such person or to pay such person or another for services rendered, regardless of whether a court may find that such agreement existed, then I hereby specifically disinherit each such person and any devise, share or interest in my estate otherwise given to each such person under this Will or to which each such person might be entitled by law, is hereby revoked and shall pass and be distributed as though each such person had predeceased me leaving no issue or heirs whatsoever.

FOURTH. I nominate and appoint (34)________________________ as (35)____________ Executor hereunder (36) without bond. In the event he/she/they should decline, become unable or, for any reason, cease to serve as Executor then I nominate and appoint (37)____________________ as Executor hereunder (36) without bond.

I authorize my Executor to sell, at either public or private sale, encumber or lease any property belonging to my estate, either with or without public notice, subject to such confirmation as may be required by law, and to hold, manage and operate any such property.

FIFTH. All type and handwritten "fill-ins" where directed above were made before the execution of this Will and are not initialed by me. All crossed through words and inter lineations were made before the execution of this Will and are initialed by me.

Except as provided otherwise herein, the masculine, feminine, and neuter gender and the singular or plural number, shall each be deemed to include the others whenever the context so indicates.

IN WITNESS WHEREOF, I have hereunto set my hand this (38)__________________ at (39)____________________, (2a)________________.

(40)______________________________

The foregoing instrument, consisting of __ pages, including the page on which this attestation clause is completed and signed, was at the date hereof by (1)___________________ signed as and declared to be his/her Will, in the presence of us who, at his/her request and in his/her presence, and in the presence of each other, have subscribed our names as witnesses thereto. Each of us observed the signing of this Will by (1)__________________ and by each other subscribing witness and knows that each signature is the true signature of the person whose name was signed.

Each of us is now an adult and a competent witness and resides at the address set forth after his or her name.

We are acquainted with (1)______________________. At this time, he/she is over the age of eighteen years, and to the best of our knowledge, he/she is of sound mind and is not acting under duress, menace, fraud, misrepresentation, or undue influence.

We declare under penalty of perjury that the foregoing is true and correct.

Executed on (38)____________________ at (39)____________________, (2a)________________.

(41)___________________________ Residing at (42)____________________________

____

(43)___________________________ Residing at (44)____________________________

____

LAST WILL AND TESTAMENT

I, (1)_____________________________, a resident of (2)______________ County, (2a)_________________, being of sound and disposing mind and memory and not acting under duress, menace, fraud or undue influence of any person whomsoever, do make, publish and declare this to be my Last Will and Testament, and I hereby expressly revoke all other wills, codicils, and testamentary writings heretofore made by me.

FIRST. I declare that I am (3)_____________________________________. My spouse's name was (4)______________________________. I have the following children:
(5)

I have a deceased child who left the following issue now surviving:
(6)

I have no other children and (7)____________________ deceased children who left issue now surviving.

SECOND. I devise all of estate to the Trustee hereinafter named, to have and to hold upon the uses, trusts, purposes and conditions hereinafter provided. I am secure in the knowledge that my Trustee will retain those items of personal use or sentimental value for my child or children in a manner I have made known or will make known to my Trustee.

My Executor, in making distribution to the Trustee, shall allocate the trust properties into as many shares as I have children then living and children then deceased who left issue then living. One such equal share shall be set aside for each of my children then living and one such equal share shall be set aside for the issue then living, by right of representation, of each of my children who are then deceased but left issue then living. Said shares shall be held, administered, and distributed as provided in the following sections:

Each share set aside for a child of mine shall be held, administered and delivered for and to such beneficiary as follows:

1. The net income from the trust while said beneficiary is under 19 years of age and not a high school graduate shall be added to principal, from which the Trustee shall pay to or for the benefit of such beneficiary such sums as in the Trustee's discretion the Trustee shall deem necessary for such beneficiary's proper care, comfort, maintenance, support or education.

In making payments for the benefit of any beneficiary pursuant to this section 1, the Trustee shall construe his or her authority liberally to permit payments reasonably necessary to ease the financial burden on the guardian of the person of such beneficiary or other suitable individual with whom they reside, and on his or her family, resulting from such beneficiary's presence in his or her household.

2. Upon the beneficiary reaching 19 years of age or finishing high school(whichever occurs first), the Trustee shall pay to or apply for his or her benefit, from his or her trust, as much of the trust principal as the Trustee, in the Trustee's discretion, considers appropriate pursuant to sections 3 and 4 following.

3. After the beneficiary attains 19 years of age or finishes high school (whichever occurs first), the Trustee may, in the Trustee's discretion, pay to or apply from her trust, such amounts necessary for her education. For purposes hereof, education shall mean enrollment, attendance, and satisfactory progression towards a degree as a student at a recognized and accredited college, university, or similar institution of higher learning, including any graduate, professional school or college or trade school. Such educational payments and benefits shall include tuition, books, all direct educational costs and fees, and all reasonable living and transportation expenses. Payments hereunder shall be made during vacation periods within the regular school term

under which the beneficiary is attending school and during "summer vacation" or similar vacation period between the regular school terms.

The Trustee may invest any portion of a beneficiary's trust share in an IRC 529 college savings plan for the benefit of said beneficiary.

4. If the beneficiary, his or her spouse, or any of his or her children should at any time or from time to time be in need, in the discretion of the Trustee, of funds due to illness, infirmity or other physical or mental disability or any emergency, the Trustee may relieve or contribute toward the relief of any such need or needs of the beneficiary by paying to him or her or using and applying for his or her benefit, such sum or sums out of the income and/or principal of his or her trust as the Trustee, in the Trustee's discretion, may deem necessary or advisable.

5. Upon the beneficiary attaining the age of 21 years, the Trustee shall begin to pay the beneficiary all of the net income, in monthly or other convenient installments, from the trust.

6. Upon the beneficiary attaining the age of (21)_______ years, the Trustee shall distribute and deliver to such beneficiary one-half of his or her trust estate. Upon each beneficiary attaining the age of (22)__________ years, the Trustee shall distribute and deliver to such beneficiary all of the remainder of his or her trust estate.

7. If, upon the attaining of the above ages, the Trustee suspects that said beneficiary may be abusing drugs and/or alcohol, the Trustee may require the beneficiary to take a reasonable drug and/or alcohol test. If the beneficiary fails said test, the trustee shall defer said principal payment to the beneficiary until the beneficiary passes said test. After a failed test, subsequent drug tests shall be administered at the request of the beneficiary but not less than six months after a prior test. In the event a beneficiary fails a drug and/or alcohol test, the Trustee may use said beneficiary's trust estate to pay for a drug and/or alcohol abuse rehabilitation program and may require the beneficiary to enroll and to complete said program as a condition precedent to the taking of a subsequent drug and/or alcohol test.

8. In the event the beneficiary should die before complete distribution to him or her of his or her trust estate, his or her entire trust estate on hand at the time of his or her death shall thereupon be apportioned and distributed to his or her surviving issue, by right of representation. If such beneficiary should die before complete distribution to him or her of his or her trust estate and leave no surviving issue, then the balance of the trust estate then on hand shall go and be distributed to my heirs to be determined according to the laws of the State of (2a)_______________ then in effect relating to the intestate succession of separate property not acquired from a predeceased spouse.

9. Each beneficiary hereunder is hereby prohibited from anticipating, encumbering, assigning, or in any other manner alienating his or her interest in either income or principal, and is without power so to do, nor shall such interest be subject to his or her liabilities or obligations, nor to attachment, execution, or other legal processes, bankruptcy proceedings or claims of creditors or others. The Trustee may, however, deposit in any bank designated in writing by a beneficiary, to his or her credit, income or principal payable to such beneficiary.

10. If, at any time, a trust created hereunder shall, in the sole judgment of the Trustee, be of the aggregate principal value of Fifty Thousand Dollars ($50,000.00) or less, the Trustee may, but need not, terminate such trust and distribute the assets thereof in the Trustee's possession to the beneficiary or beneficiaries, at the time of the current income thereof, and if there is more than one beneficiary, in the proportion in which they are beneficiaries.

11. I nominate and appoint (25)____________________ as (26)_____________ Trustee hereunder (27) without bond. In the event he/she or both of them should die, decline to act, or for any other reason, be unable to act as Trustee then I appoint (28)_________________ as Trustee hereunder (27) without bond.

THIRD. I have intentionally and with full knowledge omitted to provide for my issue, ancestors, relatives and heirs living at the time of my demise, except for such provisions as are made specifically herein.

If any person who is or claims under or through a beneficiary of this Will, or if any person who would be entitled to share in my estate if I died intestate, should in any manner whatsoever, directly or indirectly, attack, contest or seek to impair or invalidate in court any provision of the following:

A. This Will or any Codicil to this Will;

B. Any revocable or irrevocable Trust established by me;

C. Any beneficiary designation executed by me with respect to any insurance policy, any "Totten trust" account, any joint tenancy, any "transfer on death" account or any pension plan, or conspire or cooperate with anyone attempting to do any of the actions or things aforesaid, then I hereby specifically disinherit each such person and any devise, share or interest in my estate otherwise given to each such person under this Will or to which each such person might be entitled by law, is hereby revoked and shall pass and be distributed as though each such person had predeceased me leaving no issue or heirs whatsoever.

Any and every individual who asserts, or conspires or cooperates with any person who asserts, any claim against my Estate based on:

D. "Quantum meruit" theory;

E. Common law marriage, Marvin v. Marvin, 18 Cal. 3d 660 (1976) type of agreement or similar theory;

F. Constructive trust theory; or,

G. Oral agreement or written agreement which is to be proved by parole evidence, claiming that I agreed to gift or devise anything to such person or to pay such person or another for services rendered, regardless of whether a court may find that such agreement existed, then I hereby specifically disinherit each such person and any devise, share or interest in my estate otherwise given to each such person under this Will or to which each such person might be entitled by law, is hereby revoked and shall pass and be distributed as though each such person had predeceased me leaving no issue or heirs whatsoever.

FOURTH. I nominate and appoint (34)__________________________ as (35)______________ Executor hereunder (36) without bond. In the event he/she or both of them should decline, become unable or, for any reason, cease to serve as Executor then I nominate and appoint (37)________________________ as Executor hereunder (36) without bond.

I authorize my Executor to sell, at either public or private sale, encumber or lease any property belonging to my estate, either with or without public notice, subject to such confirmation as may be required by law, and to hold, manage and operate any such property.

FIFTH. All typed and handwritten "fill-ins" where directed above were made before the execution of this Will and are not initialed by me. All crossed through words and inter-lineations were made before the execution of this Will and are initialed by me.

The masculine, feminine, and neuter gender and the singular or plural number, shall each be deemed to include the others whenever the context so indicates.

IN WITNESS WHEREOF, I have hereunto set my hand this (38)_____________________ at (39)______________________, (2a)____________________.

(40)__________________________________

The foregoing instrument, consisting of __ pages, including the page on which this attestation clause is completed and signed, was at the date hereof by (1)__________________ signed as and declared to be his/her Will, in the presence of us who, at his/her request and in his/her presence, and in the presence of each other, have subscribed our names as witnesses thereto. Each of us observed the signing of this Will by (1)__________________ and by each other subscribing witness and knows that each signature is the true signature of the person whose name was signed.

Each of us is now an adult and a competent witness and resides at the address set forth after his or her name.

We are acquainted with (1)______________________. At this time, he/she is over the age of eighteen years, and to the best of our knowledge, he/she is of sound mind and is not acting under duress, menace, fraud, misrepresentation, or undue influence.

We declare under penalty of perjury that the foregoing is true and correct.

Executed on (38)__________________ at (39)__________________, (2a)_______________.

(41)_________________________ Residing at (42)_________________________

____

(43)_________________________ Residing at (44)_________________________

____

LAST WILL AND TESTAMENT

I, (1)____________________________, a resident of (2)______________ County, (2a)________________, being of sound and disposing mind and memory and not acting under duress, menace, fraud or undue influence of any person whomsoever, do make, publish and declare this to be my Last Will and Testament, and I hereby expressly revoke all other wills, codicils, and testamentary writings heretofore made by me.

FIRST. I declare that I am (3)________________________________. My spouse's name was (4)______________________________. I have no children, living and no deceased who left issue now living.

SECOND. I devise the following personal, tangible property:
(8)

I devise to (9)__________________________________ all of my remaining personal effects, household furniture and furnishings, trailers, boats, pictures, works of art and art objects, collections, jewelry, silverware, wearing apparel, collections, sporting goods, and all other articles of household or personal use or ornament at whatsoever time acquired by me and wheresoever situated.

I devise to the following persons the cash amount listed after their respective names:
(10)

I devise to the following persons the real property described after their respective names. (12) Said real property is given free of all encumbrances or liens thereon.
(11)

In the event any of the above named persons should predecease me or fail to survive me then his or her share shall lapse unless I have specifically named a person to take said bequest in the event of the first beneficiary's death.

Any beneficiary above who fails to survive me by thirty days shall be deemed to have predeceased me.

I devise all of the rest, residue and remainder of my estate, real, personal and mixed, of whatsoever kind or character and wheresoever situated, of which I die possessed or to which I may in any manner be entitled, to the following persons or entities (16) in the pro-portions listed after their names or (17) in equal shares.
(18)

and
(19)______ shares to the Trustee hereinafter named, to have and to hold for the benefit of (20)_____________________upon the uses, trusts, purposes and conditions hereinafter provided. 1. If the beneficiary, his or her spouse, or any of his or her children should at any time or from time to time be in need, in the discretion of the Trustee, of funds due to illness, infirmity or other physical or mental disability or any emergency, the Trustee may relieve or contribute toward the relief of any such need or needs of the beneficiary by paying to him or her or using and applying for his or her benefit, such sum or sums out of the income and/or principal of his or her trust as the Trustee, in the Trustee's discretion, may deem necessary or advisable.

2. The Trustee shall pay the beneficiary all of the net income, in monthly or other convenient installments, from the trust.

3.a. (47—Option 1 Start) Upon the beneficiary attaining the age of (21)_______ years, the Trustee shall distribute and deliver to such beneficiary one-half of his or her trust estate. Upon the beneficiary attaining the age of (22)_______ years, the Trustee shall distribute and deliver to such beneficiary all of the remainder of his or her trust estate.
3.b. If, upon the attaining of the above ages, the Trustee suspects that said beneficiary may be abusing drugs and/or alcohol, the Trustee may require the beneficiary to take a reasonable drug and/or alcohol test. If the beneficiary fails said test, the trustee shall defer said principal payment to the beneficiary until the beneficiary passes said test. After a failed test, subsequent drug tests shall be administered at the request of the beneficiary but not less than six months after a prior test. In the event a beneficiary fails a drug and/or alcohol test, the Trustee may use said beneficiary's trust estate to pay for a drug and/or alcohol abuse rehabilitation program and may require the beneficiary to enroll and to complete said program as a condition precedent to the taking of a subsequent drug and/or alcohol test.
3.c.In the event the beneficiary should die before complete distribution to him or her of his or her trust estate, his or her entire trust estate on hand at the time of his or her death shall thereupon be apportioned and distributed to his or her surviving issue, by right of representation. If such beneficiary should die before complete distribution to him or her of his or her trust estate and leave no surviving issue, then the balance of the trust estate then on hand shall go and be distributed to my heirs to be determined according to the laws of the State of (2a)________________ then in effect relating to the intestate succession of separate property not acquired from a predeceased spouse. (47—Option 1 End)
OR
3.a. (47—Option 2 Start) In addition to any other payments to the beneficiary hereunder, the Trustee shall, upon the written request of the beneficiary in December of each calendar year, pay to the beneficiary amounts from principal that the beneficiary requests, not exceeding in any single calendar year the greater of the following amounts: $5,000.00 or 5 percent of the value of the principal of the beneficiary's trust estate; determined as of the end of the calendar year. This right of withdrawal is noncumulative, so that if the beneficiary does not withdraw the full amount permitted to be withdrawn during any calendar year, the right to withdraw the remaining amount will lapse at the end of the calendar year.
b.On the death of the beneficiary his or her entire trust estate on hand at the time of his or her death shall thereupon be apportioned and distributed to:
(23)__________________________ if (23)____________________is then deceased then the trust estate then on hand shall go to (24)__________________________. (47—Option 2A End)
OR:
the beneficiary's surviving issue, by right of representation. If such beneficiary should die before complete distribution to him or her of his or her trust estate and leave no surviving issue, then the balance of the trust estate then on hand shall go and be distributed to my heirs to be determined according to the laws of the State of (2a)__________________ then in effect relating to the intestate succession of separate property not acquired from a predeceased spouse. (47—Option 2B End)

4. Each beneficiary hereunder is hereby prohibited from anticipating, encumbering, assigning, or in any other manner alienating his or her interest in either income or principal, and is without power so to do, nor shall such interest be subject to his or her liabilities or obligations, nor to attachment, execution, or other legal processes, bankruptcy proceedings or claims of creditors or others. The Trustee may, however, deposit in any bank designated in writing by a beneficiary, to his or her credit, income or principal payable to such beneficiary.

5. If, at any time, a trust created hereunder shall, in the sole judgment of the Trustee, be of the aggregate principal value of Fifty Thousand Dollars ($50,000.00) or less, the Trustee may, but need not, terminate such trust and distribute the assets thereof in the Trustee's possession to the beneficiary or beneficiaries, at the

time of the current income thereof, and if there is more than one beneficiary, in the proportion in which they are beneficiaries.

6. I nominate and appoint (25)________________ as (26)_____ Trustee hereunder (27) without bond. In the event he/she/or both of them should die, decline to act, or for any other reason, be unable to act as Trustee then I appoint (28)____________________________ as Trustee hereunder (27) without bond.

THIRD. I have intentionally and with full knowledge omitted to provide for my issue, ancestors, relatives and heirs living at the time of my demise, except for such provisions as are made specifically herein.

If any person who is or claims under or through a beneficiary of this Will, or if any person who would be entitled to share in my estate if I died intestate, should in any manner whatsoever, directly or indirectly, attack, contest or seek to impair or invalidate in court any provision of the following:

A. This Will or any Codicil to this Will;

B. Any revocable or irrevocable Trust established by me;

C. Any beneficiary designation executed by me with respect to any insurance policy, any "Totten trust" account, any joint tenancy, any "transfer on death" account or any pension plan, or conspire or cooperate with anyone attempting to do any of the actions or things aforesaid, then I hereby specifically disinherit each such person and any devise, share or interest in my estate otherwise given to each such person under this Will or to which each such person might be entitled by law, is hereby revoked and shall pass and be distributed as though each such person had predeceased me leaving no issue or heirs whatsoever.

Any and every individual who asserts, or conspires or cooperates with any person who asserts, any claim against my Estate based on:

D. "Quantum meruit" theory;

E. Common law marriage, Marvin v. Marvin, 18 Cal. 3d 660 (1976) type of agreement or similar theory;

F. Constructive trust theory; or,

G. Oral agreement or written agreement which is to be proved by parole evidence, claiming that I agreed to gift or devise anything to such person or to pay such person or another for services rendered, regardless of whether a court may find that such agreement existed, then I hereby specifically disinherit each such person and any devise, share or interest in my estate otherwise given to each such person under this Will or to which each such person might be entitled by law, is hereby revoked and shall pass and be distributed as though each such person had predeceased me leaving no issue or heirs whatsoever.

FOURTH. I nominate and appoint (34)_________________________ as (35)____________ Executor hereunder (36) without bond. In the event he/she/or both of them should decline, become unable or, for any reason, cease to serve as Executor then I nominate and appoint (37)_______________ ___ as Executor hereunder (36) without bond.

I authorize my Executor to sell, at either public or private sale, encumber or lease any property belonging to my estate, either with or without public notice, subject to such confirmation as may be required by law, and to hold, manage and operate any such property.

FIFTH. All typed and handwritten "fill-ins" where directed above were made before the execution of this Will and are not initialed by me. All crossed through words and inter-lineations were made before the execution of this Will and are initialed by me.

Except as provided otherwise herein, the masculine, feminine, and neuter gender and the singular or plural number, shall each be deemed to include the others whenever the context so indicates.

IN WITNESS WHEREOF, I have hereunto set my hand this (38)__________________ at (39)____________________, (2a)________________.

(40)______________________________

The foregoing instrument, consisting of __ pages, including the page on which this attestation clause is completed and signed, was at the date hereof by (40)________________ signed as and declared to be his/her Will, in the presence of us who, at his/her request and in his/her presence, and in the presence of each other, have subscribed our names as witnesses thereto. Each of us observed the signing of this Will by (40)_________________ and by each other subscribing witness and knows that each signature is the true signature of the person whose name was signed.

Each of us is now an adult and a competent witness and resides at the address set forth after his or her name.

We are acquainted with (40)______________________. At this time, he/she is over the age of eighteen years, and to the best of our knowledge, he/she is of sound mind and is not acting under duress, menace, fraud, misrepresentation, or undue influence.

We declare under penalty of perjury that the foregoing is true and correct.

Executed on (38)__________________ at (39)__________________, (2a)______________.

(41)________________________ Residing at (42)_________________________

____

(43)________________________ Residing at (44)_________________________

____

LAST WILL AND TESTAMENT

I, (1)_____________________________, a resident of (2)______________ County, (2a)__________________, being of sound and disposing mind and memory and not acting under duress, menace, fraud or undue influence of any person whomsoever, do make, publish and declare this to be my Last Will and Testament, and I hereby expressly revoke all other wills, codicils, and testamentary writings heretofore made by me.

FIRST. I declare that I am (3)____. My spouse's name was (4)_________________________________. I have no children, living and no deceased children who left issue now living.

SECOND. I devise the following personal, tangible property:
(8)

I devise to (9)____ all of my remaining personal effects, household furniture and furnishings, trailers, boats, pictures, works of art and art objects, collections, jewelry, silverware, wearing apparel, collections, sporting goods, and all other articles of household or personal use or ornament at whatsoever time acquired by me and wheresoever situated.

I devise to the following persons the cash amount listed after their respective names:
(10)

I devise to the following persons the real property described after their respective names. (12) Said real property is given free of all encumbrances or liens thereon.
(11)

I devise all of the rest, residue and remainder of my estate, real, personal and mixed, of whatsoever kind or character and wheresoever situated, of which I die possessed or to which I may in any manner be entitled, to the following persons or entities (16) in the pro-portions listed after their names (17) in equal shares.
(18)

In the event any of the above named persons should predecease me or fail to survive me then his or her share shall lapse unless I have specifically named a person to take said bequest in the event of the first beneficiary's death.
Any beneficiary above who fails to survive me by thirty days shall be deemed to have predeceased me.

THIRD. I have intentionally and with full knowledge omitted to provide for my issue, ancestors, relatives and heirs living at the time of my demise, except for such provisions as are made specifically herein.

If any person who is or claims under or through a beneficiary of this Will, or if any person who would be entitled to share in my estate if I died intestate, should in any manner whatsoever, directly or indirectly, attack, contest or seek to impair or invalidate in court any provision of the following:

A. This Will or any Codicil to this Will;

B. Any revocable or irrevocable Trust established by me;

C. Any beneficiary designation executed by me with respect to any insurance policy, any "Totten trust" account, any joint tenancy, any "transfer on death" account or any pension plan, or conspire or cooperate with anyone attempting to do any of the actions or things aforesaid, then I hereby specifically disinherit each such person and any devise, share or interest in my estate otherwise given to each such person under this Will or to which each such person might be entitled by law, is hereby revoked and shall pass and be distributed as though each such person had predeceased me leaving no issue or heirs whatsoever.

Any and every individual who asserts, or conspires or cooperates with any person who asserts, any claim against my Estate based on:

D. "Quantum meruit" theory;

E. Common law marriage, Marvin v. Marvin, 18 Cal. 3d 660 (1976) type of agreement or similar theory;

F. Constructive trust theory; or,

G. Oral agreement or written agreement which is to be proved by parole evidence, claiming that I agreed to gift or devise anything to such person or to pay such person or another for services rendered, regardless of whether a court may find that such agreement existed, then I hereby specifically disinherit each such person and any devise, share or interest in my estate otherwise given to each such person under this Will or to which each such person might be entitled by law, is hereby revoked and shall pass and be distributed as though each such person had predeceased me leaving no issue or heirs whatsoever.

FOURTH. I nominate and appoint (34)________________________ as (35)___Executor_ hereunder (36) without bond. In the event he/she/they should decline, become unable or, for any reason, cease to serve as Executor then I nominate and appoint (37)__________________ as Executor hereunder (36) without bond.

I authorize my Executor to sell, at either public or private sale, encumber or lease any property belonging to my estate, either with or without public notice, subject to such confirmation as may be required by law, and to hold, manage and operate any such property.

FIFTH. All typed and handwritten "fill-ins" where directed above were made before the execution of this Will and are not initialed by me. All crossed through words and inter-lineations were made before the execution of this Will and are initialed by me.

The masculine, feminine, and neuter gender and the singular or plural number, shall each be deemed to include the others whenever the context so indicates.

IN WITNESS WHEREOF, I have hereunto set my hand this (38)__________________ at (39)____________________, (2a)________________.

(40)______________________________

The foregoing instrument, consisting of __ pages, including the page on which this attestation clause is completed and signed, was at the date hereof by (1)__________________ signed as and declared to be his/her Will, in the presence of us who, at his/her request and in his/her presence, and in the presence of each other, have subscribed our names as witnesses thereto. Each of us observed the signing of this Will by (1)________________ and by each other subscribing witness and knows that each signature is the true signature of the person whose name was signed.

Each of us is now an adult and a competent witness and resides at the address set forth after his or her name.

We are acquainted with (1)____________________. At this time, he/she is over the age of eighteen years, and to the best of our knowledge, he/she is of sound mind and is not acting under duress, menace, fraud, misrepresentation, or undue influence.

We declare under penalty of perjury that the foregoing is true and correct.

Executed on (38)__________________ at (39)__________________, (2a)_______________.

(41)________________________ Residing at (42)________________________

____

(43)________________________ Residing at (44)________________________

____

LAST WILL AND TESTAMENT

I, (1)____________________________, a resident of (2)______________ County, (2a)___________________, being of sound and disposing mind and memory and not acting under duress, menace, fraud or undue influence of any person whomsoever, do make, publish and declare this to be my Last Will and Testament, and I hereby expressly revoke all other wills, codicils, and testamentary writings heretofore made by me.

FIRST. I declare that I am (3)_____________________________________. My spouse's name was (4)_____________________________________. I have no children, living and no deceased children who left issue now living.

SECOND. I devise the following personal, tangible property:
(8)

I devise to (9)_____________________________________ all of my remaining personal effects, household furniture and furnishings, trailers, boats, pictures, works of art and art objects, collections, jewelry, silverware, wearing apparel, collections, sporting goods, and all other articles of household or personal use or ornament at whatsoever time acquired by me and wheresoever situated.

I devise to the following persons the cash amount listed after their respective names:
(10)

I devise to the following persons the real property described after their respective names. (12) Said real property is given free of all encumbrances or liens thereon.
(11)

I devise to (13)____________________ a life estate in the following property located at: (14)__________________________. After the death of (13)______________________ said property shall go, outright, to (15)______________________________ as the remainder person(s).

I devise all of the rest, residue and remainder of my estate, real, personal and mixed, of whatsoever kind or character and wheresoever situated, of which I die possessed or to which I may in any manner be entitled, to the following persons or entities (16) in the pro-portions listed after their names (17) in equal shares.
(18)

In the event any of the above named persons should predecease me or fail to survive me then his or her share shall lapse unless I have specifically named a person to take said bequest in the event of the first beneficiary's death.
Any beneficiary above who fails to survive me by thirty days shall be deemed to have predeceased me.

THIRD. I have intentionally and with full knowledge omitted to provide for my issue, ancestors, relatives and heirs living at the time of my demise, except for such provisions as are made specifically herein.

If any person who is or claims under or through a beneficiary of this Will, or if any person who would be entitled to share in my estate if I died intestate, should in any manner whatsoever, directly or indirectly, attack, contest or seek to impair or invalidate in court any provision of the following:

A. This Will or any Codicil to this Will;

B. Any revocable or irrevocable Trust established by me;

C. Any beneficiary designation executed by me with respect to any insurance policy, any "Totten trust" account, any joint tenancy, any "transfer on death" account or any pension plan, or conspire or cooperate with anyone attempting to do any of the actions or things aforesaid, then I hereby specifically disinherit each such person and any devise, share or interest in my estate otherwise given to each such person under this Will or to which each such person might be entitled by law, is hereby revoked and shall pass and be distributed as though each such person had predeceased me leaving no issue or heirs whatsoever.

Any and every individual who asserts, or conspires or cooperates with any person who asserts, any claim against my Estate based on:

D. "Quantum meruit" theory;

E. Common law marriage, Marvin v. Marvin, 18 Cal. 3d 660 (1976) type of agreement or similar theory;

F. Constructive trust theory; or,

G. Oral agreement or written agreement which is to be proved by parole evidence, claiming that I agreed to gift or devise anything to such person or to pay such person or another for services rendered, regardless of whether a court may find that such agreement existed, then I hereby specifically disinherit each such person and any devise, share or interest in my estate otherwise given to each such person under this Will or to which each such person might be entitled by law, is hereby revoked and shall pass and be distributed as though each such person had predeceased me leaving no issue or heirs whatsoever.

FOURTH. I nominate and appoint (34)_________________________ as (35)_____________ Executor hereunder (36) without bond. In the event he/she/they should decline, become unable or, for any reason, cease to serve as Executor then I nominate and appoint (37)____________________ as Executor hereunder (36) without bond.

I authorize my Executor to sell, at either public or private sale, encumber or lease any property belonging to my estate, either with or without public notice, subject to such confirmation as may be required by law, and to hold, manage and operate any such property.

FIFTH. All typed and handwritten "fill-ins" where directed above were made before the execution of this Will and are not initialed by me. All crossed through words inter-lineations were made before the execution of this Will and are initialed by me.

The masculine, feminine, and neuter gender and the singular or plural number, shall each be deemed to include the others whenever the context so indicates.

IN WITNESS WHEREOF, I have hereunto set my hand this (38)__________________ at (39)____________________, (2a)__________________.

(40)_________________________________

The foregoing instrument, consisting of __ pages, including the page on which this attestation clause is completed and signed, was at the date hereof by (1)__________________ signed as and declared to be his/her Will, in the presence of us who, at his/her request and in his/her presence, and in the presence of each other, have subscribed our names as witnesses thereto. Each of us observed the signing of this Will by (1)__________________ and by each other subscribing witness and knows that each signature is the true signature of the person whose name was signed.

Each of us is now an adult and a competent witness and resides at the address set forth after his or her name.

We are acquainted with (1)____________________. At this time, he/she is over the age of eighteen years, and to the best of our knowledge, he/she is of sound mind and is not acting under duress, menace, fraud, misrepresentation, or undue influence.

We declare under penalty of perjury that the foregoing is true and correct.

Executed on (38)____________________ at (39)____________________, (2a)____________________.

(41)____________________ Residing at (42)____________________

____

(43)____________________ Residing at (44)____________________

____

LAST WILL AND TESTAMENT

I, (1)_____________________________, a resident of (2)_____________ County, (2a)__________________, being of sound and disposing mind and memory and not acting under duress, menace, fraud or undue influence of any person whomsoever, do make, publish and declare this to be my Last Will and Testament, and I hereby expressly revoke all other wills, codicils, and testamentary writings heretofore made by me.

FIRST. I declare that I am (3)_________________________________. My spouse's name was (4)________________________________. I have no children, living and no deceased children who left issue now living.

SECOND. I devise the following personal, tangible property to the follow persons:
(8)

I devise to (9)_________________________________ all of my remaining personal effects, household furniture and furnishings, trailers, boats, pictures, works of art and art objects, collections, jewelry, silverware, wearing apparel, collections, sporting goods, and all other articles of household or personal use or ornament at whatsoever time acquired by me and wheresoever situated.

I devise to the following persons the cash amount listed after their respective names:
(10)

I devise to the following persons the real property described after their respective names. (12) Said real property is given free of all encumbrances or liens thereon.
(11)

I devise all of the rest, residue and remainder of my estate, real, personal and mixed, of whatsoever kind or character and wheresoever situated, of which I die possessed or to which I may in any manner be entitled, to (16) in the pro-portions listed after their names (17) in equal shares.
(18)

and
(19)______ shares to the Trustee hereinafter named, to have and to hold for the benefit of (20)__________________ _upon the uses, trusts, purposes and conditions hereinafter provided.

1. If the beneficiary, his or her spouse, or any of his or her children should at any time or from time to time be in need, in the discretion of the Trustee, of funds due to illness, infirmity or other physical or mental disability or any emergency, the Trustee may relieve or contribute toward the relief of any such need or needs of the beneficiary by paying to him or her or using and applying for his or her benefit, such sum or sums out of the income and/or principal of his or her trust as the Trustee, in the Trustee's discretion, may deem necessary or advisable.

2. The Trustee shall pay the beneficiary all of the net income, in monthly or other convenient installments, from the trust.

3.a. (47—Option 1 Start) Upon the beneficiary attaining the age of (21)_______ years, the Trustee shall distribute and deliver to such beneficiary one-half of his or her trust estate. Upon the beneficiary attaining the age of (22)_______ years, the Trustee shall distribute and deliver to such beneficiary all of the remainder of his or her trust estate.

3.b. If, upon the attaining of the above ages, the Trustee suspects that said beneficiary may be abusing drugs and/or alcohol, the Trustee may require the beneficiary to take a reasonable drug and/or alcohol test. If the beneficiary fails said test, the trustee shall defer said principal payment to the beneficiary until the beneficiary passes said test. After a failed test, subsequent drug tests shall be administered at the request of the beneficiary but not less than six months after a prior test. In the event a beneficiary fails a drug and/or alcohol test, the Trustee may use said beneficiary's trust estate to pay for a drug and/or alcohol abuse rehabilitation program and may require the beneficiary to enroll and to complete said program as a condition precedent to the taking of a subsequent drug and/or alcohol test.
3.c.In the event the beneficiary should die before complete distribution to him or her of his or her trust estate, his or her entire trust estate on hand at the time of his or her death shall thereupon be apportioned and distributed to his or her surviving issue, by right of representation. If such beneficiary should die before complete distribution to him or her of his or her trust estate and leave no surviving issue, then the balance of the trust estate then on hand shall go and be distributed to my heirs to be determined according to the laws of the State of (2a)_________________ then in effect relating to the intestate succession of separate property not acquired from a predeceased spouse. (47—Option 1 End)
OR
3.a. (47—Option 2 Start) In addition to any other payments to the beneficiary hereunder, the Trustee shall, upon the written request of the beneficiary in December of each calendar year, pay to the beneficiary amounts from principal that the beneficiary requests, not exceeding in any single calendar year the greater of the following amounts: $5,000.00 or 5 percent of the value of the principal of the beneficiary's trust estate; determined as of the end of the calendar year. This right of withdrawal is noncumulative, so that if the beneficiary does not withdraw the full amount permitted to be withdrawn during any calendar year, the right to withdraw the remaining amount will lapse at the end of the calendar year.
3.b.On the death of the beneficiary his or her entire trust estate on hand at the time of his or her death shall thereupon be apportioned and distributed to: (23)___________________________.
If (23)______________________is then deceased then the trust estate then on hand shall go to (24)____________________________, if he/she is then living. (47—Option 2A End)
OR:
the beneficiary's surviving issue, by right of representation. If such beneficiary should die before complete distribution to him or her of his or her trust estate and leave no surviving issue, then the balance of the trust estate then on hand shall go and be distributed to my heirs to be determined according to the laws of the State of (2a)___________________ then in effect relating to the intestate succession of separate property not acquired from a predeceased spouse. (47—Option 2B End)

4. Each beneficiary hereunder is hereby prohibited from anticipating, encumbering, assigning, or in any other manner alienating his or her interest in either income or principal, and is without power so to do, nor shall such interest be subject to his or her liabilities or obligations, nor to attachment, execution, or other legal processes, bankruptcy proceedings or claims of creditors or others. The Trustee may, however, deposit in any bank designated in writing by a beneficiary, to his or her credit, income or principal payable to such beneficiary.

5. If, at any time, a trust created hereunder shall, in the sole judgment of the Trustee, be of the aggregate principal value of Fifty Thousand Dollars ($50,000.00) or less, the Trustee may, but need not, terminate such trust and distribute the assets thereof in the Trustee's possession to the beneficiary or beneficiaries, at the time of the current income thereof, and if there is more than one beneficiary, in the proportion in which they are beneficiaries.

6. I nominate and appoint (25)________________________ as (26)___________ Trustee hereunder (27) without bond. In the event he/she/they should die, decline to act, or for any other reason, be unable to

act as Trustee then I appoint (28)____________________________ as Trustee hereunder (27) without bond.

7. In the event any of the above named persons should predecease me or fail to survive me then his or her share shall lapse unless I have specifically named a person to take said bequest in the event of the first beneficiary's death.

Any beneficiary above who fails to survive me by thirty days shall be deemed to have predeceased me.

THIRD. I have intentionally and with full knowledge omitted to provide for my issue, ancestors, relatives and heirs living at the time of my demise, except for such provisions as are made specifically herein.

If any person who is or claims under or through a beneficiary of this Will, or if any person who would be entitled to share in my estate if I died intestate, should in any manner whatsoever, directly or indirectly, attack, contest or seek to impair or invalidate in court any provision of the following:

A. This Will or any Codicil to this Will;

B. Any revocable or irrevocable Trust established by me;

C. Any beneficiary designation executed by me with respect to any insurance policy, any "Totten trust" account, any joint tenancy, any "transfer on death" account or any pension plan, or conspire or cooperate with anyone attempting to do any of the actions or things aforesaid, then I hereby specifically disinherit each such person and any devise, share or interest in my estate otherwise given to each such person under this Will or to which each such person might be entitled by law, is hereby revoked and shall pass and be distributed as though each such person had predeceased me leaving no issue or heirs whatsoever.

Any and every individual who asserts, or conspires or cooperates with any person who asserts, any claim against my Estate based on:

D. "Quantum meruit" theory;

E. Common law marriage, Marvin v. Marvin, 18 Cal. 3d 660 (1976) type of agreement or similar theory;

F. Constructive trust theory; or,

G. Oral agreement or written agreement which is to be proved by parole evidence, claiming that I agreed to gift or devise anything to such person or to pay such person or another for services rendered, regardless of whether a court may find that such agreement existed, then I hereby specifically disinherit each such person and any devise, share or interest in my estate otherwise given to each such person under this Will or to which each such person might be entitled by law, is hereby revoked and shall pass and be distributed as though each such person had predeceased me leaving no issue or heirs whatsoever.

FOURTH. I nominate and appoint (34)_______________________ as (35)___Executor_ hereunder (36) without bond. In the event he/she/they should decline, become unable or, for any reason, cease to serve as Executor then I nominate and appoint (37)_______ ____________ as Executor hereunder (36) without bond.

I authorize my Executor to sell, at either public or private sale, encumber or lease any property belonging to my estate, either with or without public notice, subject to such confirmation as may be required by law, and to hold, manage and operate any such property.

FIFTH. All typed and handwritten "fill-ins" where directed above were made before the execution of this Will and are not initialed by me. All crossed through words and inter-lineations were made before the execution of this Will and are initialed by me.

The masculine, feminine, and neuter gender and the singular or plural number, shall each be deemed to include the others whenever the context so indicates.

IN WITNESS WHEREOF, I have hereunto set my hand this (38)__________________________ at (39)______________________, (2a)____________________.

(40)___________________________________

The foregoing instrument, consisting of __ pages, including the page on which this attestation clause is completed and signed, was at the date hereof by (1)____________________ signed as and declared to be his/her Will, in the presence of us who, at his/her request and in his/her presence, and in the presence of each other, have subscribed our names as witnesses thereto. Each of us observed the signing of this Will by (1)__________________ and by each other subscribing witness and knows that each signature is the true signature of the person whose name was signed.

Each of us is now an adult and a competent witness and resides at the address set forth after his or her name.

We are acquainted with (1)______________________. At this time, he/she is over the age of eighteen years, and to the best of our knowledge, he/she is of sound mind and is not acting under duress, menace, fraud, misrepresentation, or undue influence.

We declare under penalty of perjury that the foregoing is true and correct.

Executed on (38)____________________ at (39)____________________, (2a)________________.

(41)___________________________ Residing at (42)_____________________________

____

(43)___________________________ Residing at (44)_____________________________

____

LAST WILL AND TESTAMENT

I, (1)______________________________, a resident of (2)______________ County, (2a)__________________, being of sound and disposing mind and memory and not acting under duress, menace, fraud or undue influence of any person whomsoever, do make, publish and declare this to be my Last Will and Testament, and I hereby expressly revoke all other wills, codicils, and testamentary writings heretofore made by me.

FIRST. I declare that I am married. My spouse's name is (4)______________________________.I have the following children:
(5)

I have a deceased child who left the following issue now surviving:
(6)

I have no other children and no (7)____________ deceased children who left issue now surviving.

SECOND. I devise the following personal, tangible property to the follow persons:
(8)

I devise to (9)__________________________________ all of my remaining personal effects, household furniture and furnishings, trailers, boats, pictures, works of art and art objects, collections, jewelry, silverware, wearing apparel, collections, sporting goods, and all other articles of household or personal use or ornament at whatsoever time acquired by me and wheresoever situated.

I devise to the following persons the cash amount listed after their respective names:
(10)

In the event any of the above named persons should predecease me or fail to survive me then his or her share shall lapse unless I have specifically named a person to take said bequest in the event of the first beneficiary's death.

Any beneficiary above who fails to survive me by thirty days shall be deemed to have predeceased me.

I devise all the rest, residue and remainder of my estate, real, personal and mixed, of whatsoever kind or character and wheresoever situated, of which I die possessed or to which I may in any manner be entitled, to the Trustee under that Trust Declaration known as THE (1a)________________________ TRUST dated (48)________________________, in which I am the or an original Trustor, to be added to and commingled with the trust property of that trust and held, managed and distributed as a part of said trust according to the terms of that Trust Declaration and not as a separate testamentary trust.

If, for any reason, the foregoing disposition to above described Trust should be inoperative or invalid, then all the rest, residue and remainder of my estate as aforesaid, shall go to the Trustee of the above described Trust, in trust, to have and to hold upon the uses, trusts, purposes and conditions as provided in the above described Trust which provisions are hereby incorporated by reference.

THIRD. I have intentionally and with full knowledge omitted to provide for my issue, ancestors, relatives and heirs living at the time of my demise, except for such provisions as are made specifically herein.

If any person who is or claims under or through a beneficiary of this Will, or if any person who would be entitled to share in my estate if I died intestate, should in any manner whatsoever, directly or indirectly, attack, contest or seek to impair or invalidate in court any provision of the following:

A. This Will or any Codicil to this Will;

B. Any revocable or irrevocable Trust established by me;

C. Any beneficiary designation executed by me with respect to any insurance policy, any "Totten trust" account, any joint tenancy, any "transfer on death" account or any pension plan,

or conspire or cooperate with anyone attempting to do any of the actions or things aforesaid, then I hereby specifically disinherit each such person and any devise, share or interest in my estate otherwise given to each such person under this Will or to which each such person might be entitled by law, is hereby revoked and shall pass and be distributed as though each such person had predeceased me leaving no issue or heirs whatsoever.

Any and every individual who asserts, or conspires or cooperates with any person who asserts, any claim against my Estate based on:

D. "Quantum meruit" theory;

E. Common law marriage, Marvin v. Marvin, 18 Cal. 3d 660 (1976) type of agreement or similar theory;

F. Constructive trust theory; or,

G. Oral agreement or written agreement which is to be proved by parole evidence, claiming that I agreed to gift or devise anything to such person or to pay such person or another for services rendered, regardless of whether a court may find that such agreement existed,

then I hereby specifically disinherit each such person and any devise, share or interest in my estate otherwise given to each such person under this Will or to which each such person might be entitled by law, is hereby revoked and shall pass and be distributed as though each such person had predeceased me leaving no issue or heirs whatsoever.

FOURTH. I nominate and appoint (34)________________________ as (35)___Executor hereunder (36) without bond. In the event he/she/they should decline, become unable or, for any reason, cease to serve as Executor then I nominate and appoint (37)____________________ as Executor hereunder (36) without bond.

I authorize my Executor to sell, at either public or private sale, encumber or lease any property belonging to my estate, either with or without public notice, subject to such confirmation as may be required by law, and to hold, manage and operate any such property.

FIFTH. All typed or handwritten "fill-ins" where directed above were made before the execution of this Will and are not initialed by me. All cross through words and inter-lineations were made before the execution of this Will and are initialed by me.

Except as provided otherwise herein, the masculine, feminine, and neuter gender and the singular or plural number, shall each be deemed to include the others whenever the context so indicates.

IN WITNESS WHEREOF, I have hereunto set my hand this (38)______________________ at (39)____________________, (2a)__________________.

(40)______________________________

The foregoing instrument, consisting of __ pages, including the page on which this attestation clause is completed and signed, was at the date hereof by (1)____________________ signed as and declared to be his/her Will, in the presence of us who, at his/her request and in his/her presence, and in the presence of each other, have subscribed our names as witnesses thereto. Each of us observed the signing of this Will by (1)__________________ and by each other subscribing witness and knows that each signature is the true signature of the person whose name was signed.

Each of us is now an adult and a competent witness and resides at the address set forth after his or her name.

We are acquainted with (1)______________________. At this time, he/she is over the age of eighteen years, and to the best of our knowledge, he/she is of sound mind and is not acting under duress, menace, fraud, misrepresentation, or undue influence.

We declare under penalty of perjury that the foregoing is true and correct.

Executed on (38)____________________ at (39)___________________, (2a)__________________.

(41)__________________________ Residing at (42)___________________________

____

(43)__________________________ Residing at (44)___________________________

____

LAST WILL AND TESTAMENT

I, (1)______________________________, a resident of (2)________________ County, (2a)____________, being of sound and disposing mind and memory and not acting under duress, menace, fraud or undue influence of any person whomsoever, do make, publish and declare this to be my Last Will and Testament, and I hereby expressly revoke all other wills, codicils, and testamentary writings heretofore made by me.

FIRST. I declare that I am (3)__________________________________. My spouse's name was (4)________________________________. I have the following children:
(5)

I have a deceased child who left the following issue now surviving:
(6)

I have no other children and no (7)______________ deceased children who left issue now surviving.

SECOND. I devise the following personal, tangible property:
(8)

I devise to (9)______________________________________ all of my remaining personal effects, household furniture and furnishings, trailers, boats, pictures, works of art and art objects, collections, jewelry, silverware, wearing apparel, collections, sporting goods, and all other articles of household or personal use or ornament at whatsoever time acquired by me and wheresoever situated.

I devise to the following persons the cash amount listed after their respective names:
(10)

In the event any of the above named persons should predecease me or fail to survive me then his or her share shall lapse unless I have specifically named a person to take said bequest in the event of the first beneficiary's death.

Any beneficiary above who fails to survive me by thirty days shall be deemed to have predeceased me. I devise all the rest, residue and remainder of my estate, real, personal and mixed, of whatsoever kind or character and wheresoever situated, of which I die possessed or to which I may in any manner be entitled, to the Trustee under that Trust Declaration known as THE (1a)____________________________ TRUST dated (48)____________________________, in which I am the or an original Trustor, to be added to and commingled with the trust property of that trust and held, managed and distributed as a part of said trust according to the terms of that Trust Declaration and not as a separate testamentary trust.

If, for any reason, the foregoing disposition to above described Trust should be inoperative or invalid, then all the rest, residue and remainder of my estate as aforesaid, shall go to the Trustee of the above described Trust, in trust, to have and to hold upon the uses, trusts, purposes and conditions as provided in the above described Trust which provisions are hereby incorporated by reference.

THIRD. I have intentionally and with full knowledge omitted to provide for my issue, ancestors, relatives and heirs living at the time of my demise, except for such provisions as are made specifically herein.

If any person who is or claims under or through a beneficiary of this Will, or if any person who would be entitled to share in my estate if I died intestate, should in any manner whatsoever, directly or indirectly, attack, contest or seek to impair or invalidate in court any provision of the following:

A. This Will or any Codicil to this Will;

B. Any revocable or irrevocable Trust established by me;

C. Any beneficiary designation executed by me with respect to any insurance policy, any "Totten trust" account, any joint tenancy, any "transfer on death" account or any pension plan,

or conspire or cooperate with anyone attempting to do any of the actions or things aforesaid, then I hereby specifically disinherit each such person and any devise, share or interest in my estate otherwise given to each such person under this Will or to which each such person might be entitled by law, is hereby revoked and shall pass and be distributed as though each such person had predeceased me leaving no issue or heirs whatsoever.

Any and every individual who asserts, or conspires or cooperates with any person who asserts, any claim against my Estate based on:

D. "Quantum meruit" theory;

E. Common law marriage, Marvin v. Marvin, 18 Cal. 3d 660 (1976) type of agreement or similar theory;

F. Constructive trust theory; or,

G. Oral agreement or written agreement which is to be proved by parole evidence, claiming that I agreed to gift or devise anything to such person or to pay such person or another for services rendered, regardless of whether a court may find that such agreement existed,

then I hereby specifically disinherit each such person and any devise, share or interest in my estate otherwise given to each such person under this Will or to which each such person might be entitled by law, is hereby revoked and shall pass and be distributed as though each such person had predeceased me leaving no issue or heirs whatsoever.

FOURTH. I nominate and appoint (34)__________________________ as (35)___Executor_ hereunder (36) without bond. In the event he/she/they should decline, become unable or, for any reason, cease to serve as Executor then I nominate and appoint (37)______________________ as Executor hereunder (36) without bond.

I authorize my Executor to sell, at either public or private sale, encumber or lease any property belonging to my estate, either with or without public notice, subject to such confirmation as may be required by law, and to hold, manage and operate any such property.

FIFTH. All typed and handwritten "fill-ins" where directed above were made before the execution of this Will and are not initialed by me. All crossed through words and inter-lineations were made before the execution of this Will and are initialed by me.

The masculine, feminine, and neuter gender and the singular or plural number, shall each be deemed to include the others whenever the context so indicates.

IN WITNESS WHEREOF, I have hereunto set my hand this (38)______________________ at (39)_______________________, (2a)______________________.

(40)___________________________________

The foregoing instrument, consisting of __ pages, including the page on which this attestation clause is completed and signed, was at the date hereof by (1)__________________ signed as and declared to be his/her Will, in the presence of us who, at his/her request and in his/her presence, and in the presence of each other, have subscribed our names as witnesses thereto. Each of us observed the signing of this Will by (1)__________________ and by each other subscribing witness and knows that each signature is the true signature of the person whose name was signed.

Each of us is now an adult and a competent witness and resides at the address set forth after his or her name.

We are acquainted with (1)______________________. At this time, he/she is over the age of eighteen years, and to the best of our knowledge, he/she is of sound mind and is not acting under duress, menace, fraud, misrepresentation, or undue influence.

We declare under penalty of perjury that the foregoing is true and correct.

Executed on (38)__________________ at (39)__________________, (2a)__________________.

(41)________________________ Residing at (42)________________________

____

(43)________________________ Residing at (44)________________________

____

LAST WILL AND TESTAMENT

I, (1)______________________________, a resident of (2)______________ County, (2a)___________, being of sound and disposing mind and memory and not acting under duress, menace, fraud or undue influence of any person whomsoever, do make, publish and declare this to be my Last Will and Testament, and I hereby expressly revoke all other wills, codicils, and testamentary writings heretofore made by me.

FIRST. I declare that I am (3)____________________________. My spouse's name was (4)______________________________. I have no children and no issue now living of a deceased child.

SECOND. I devise the following personal, tangible property:
(8)

I devise to (9)____________________________________ all of my remaining personal effects, household furniture and furnishings, trailers, boats, pictures, works of art and art objects, collections, jewelry, silverware, wearing apparel, collections, sporting goods, and all other articles of household or personal use or ornament at whatsoever time acquired by me and wheresoever situated.

I devise to the following persons the cash amount listed after their respective names:
(10)

In the event any of the above named persons should predecease me or fail to survive me then his or her share shall lapse unless I have specifically named a person to take said bequest in the event of the first beneficiary's death.

Any beneficiary above who fails to survive me by thirty days shall be deemed to have predeceased me.

I devise all the rest, residue and remainder of my estate, real, personal and mixed, of whatsoever kind or character and wheresoever situated, of which I die possessed or to which I may in any manner be entitled, to the Trustee under that Trust Declaration known as THE (1a)________________________ TRUST dated (48)________________________, in which I am the or an original Trustor, to be added to and commingled with the trust property of that trust and held, managed and distributed as a part of said trust according to the terms of that Trust Declaration and not as a separate testamentary trust.

If, for any reason, the foregoing disposition to above described Trust should be inoperative or invalid, then all the rest, residue and remainder of my estate as aforesaid, shall go to the Trustee of the above described Trust, in trust, to have and to hold upon the uses, trusts, purposes and conditions as provided in the above described Trust which provisions are hereby incorporated by reference.

THIRD. I have intentionally and with full knowledge omitted to provide for my issue, ancestors, relatives and heirs living at the time of my demise, except for such provisions as are made specifically herein.

If any person who is or claims under or through a beneficiary of this Will, or if any person who would be entitled to share in my estate if I died intestate, should in any manner whatsoever, directly or indirectly, attack, contest or seek to impair or invalidate in court any provision of the following:

A. This Will or any Codicil to this Will;

B. Any revocable or irrevocable Trust established by me;

C. Any beneficiary designation executed by me with respect to any insurance policy, any "Totten trust" account, any joint tenancy, any "transfer on death" account or any pension plan, or conspire or cooperate with anyone attempting to do any of the actions or things aforesaid, then I hereby specifically disinherit each such person and any devise, share or interest in my estate otherwise given to each such person under this Will or to which each such person might be entitled by law, is hereby revoked and shall pass and be distributed as though each such person had predeceased me leaving no issue or heirs whatsoever.

Any and every individual who asserts, or conspires or cooperates with any person who asserts, any claim against my Estate based on:

D. "Quantum meruit" theory;

E. Common law marriage, Marvin v. Marvin, 18 Cal. 3d 660 (1976) type of agreement or similar theory;

F. Constructive trust theory; or,

G. Oral agreement or written agreement which is to be proved by parole evidence, claiming that I agreed to gift or devise anything to such person or to pay such person or another for services rendered, regardless of whether a court may find that such agreement existed,

then I hereby specifically disinherit each such person and any devise, share or interest in my estate otherwise given to each such person under this Will or to which each such person might be entitled by law, is hereby revoked and shall pass and be distributed as though each such person had predeceased me leaving no issue or heirs whatsoever.

FOURTH. I nominate and appoint (34)__________________________ as (35)___Executor_ hereunder (36) without bond. In the event he/she/they should decline, become unable or, for any reason, cease to serve as Executor then I nominate and appoint (37)____________________ as Executor hereunder (36) without bond.

I authorize my Executor to sell, at either public or private sale, encumber or lease any property belonging to my estate, either with or without public notice, subject to such confirmation as may be required by law, and to hold, manage and operate any such property.

FIFTH. All typed and handwritten "fill-ins" where directed above were made before the execution of this Will and are not initialed by me. All crossed through words and inter-lineations were made before the execution of this Will and are initialed by me.

The masculine, feminine, and neuter gender and the singular or plural number, shall each be deemed to include the others whenever the context so indicates.

IN WITNESS WHEREOF, I have hereunto set my hand this (38)______________________ at (39)______________________, (2a)__________________.

(40)________________________________

The foregoing instrument, consisting of __ pages, including the page on which this attestation clause is completed and signed, was at the date hereof by (1)___________________ signed as and declared to be his/her Will, in the presence of us who, at his/her request and in his/her presence, and in the presence of each other, have subscribed our names as witnesses thereto. Each of us observed the signing of this Will by (1)__________________ and by each other subscribing witness and knows that each signature is the true signature of the person whose name was signed.

Each of us is now an adult and a competent witness and resides at the address set forth after his or her name.

We are acquainted with (1)_______________________. At this time, he/she is over the age of eighteen years, and to the best of our knowledge, he/she is of sound mind and is not acting under duress, menace, fraud, misrepresentation, or undue influence.

We declare under penalty of perjury that the foregoing is true and correct.

Executed on (38)____________________ at (39)____________________, (2a)__________________.

(41)____________________________ Residing at (42)____________________________

____

(43)____________________________ Residing at (44)____________________________

____

LAST WILL AND TESTAMENT

I, (1)______________________________, a resident of (2)______________ County, (2a)__________________, being of sound and disposing mind and memory and not acting under duress, menace, fraud or undue influence of any person whomsoever, do make, publish and declare this to be my Last Will and Testament, and I hereby expressly revoke all other wills, codicils, and testamentary writings heretofore made by me.

FIRST. I declare that I am married. My spouse's name is (4)________________________________. I have no children and no issue now living of a deceased child.

SECOND. I devise the following personal, tangible property to the follow persons:
(8)

I devise to (9)____________________________________ all of my remaining personal effects, household furniture and furnishings, trailers, boats, pictures, works of art and art objects, collections, jewelry, silverware, wearing apparel, collections, sporting goods, and all other articles of household or personal use or ornament at whatsoever time acquired by me and wheresoever situated.

I devise to the following persons the cash amount listed after their respective names:
(10)

In the event any of the above named persons should predecease me or fail to survive me then his or her share shall lapse unless I have specifically named a person to take said bequest in the event of the first beneficiary's death.

Any beneficiary above who fails to survive me by thirty days shall be deemed to have predeceased me.

I devise all the rest, residue and remainder of my estate, real, personal and mixed, of whatsoever kind or character and wheresoever situated, of which I die possessed or to which I may in any manner be entitled, to the Trustee under that Trust Declaration known as THE (1a)___________________________ TRUST dated (48)__________________________, in which I am the or an original Trustor, to be added to and commingled with the trust property of that trust and held, managed and distributed as a part of said trust according to the terms of that Trust Declaration and not as a separate testamentary trust.

If, for any reason, the foregoing disposition to above described Trust should be inoperative or invalid, then all the rest, residue and remainder of my estate as aforesaid, shall go to the Trustee of the above described Trust, in trust, to have and to hold upon the uses, trusts, purposes and conditions as provided in the above described Trust which provisions are hereby incorporated by reference.

THIRD. I have intentionally and with full knowledge omitted to provide for my issue, ancestors, relatives and heirs living at the time of my demise, except for such provisions as are made specifically herein.

If any person who is or claims under or through a beneficiary of this Will, or if any person who would be entitled to share in my estate if I died intestate, should in any manner whatsoever, directly or indirectly, attack, contest or seek to impair or invalidate in court any provision of the following:

A. This Will or any Codicil to this Will;

B. Any revocable or irrevocable Trust established by me;

C. Any beneficiary designation executed by me with respect to any insurance policy, any "Totten trust" account, any joint tenancy, any "transfer on death" account or any pension plan, or conspire or cooperate with anyone attempting to do any of the actions or things aforesaid, then I hereby specifically disinherit each such person and any devise, share or interest in my estate otherwise given to each such person under this Will or to which each such person might be entitled by law, is hereby revoked and shall pass and be distributed as though each such person had predeceased me leaving no issue or heirs whatsoever.

Any and every individual who asserts, or conspires or cooperates with any person who asserts, any claim against my Estate based on:

D. "Quantum meruit" theory;

E. Common law marriage, Marvin v. Marvin, 18 Cal. 3d 660 (1976) type of agreement or similar theory;

F. Constructive trust theory; or,

G. Oral agreement or written agreement which is to be proved by parole evidence, claiming that I agreed to gift or devise anything to such person or to pay such person or another for services rendered, regardless of whether a court may find that such agreement existed, then I hereby specifically disinherit each such person and any devise, share or interest in my estate otherwise given to each such person under this Will or to which each such person might be entitled by law, is hereby revoked and shall pass and be distributed as though each such person had predeceased me leaving no issue or heirs whatsoever.

FOURTH. I nominate and appoint (34)_________________________ as (35)___Executor_ hereunder (36) without bond. In the event he/she/they should decline, become unable or, for any reason, cease to serve as Executor then I nominate and appoint (37)____________________ as Executor hereunder (36) without bond.

I authorize my Executor to sell, at either public or private sale, encumber or lease any property belonging to my estate, either with or without public notice, subject to such confirmation as may be required by law, and to hold, manage and operate any such property.

FIFTH. All typed or handwritten "fill-ins" where directed above were made before the execution of this Will and are not initialed by me. All cross through words and inter-lineations were made before the execution of this Will and are initialed by me.

Except as provided otherwise herein, the masculine, feminine, and neuter gender and the singular or plural number, shall each be deemed to include the others whenever the context so indicates.

IN WITNESS WHEREOF, I have hereunto set my hand this (38)_ ____________________ at (39)_____________________, (2a)_______________________.

(40)________________________________

The foregoing instrument, consisting of __ pages, including the page on which this attestation clause is completed and signed, was at the date hereof by (1)___________________ signed as and declared to be his/her Will, in the presence of us who, at his/her request and in his/her presence, and in the presence of each other, have subscribed our names as witnesses thereto. Each of us observed the signing of this Will by (1)___________________ and by each other subscribing witness and knows that each signature is the true signature of the person whose name was signed.

Each of us is now an adult and a competent witness and resides at the address set forth after his or her name.

We are acquainted with (1)______________________. At this time, he/she is over the age of eighteen years, and to the best of our knowledge, he/she is of sound mind and is not acting under duress, menace, fraud, misrepresentation, or undue influence.

We declare under penalty of perjury that the foregoing is true and correct.

Executed on (38)____________________ at (39)____________________, (2a)____________________.

(41)____________________________ Residing at (42)____________________________

____

(43)____________________________ Residing at (44)____________________________

____

SELF-PROVED WILL/CODICIL AFFIDAVIT

"I, (1)_____, the testator, sign my name to this instrument this ______ day of _____, 200__, and being first duly sworn, do hereby declare to the undersigned authority that I sign and execute this instrument as my (62) codicil to my last will and that I sign it willingly (or willingly direct another to sign for me), that I execute it as my free and voluntary act for the purposes therein expressed, and that I am 18 years of age or older, of sound mind, and under no constraint or undue influence."

(41)__________________________
Witness

(43)__________________________
Witness

State of (2a)________________
County of (2)_______________

Subscribed, sworn to and acknowledged before me by (1)________________, the testator and subscribed and sworn to before me by (41a)_________________, and (43a)_________________, witnesses, this _____ day of _____, 200__.

__________________________ Notary

SELF-PROVED WILL/CODICIL AFFIDAVIT

STATE OF (2a)____________
COUNTY of (2)__________

Before me, the undersigned authority, on this day personally appeared (1)______________________, (41a)______________________, and (43a)________________, known to me to be the testator and the witnesses, respectively, whose names are subscribed to the annexed or foregoing instrument in their respective capacities, and all of said individuals being by me duly sworn, (1)______________________, testator, declared to me and to the witnesses in my presence that said instrument is the last will and testament or a codicil to the last will and testament of the testator and that the testator had willingly made and executed it as a free act and deed for the purposes expressed therein. The witnesses, each on oath, stated to me in the presence and hearing of the testator that the testator had declared to them that the instrument is the testator's last will and testament or a codicil to the testator's last will and testament and that the testator executed the instrument as such and wished each of them to sign it as a witness; and under oath each witness stated further that the witness had signed the same as witness in the presence of the testator and at the testator's request; that the testator was of legal age or over and of sound mind; and that each of the witnesses was then of legal age or over.

(40)______________________ Testator

(41)______________________ Witness (43)______________________ Witness

Sworn to and subscribed before me by (1)______________________, testator, and sworn to and subscribed before me by (41a)______________________ and (43a)______________________, witnesses, this ______ day of ______________, 200___. (SEAL)

(Signed)______________________________ (Official Capacity of Officer)

SELF-PROVED WILL/CODICIL AFFIDAVIT—TEXAS

THE STATE OF TEXAS
COUNTY OF (2)________________

Before me, the undersigned authority, on this day personally appeared (1)________________, (41a)________________, and (43a)________________, known to me to be the testator and the witnesses, respectively, whose names are subscribed to the annexed or foregoing instrument in their respective capacities, and, all of said persons being by me duly sworn, the said (1)______________, testator, declared to me and to the said witnesses in my presence that said instrument is his/her (60) codicil to his/her last will and testament, and that he/she had willingly made and executed it as his/her free act and deed; and the said witnesses, each on his or her oath stated to me, in the presence and hearing of the said testator, that the said testator had declared to them that said instrument is his/her (60) codicil to his/her last will and testament, and that he/she executed same as such and wanted each of them to sign it as a witness; and upon their oaths each witness stated further that they did sign the same as witnesses in the presence of the said testator and at his/her request; that he/she was at that time eighteen years of age or over (or being under such age, was or had been lawfully married, or was then a member of the armed forces of the United States or of an auxiliary thereof or of the Maritime Service) and was of sound mind; and that each of said witnesses was then at least fourteen years of age.

(40)__________________________
Testator

(41)__________________________
Witness

(43)__________________________
Witness

Subscribed and sworn to before me by the said _____________, testator, and by the said ________________ and ________________, witnesses, this ______ day of ________________ A.D. ________________.
(SEAL)
(Signed)______________________________
(Official Capacity of Officer)

SELF-PROVED WILL/CODICIL AFFIDAVIT—NEW HAMPSHIRE

The foregoing instrument was acknowledge before me this ____________________ day, by (1)____________________, the testator, (41a)____________________, and (43a)____________________, the witnesses, who under oath swear as follows:

1. The testator signed the instrument as his or her (60) codicil to his/her will or expressly directed another to sign for him.
2. This was the testator's free and voluntary act for the purposes expressed in the (60) codicil to his or her will.
3. Each witness signed at the request of the testator, in his or her presence, and in the presence of the other witness.
4. To the best of my knowledge, at the time of the signing the testator was at least 18 years of age, or if under 18 years was a married person, and was of sane mind and under no constraint or undue influence.

____
Notary

____
Official Capacity

SELF-PROVED WILL/CODICIL AFFIDAVIT—LOUISIANA

STATE OF LOUISIANA
PARISH OF (2)______________

The testator has signed his or her (60) codicil to his/her will at the end and on each separate page, and has declared or signified in our presence that it is his/her (60) codicil to his/her last will and testament, and in the presence of the testator and each other we have herunto subscribed our names this _______ day of __________, 200__.

(40)__________________
Testator

(41)____________________
Witness

(43)______________________
Witness

On this _________ day of ____________, 200__, before me personally appeared (1)______________, the testator, and (41a)______________ and (43a)_________________, the witnesses, to me known to be the persons described in and who executed the foregoing instrument, and acknowledged that they executed it as their free act and deed.

____
Notary

SELF-PROVED WILL/CODICIL AFFADAVIT—IOWA

(Attach to Will/Codicil)

State of (2a)_________________)
County of (2)_________________) ss

We, the undersigned, (1)________________ and (41a)__________________ and (43a)_________________, the testator and the witnesses, respectively, whose names are signed to the attached or foregoing instrument, being first duly sworn, declare to the undersigned authority that said instrument is the testator's (60) codicil to his/her will and that the testator willingly signed and executed such instrument, or expressly directed another to sign the same in the presence of the witnesses, as a free and voluntary act for the purposes therein expressed; that said witnesses, and each of them, declare to the undersigned authority that such (60) codicil to his/her will was executed and acknowledged by the testator as the testator's (60) codicil to his/her will in their presence and that they, in the testator's presence, at the testator's request, and in the presence of each other, did subscribe their names thereto as attesting witnesses on the date of the date of such (60) codicil to his/her will; and that the testator, at the time of the execution of such instrument, was of full age and of sound mind and that the witnesses were sixteen years of age or older and otherwise competent to be witnesses.

(40)_________________________
Testator

(41)_________________________
Witness

(43)_________________________
Witness

Subscribed, sworn and acknowledged before me by (1)_______________, the testator; and subscribed and sworn before me by (41a)________________ and (43a)__________________, witnesses, this ___ day of ___________, 200___.

____
Notary Public, or other officer authorized to take and certify acknowledgments and administer oaths
(Seal)

CODICIL TO LAST WILL AND TESTAMENT

I, (1)__________________________, a resident of (2)______________ County, (2a)______________, being of sound and disposing mind and memory and not acting under duress, menace, fraud or undue influence of any person whomsoever, do make, publish and declare this to be the (31)___________ codicil to my Last Will and Testament dated (45)____________________

1. Paragraph ___________________ is amended as follows:
(46)

2. All typed and handwritten "fill-ins" where directed above were made before the execution of this Will and are not initialed by me. All crossed through words and inter-lineations were made before the execution of this Will and are initialed by me.

3. I hereby ratify, confirm and republish my said Last Will and Testament, as modified by this Codicil thereto.

IN WITNESS WHEREOF, I have hereunto set my hand this (38)______________________ at (39) _____________________, (2a)____________________.

(40)_________________________________

The foregoing instrument, consisting of __ pages, including the page on which this attestation clause is completed and signed, was at the date hereof by (1)__________________ signed as and declared to be his/her Codicil, in the presence of us who, at his/her request and in his/her presence, and in the presence of each other, have subscribed our names as witnesses thereto. Each of us observed the signing of this Codicil by (1)___________________ and by each other subscribing witness and knows that each signature is the true signature of the person whose name was signed.

Each of us is now an adult and a competent witness and resides at the address set forth after his or her name.

We are acquainted with (1)______________________. At this time, he/she is over the age of eighteen years, and to the best of our knowledge, he/she is of sound mind and is not acting under duress, menace, fraud, misrepresentation, or undue influence.

We declare under penalty of perjury that the foregoing is true and correct.

Executed on (38)____________________ at (39)___________________, (2a)________________.

(41)__________________________ Residing at (42)___________________________

____

(43)__________________________ Residing at (44)___________________________

____

INTER-VIVOS TRUST

THE (1a)____________________TRUST

The Settlor named below hereby declares as follows:

ARTICLE I
ESTABLISHMENT OF TRUST

Paragraph 1.01. Creation of Trust. This Trust Declaration has been entered into between (1)______________________________ as Settlor and himself/herself as the Trustee. The Settlor, of (2)________ County, (2a)____________________, has transferred, or will transfer, to the Trustee of this Trust Declaration the property described in the attached Exhibit "A" which will constitute, together with any other property that may be added to this Trust Declaration, the Trust Estate of an express trust which shall be held, administered and distributed by the Trustee as provided in this Trust Declaration.

Paragraph 1.02. Trust Name. This Trust Declaration shall be known as the (1a)"________________________ TRUST" dated (48)________________________.

Paragraph 1.03. Definitions. As used in this Trust Declaration:

A. Settlor: The term "Settlor" shall refer to (1)____________________________________.

B. Trustee: The term "Trustee" or "Trustees" shall refer to whoever is serving as Trustee or Trustees under this Trust Declaration.

C. Trust Estate: The term "Trust Estate" shall refer to the property subject to this Trust Declaration.

ARTICLE II
OPERATION OF TRUST DURING THE LIFE OF SETTLOR

Paragraph 2.01. Net Income. During the life of Settlor the Trustee shall pay to or apply for the benefit of Settlor, in monthly or more frequent intervals, all of the net income of the Trust Estate.

Paragraph 2.02. Withdrawal of Principal. During the life of Settlor the Trustee shall also pay to or apply for the benefit of Settlor so much of the principal of the Trust Estate, up to the whole thereof, as Settlor shall direct.

Paragraph 2.03. Incapacity of Settlor. If, at any time during the life of the Settlor he or she shall become physically or mentally incapacitated so as to be unable to manage his or her affairs, whether or not a court of competent jurisdiction has declared him/her incompetent, mentally ill, or in need of a conservator, the Trustee shall pay to the Settlor or apply for the benefit of the Settlor such amounts of income or principal so that the Settlor enjoys a high standard of living commensurate with his/her estate and life expectancy. The interests of any other beneficiaries of this Trust are to be subordinated to the generous support of the Settlor. In this context "incapacitated" shall be determined by two physicians, at least one of whom is a geriatric specialist.

In regards to the amount of principal invasion by the Trustee for the Settlor, the Settlor is the primary beneficiary of this Trust Estate. The Settlor does not care if at his or her death the entire Trust Estate has been consumed by his or her needs. It is also the intent and desire of the Settlor that he/she live in his/her own home at all times, even if that requires the purchase of a new home to accommodate the in-home placement of twenty-four (24) hour nursing care.

The payments specified in this Section shall be made until the Settlor is again able to manage his or her own affairs, or until the death of the Settlor, whichever event may occur earlier.

Paragraph 2.04. Revocation of Trust. At any time during the life of the Settlor he or she may, by serving written notice on the Trustee, revoke the Trust created by this Trust Declaration, in whole or in part.

Paragraph 2.05. Amendment of Trust. At any time during the life of the Settlor, he or she may, by serving written notice on the Trustee, alter, modify or amend the Trust created by this Trust Declaration in any respect.

ARTICLE III
OPERATION OF TRUST AFTER DEATH OF SETTLOR

Paragraph 3.01. Collection of Assets and Payment of Debts: On the death of the Settlor the Trustee shall collect all assets belonging to the Trust Estate. As soon as practicable after the death of the Trustee, except as otherwise provided herein, shall pay from the Trust Estate the just debts of the Settlor (excluding any debts barred by provisions of law or not yet due), funeral expenses of the Settlor, and any inheritance, estate, or other death taxes that shall, by reason of the death of the Settlor, be attributable to the Trust Estate. This is not and shall not constitute a direction to pay all inheritance, estate or other death taxes from or charge the same to, the Trust Estate without apportionment.

Paragraph 3.02. Distribution of Trust Estate. Upon the death of the Settlor, and after payment of expenses as set forth in Paragraph 3.01, the Trustee shall hold, administer and distribute the Trust Estate as follows:

A. The Trustee shall distribute to the following persons the cash amount listed after their respective names:
(10)

B. The Trustee shall distribute to the following persons the real property described after their respective names. (12) Said real property is given free of all encumbrances or liens thereon.
(11)

C. The Trustee shall distribute to (13)____________________ a life estate in the following property located at: (14)__________________________. After the death of (13)_____________________ said property shall go, outright, to (15)______________________________ as the remainder person(s).

D. The Trustee shall distribute all of the rest, residue and remainder of the Trust Estate, real, personal and mixed, of whatsoever kind or character and wheresoever situated, to the following persons or entities (16) in the proportions listed after their names (17) in equal shares.
(18)

E. Distribution of Trust Assets. With respect to the distribution of any trust estate upon termination of any trust, and partial distribution of any trust, the liquidation and distribution by the Trustee of the Trust Estate involved or the distributable portion shall commence immediately and be accomplished as rapidly as possible, and deliveries of the trust properties to the beneficiary or beneficiaries may be made in installments or series, retaining only reasonable reserves for final charges and expenses. In no event shall it be necessary for the Trustee to await an accounting to the Court, or any Court order, before releasing and distributing the majority of the Trust Estate to be distributed.

F. Undistributed Income. All the net income of the respective trusts or trust estates, not distributed, used or applied as otherwise provided herein, shall be accumulated and added to the principals of the respective trusts.

Upon the change or succession of any beneficiary, distribution of trust properties or any trust estate or any portion thereof, or upon setting aside, apportionment or division of any trust estate or upon the termination of a trust or any interest therein, the beneficial interest, properties or balance of trust estate at the applicable time and to be dealt with shall include any and all income accumulated, accrued, uncollected or held undistributed and all of such income shall likewise be distributed, set aside or apportioned to the next or succeeding beneficiaries, distributees, shares or trusts, retaining its character as income.

ARTICLE IV
TRUSTEES

Paragraph 4.01. Appointment of Trustees. (49)____________________________________ is appointed and confirmed as the Trustee(s). In the event (49)________________________________ should die, refuse to act, or for any other reason be unable to act as Trustee then (25)______________________ shall act as (26)____Trustee_ hereunder (27) without bond. In the event he/she/they should die, decline to act, or for any other reason, be unable to act as Trustee then (28)______________________________ shall act as Trustee hereunder (27) without bond.

Paragraph 4.02. Substitute Trustee. The Settlor may appoint a substitute or successor Trustee to act as Trustee of any trust or trusts created hereunder in the place and stead of, or as successor to, any Trustee named in Section 4.01 above. Such substitution shall be in writing.

Paragraph 4.03. Trustee Liability. No person named as Trustee in this instrument or appointed as Trustee in the manner specified herein shall be liable to any beneficiary or to any heir of Settlor for the Trustee's acts or failure to act, except for willful misconduct or gross negligence. No such Trustee shall be liable or responsible for any act, omission or default of any other Trustee provided that they shall have had no knowledge of facts that might reasonably be expected to put the Trustee on notice of it.

Paragraph 4.04. Trustee Compensation. The Trustee shall be entitled to reasonable compensation for services rendered to the Trust or Trusts created hereunder.

Paragraph 4.05. Title to Trust Estate. The legal title to all property held in trust hereunder shall be, remain and become vested in the Trustee or successor Trustee from time to time acting hereunder, without any act of conveyance or transfer to or by or acceptance from, any succeeding, retiring or predecessor Trustee; however, any removed or resigning Trustee shall execute and deliver any and all conveyances and documents requested and reasonably necessary to transfer the trust estate and its assets to a successor Trustee. Each successor Trustee from time to time acting hereunder shall have all the rights, powers immunities and authorities, discretionary or otherwise and the duties and obligations herein granted to the original Trustee. No successor

Trustee shall be obligated to inquire into or be in any way responsible for the previous administration of any trust created herein or of the trust estate or for any act or default of any predecessor Trustee.

Paragraph 4.06. Powers of Trustee. To carry out the purposes of any trust created under this Trust Declaration, and subject to any limitations stated elsewhere in this Trust Declaration, the Trustee is vested with the following powers with respect to the Trust Estate, and any part of it, in addition to those powers now or hereafter conferred by law.

A. Power to Invest. To invest and reinvest the Trust Estate in every kind of property, real, personal or mixed, and every kind of investment, specifically including but not by way of limitation, corporate obligations of every kind, stocks, preferred or common, shares of investment trusts, investment companies, mutual funds, market index funds and mortgage participations which individuals of prudence, discretion and intelligence acquire for their own account, and any common trust fund administered by any Trustee under this Trust Declaration.

B. Power to Retain Property. To retain any property which was an asset of the Trust Estate during the Settlor's lifetime or received without consideration by the Trustee as long as the Trustee deems advisable whether or not of the character permitted by law for the investment of trust funds. The trust properties and investment need not be diversified and the Trustee shall have no duty to dispose or convert any trust assets to effect diversification.

C. Power to Manage Securities. With respect to securities held in this Trust Declaration, to have all the rights, powers and privileges of an owner, including but not by way of limitation, the power to vote, give proxies and pay assessments, to participate in voting trusts, pooling agreements, foreclosures, reorganizations, consolidations, mergers, liquidations, sales and leases and, incident to such participation, to deposit securities with and transfer title to any protective or other committee on such terms as the Trustee may deem advisable, to exercise and sell stock subscription or conversion rights and to hold securities in "street name".

D. Power of Sale, Exchange, Repair. To manage, control, foreclose, repossess, grant options on, grant easements on, sell (for cash), convey, exchange, partition, divide, improve and repair trust property.

The power to sell, at the termination of the trust, any trust property if the Trustee feels said disposition would assist in the distribution of the trust property at termination.

E. Power to Lease. To lease trust property for terms within or beyond the term of the trust and for any purpose, including exploration for and removal of gas, oil and other minerals; and to enter into community oil leases, pooling and unitization agreements, operating agreements or otherwise, and to create restrictions, easements or other servitudes thereon, to assign, partition, divide, subdivide, transfer to a corporation in exchange for stock, improve, repair, loan, reloan, invest and reinvest the trust estate or any part thereof.

F. Power to Insure. To carry, at the expense of the Trust Estate, insurance of such kinds and in such amounts as the Trustee shall deem advisable to protect the Trust Estate and the Trustee against any hazard.

G. Power to Commence or Defend Litigation. To commence or defend such litigation with respect to the Trust or any property of the Trust Estate as the Trustee may deem advisable, at the expense of the Trust Declaration.

H. Power to Compromise Claim. To compromise or otherwise adjust any claims or litigation against or in favor of the Trust Declaration.

I. Power to Employ Consultants. To employ any custodian, investment advisor, attorney, accountant or other agents to assist the Trustee in administration of this Trust Declaration and to rely upon the advice given by these agents. Reasonable compensation shall be paid to these agents for all services performed.

J. Power to Adjust for Tax Consequences. To take any action and to make any election the Trustee shall deem advisable to minimize the tax liabilities of this trust and its beneficiaries, to allocate the benefits among the various beneficiaries and to make adjustments in the rights of any beneficiaries or group of beneficiaries or between principal and income accounts, to compensate for the consequences of any tax election or any investment decision or administrative decision that has the effect of preferring one beneficiary or group of beneficiaries over others, provided such discretion shall not be exercised in any manner which will cause a loss of or a decrease in any marital or charitable deduction otherwise allowable in computing the Settlor's federal estate tax.

ARTICLE V
MISCELLANEOUS

Paragraph 5.01. No Assignment. Each beneficiary hereunder is hereby prohibited from anticipating, encumbering, assigning or in any other manner, alienating or her or his interest in either income or principal of any trust created under this Trust Declaration and is without power to do so nor shall such interest be subject to her or his liabilities or obligations nor to attachment, execution or other legal processes, bankruptcy proceedings or claims of creditors or others. The Trustee may require the personal receipt of a beneficiary as a condition precedent to payment, distribution or delivery of any amount, property or benefit hereunder. The Trustee may, however, deposit in any bank designated in writing, by a beneficiary, to her or his credit, income or principal payable to such beneficiary.

Paragraph 5.02. Principal and Income. Except as otherwise specifically provided in this Trust Declaration, the determination of all matters with respect to what shall constitute principal and income of each trust estate, gross income therefrom and net income distributable under the terms of the Trust Declaration, shall be governed by the provisions of the Revised Uniform Principal and Income Act as enacted in the State of (2a)____________________, from time to time existing. All taxes, assessments, fees, charges and other expenses incurred by the Trustee in the administration, protection and distribution of each trust, shall be a charge upon the trust estate and shall be paid out of the income and/or principal, in accordance with the aforesaid Act.

Paragraph 5.03. Savings Clause. Unless sooner terminated in accordance with other provisions of this Trust Declaration, any trust created hereunder shall terminate twenty-one (21) years after the death of the last surviving member of the group consisting of the Settlor and the issue of the Settlor who are living and in being at the date of death of the Settlor.

Paragraph 5.04. Payments to Minors and Incompetents. The Trustee, in the Trustee's discretion, may apply payments directly for the benefit of any beneficiary, rather than directly to such beneficiary and, in the case of a beneficiary who is a minor or who is under any other disability, make payment to the guardian, conservator of the person or estate of such beneficiary, custodian under the Uniform Transfers to Minors Act, parent or any other suitable adult with whom the beneficiary resides or by expending the same for the care, education, maintenance or other benefit of said beneficiary. In addition, the Trustee, in the Trustee's discretion, may make payments directly to a beneficiary who is a minor if, in the Trustee's judgment, the minor is of sufficient age and maturity to properly manage the money or property so paid. The Trustee shall not be required to see to the application of any such payment so made to any said persons, but his, her or their receipt therefor shall be a full discharge to the Trustee.

Paragraph 5.05. No Physical Segregation. There need be no physical segregation or division of the various trusts except as segregation or division may be required by the termination of any of the trusts or as specifically provided, but the Trustee shall keep separate accounts for the different undivided interests.

Paragraph 5.06. Distribution. In any case in which the Trustee is required, pursuant to the provisions of the Trust, to divide any parts or shares for the purposes of distribution or otherwise, except as the donee of any power of appointment affecting such property may have expressly provided otherwise in the instrument exercising such power, the Trustee is authorized, in the Trustee's absolute discretion, to make the division and distribution (pro rata or otherwise) in kind, including an undivided interest in any property or partly in kind and partly in money, and for this purpose, to make such sales of the trust property as the Trustee may deem necessary, on such terms and conditions as the Trustee shall see fit. Any asset which is encumbered shall be assigned subject thereto, and its value or amount shall be given effect less such indebtedness.

Paragraph 5.07. Non-Pro Rata Distributions. As to distribution or division of property in kind under and for the several trusts, excepting the initial establishment of any trust for a pecuniary amount, the Trustee shall be cognizant of the differences between the tax cost bases and current value and shall endeavor, insofar as is practicable to distribute or set aside to or for each beneficiary or distributee, assets or property carrying amount or portions of the total unrealized taxable gains or losses embodied in all the assets and properties involved commensurate with the share or portion of each beneficiary or distributee.

Paragraph 5.08. Distribution If All Beneficiaries Die Before Full Distribution. If at any time before full distribution of the Trust Estate, the Settlor is deceased and no disposition of the property is directed by this Trust Declaration, the Trust Estate or the portion of it not disposed of under the Trust Declaration, whichever the case may be, shall thereupon be distributed to the Settlor's heirs at law under the laws of intestate succession of the State of (2a)________________ then in effect for separate property not acquired from a predeceased spouse.

Paragraph 5.09. Additional Property. With consent of the Trustee, additional property may be added at any time from any source to any trust held under this Trust Declaration. No person dealing with the Trustee in any manner shall be under any obligation to see to the application of any money paid to the Trustee or to inquire into the validity, expediency or propriety of any act of the Trustee or into any of the provisions of any trust hereunder.

Paragraph 5.10. Fiduciary Capacity. All of the powers of the Trustee provided in this Trust Declaration shall be exercisable by the Trustee in the Trustee's fiduciary capacity and only in such capacity.

Paragraph 5.11. Corporate Office. No person shall, by reason of acting as Trustee, be in any way restricted or prohibited from holding office in any corporation in which any trust under this Trust Declaration holds securities or from receiving compensation from any such corporation for services performed as a director, officer or employee of such corporation or from purchasing, selling or otherwise dealing with the stock of any such corporation for the individual account of such Trustee or from voting the stock of any such corporation held by such trust, including voting those shares in favor of the Settlor or any other person.

Paragraph 5.12. Disclaimer of Powers. The Settlor may disclaim, release or restrict the scope of any power held in connection with any trust created under this Trust Declaration, including any administrative power, whether such power is expressly granted in this Trust Declaration or implied by law, by a written instrument specifying the power to be disclaimed, released or restricted and the nature of any such restriction. Any power disclaimed or released by the Settlor shall be extinguished except to the extent this Trust Declaration expressly provides that such power pass to another. This power shall be personal to the Settlor only and may not be exercised by any other person acting on behalf of the Settlor, including, but not limited to, any Trustee (other than the Settlor), Conservator, agent or guardian.

Paragraph 5.13. Notice. Unless the Trustee has received written notice of the occurrence of an event affecting the beneficial interest in any trust held under this Trust Declaration, the Trustee shall not be liable to any beneficiary of such trust for any distributions made or other actions taken by the Trustee in good faith as though such event had not occurred.

Paragraph 5.14. Invalidity of Any Provision. Should any provision of this Trust Declaration be or become invalid or unenforceable, the remaining provisions of this Trust Declaration shall be and continue to be fully effective.

Paragraph 5.15. Gender and Number. Except as provided otherwise herein, the masculine, feminine and neuter gender, and the singular or plural number, shall each be deemed to include the others whenever the context so indicates.

Paragraph 5.16. Law of Construction of Trust. This Trust Declaration, its validity, the construction of and all rights under the Trusts provided for in this Trust Declaration shall be governed by the laws of the State of (2a)___________________.

Paragraph 5.17. No Contest. The Settlor has intentionally and with full knowledge omitted to provide for his/her issue, ancestors, relatives and heirs living at the time of his/her demise, except for such provisions as are made specifically herein.

If any person who is or claims under or through a beneficiary of this Trust, or if any person who would be entitled to share in the Settlor's estate if the Settlor died intestate, should in any manner whatsoever, directly or indirectly, attack, contest or seek to impair or invalidate in court any provision of the following:

A. This Trust or any Amendment to this Trust;

B. Any Will or Codicil to any Will executed by the Settlor;

C. Any beneficiary designation executed by the Settlor with respect to any insurance policy, any "Totten trust" account, any joint tenancy or tenancy by the entirety, any "transfer on death" account or any pension plan or conspire or cooperate with anyone attempting to do any of the actions or things aforesaid, then each such person and any devise, share or interest in the Trust or the Settlor's Estate otherwise given to each such person under this Trust or the Settlor's Estate to which each such person might be entitled by law, is hereby revoked and shall pass and be distributed as though each such person had predeceased the Settlor leaving no issue or heirs whatsoever.

Any and every individual who asserts, or conspires or cooperates with any person who asserts, any claim against this Trust or the Estate of the Settlor of this Trust based on:

D. "Quantum meruit" theory;

E. Common law marriage, Marvin v. Marvin, 18 Cal. 3d 660 (1976) type of agreement or similar theory;

F. Constructive trust theory; or,

G. Oral agreement or written agreement which is to be proved by parole evidence, claiming that Settlor agreed to gift or devise anything to such person or to pay such person or another for services rendered, regardless of whether a court may find that such agreement existed, then each such person is disinherited and any devise, share or interest in this Trust or the Settlor's Estate otherwise given to each such person under this

Trust or the Settlor's Estate or to which each such person might be entitled by law, is hereby revoked and shall pass and be distributed as though each such person had predeceased the Settlor leaving no issue or heirs whatsoever.

The Trustee is specifically authorized to defend any such attack, contest, claim or other proceeding of any nature concerning this Trust or of any provision hereof, and to employ legal counsel therefor, all at the expense of the Trust.

Paragraph 5.18. Survival. If any person fails to survive the Settlor by thirty (30) days, for all purposes of this Trust Declaration the person shall be considered to have predeceased the Settlor.

Paragraph 5.19. All typed and handwritten "fill-ins" where directed above were made before the execution of this Declaration of Trust and are not initialed by the Settlor. All crossed through words and inter-lineations were made before the execution of this Trust and are initialed by the Settlor.

CERTIFICATION OF SETTLOR

I certify that:

A. I have read the foregoing Trust Declaration;

B. The foregoing Trust Declaration correctly states the terms and conditions under which the Trust Estate is to be held, managed, administered and disposed of by the Trustee;

C. As the Settlor named in such Trust Declaration, I approve such Trust Declaration in all particulars; and,

D. As the Trustee named in such Trust Declaration, I approve and accept the Trust provided for in such Declaration.

Dated: (40)________________________

(1)____________________, Settlor

(54)________________________

(49)____________________, Trustee

STATE OF (2a)____________________)
) ss.
COUNTY OF (2)____________________)

On ______________, 200__ before me, the undersigned, a Notary Public in and for said county and state, personally appeared (1)____________________, personally known to me (or proved to me on the basis of satisfactory evidence) to be the person(s) whose name(s) is/are subscribed to the within instrument and acknowledged that he/she/they executed the same in his/her/their authorized capacity(ies), and that by his/her/their signature(s) on the instrument the person(s), or the entity upon behalf of which the person(s) acted, executed the instrument.

WITNESS my hand and official seal.

____

Notary Public in and for said County and State

EXHIBIT A

Property Declared to be assets of the (1a)________________________________ TRUST dated (48)______________:

(55)
1.

INTER-VIVOS TRUST

THE (1a)____________________ TRUST

The Settlor named below hereby declares as follows:

ARTICLE I
ESTABLISHMENT OF TRUST

Paragraph 1.01. Creation of Trust. This Trust Declaration has been entered into between (1)____________________________________ as Settlor and himself/herself as the Trustee. The Settlor, of (2)___________________ County, (2a)_____________________, has transferred, or will transfer, to the Trustee of this Trust Declaration the property described in the attached Exhibit "A" which will constitute, together with any other property that may be added to this Trust Declaration, the Trust Estate of an express trust which shall be held, administered and distributed by the Trustee as provided in this Trust Declaration.

Paragraph 1.02. Trust Name. This Trust Declaration shall be known as the (1a)"_________________________ TRUST" dated (48)____________________________.

Paragraph 1.03. Definitions. As used in this Trust Declaration:

A. Settlor: The term "Settlor" shall refer to (1)____.

B. Trustee: The term "Trustee" or "Trustees" shall refer to whoever is serving as Trustee or Trustees under this Trust Declaration.

C. Trust Estate: The term "Trust Estate" shall refer to the property subject to this Trust Declaration.

ARTICLE II
OPERATION OF TRUST DURING THE LIFE OF SETTLOR

Paragraph 2.01. Net Income. During the life of Settlor the Trustee shall pay to or apply for the benefit of Settlor, in monthly or more frequent intervals, all of the net income of the Trust Estate.

Paragraph 2.02. Withdrawal of Principal. During the life of Settlor the Trustee shall also pay to or apply for the benefit of Settlor so much of the principal of the Trust Estate, up to the whole thereof, as Settlor shall direct.

Paragraph 2.03. Incapacity of Settlor. If, at any time during the life of the Settlor he/she shall become physically or mentally incapacitated so as to be unable to manage his or her affairs, whether or not a court of competent jurisdiction has declared him or her incompetent, mentally ill, or in need of a conservator, the Trustee shall pay to the Settlor or apply for the benefit of the Settlor such amounts of income or principal so that the Settlor enjoys a high standard of living commensurate with his/her estate and life expecancy. The interests of any other beneficiaries of this Trust are to be subordinated to the generous support of the Settlor. In this context "incapacitated" shall be determined by two physicians, at least one of whom is a geriatric specialists.

In regards to the amount of principal invasion by the Trustee for the Settlor, the Settlor is the primary beneficiary of this Trust Estate. The Settlor does not care if at his or her death the entire Trust Estate has been consumed by his or her needs. It is also the intent and desire of the Settlor that he/she live in his/her own home at all times, even if that requires the purchase of a new home to accommodate the in-home placement of twenty-four (24) hour nursing care.

The payments specified in this Section shall be made until the Settlor is again able to manage his or her own affairs, or until the death of the Settlor, whichever event may occur earlier.

Paragraph 2.04. Revocation of Trust. At any time during the life of the Settlor he/she may, by serving written notice on the Trustee, revoke the Trust created by this Trust Declaration, in whole or in part.

Paragraph 2.05. Amendment of Trust. At any time during the life of the Settlor, he/she may, by serving written notice on the Trustee, alter, modify or amend the Trust created by this Trust Declaration in any respect.

ARTICLE III

OPERATION OF TRUST AFTER DEATH OF SETTLOR

Paragraph 3.01. Collection of Assets and Payment of Debts: On the death of the Settlor the Trustee shall collect all assets belonging to the Trust Estate. As soon as practicable after the death of the Trustee, except as otherwise provided herein, shall pay from the Trust Estate the just debts of the Settlor (excluding any debts barred by provisions of law or not yet due), funeral expenses of the Settlor, and any inheritance, estate, or other death taxes that shall, by reason of the death of the Settlor, be attributable to the Trust Estate. This is not and shall not constitute a direction to pay all inheritance, estate or other death taxes from or charge the same to, the Trust Estate without apportionment.

Paragraph 3.02. Distribution of Trust Estate. Upon the death of the Settlor, and after payment of expenses as set forth in Paragraph 3.01, the Trustee shall hold, administer and distribute the Trust Estate as follows:

A. The Trustee shall distribute to the following persons the cash amount listed after their respective names:

(10)

B. The Trustee shall distribute to the following persons the real property described after their respective names. (12) Said real property is given free of all encumbrances or liens thereon.

(11)

C. The Trustee shall distribute to (13)__________________ a life estate in the following property located at: (14)__________________________. After the death of (13)__________________ said property shall go, outright, to (15)______________________________ as the remainder person(s).

D. The Trustee shall distribute all of the rest, residue and remainder of the Trust Estate, real, personal and mixed, of whatsoever kind or character and wheresoever situated, to the following persons or entities (16) in the proportions listed after their names (17) in equal shares.

(18)

and (19)______ shares to the Trustee hereinafter named, to have and to hold for the benefit of (20)______________ upon the uses, trusts, purposes and conditions hereinafter provided.

1. If (20)_______________ should at any time or from time to time be in need, in the discretion of the Trustee, of funds due to illness, infirmity or other physical or mental disability or any emergency, the Trustee may relieve or contribute toward the relief of any such need or needs of (20)__________________by paying to him or her or using and applying for his or her benefit, such sum or sums out of the income and/or principal of his or her trust as the Trustee, in the Trustee's discretion, may deem necessary or advisable.

2. The Trustee shall pay (20)____________________ all of the net income, in monthly or other convenient installments, from the trust.

3. (20)______________________shall have the right to require the Trustee to convert any non-income producing asset into an income producing asset.

4. Upon the death of (20)____________________ the Trustee shall distribute, free of trust, the remaining trust properties to: (23)______________________________.

E. Distribution of Trust Assets. With respect to the distribution of any trust estate upon termination of any trust, and partial distribution of any trust, the liquidation and distribution by the Trustee of the Trust Estate involved or the distributable portion shall commence immediately and be accomplished as rapidly as possible, and deliveries of the trust properties to the beneficiary or beneficiaries may be made in installments or series, retaining only reasonable reserves for final charges and expenses. In no event shall it be necessary for the Trustee to await an accounting to the Court, or any Court order, before releasing and distributing the majority of the Trust Estate to be distributed.

F. Undistributed Income. All the net income of the respective trusts or trust estates, not distributed, used or applied as otherwise provided herein, shall be accumulated and added to the principals of the respective trusts.

Upon the change or succession of any beneficiary, distribution of trust properties or any trust estate or any portion thereof, or upon setting aside, apportionment or division of any trust estate or upon the termination of a trust or any interest therein, the beneficial interest, properties or balance of trust estate at the applicable time and to be dealt with shall include any and all income accumulated, accrued, uncollected or held undistributed and all of such income shall likewise be distributed, set aside or apportioned to the next or succeeding beneficiaries, distributees, shares or trusts, retaining its character as income.

ARTICLE IV
TRUSTEES

Paragraph 4.01. Appointment of Trustees. (49)___________________________________ is appointed and confirmed as the Trustee(s). In the event (49)____________________________ should die, refuse to act, or for any other reason be unable to act as Trustee then (25)____________________ shall act as (26)____Trustee_ hereunder (27) without bond. In the event he/she/they should die, decline to act, or for any other reason, be unable to act as Trustee then (28)___________________________ shall act as Trustee hereunder (27) without bond.

Paragraph 4.02. Substitute Trustee. The Settlor may appoint a substitute or successor Trustee to act as Trustee of any trust or trusts created hereunder in the place and stead of, or as successor to, any Trustee named in Section 4.01 above. Such substitution shall be in writing.

Paragraph 4.03. Trustee Liability. No person named as Trustee in this instrument or appointed as Trustee in the manner specified herein shall be liable to any beneficiary or to any heir of Settlor for the Trustee's acts or failure to act, except for willful misconduct or gross negligence. No such Trustee shall be liable or responsible for any act, omission or default of any other Trustee provided that they shall have had no knowledge of facts that might reasonably be expected to put the Trustee on notice of it.

Paragraph 4.04. Trustee Compensation. The Trustee shall be entitled to reasonable compensation for services rendered to the Trust or Trusts created hereunder.

Paragraph 4.05. Title to Trust Estate. The legal title to all property held in trust hereunder shall be, remain and become vested in the Trustee or successor Trustee from time to time acting hereunder, without any act of conveyance or transfer to or by or acceptance from, any succeeding, retiring or predecessor Trustee; however, any removed or resigning Trustee shall execute and deliver any and all conveyances and documents requested and reasonably necessary to transfer the trust estate and its assets to a successor Trustee. Each successor Trustee from time to time acting hereunder shall have all the rights, powers immunities and authorities, discretionary or otherwise and the duties and obligations herein granted to the original Trustee. No successor Trustee shall be obligated to inquire into or be in any way responsible for the previous administration of any trust created herein or of the trust estate or for any act or default of any predecessor Trustee.

Paragraph 4.06. Powers of Trustee. To carry out the purposes of any trust created under this Trust Declaration, and subject to any limitations stated elsewhere in this Trust Declaration, the Trustee is vested with the following powers with respect to the Trust Estate, and any part of it, in addition to those powers now or hereafter conferred by law.

A. Power to Invest. To invest and reinvest the Trust Estate in every kind of property, real, personal or mixed, and every kind of investment, specifically including but not by way of limitation, corporate obligations of every kind, stocks, preferred or common, shares of investment trusts, investment companies, mutual funds, market index funds and mortgage participations which individuals of prudence, discretion and intelligence acquire for their own account, and any common trust fund administered by any Trustee under this Trust Declaration.

B. Power to Retain Property. To retain any property which was an asset of the Trust Estate during the Settlor's lifetime or received without consideration by the Trustee as long as the Trustee deems advisable whether or not of the character permitted by law for the investment of trust funds. The trust properties and investment need not be diversified and the Trustee shall have no duty to dispose or convert any trust assets to effect diversification.

C. Power to Manage Securities. With respect to securities held in this Trust Declaration, to have all the rights, powers and privileges of an owner, including but not by way of limitation, the power to vote, give proxies and pay assessments, to participate in voting trusts, pooling agreements, foreclosures, reorganizations, consolidations, mergers, liquidations, sales and leases and, incident to such participation, to deposit securities with and transfer title to any protective or other committee on such terms as the Trustee may deem advisable, to exercise and sell stock subscription or conversion rights and to hold securities in "street name".

D. Power of Sale, Exchange, Repair. To manage, control, foreclose, repossess, grant options on, grant easements on, sell (for cash), convey, exchange, partition, divide, improve and repair trust property.

The power to sell, at the termination of the trust, any trust property if the Trustee feels said disposition would assist in the distribution of the trust property at termination.

E. Power to Lease. To lease trust property for terms within or beyond the term of the trust and for any purpose, including exploration for and removal of gas, oil and other minerals; and to enter into community oil leases, pooling and unitization agreements, operating agreements or otherwise, and to create restrictions, easements or other servitudes thereon, to assign, partition, divide, subdivide, transfer to a corporation in exchange for stock, improve, repair, loan, reloan, invest and reinvest the trust estate or any part thereof.

F. Power to Insure. To carry, at the expense of the Trust Estate, insurance of such kinds and in such amounts as the Trustee shall deem advisable to protect the Trust Estate and the Trustee against any hazard.

G. Power to Commence or Defend Litigation. To commence or defend such litigation with respect to the Trust or any property of the Trust Estate as the Trustee may deem advisable, at the expense of the Trust Declaration.

H. Power to Compromise Claim. To compromise or otherwise adjust any claims or litigation against or in favor of the Trust Declaration.

I. Power to Employ Consultants. To employ any custodian, investment advisor, attorney, accountant or other agents to assist the Trustee in administration of this Trust Declaration and to rely upon the advice given by these agents. Reasonable compensation shall be paid to these agents for all services performed.

J. Power to Adjust for Tax Consequences. To take any action and to make any election the Trustee shall deem advisable to minimize the tax liabilities of this trust and its beneficiaries, to allocate the benefits among the various beneficiaries and to make adjustments in the rights of any beneficiaries or group of beneficiaries or between principal and income accounts, to compensate for the consequences of any tax election or any investment decision or administrative decision that has the effect of preferring one beneficiary or group of beneficiaries over others, provided such discretion shall not be exercised in any manner which will cause a loss of or a decrease in any marital or charitable deduction otherwise allowable in computing the Settlor's federal estate tax.

ARTICLE V
MISCELLANEOUS

Paragraph 5.01. No Assignment. Each beneficiary hereunder is hereby prohibited from anticipating, encumbering, assigning or in any other manner, alienating her or his interest in either income or principal of any trust created under this Trust Declaration and is without power to do so nor shall such interest be subject to her or his liabilities or obligations nor to attachment, execution or other legal processes, bankruptcy proceedings or claims of creditors or others. The Trustee may require the personal receipt of a beneficiary as a condition precedent to payment, distribution or delivery of any amount, property or benefit hereunder. The Trustee may, however, deposit in any bank designated in writing, by a beneficiary, to her or his credit, income or principal payable to such beneficiary.

Paragraph 5.02. Principal and Income. Except as otherwise specifically provided in this Trust Declaration, the determination of all matters with respect to what shall constitute principal and income of each trust estate, gross income therefrom and net income distributable under the terms of the Trust Declaration, shall be governed by the provisions of the Revised Uniform Principal and Income Act as enacted in the State of (2a)________________, from time to time existing. All taxes, assessments, fees, charges and other expenses incurred by the Trustee in the administration, protection and distribution of each trust, shall be a charge upon the trust estate and shall be paid out of the income and/or principal, in accordance with the aforesaid Act.

Paragraph 5.03. Savings Clause. Unless sooner terminated in accordance with other provisions of this Trust Declaration, any trust created hereunder shall terminate twenty-one (21) years after the death of the last surviving member of the group consisting of the Settlor and the issue of the Settlor who are living and in being at the date of death of the Settlor.

Paragraph 5.04. Payments to Minors and Incompetents. The Trustee, in the Trustee's discretion, may apply payments directly for the benefit of any beneficiary, rather than directly to such beneficiary and, in the case of a beneficiary who is a minor or who is under any other disability, make payment to the guardian, conservator of the person or estate of such beneficiary, custodian under the Uniform Transfers to Minors Act, parent or any other suitable adult with whom the beneficiary resides or by expending the same for the care, education, maintenance or other benefit of said beneficiary. In addition, the Trustee, in the Trustee's discretion, may make payments directly to a beneficiary who is a minor if, in the Trustee's judgment, the minor is of sufficient age and maturity to properly manage the money or property so paid. The Trustee shall not be required to see to the application of any such payment so made to any said persons, but his, her or their receipt therefor shall be a full discharge to the Trustee.

Paragraph 5.05. No Physical Segregation. There need be no physical segregation or division of the various trusts except as segregation or division may be required by the termination of any of the trusts or as specifically provided, but the Trustee shall keep separate accounts for the different undivided interests.

Paragraph 5.06. Distribution. In any case in which the Trustee is required, pursuant to the provisions of the Trust, to divide any parts or shares for the purposes of distribution or otherwise, except as the donee of any power of appointment affecting such property may have expressly provided otherwise in the instrument exercising such power, the Trustee is authorized, in the Trustee's absolute discretion, to make the division and distribution (pro rata or otherwise) in kind, including an undivided interest in any property or partly in kind and partly in money, and for this purpose, to make such sales of the trust property as the Trustee may deem necessary, on such terms and conditions as the Trustee shall see fit. Any asset which is encumbered shall be assigned subject thereto, and its value or amount shall be given effect less such indebtedness.

Paragraph 5.07. Non-Pro Rata Distributions. As to distribution or division of property in kind under and for the several trusts, excepting the initial establishment of any trust for a pecuniary amount, the Trustee shall be cognizant of the differences between the tax cost bases and current value and shall endeavor, insofar as is practicable to distribute or set aside to or for each beneficiary or distributee, assets or property carrying amount or portions of the total unrealized taxable gains or losses embodied in all the assets and properties involved commensurate with the share or portion of each beneficiary or distributee.

Paragraph 5.08. Distribution If All Beneficiaries Die Before Full Distribution. If at any time before full distribution of the Trust Estate, the Settlor is deceased and no disposition of the property is directed by this Trust Declaration, the Trust Estate or the portion of it not disposed of under the Trust Declaration, whichever the case may be, shall thereupon be distributed to the Settlor's heirs at law under the laws of intestate succession of the State of (2a)________________ then in effect for separate property not acquired from a predeceased spouse.

Paragraph 5.09. Additional Property. With consent of the Trustee, additional property may be added at any time from any source to any trust held under this Trust Declaration. No person dealing with the Trustee in any manner shall be under any obligation to see to the application of any money paid to the Trustee or to inquire into the validity, expediency or propriety of any act of the Trustee or into any of the provisions of any trust hereunder.

Paragraph 5.10. Fiduciary Capacity. All of the powers of the Trustee provided in this Trust Declaration shall be exercisable by the Trustee in the Trustee's fiduciary capacity and only in such capacity.

Paragraph 5.11. Corporate Office. No person shall, by reason of acting as Trustee, be in any way restricted or prohibited from holding office in any corporation in which any trust under this Trust Declaration holds securities or from receiving compensation from any such corporation for services performed as a director, officer or employee of such corporation or from purchasing, selling or otherwise dealing with the stock of any such corporation for the individual account of such Trustee or from voting the stock of any such corporation held by such trust, including voting those shares in favor of the Settlor or any other person.

Paragraph 5.12. Disclaimer of Powers. The Settlor may disclaim, release or restrict the scope of any power held in connection with any trust created under this Trust Declaration, including any administrative power, whether such power is expressly granted in this Trust Declaration or implied by law, by a written instrument specifying the power to be disclaimed, released or restricted and the nature of any such restriction. Any power disclaimed or released by the Settlor shall be extinguished except to the extent this Trust Declaration expressly provides that such power pass to another. This power shall be personal to the Settlor only and may not be exercised by any other person acting on behalf of the Settlor, including, but not limited to, any Trustee (other than the Settlor), Conservator, agent or guardian.

Paragraph 5.13. Notice. Unless the Trustee has received written notice of the occurrence of an event affecting the beneficial interest in any trust held under this Trust Declaration, the Trustee shall not be liable to any beneficiary of such trust for any distributions made or other actions taken by the Trustee in good faith as though such event had not occurred.

Paragraph 5.14. Invalidity of Any Provision. Should any provision of this Trust Declaration be or become invalid or unenforceable, the remaining provisions of this Trust Declaration shall be and continue to be fully effective.

Paragraph 5.15. Gender and Number. Except as provided otherwise herein, the masculine, feminine and neuter gender, and the singular or plural number, shall each be deemed to include the others whenever the context so indicates.

Paragraph 5.16. Law of Construction of Trust. This Trust Declaration, its validity, the construction of and all rights under the Trusts provided for in this Trust Declaration shall be governed by the laws of the State of (2a)____________________.

Paragraph 5.17. No Contest. The Settlor has intentionally and with full knowledge omitted to provide for his/her issue, ancestors, relatives and heirs living at the time of his/her demise, except for such provisions as are made specifically herein.

If any person who is or claims under or through a beneficiary of this Trust, or if any person who would be entitled to share in the Settlor's estate if the Settlor died intestate, should in any manner whatsoever, directly or indirectly, attack, contest or seek to impair or invalidate in court any provision of the following:

A. This Trust or any Amendment to this Trust;

B. Any Will or Codicil to any Will executed by the Settlor;

C. Any beneficiary designation executed by the Settlor with respect to any insurance policy, any "Totten trust" account, any joint tenancy or tenancy by the entirety, any "transfer on death" account or any pension plan, or conspire or cooperate with anyone attempting to do any of the actions or things aforesaid, then each such person and any devise, share or interest in the Trust or the Settlor's Estate otherwise given to each such person under this Trust or the Settlor's Estate to which each such person might be entitled by law, is hereby revoked and shall pass and be distributed as though each such person had predeceased the Settlor leaving no issue or heirs whatsoever.

Any and every individual who asserts, or conspires or cooperates with any person who asserts, any claim against this Trust or the Estate of the Settlor of this Trust based on:

D. "Quantum meruit" theory;

E. Common law marriage, Marvin v. Marvin, 18 Cal. 3d 660 (1976) type of agreement or similar theory;

F. Constructive trust theory; or,

G. Oral agreement or written agreement which is to be proved by parole evidence, claiming that Settlor agreed to gift or devise anything to such person or to pay such person or another for services rendered, regardless of whether a court may find that such agreement existed, then each such person is disinherited and any devise, share or interest in this Trust or the Settlor's Estate otherwise given to each such person under this Trust or the Settlor's Estate or to which each such person might be entitled by law, is hereby revoked and shall pass and be distributed as though each such person had predeceased the Settlor leaving no issue or heirs whatsoever.

The Trustee is specifically authorized to defend any such attack, contest, claim or other proceeding of any nature concerning this Trust or of any provision hereof, and to employ legal counsel therefor, all at the expense of the Trust.

Paragraph 5.18. Survival. If any person fails to survive the Settlor by thirty (30) days, for all purposes of this Trust Declaration the person shall be considered to have predeceased the Settlor.

Paragraph 5.19. All typed and handwritten "fill-ins" where directed above were made before the execution of this Declaration of Trust and are not initialed by the Settlors. All crossed through words and inter-lineations were made before the execution of this Trust and are initialed by the Settlors.

CERTIFICATION OF SETTLOR

I certify that:

A. I have read the foregoing Trust Declaration;

B. The foregoing Trust Declaration correctly states the terms and conditions under which the Trust Estate is to be held, managed, administered and disposed of by the Trustee;

C. As the Settlor named in such Trust Declaration, I approve such Trust Declaration in all particulars; and,

D. As the Trustee named in such Trust Declaration, I approve and accept the Trust provided for in such Declaration.

Dated: (40)______________________________

(1)________________________,Settlor

(54)______________________________

(49)________________________, Trustee

STATE OF (2a)__________________________)
) ss.
COUNTY OF (2)__________________________)

On ________________, 200__ before me, the undersigned, a Notary Public in and for said county and state, personally appeared (1)______________________, personally known to me (or proved to me on the basis of satisfactory evidence) to be the person(s) whose name(s) is/are subscribed to the within instrument and acknowledged that he/she/they executed the same in his/her/their authorized capacity(ies), and that by his/her/their signature(s) on the instrument the person(s), or the entity upon behalf of which the person(s) acted, executed the instrument.

WITNESS my hand and official seal.

____
Notary Public in and for said County and State

EXHIBIT A

Property Declared to be assets of the (1a)________________________ TRUST dated (48)____________:

(55)
1.

INTER-VIVOS TRUST

THE (1a)____________________ TRUST

The Settlor named below hereby declares as follows:

ARTICLE I
ESTABLISHMENT OF TRUST

Paragraph 1.01. Creation of Trust. This Trust Declaration has been entered into between (1)______________________________ as Settlor and himself/herself as the Trustee. The Settlor, of (2)________ County, (2a)____________________, has transferred, or will transfer, to the Trustee of this Trust Declaration the property described in the attached Exhibit "A" which will constitute, together with any other property that may be added to this Trust Declaration, the Trust Estate of an express trust which shall be held, administered and distributed by the Trustee as provided in this Trust Declaration.

Paragraph 1.02. Trust Name. This Trust Declaration shall be known as the (1a)"____________________ TRUST" dated (48)________________________.

Paragraph 1.03. Definitions. As used in this Trust Declaration:

A. Settlor: The term "Settlor" shall refer to (1)________________________________.

B. Trustee: The term "Trustee" or "Trustees" shall refer to whoever is serving as Trustee or Trustees under this Trust Declaration.

C. Trust Estate: The term "Trust Estate" shall refer to the property subject to this Trust Declaration.

D. Issue: The term "issue" shall refer only to a person who is a lineal descendant of any degree of the Settlor and shall (59) not include adopted persons.

ARTICLE II
OPERATION OF TRUST DURING THE LIFE OF SETTLOR

Paragraph 2.01. Net Income. During the life of Settlor the Trustee shall pay to or apply for the benefit of Settlor, in monthly or more frequent intervals, all of the net income of the Trust Estate.

Paragraph 2.02. Withdrawal of Principal. During the life of Settlor the Trustee shall also pay to or apply for the benefit of Settlor so much of the principal of the Trust Estate, up to the whole thereof, as Settlor shall direct.

Paragraph 2.03. Incapacity of Settlor. If, at any time during the life of the Settlor he/she shall become physically or mentally incapacitated so as to be unable to manage his or her affairs, whether or not a court of competent jurisdiction has declared him or her incompetent, mentally ill, or in need of a conservator, the Trustee shall pay to the Settlor or apply for the benefit of the Settlor such amounts of income or principal so that the Settlor enjoys a high standard of living commensurate with his/her estate or life expectancy. The interests of any other beneficiaries of this Trust are to be subordinated to the generous support of the Settlor. In this context "incapacitated" shall be determined by two physicians, at least one of whom is a geriatric specialists.

In regards to the amount of principal invasion by the Trustee for the Settlor, the Settlor is the primary beneficiary of this Trust Estate. The Settlor does not care if at his or her death the entire Trust Estate has been consumed by his or her needs. It is also the intent and desire of the Settlor that he/she live in his/her own home at all times, even if that requires the purchase of a new home to accommodate the in-home placement of twenty-four (24) hour nursing care.

The payments specified in this Section shall be made until the Settlor is again able to manage his or her own affairs, or until the death of the Settlor, whichever event may occur earlier.

Paragraph 2.04. Revocation of Trust. At any time during the life of the Settlor he/she may, by serving written notice on the Trustee, revoke the Trust created by this Trust Declaration, in whole or in part.

Paragraph 2.05. Amendment of Trust. At any time during the life of the Settlor, he/she may, by serving written notice on the Trustee, alter, modify or amend the Trust created by this Trust Declaration in any respect.

ARTICLE III
OPERATION OF TRUST AFTER DEATH OF SETTLOR

Paragraph 3.01. Collection of Assets and Payment of Debts: On the death of the Settlor the Trustee shall collect all assets belonging to the Trust Estate. As soon as practicable after the death of the Trustee, except as otherwise provided herein, shall pay from the Trust Estate the just debts of the Settlor (excluding any debts barred by provisions of law or not yet due), funeral expenses of the Settlor, and any inheritance, estate, or other death taxes that shall, by reason of the death of the Settlor, be attributable to the Trust Estate. This is not and shall not constitute a direction to pay all inheritance, estate or other death taxes from or charge the same to, the Trust Estate without apportionment.

Paragraph 3.02. Distribution of Trust Estate. Upon the death of the Settlor, and after payment of expenses as set forth in Paragraph 3.01, the Trustee shall hold, administer and distribute the Trust Estate as follows:

A. The Trustee shall distribute to the following persons the cash amount listed after their respective names:

(10)

B. The Trustee shall distribute to the following persons the real property described after their respective names. (12) Said real property is given free of all encumbrances or liens thereon.

(11)

C. The Trustee shall distribute to (13)___________________ a life estate in the following property located at: (14)_________________________. After the death of (13)___________________ said property shall go, outright, to (15)_____________________________ as the remainder person(s).

D. The Trustee shall distribute all of the rest, residue and remainder of the Trust Estate, real, personal and mixed, of whatsoever kind or character and wheresoever situated, to the following persons or entities (16) in the proportions listed after their names (17) in equal shares.

(18)

and (19)______ shares to the Trustee hereinafter named, to have and to hold for the benefit of (20)_____________ upon the uses, trusts, purposes and conditions hereinafter provided.

The Trustee, shall allocate the trust properties into as many shares as there are children of the Settlor then living and children of the Settlor then deceased who left issue then living. One such equal share shall be set aside for each of the Settlor's children then living and one such equal share shall be set aside for the issue then living, by right of representation, of each of the Settlor's children who are then deceased but left issue then living. Said shares shall be held, administered, and distributed as provided in the following sections:

Each share set aside for a child of the Settlor shall be held, administered and delivered for and to such beneficiary as follows:

1. The net income from the trust while said beneficiary is under 19 years of age and not a high school graduate shall be added to principal, from which the Trustee shall pay to or for the benefit of such beneficiary such sums as in the Trustee's discretion the Trustee shall deem necessary for such beneficiary's proper care, comfort, maintenance, support or education.

In making payments for the benefit of any beneficiary pursuant to this section 1, the Trustee shall construe his or her authority liberally to permit payments reasonably necessary to ease the financial burden on the guardian of the person of such beneficiary or other suitable individual with whom they reside, and on his or her family, resulting from such beneficiary's presence in his or her household.

2. Upon the beneficiary reaching 19 years of age or finishing high school(whichever occurs first), the Trustee shall pay to or apply for his or her benefit, from his or her trust, as much of the trust principal as the Trustee, in the Trustee's discretion, considers appropriate pursuant to sections 3 and 4 following.

3. After the beneficiary attains 19 years of age or finishes high school (whichever occurs first), the Trustee may, in the Trustee's discretion, pay to or apply from his or her trust, such amounts necessary for his or her education. For purposes hereof, education shall mean enrollment, attendance, and satisfactory progression towards a degree as a student at a recognized and accredited college, university, or similar institution of higher learning, including any graduate, professional school or college or trade school. Such educational payments and benefits shall include tuition, books, all direct educational costs and fees, and all reasonable living and transportation expenses. Payments hereunder shall be made during vacation periods within the regular school term under which the beneficiary is attending school and during "summer vacation" or similar vacation period between the regular school terms.

The Trustee may invest any portion of a beneficiary's trust share in an IRC 529 college savings plan for the benefit of said beneficiary.

4. If the beneficiary, his or her spouse, or any of his or her children should at any time or from time to time be in need, in the discretion of the Trustee, of funds due to illness, infirmity or other physical or mental disability or any emergency, the Trustee may relieve or contribute toward the relief of any such need or needs of the beneficiary by paying to him or her or using and applying for his or her benefit, such sum or sums out of the income and/or principal of his or her trust as the Trustee, in the Trustee's discretion, may deem necessary or advisable.

5. Upon the beneficiary attaining the age of 21 years, the Trustee shall begin to pay the beneficiary all of the net income, in monthly or other convenient installments, from the trust.

6. Upon the beneficiary attaining the age of (21)________ years, the Trustee shall distribute and deliver to such beneficiary one-half of his or her trust estate. Upon each beneficiary attaining the age of (22)________ years, the Trustee shall distribute and deliver to such beneficiary all of the remainder of his or her trust estate.

7. If, upon the attaining of the above ages, the Trustee suspects that said beneficiary may be abusing drugs, the Trustee may require the beneficiary to take a reasonable drug test. If the beneficiary fails said drug test, the Trustee shall defer said principal payment to the beneficiary until the beneficiary passes said drug test. After a failed drug test, subsequent drug tests shall be administered at six month intervals. In the event a beneficiary fails a drug test, the Trustee may use said beneficiary's trust estate to pay for a drug abuse rehabilitation pro-

gram and may require the beneficiary to enroll and to complete said program as a condition precedent to the taking of a subsequent drug test.

8. In the event the beneficiary should die before complete distribution to him or her of his or her trust estate, his or her entire trust estate on hand at the time of his or her death shall thereupon be apportioned and distributed to his or her surviving issue, by right of representation. If such beneficiary should die before complete distribution to him or her of his or her trust estate and leave no surviving issue, then the balance of the trust estate then on hand shall go and be distributed to the Settlor's heirs to be determined according to the laws of the State of (2a)________________ then in effect relating to the intestate succession of separate property not acquired from a predeceased spouse.

9. If, at any time, a trust created hereunder shall, in the sole judgment of the Trustee, be of the aggregate principal value of Fifty Thousand Dollars ($50,000.00) or less, the Trustee may, but need not, terminate such trust and distribute the assets thereof in the Trustee's possession to the beneficiary or beneficiaries, at the time of the current income thereof, and if there is more than one beneficiary, in the proportion in which they are beneficiaries.

E. Distribution of Trust Assets. With respect to the distribution of any trust estate upon termination of any trust, and partial distribution of any trust, the liquidation and distribution by the Trustee of the Trust Estate involved or the distributable portion shall commence immediately and be accomplished as rapidly as possible, and deliveries of the trust properties to the beneficiary or beneficiaries may be made in installments or series, retaining only reasonable reserves for final charges and expenses. In no event shall it be necessary for the Trustee to await an accounting to the Court, or any Court order, before releasing and distributing the majority of the Trust Estate to be distributed.

F. Undistributed Income. All the net income of the respective trusts or trust estates, not distributed, used or applied as otherwise provided herein, shall be accumulated and added to the principals of the respective trusts.

Upon the change or succession of any beneficiary, distribution of trust properties or any trust estate or any portion thereof, or upon setting aside, apportionment or division of any trust estate or upon the termination of a trust or any interest therein, the beneficial interest, properties or balance of trust estate at the applicable time and to be dealt with shall include any and all income accumulated, accrued, uncollected or held undistributed and all of such income shall likewise be distributed, set aside or apportioned to the next or succeeding beneficiaries, distributees, shares or trusts, retaining its character as income.

ARTICLE IV
TRUSTEES

Paragraph 4.01. Appointment of Trustees. (49)________________________________ is appointed and confirmed as the Trustee(s). In the event (49)____________________________ should die, refuse to act, or for any other reason be unable to act as Trustee then (25)____________________ shall act as (26)____Trustee_ hereunder (27) without bond. In the event he/she/they should die, decline to act, or for any other reason, be unable to act as Trustee then (28)__________________________ shall act as Trustee hereunder (27) without bond.

Paragraph 4.02. Substitute Trustee. The Settlor may appoint a substitute or successor Trustee to act as Trustee of any trust or trusts created hereunder in the place and stead of, or as successor to, any Trustee named in Section 4.01 above. Such substitution shall be in writing.

Paragraph 4.03. Trustee Liability. No person named as Trustee in this instrument or appointed as Trustee in the manner specified herein shall be liable to any beneficiary or to any heir of Settlor for the Trustee's acts or failure to act, except for willful misconduct or gross negligence. No such Trustee shall be liable or responsible for any act, omission or default of any other Trustee provided that they shall have had no knowledge of facts that might reasonably be expected to put the Trustee on notice of it.

Paragraph 4.04. Trustee Compensation. The Trustee shall be entitled to reasonable compensation for services rendered to the Trust or Trusts created hereunder.

Paragraph 4.05. Title to Trust Estate. The legal title to all property held in trust hereunder shall be, remain and become vested in the Trustee or successor Trustee from time to time acting hereunder, without any act of conveyance or transfer to or by or acceptance from, any succeeding, retiring or predecessor Trustee; however, any removed or resigning Trustee shall execute and deliver any and all conveyances and documents requested and reasonably necessary to transfer the trust estate and its assets to a successor Trustee. Each successor Trustee from time to time acting hereunder shall have all the rights, powers immunities and authorities, discretionary or otherwise and the duties and obligations herein granted to the original Trustee. No successor Trustee shall be obligated to inquire into or be in any way responsible for the previous administration of any trust created herein or of the trust estate or for any act or default of any predecessor Trustee.

Paragraph 4.06. Powers of Trustee. To carry out the purposes of any trust created under this Trust Declaration, and subject to any limitations stated elsewhere in this Trust Declaration, the Trustee is vested with the following powers with respect to the Trust Estate, and any part of it, in addition to those powers now or hereafter conferred by law.

A. Power to Invest. To invest and reinvest the Trust Estate in every kind of property, real, personal or mixed, and every kind of investment, specifically including but not by way of limitation, corporate obligations of every kind, stocks, preferred or common, shares of investment trusts, investment companies, mutual funds, market index funds and mortgage participations which individuals of prudence, discretion and intelligence acquire for their own account, and any common trust fund administered by any Trustee under this Trust Declaration.

B. Power to Retain Property. To retain any property which was an asset of the Trust Estate during the Settlor's lifetime or received without consideration by the Trustee as long as the Trustee deems advisable whether or not of the character permitted by law for the investment of trust funds. The trust properties and investment need not be diversified and the Trustee shall have no duty to dispose or convert any trust assets to effect diversification.

C. Power to Manage Securities. With respect to securities held in this Trust Declaration, to have all the rights, powers and privileges of an owner, including but not by way of limitation, the power to vote, give proxies and pay assessments, to participate in voting trusts, pooling agreements, foreclosures, reorganizations, consolidations, mergers, liquidations, sales and leases and, incident to such participation, to deposit securities with and transfer title to any protective or other committee on such terms as the Trustee may deem advisable, to exercise and sell stock subscription or conversion rights and to hold securities in "street name".

D. Power of Sale, Exchange, Repair. To manage, control, foreclose, repossess, grant options on, grant easements on, sell (for cash), convey, exchange, partition, divide, improve and repair trust property.

The power to sell, at the termination of the trust, any trust property if the Trustee feels said disposition would assist in the distribution of the trust property at termination.

E. Power to Lease. To lease trust property for terms within or beyond the term of the trust and for any purpose, including exploration for and removal of gas, oil and other minerals; and to enter into community oil leases, pooling and unitization agreements, operating agreements or otherwise, and to create restrictions, easements or other servitudes thereon, to assign, partition, divide, subdivide, transfer to a corporation in exchange for stock, improve, repair, loan, reloan, invest and reinvest the trust estate or any part thereof.

F. Power to Insure. To carry, at the expense of the Trust Estate, insurance of such kinds and in such amounts as the Trustee shall deem advisable to protect the Trust Estate and the Trustee against any hazard.

G. Power to Commence or Defend Litigation. To commence or defend such litigation with respect to the Trust or any property of the Trust Estate as the Trustee may deem advisable, at the expense of the Trust Declaration.

H. Power to Compromise Claim. To compromise or otherwise adjust any claims or litigation against or in favor of the Trust Declaration.

I. Power to Employ Consultants. To employ any custodian, investment advisor, attorney, accountant or other agents to assist the Trustee in administration of this Trust Declaration and to rely upon the advice given by these agents. Reasonable compensation shall be paid to these agents for all services performed.

J. Power to Adjust for Tax Consequences. To take any action and to make any election the Trustee shall deem advisable to minimize the tax liabilities of this trust and its beneficiaries, to allocate the benefits among the various beneficiaries and to make adjustments in the rights of any beneficiaries or group of beneficiaries or between principal and income accounts, to compensate for the consequences of any tax election or any investment decision or administrative decision that has the effect of preferring one beneficiary or group of beneficiaries over others, provided such discretion shall not be exercised in any manner which will cause a loss of or a decrease in any marital or charitable deduction otherwise allowable in computing the Settlor's federal estate tax.

ARTICLE V
MISCELLANEOUS

Paragraph 5.01. No Assignment. Each beneficiary hereunder is hereby prohibited from anticipating, encumbering, assigning or in any other manner, alienating her or his interest in either income or principal of any trust created under this Trust Declaration and is without power to do so nor shall such interest be subject to her or his liabilities or obligations nor to attachment, execution or other legal processes, bankruptcy proceedings or claims of creditors or others. The Trustee may require the personal receipt of a beneficiary as a condition precedent to payment, distribution or delivery of any amount, property or benefit hereunder. The Trustee may, however, deposit in any bank designated in writing, by a beneficiary, to her or his credit, income or principal payable to such beneficiary.

Paragraph 5.02. Principal and Income. Except as otherwise specifically provided in this Trust Declaration, the determination of all matters with respect to what shall constitute principal and income of each trust estate, gross income therefrom and net income distributable under the terms of the Trust Declaration, shall be governed by the provisions of the Revised Uniform Principal and Income Act as enacted in the State of (2a)_______________, from time to time existing. All taxes, assessments, fees, charges and other expenses incurred by the Trustee in the administration, protection and distribution of each trust, shall be a charge upon the trust estate and shall be paid out of the income and/or principal, in accordance with the aforesaid Act.

Paragraph 5.03. Savings Clause. Unless sooner terminated in accordance with other provisions of this Trust Declaration, any trust created hereunder shall terminate twenty-one (21) years after the death of the last surviving member of the group consisting of the Settlor and the issue of the Settlor who are living and in being at the date of death of the Settlor.

Paragraph 5.04. Payments to Minors and Incompetents. The Trustee, in the Trustee's discretion, may apply payments directly for the benefit of any beneficiary, rather than directly to such beneficiary and, in the case of a beneficiary who is a minor or who is under any other disability, make payment to the guardian, conservator of the person or estate of such beneficiary, custodian under the Uniform Transfers to Minors Act, parent or any other suitable adult with whom the beneficiary resides or by expending the same for the care, education, maintenance or other benefit of said beneficiary. In addition, the Trustee, in the Trustee's discretion, may make payments directly to a beneficiary who is a minor if, in the Trustee's judgment, the minor is of sufficient age and maturity to properly manage the money or property so paid. The Trustee shall not be required to see to the application of any such payment so made to any said persons, but his, her or their receipt therefor shall be a full discharge to the Trustee.

Paragraph 5.05. No Physical Segregation. There need be no physical segregation or division of the various trusts except as segregation or division may be required by the termination of any of the trusts or as specifically provided, but the Trustee shall keep separate accounts for the different undivided interests.

Paragraph 5.06. Distribution. In any case in which the Trustee is required, pursuant to the provisions of the Trust, to divide any parts or shares for the purposes of distribution or otherwise, except as the donee of any power of appointment affecting such property may have expressly provided otherwise in the instrument exercising such power, the Trustee is authorized, in the Trustee's absolute discretion, to make the division and distribution (pro rata or otherwise) in kind, including an undivided interest in any property or partly in kind and partly in money, and for this purpose, to make such sales of the trust property as the Trustee may deem necessary, on such terms and conditions as the Trustee shall see fit. Any asset which is encumbered shall be assigned subject thereto, and its value or amount shall be given effect less such indebtedness.

Paragraph 5.07. Non-Pro Rata Distributions. As to distribution or division of property in kind under and for the several trusts, excepting the initial establishment of any trust for a pecuniary amount, the Trustee shall be cognizant of the differences between the tax cost bases and current value and shall endeavor, insofar as is practicable to distribute or set aside to or for each beneficiary or distributee, assets or property carrying amount or portions of the total unrealized taxable gains or losses embodied in all the assets and properties involved commensurate with the share or portion of each beneficiary or distributee.

Paragraph 5.08. Distribution If All Beneficiaries Die Before Full Distribution. If at any time before full distribution of the Trust Estate, the Settlor is deceased and no disposition of the property is directed by this Trust Declaration, the Trust Estate or the portion of it not disposed of under the Trust Declaration, whichever the case may be, shall thereupon be distributed to the Settlor's heirs at law under the laws of intestate succession of the State of (2a)_________________ then in effect for separate property not acquired from a predeceased spouse.

Paragraph 5.09. Additional Property. With consent of the Trustee, additional property may be added at any time from any source to any trust held under this Trust Declaration. No person dealing with the Trustee in any manner shall be under any obligation to see to the application of any money paid to the Trustee or to inquire into the validity, expediency or propriety of any act of the Trustee or into any of the provisions of any trust hereunder.

Paragraph 5.10. Fiduciary Capacity. All of the powers of the Trustee provided in this Trust Declaration shall be exercisable by the Trustee in the Trustee's fiduciary capacity and only in such capacity.

Paragraph 5.11. Corporate Office. No person shall, by reason of acting as Trustee, be in any way restricted or prohibited from holding office in any corporation in which any trust under this Trust Declaration holds securities or from receiving compensation from any such corporation for services performed as a director, officer or employee of such corporation or from purchasing, selling or otherwise dealing with the stock of any such corporation for the individual account of such Trustee or from voting the stock of any such corporation held by such trust, including voting those shares in favor of the Settlor or any other person.

Paragraph 5.12. Disclaimer of Powers. The Settlor may disclaim, release or restrict the scope of any power held in connection with any trust created under this Trust Declaration, including any administrative power, whether such power is expressly granted in this Trust Declaration or implied by law, by a written instrument specifying the power to be disclaimed, released or restricted and the nature of any such restriction. Any power disclaimed or released by the Settlor shall be extinguished except to the extent this Trust Declaration expressly provides that such power pass to another. This power shall be personal to the Settlor only and may not be exercised by any other person acting on behalf of the Settlor, including, but not limited to, any Trustee (other than the Settlor), Conservator, agent or guardian.

Paragraph 5.13. Notice. Unless the Trustee has received written notice of the occurrence of an event affecting the beneficial interest in any trust held under this Trust Declaration, the Trustee shall not be liable to any beneficiary of such trust for any distributions made or other actions taken by the Trustee in good faith as though such event had not occurred.

Paragraph 5.14. Invalidity of Any Provision. Should any provision of this Trust Declaration be or become invalid or unenforceable, the remaining provisions of this Trust Declaration shall be and continue to be fully effective.

Paragraph 5.15. Gender and Number. Except as provided otherwise herein, the masculine, feminine and neuter gender, and the singular or plural number, shall each be deemed to include the others whenever the context so indicates.

Paragraph 5.16. Law of Construction of Trust. This Trust Declaration, its validity, the construction of and all rights under the Trusts provided for in this Trust Declaration shall be governed by the laws of the State of (2a)____________________.

Paragraph 5.17. No Contest. The Settlor has intentionally and with full knowledge omitted to provide for his/her issue, ancestors, relatives and heirs living at the time of his/her demise, except for such provisions as are made specifically herein.

If any person who is or claims under or through a beneficiary of this Trust, or if any person who would be entitled to share in the Settlor's estate if the Settlor died intestate, should in any manner whatsoever, directly or indirectly, attack, contest or seek to impair or invalidate in court any provision of the following:

A. This Trust or any Amendment to this Trust;

B. Any Will or Codicil to any Will executed by the Settlor;

C. Any beneficiary designation executed by the Settlor with respect to any insurance policy, any "Totten trust" account, any joint tenancy or tenancy by the entirety, any "transfer on death" account or any pension plan, or conspire or cooperate with anyone attempting to do any of the actions or things aforesaid, then each such person and any devise, share or interest in the Trust or the Settlor's Estate otherwise given to each such person under this Trust or the Settlor's Estate to which each such person might be entitled by law, is hereby revoked and shall pass and be distributed as though each such person had predeceased the Settlor leaving no issue or heirs whatsoever.

Any and every individual who asserts, or conspires or cooperates with any person who asserts, any claim against this Trust or the Estate of the Settlor of this Trust based on:

D. "Quantum meruit" theory;

E. Common law marriage, Marvin v. Marvin, 18 Cal. 3d 660 (1976) type of agreement or similar theory;

F. Constructive trust theory; or,

G. Oral agreement or written agreement which is to be proved by parole evidence, claiming that Settlor agreed to gift or devise anything to such person or to pay such person or another for services rendered, regardless of whether a court may find that such agreement existed, then each such person is disinherited and any devise, share or interest in this Trust or the Settlor's Estate otherwise given to each such person under this Trust or the Settlor's Estate or to which each such person might be entitled by law, is hereby revoked and shall pass and be distributed as though each such person had predeceased the Settlor leaving no issue or heirs whatsoever.

The Trustee is specifically authorized to defend any such attack, contest, claim or other proceeding of any nature concerning this Trust or of any provision hereof, and to employ legal counsel therefor, all at the expense of the Trust.

Paragraph 5.18. Survival. If any person fails to survive the Settlor by thirty (30) days, for all purposes of this Trust Declaration the person shall be considered to have predeceased the Settlor.

Paragraph 5.19. All typed and handwritten "fill-ins" where directed above were made before the execution of this Declaration of Trust and are not initialed by the Settlor. All crossed through words and inter-lineations were made before the execution of this Trust and are initialed by the Settlor.

CERTIFICATION OF SETTLOR

I certify that:

A. I have read the foregoing Trust Declaration;

B. The foregoing Trust Declaration correctly states the terms and conditions under which the Trust Estate is to be held, managed, administered and disposed of by the Trustee;

C. As the Settlor named in such Trust Declaration, I approve such Trust Declaration in all particulars; and,

D. As the Trustee named in such Trust Declaration, I approve and accept the Trust provided for in such Declaration.

Dated: (40)________________________________

(1)________________________________, Settlor

(54)________________________________

(49)________________________________, Trustee

STATE OF (2a)________________________)
) ss.
COUNTY OF (2)________________________)

On ________________, 200__ before me, the undersigned, a Notary Public in and for said county and state, personally appeared (1)_____________ _________, personally known to me (or proved to me on the basis of satisfactory evidence) to be the person(s) whose name(s) is/are subscribed to the within instrument and acknowledged that he/she/they executed the same in his/her/their authorized capacity(ies), and that by his/her/their signature(s) on the instrument the person(s), or the entity upon behalf of which the person(s) acted, executed the instrument.

WITNESS my hand and official seal.

____

Notary Public in and for said County and State

EXHIBIT A

Property Declared to be assets of the (1a)______________________________ TRUST dated (48)________________:

(55)

1.

INTER-VIVOS TRUST

THE (1a)____________________

The Settlors named below hereby declare as follows:

ARTICLE I
ESTABLISHMENT OF TRUST

Paragraph 1.01. Creation of Trust. This Trust Declaration has been entered into between (1)__________________and (4)_____________________ as Settlors and themselves as the Trustees. The Settlors, of (2)_________ County, (2a)___________, have transferred, or will transfer, to the Trustees of this Trust Declaration the property described in the attached Exhibit "A" which will constitute, together with any other property that may be added to this Trust Declaration, the Trust Estate of an express trust which shall be held, administered and distributed by the Trustee as provided in this Trust Declaration.

Paragraph 1.02. Trust Name. This Trust Declaration shall be known as the (1a)"______________________TRUST" dated (48)______________________.

Paragraph 1.03. Definitions. As used in this Trust Declaration:

A. Husband: The term "Husband" shall mean (1)________________________.

B. Wife: The term "Wife" shall mean (4)__________________________.

C. Settlors: The term "Settlors" shall refer collectively to Husband and Wife.

D. Deceased Settlor: The term "deceased Settlor" shall refer to the Settlor who is first to die. However, the term, "then deceased Settlor" shall refer to the Settlor then deceased and may thus refer to the otherwise surviving Settlor.

E. Surviving Settlor: The term "surviving Settlor" shall refer to the Settlor who is last to die.

F. Trustee: The term "Trustee" or "Trustees" shall refer to whoever is serving as Trustee or Trustees under this Trust Declaration.

G. Trust Estate: The term "Trust Estate" shall refer to the property subject to this Trust Declaration.

Paragraph 1.04. Property to Retain Status. All property now or hereafter transferred to the Trustee which was community property, quasi-community property or separate property at the time of such transfer, shall remain, respectively, community property, quasi-community property or the separate property of the spouse or spouses transferring such property to the Trustee.

ARTICLE II
OPERATION OF TRUST DURING THE LIFE OF HUSBAND AND WIFE

Paragraph 2.01. Net Income. During the life of Husband and/or Wife, the Trustee shall pay to or apply for the benefit of both Husband and Wife, or the survivor thereof, in monthly or more frequent intervals, all of the net income of the community Trust Estate and shall pay to or apply for the benefit of the contributing spouse, in monthly or more frequent intervals, all of the net income of the separate property contributed or owned by that spouse.

Paragraph 2.02. Withdrawal of Principal. During the life of Husband and/or Wife, the Trustee shall also pay to or apply for the benefit of both Husband and Wife, or either, or the survivor thereof, so much of the community principal of the Trust Estate, up to the whole thereof, as both Husband and Wife shall direct, and shall, at the discretion of a spouse, pay to or apply for the benefit of that spouse so much of the principal of the Trust Estate, up to the whole thereof, as is that spouse's separate property.

Paragraph 2.03. Incapacity of Husband or Wife. If, at any time either Husband or Wife has become physically or mentally incapacitated so as to be unable to manage his or her affairs, whether or not a court of competent jurisdiction has declared him or her incompetent, mentally ill, or in need of a conservator, the Trustee shall pay to the non-incapacitated spouse or apply for the benefit of either spouse such amounts of the principal and/or income of the community estate as may be necessary, in the Trustee's discretion, for the care, maintenance and support of both spouses in accordance with their accustomed manner of living. The Trustee shall also pay to or apply for the benefit of the incapacitated spouse such amounts of income or principal of the separate property contributed by the incapacitated spouse as may be necessary, in the Trustee's discretion, for the care, maintenance, and support of the incapacitated spouse in accordance with his or her accustomed manner of living, taking into account payments made by the Trustee from the community Trust Estate. If a conservator of the person or estate is appointed for the incapacitated spouse, the Trustee shall take into account any payments made for the incapacitated spouse's benefit by the conservator.

The payments specified in this Section shall be made until the incapacitated spouse is again able to manage his or her own affairs, or until the death of the first spouse to die, whichever event may occur earlier.

Paragraph 2.04. Revocation of Trust. At any time during their joint lives, either Husband or Wife as to community property, and either spouse as to his or her separate property, may, by serving written notice on the Trustee, revoke the Trust created by this Trust Declaration, in whole or in part. Any community property withdrawn from the Trust Estate by reason of any such revocation shall be delivered by the Trustee to both Husband and Wife and any separate property withdrawn from the Trust shall be delivered by the Trustee to the spouse revoking the Trust.

Paragraph 2.05. Amendment of Trust. At any time during their joint lives, Husband and Wife, jointly as to community property, and either spouse as to his or her separate property, may, by serving written notice on the Trustee, alter, modify or amend the Trust created by this Trust Declaration in any respect. After the death of the predeceasing Trustor the surviving Trustor may, by serving written notice on the Trustee, alter, modify or amend the Trust created by this Trust Declaration in any respect.

ARTICLE III
OPERATION OF TRUST AFTER DEATH OF DECEASED SETTLOR
AND DEATH OF SURVIVING SETTLOR

Paragraph 3.01. Collection of Assets and Payment of Debts: On the death of each Settlor the Trustee shall collect all assets belonging to the Trust Estate. As soon as practicable after the death of each Settlor the Trustee, except as otherwise provided herein, shall pay from the Trust Estate the just debts of the then deceased Settlor, as the case may be, (excluding any debts barred by provisions of law or not yet due), funeral expenses of the then deceased Settlor, and any inheritance, estate, or other death taxes that shall, by reason of the death of the then deceased Settlor, be attributable to the Trust Estate. This is not and shall not constitute a direction to pay all inheritance, estate or other death taxes from or charge the same to, the Trust Estate without apportionment.

Upon the death of the deceased Settlor all assets subject to this Declaration of Trust shall be and are confirmed as the separate property of the surviving Settlor.

Paragraph 3.02. Distribution of Trust Estate. Upon the death of the surviving Settlor, and after payment of expenses as set forth in Paragraph 3.01, the Trustee shall hold, administer and distribute the Trust Estate as follows:

A. The Trustee shall distribute to the following persons the cash amount listed after their respective names:

(10)

B. The Trustee shall distribute to the following persons the real property described after their respective names. (12) Said real property is given free of all encumbrances or liens thereon.

(11)

C. The Trustee shall distribute to (13)____________________ a life estate in the following property located at: (14)__________________________. After the death of (13)____________________ said property shall go, outright, to (15)______________________________ as the remainder person(s).

D. The Trustee shall distribute all of the rest, residue and remainder of the Trust Estate, real, personal and mixed, of whatsoever kind or character and wheresoever situated, to the following persons or entities (16) in the proportions listed after their names (17) in equal shares.

(18)

E. Distribution of Trust Assets. With respect to the distribution of any trust estate upon termination of any trust, and partial distribution of any trust, the liquidation and distribution by the Trustee of the Trust Estate involved or the distributable portion shall commence immediately and be accomplished as rapidly as possible, and deliveries of the trust properties to the beneficiary or beneficiaries may be made in installments or series, retaining only reasonable reserves for final charges and expenses. In no event shall it be necessary for the Trustee to await an accounting to the Court, or any Court order, before releasing and distributing the majority of the Trust Estate to be distributed.

F. Undistributed Income. All the net income of the respective trusts or trust estates, not distributed, used or applied as otherwise provided herein, shall be accumulated and added to the principals of the respective trusts.

Upon the change or succession of any beneficiary, distribution of trust properties or any trust estate or any portion thereof, or upon setting aside, apportionment or division of any trust estate or upon the termination of a trust or any interest therein, the beneficial interest, properties or balance of trust estate at the applicable time and to be dealt with shall include any and all income accumulated, accrued, uncollected or held undistributed and all of such income shall likewise be distributed, set aside or apportioned to the next or succeeding beneficiaries, distributees, shares or trusts, retaining its character as income.

ARTICLE IV

TRUSTEES

Paragraph 4.01. Appointment of Trustees. Settlors, (1a)____________________ and (4)____________________ are appointed and confirmed as the Trustees, without bond. In the event either original Trustee should resign, die or become mentally incapacitated, the remaining Trustee shall act as sole Trustee. If either original Trustee should cease to act as Trustee due to a mental incapacity, his/her restoration of mental capacity shall result in his immediate return as Trustee or Co-Trustee hereunder. If either original

Trustee should cease to act as sole Trustee or a Co-Trustee with the other original Trustee due to his/her resignation, he/she may at any time subsequent, elect to act again as sole Trustee or a Co-Trustee with the other original Trustee. Said election shall be made by filing same with either of the then acting Trustee or by recording said election in the County of residence of said Trustee making such election.

In the event both (1)__________________ and (4)_____________should die, refuse to act, or for any other reason be unable to act, then (25)_____________________ shall act as (26)____Trustee_ hereunder (27) without bond. In the event he/she/they should die, decline to act, or for any other reason, be unable to act as Trustee then (28)___________________________ shall act as Trustee hereunder (27) without bond.

Paragraph 4.02. Substitute Trustee. The Settlors jointly, or the surviving Settlor upon the death of the predeceased Settlor, may appoint a substitute or successor Trustee to act as Trustee of any trust or trusts created hereunder in the place and stead of, or as successor to, any Trustee named in Section 4.01 above. Such substitution shall be in writing.

Paragraph 4.03. Trustee Liability. No person named as Trustee in this instrument or appointed as Trustee in the manner specified herein shall be liable to any beneficiary or to any heir of either Settlor for the Trustee's acts or failure to act, except for willful misconduct or gross negligence. No such Trustee shall be liable or responsible for any act, omission or default of any other Trustee provided that they shall have had no knowledge of facts that might reasonably be expected to put the Trustee on notice of it.

Paragraph 4.04. Title to Trust Estate. The legal title to all property held in trust hereunder shall be, remain and become vested in the Trustee or successor Trustee from time to time acting hereunder, without any act of conveyance or transfer to or by or acceptance from, any succeeding, retiring or predecessor Trustee; however, any removed or resigning Trustee shall execute and deliver any and all conveyances and documents requested and reasonably necessary to transfer the trust estate and its assets to a successor Trustee. Each successor Trustee from time to time acting hereunder shall have all the rights, powers immunities and authorities, discretionary or otherwise and the duties and obligations herein granted to the original Trustee. No successor Trustee shall be obligated to inquire into or be in any way responsible for the previous administration of any trust created herein or of the trust estate or for any act or default of any predecessor Trustee.

Paragraph 4.05. Powers of Trustee. To carry out the purposes of any trust created under this Trust Declaration, and subject to any limitations stated elsewhere in this Trust Declaration, the Trustee is vested with the following powers with respect to the Trust Estate, and any part of it, in addition to those powers now or hereafter conferred by law.

A. Power to Invest. To invest and reinvest the Trust Estate in every kind of property, real, personal or mixed, and every kind of investment, specifically including but not by way of limitation, corporate obligations of every kind, stocks, preferred or common, shares of investment trusts, investment companies, mutual funds, market index funds and mortgage participations which individuals of prudence, discretion and intelligence acquire for their own account, and any common trust fund administered by any Trustee under this Trust Declaration.

B. Power to Retain Property. To retain any property which was an asset of the Trust Estate during the Settlor's lifetime or received without consideration by the Trustee as long as the Trustee deems advisable whether or not of the character permitted by law for the investment of trust funds. The trust properties and investment need not be diversified and the Trustee shall have no duty to dispose or convert any trust assets to effect diversification.

C. Power to Manage Securities. With respect to securities held in this Trust Declaration, to have all the rights, powers and privileges of an owner, including but not by way of limitation, the power to vote, give proxies and pay assessments, to participate in voting trusts, pooling agreements, foreclosures, reorganizations, consolidations, mergers, liquidations, sales and leases and, incident to such participation, to deposit securities with and transfer title to any protective or other committee on such terms as the Trustee may deem advisable, to exercise and sell stock subscription or conversion rights and to hold securities in "street name".

D. Power of Sale, Exchange, Repair. To manage, control, foreclose, repossess, grant options on, grant easements on, sell (for cash), convey, exchange, partition, divide, improve and repair trust property.

The power to sell, at the termination of the trust, any trust property if the Trustee feels said disposition would assist in the distribution of the trust property at termination.

E. Power to Lease. To lease trust property for terms within or beyond the term of the trust and for any purpose, including exploration for and removal of gas, oil and other minerals; and to enter into community oil leases, pooling and unitization agreements, operating agreements or otherwise, and to create restrictions, easements or other servitudes thereon, to assign, partition, divide, subdivide, transfer to a corporation in exchange for stock, improve, repair, loan, reloan, invest and reinvest the trust estate or any part thereof.

F. Power to Insure. To carry, at the expense of the Trust Estate, insurance of such kinds and in such amounts as the Trustee shall deem advisable to protect the Trust Estate and the Trustee against any hazard.

G. Power to Commence or Defend Litigation. To commence or defend such litigation with respect to the Trust or any property of the Trust Estate as the Trustee may deem advisable, at the expense of the Trust Declaration.

H. Power to Compromise Claim. To compromise or otherwise adjust any claims or litigation against or in favor of the Trust Declaration.

I. Power to Employ Consultants. To employ any custodian, investment advisor, attorney, accountant or other agents to assist the Trustee in administration of this Trust Declaration and to rely upon the advice given by these agents. Reasonable compensation shall be paid to these agents for all services performed.

J. Power to Adjust for Tax Consequences. To take any action and to make any election the Trustee shall deem advisable to minimize the tax liabilities of this trust and its beneficiaries, to allocate the benefits among the various beneficiaries and to make adjustments in the rights of any beneficiaries or group of beneficiaries or between principal and income accounts, to compensate for the consequences of any tax election or any investment decision or administrative decision that has the effect of preferring one beneficiary or group of beneficiaries over others, provided such discretion shall not be exercised in any manner which will cause a loss of or a decrease in any marital or charitable deduction otherwise allowable in computing the then deceased Settlor's federal estate tax.

K. Trust Bank and Securities Accounts. During the joint lives of the Settlors, if the Settlors are serving as co-Trustees hereunder, the signature of either Trustor shall be sufficient to create, negotiate or endorse trust checks or to deposit or withdraw trust funds from trust bank or securities accounts or to trade securities in said securities accounts.

ARTICLE V
MISCELLANEOUS

Paragraph 5.01. No Assignment. Each beneficiary hereunder is hereby prohibited from anticipating, encumbering, assigning or in any other manner, alienating her or his interest in either income or principal of any trust created under this Trust Declaration and is without power to do so nor shall such interest be subject to her or his liabilities or obligations nor to attachment, execution or other legal processes, bankruptcy proceedings or claims of creditors or others. The Trustee may require the personal receipt of a beneficiary as a condition precedent to payment, distribution or delivery of any amount, property or benefit hereunder. The

Trustee may, however, deposit in any bank designated in writing, by a beneficiary, to her or his credit, income or principal payable to such beneficiary.

Paragraph 5.02. Principal and Income. Except as otherwise specifically provided in this Trust Declaration, the determination of all matters with respect to what shall constitute principal and income of each trust estate, gross income therefrom and net income distributable under the terms of the Trust Declaration, shall be governed by the provisions of the Revised Uniform Principal and Income Act as enacted in the State of (2a)____________________, from time to time existing. All taxes, assessments, fees, charges and other expenses incurred by the Trustee in the administration, protection and distribution of each trust, shall be a charge upon the trust estate and shall be paid out of the income and/or principal, in accordance with the aforesaid Act.

Paragraph 5.03. Savings Clause. Unless sooner terminated in accordance with other provisions of this Trust Declaration, any trust created hereunder shall terminate twenty-one (21) years after the death of the last surviving member of the group consisting of the Settlor and the issue of the Settlor who are living and in being at the date of death of the Settlor.

Paragraph 5.04. Payments to Minors and Incompetents. The Trustee, in the Trustee's discretion, may apply payments directly for the benefit of any beneficiary, rather than directly to such beneficiary and, in the case of a beneficiary who is a minor or who is under any other disability, make payment to the guardian, conservator of the person or estate of such beneficiary, custodian under the Uniform Transfers to Minors Act, parent or any other suitable adult with whom the beneficiary resides or by expending the same for the care, education, maintenance or other benefit of said beneficiary. In addition, the Trustee, in the Trustee's discretion, may make payments directly to a beneficiary who is a minor if, in the Trustee's judgment, the minor is of sufficient age and maturity to properly manage the money or property so paid. The Trustee shall not be required to see to the application of any such payment so made to any said persons, but his, her or their receipt therefor shall be a full discharge to the Trustee.

Paragraph 5.05. No Physical Segregation. There need be no physical segregation or division of the various trusts except as segregation or division may be required by the termination of any of the trusts or as specifically provided, but the Trustee shall keep separate accounts for the different undivided interests.

Paragraph 5.06. Distribution. In any case in which the Trustee is required, pursuant to the provisions of the Trust, to divide any parts or shares for the purposes of distribution or otherwise, except as the donee of any power of appointment affecting such property may have expressly provided otherwise in the instrument exercising such power, the Trustee is authorized, in the Trustee's absolute discretion, to make the division and distribution (pro rata or otherwise) in kind, including an undivided interest in any property or partly in kind and partly in money, and for this purpose, to make such sales of the trust property as the Trustee may deem necessary, on such terms and conditions as the Trustee shall see fit. Any asset which is encumbered shall be assigned subject thereto, and its value or amount shall be given effect less such indebtedness.

Paragraph 5.07. Non-Pro Rata Distributions. As to distribution or division of property in kind under and for the several trusts, excepting the initial establishment of any trust for a pecuniary amount, the Trustee shall be cognizant of the differences between the tax cost bases and current value and shall endeavor, insofar as is practicable to distribute or set aside to or for each beneficiary or distributee, assets or property carrying amount or portions of the total unrealized taxable gains or losses embodied in all the assets and properties involved commensurate with the share or portion of each beneficiary or distributee.

Paragraph 5.08. Distribution If All Beneficiaries Die Before Full Distribution. If at any time before full distribution of the Trust Estate, the Settlor is deceased and no disposition of the property is directed by this Trust Declaration, the Trust Estate or the portion of it not disposed of under the Trust Declaration, whichever the case may be, shall thereupon be distributed one-half to those persons who would be the legal heirs of Husband and one-half to the legal heirs of Wife their identities and respective shares to be determined as though the death of Husband and Wife had occurred immediately following the event requiring distribution and according to the laws of the State of (2a)________________ then in effect relating to the succession of separate property not acquired from a parent, grandparent or previously deceased spouse.

Paragraph 5.09. Additional Property. With consent of the Trustee, additional property may be added at any time from any source to any trust held under this Trust Declaration. No person dealing with the Trustee in any manner shall be under any obligation to see to the application of any money paid to the Trustee or to inquire into the validity, expediency or propriety of any act of the Trustee or into any of the provisions of any trust hereunder.

Paragraph 5.10. Fiduciary Capacity. All of the powers of the Trustee provided in this Trust Declaration shall be exercisable by the Trustee in the Trustee's fiduciary capacity and only in such capacity.

Paragraph 5.11. Corporate Office. No person shall, by reason of acting as Trustee, be in any way restricted or prohibited from holding office in any corporation in which any trust under this Trust Declaration holds securities or from receiving compensation from any such corporation for services performed as a director, officer or employee of such corporation or from purchasing, selling or otherwise dealing with the stock of any such corporation for the individual account of such Trustee or from voting the stock of any such corporation held by such trust, including voting those shares in favor of the Settlor or any other person.

Paragraph 5.12. Disclaimer of Powers. The Trustee may disclaim, release or restrict the scope of any power held in connection with any trust created under this Trust Declaration, including any administrative power, whether such power is expressly granted in this Trust Declaration or implied by law, by a written instrument specifying the power to be disclaimed, released or restricted and the nature of any such restriction. Any power disclaimed or released by the Trustee shall be extinguished except to the extent this Trust Declaration expressly provides that such power pass to another. This power shall be personal to the Trustee only and may not be exercised by any other person acting on behalf of the Trustee, including, but not limited to, any Trustee (other than the Trustee), Conservator, agent or guardian.

Paragraph 5.13. Notice. Unless the Trustee has received written notice of the occurrence of an event affecting the beneficial interest in any trust held under this Trust Declaration, the Trustee shall not be liable to any beneficiary of such trust for any distributions made or other actions taken by the Trustee in good faith as though such event had not occurred.

Paragraph 5.14. Invalidity of Any Provision. Should any provision of this Trust Declaration be or become invalid or unenforceable, the remaining provisions of this Trust Declaration shall be and continue to be fully effective.

Paragraph 5.15. Gender and Number. Except as provided otherwise herein, the masculine, feminine and neuter gender, and the singular or plural number, shall each be deemed to include the others whenever the context so indicates.

Paragraph 5.16. Law of Construction of Trust. This Trust Declaration, its validity, the construction of and all rights under the Trusts provided for in this Trust Declaration shall be governed by the laws of the State of (2a)____________________.

Paragraph 5.17. No Contest. The Settlors have intentionally and with full knowledge omitted to provide for his/her issue, ancestors, relatives and heirs living at the time of his/her demise, except for such provisions as are made specifically herein.

If any person who is or claims under or through a beneficiary of this Trust, or if any person who would be entitled to share in either Settlor's estate if either or both Settlors died intestate, should in any manner whatsoever, directly or indirectly, attack, contest or seek to impair or invalidate in court any provision of the following:

A. This Trust or any Amendment to this Trust;

B. Any Will or Codicil to any Will executed by either Settlor;

C. Any beneficiary designation executed by either Settlor with respect to any insurance policy, any "Totten trust" account, any joint tenancy or tenancy by the entirety, any "transfer on death" account or any pension plan, or conspire or cooperate with anyone attempting to do any of the actions or things aforesaid, then each such person and any devise, share or interest in the Trust or either Settlor's Estate otherwise given to each such person under this Trust or either Settlor's Estate to which each such person might be entitled by law, is hereby revoked and shall pass and be distributed as though each such person had predeceased either Settlor leaving no issue or heirs whatsoever.

Any and every individual who asserts, or conspires or cooperates with any person who asserts, any claim against this Trust or the Estate of either Settlor of this Trust based on.

D. "Quantum meruit" theory;

E. Common law marriage, Marvin v. Marvin, 18 Cal. 3d 660 (1976) type of agreement or similar theory;

F. Constructive trust theory; or,

G. Oral agreement or written agreement which is to be proved by parole evidence, claiming that either Settlor agreed to gift or devise anything to such person or to pay such person or another for services rendered, regardless of whether a court may find that such agreement existed, then each such person is disinherited and any devise, share or interest in this Trust or either Settlor's Estate otherwise given to each such person under this Trust or either Settlor's Estate or to which each such person might be entitled by law, is hereby revoked and shall pass and be distributed as though each such person had predeceased both Settlors leaving no issue or heirs whatsoever.

The Trustee is specifically authorized to defend any such attack, contest, claim or other proceeding of any nature concerning this Trust or of any provision hereof, and to employ legal counsel therefor, all at the expense of the Trust.

Paragraph 5.18. Survival. If any person fails to survive a Settlor by thirty (30) days, for all purposes of this Trust Declaration the person shall be considered to have predeceased such Settlor.

Paragraph 5.19. All typed and handwritten "fill-ins" where directed above were made before the execution of this Declaration of Trust and are not initialed by the Settlors. All crossed through words and inter-lineations were made before the execution of this Trust and are initialed by the Settlors.

CERTIFICATION OF HUSBAND AND WIFE

We, and each of us, certify that:

A. We, and each of us, have read the foregoing Trust Declaration;

B. The foregoing Trust Declaration correctly states the terms and conditions under which the Trust Estate is to be held, managed, administered and disposed of by the Trustee;

C. As the Settlors named in such Trust Declaration, we, and each of us, approve such Trust Declaration in all particulars; and

D. As the Trustees named in such Trust Declaration, we, and each of us, approve and accept the Trust provided for in such Declaration.

Dated: (40)______________________________

(1)______________________________, Settlor, Trustee

(1b)______________________________

(4)______________________________, Settlor, Trustee

STATE OF (2a)________________________)
) ss.
COUNTY OF (2)________________________)

On ________________, 200__ before me, the undersigned, a Notary Public in and for said county and state, personally appeared (1)__ _________ and (4)___________, personally known to me (or proved to me on the basis of satisfactory evidence) to be the person(s) whose name(s) is/are subscribed to the within instrument and acknowledged that he/she/they executed the same in his/her/their authorized capacity(ies), and that by his/her/their signature(s) on the instrument the person(s), or the entity upon behalf of which the person(s) acted, executed the instrument.

WITNESS my hand and official seal.

____
Notary Public in and for said County and State

EXHIBIT A

Property Declared to be assets of the (1a)________________and (4)_____________________ TRUST dated (48)________________:

(55)

1.

INTER-VIVOS TRUST

THE (1a)________________________________ TRUST

The Settlors named below hereby declare as follows:

ARTICLE I
ESTABLISHMENT OF TRUST

Paragraph 1.01. Creation of Trust. This Trust Declaration has been entered into between (1)_________________and (4)___________________ as Settlors and themselves as the Trustees. The Settlors, of (2)______________________ County, (2a)___________, have transferred, or will transfer, to the Trustees of this Trust Declaration the property described in the attached Exhibit "A" which will constitute, together with any other property that may be added to this Trust Declaration, the Trust Estate of an express trust which shall be held, administered and distributed by the Trustee as provided in this Trust Declaration.

Paragraph 1.02. Trust Name. This Trust Declaration shall be known as the (1a)"____ TRUST" dated (48)________________________.

Paragraph 1.03. Definitions. As used in this Trust Declaration:

A. Husband: The term "Husband" shall mean (1)__________.

B. Wife: The term "Wife" shall mean (4)______________.

C. Settlors: The term "Settlors" shall refer collectively to Husband and Wife.

D. Deceased Settlor: The term "deceased Settlor" shall refer to the Settlor who is first to die. However, the term, "then deceased Settlor" shall refer to the Settlor then deceased and may thus refer to the otherwise surviving Settlor.

E. Surviving Settlor: The term "surviving Settlor" shall refer to the Settlor who is last to die.

F. Trustee: The term "Trustee" or "Trustees" shall refer to whoever is serving as Trustee or Trustees under this Trust Declaration.

G. Trust Estate: The term "Trust Estate" shall refer to the property subject to this Trust Declaration.

H. Issue: The term "issue" shall refer only to a person who is a lineal descendant of any degree of either the Husband and the Wife and shall(59) not include adopted persons.

Paragraph 1.04. Property to Retain Status. All property now or hereafter transferred to the Trustee which was community property, quasi-community property or separate property at the time of such transfer, shall remain, respectively, community property, quasi-community property or the separate property of the spouse or spouses transferring such property to the Trustee.

ARTICLE II
OPERATION OF TRUST DURING THE LIFE OF HUSBAND AND WIFE

Paragraph 2.01. Net Income. During the life of Husband and/or Wife, the Trustee shall pay to or apply for the benefit of both Husband and Wife, or the survivor thereof, in monthly or more frequent intervals, all of the net income of the community Trust Estate and shall pay to or apply for the benefit of the contributing spouse, in monthly or more frequent intervals, all of the net income of the separate property contributed or owned by that spouse.

Paragraph 2.02. Withdrawal of Principal. During the life of Husband and/or Wife, the Trustee shall also pay to or apply for the benefit of both Husband and Wife, or either, or the survivor thereof, so much of the community principal of the Trust Estate, up to the whole thereof, as both Husband and Wife shall direct, and shall, at the discretion of a spouse, pay to or apply for the benefit of that spouse so much of the principal of the Trust Estate, up to the whole thereof, as is that spouse's separate property.

Paragraph 2.03. Incapacity of Husband or Wife. If, at any time either Husband or Wife has become physically or mentally incapacitated so as to be unable to manage his or her affairs, whether or not a court of competent jurisdiction has declared him or her incompetent, mentally ill, or in need of a conservator, the Trustee shall pay to the non-incapacitated spouse or apply for the benefit of either spouse such amounts of the principal and/or income of the community estate as may be necessary, in the Trustee's discretion, for the care, maintenance and support of both spouses in accordance with their accustomed manner of living. The Trustee shall also pay to or apply for the benefit of the incapacitated spouse such amounts of income or principal of the separate property contributed by the incapacitated spouse as may be necessary, in the Trustee's discretion, for the care, maintenance, and support of the incapacitated spouse in accordance with his or her accustomed manner of living, taking into account payments made by the Trustee from the community Trust Estate. If a conservator of the person or estate is appointed for the incapacitated spouse, the Trustee shall take into account any payments made for the incapacitated spouse's benefit by the conservator.

The payments specified in this Section shall be made until the incapacitated spouse is again able to manage his or her own affairs, or until the death of the first spouse to die, whichever event may occur earlier.

Paragraph 2.04. Revocation of Trust. At any time during their joint lives, either Husband or Wife as to community property, and either spouse as to his or her separate property, may, by serving written notice on the Trustee, revoke the Trust created by this Trust Declaration, in whole or in part. Any community property withdrawn from the Trust Estate by reason of any such revocation shall be delivered by the Trustee to both Husband and Wife and any separate property withdrawn from the Trust shall be delivered by the Trustee to the spouse revoking the Trust.

Paragraph 2.05. Amendment of Trust. At any time during their joint lives, Husband and Wife, jointly as to community property, and either spouse as to his or her separate property, may, by serving written notice on the Trustee, alter, modify or amend the Trust created by this Trust Declaration in any respect. After the death of the deceased Settlor the surviving Settlor may, by serving written notice on the Trustee, alter, modify or amend the Trust created by this Trust Declaration in any respect.

ARTICLE III
OPERATION OF TRUST AFTER DEATH OF DECEASED SETTLOR AND DEATH OF SURVIVING SETTLOR

Paragraph 3.01. Collection of Assets and Payment of Debts: On the death of each Settlor the Trustee shall collect all assets belonging to the Trust Estate. As soon as practicable after the death of each Settlor the Trustee, except as otherwise provided herein, shall pay from the Trust Estate the just debts of the then deceased Settlor, as the case may be, (excluding any debts barred by provisions of law or not yet due), funeral expenses of the then deceased Settlor, and any inheritance, estate, or other death taxes that shall, by reason of the death of the then deceased Settlor, be attributable to the Trust Estate. This is not and shall not constitute a direction to pay all inheritance, estate or other death taxes from or charge the same to, the Trust Estate without apportionment.

Upon the death of the deceased Settlor all assets subject to this Declaration of Trust shall be and are confirmed as the separate property of the surviving Settlor.

Paragraph 3.02. Distribution of Trust Estate. Upon the death of the surviving Settlor, and after payment of expenses as set forth in Paragraph 3.01, the Trustee shall hold, administer and distribute the Trust Estate as follows:

A. The Trustee shall distribute to the following persons the cash amount listed after their respective names:

(10)

B The Trustee shall distribute to the following persons the real property described after their respective names. (12) Said real property is given free of all encumbrances or liens thereon.

(11)

C. The Trustee shall distribute to (13)____________________ a life estate in the following property located at: (14)__________________________. After the death of (13)_____________________ said property shall go, outright, to (15)______________________________ as the remainder person(s).

D. The Trustee shall distribute all of the rest, residue and remainder of the Trust Estate, real, personal and mixed, of whatsoever kind or character and wheresoever situated, to the Trustee hereinafter named, to have and to hold upon the uses, trusts, purposes and conditions hereinafter provided.

The Trustee, shall allocate the trust properties into as many shares as there are children of the joint Settlors then living and children of the joint Settlors then deceased who left issue then living. One such equal share shall be set aside for each of the joint Settlors' children then living and one such equal share shall be set aside for the issue then living, by right of representation, of each of the joint Settlors' children who are then deceased but left issue then living. Said shares shall be held, administered, and distributed as provided in the following sections:

Each share set aside for a child of the joint Settlors shall be held, administered and delivered for and to such beneficiary as follows:

1. The net income from the trust while said beneficiary is under 19 years of age and not a high school graduate shall be added to principal, from which the Trustee shall pay to or for the benefit of such beneficiary such sums as in the Trustee's discretion the Trustee shall deem necessary for such beneficiary's proper care, comfort, maintenance, support or education.

In making payments for the benefit of any beneficiary pursuant to this section 1, the Trustee shall construe his or her authority liberally to permit payments reasonably necessary to ease the financial burden on the guardian of the person of such beneficiary or other suitable individual with whom they reside, and on his or her family, resulting from such beneficiary's presence in his or her household.

2. Upon the beneficiary reaching 19 years of age or finishing high school(whichever occurs first), the Trustee shall pay to or apply for his or her benefit, from his or her trust, as much of the trust principal as the Trustee, in the Trustee's discretion, considers appropriate pursuant to sections 3 and 4 following.

3. After the beneficiary attains 19 years of age or finishes high school (whichever occurs first), the Trustee may, in the Trustee's discretion, pay to or apply from his or her trust, such amounts necessary for his or her educa-

tion. For purposes hereof, education shall mean enrollment, attendance, and satisfactory progression towards a degree as a student at a recognized and accredited college, university, or similar institution of higher learning, including any graduate, professional school or college or trade school. Such educational payments and benefits shall include tuition, books, all direct educational costs and fees, and all reasonable living and transportation expenses. Payments hereunder shall be made during vacation periods within the regular school term under which the beneficiary is attending school and during "summer vacation" or similar vacation period between the regular school terms.
The Trustee may invest any portion of a beneficiary's trust share in an IRC 529 college savings plan for the benefit of said beneficiary.

4. If the beneficiary, his or her spouse, or any of his or her children should at any time or from time to time be in need, in the discretion of the Trustee, of funds due to illness, infirmity or other physical or mental disability or any emergency, the Trustee may relieve or contribute toward the relief of any such need or needs of the beneficiary by paying to him or her or using and applying for his or her benefit, such sum or sums out of the income and/or principal of his or her trust as the Trustee, in the Trustee's discretion, may deem necessary or advisable.

5. Upon the beneficiary attaining the age of 21 years, the Trustee shall begin to pay the beneficiary all of the net income, in monthly or other convenient installments, from the trust.

6. Upon the beneficiary attaining the age of (21)_______ years, the Trustee shall distribute and deliver to such beneficiary one-half of his trust estate. Upon each beneficiary attaining the age of (22)_______ years, the Trustee shall distribute and deliver to such beneficiary all of the remainder of his or her trust estate.

7. If, upon the attaining of the above ages, the Trustee suspects that said beneficiary may be abusing drugs, the Trustee may require the beneficiary to take a reasonable drug test. If the beneficiary fails said drug test, the Trustee shall defer said principal payment to the beneficiary until the beneficiary passes said drug test. After a failed drug test, subsequent drug tests shall be administered at six month intervals. In the event a beneficiary fails a drug test, the Trustee may use said beneficiary's trust estate to pay for a drug abuse rehabilitation program and may require the beneficiary to enroll and to complete said program as a condition precedent to the taking of a subsequent drug test.

8. In the event the beneficiary should die before complete distribution to him or her of his or her trust estate, his or her entire trust estate on hand at the time of his or her death shall thereupon be apportioned and distributed to his or her surviving issue, by right of representation. If such beneficiary should die before complete distribution to him or her of his or her trust estate and leave no surviving issue, then the balance of the trust estate then on hand shall go and be distributed one-half to those persons who would be the legal heirs of Husband and one-half to the legal heirs of Wife their identities and respective shares to be determined as though the death of Husband and Wife had occurred immediately following the event requiring distribution and according to the laws of the State of (2a)_________________ then in effect relating to the succession of separate property not acquired from a parent, grandparent or previously deceased spouse.

9. If, at any time, a trust created hereunder shall, in the sole judgment of the Trustee, be of the aggregate principal value of Fifty Thousand Dollars ($50,000.00) or less, the Trustee may, but need not, terminate such trust and distribute the assets thereof in the Trustee's possession to the beneficiary or beneficiaries, at the time of the

current income thereof, and if there is more than one beneficiary, in the proportion in which they are beneficiaries.

E. Distribution of Trust Assets. With respect to the distribution of any trust estate upon termination of any trust, and partial distribution of any trust, the liquidation and distribution by the Trustee of the Trust Estate involved or the distributable portion shall commence immediately and be accomplished as rapidly as possible, and deliveries of the trust properties to the beneficiary or beneficiaries may be made in installments or series, retaining only reasonable reserves for final charges and expenses. In no event shall it be necessary for the Trustee to await an accounting to the Court, or any Court order, before releasing and distributing the majority of the Trust Estate to be distributed.

F. Undistributed Income. All the net income of the respective trusts or trust estates, not distributed, used or applied as otherwise provided herein, shall be accumulated and added to the principals of the respective trusts.

Upon the change or succession of any beneficiary, distribution of trust properties or any trust estate or any portion thereof, or upon setting aside, apportionment or division of any trust estate or upon the termination of a trust or any interest therein, the beneficial interest, properties or balance of trust estate at the applicable time and to be dealt with shall include any and all income accumulated, accrued, uncollected or held undistributed and all of such income shall likewise be distributed, set aside or apportioned to the next or succeeding beneficiaries, distributees, shares or trusts, retaining its character as income.

ARTICLE IV
TRUSTEES

Paragraph 4.01. Appointment of Trustees. Settlors, (1)_______________and (4)__________________ are appointed and confirmed as the Trustees, without bond. In the event either original Trustee should resign, die or become mentally incapacitated, the remaining Trustee shall act as sole Trustee. If either original Trustee should cease to act as Trustee due to a mental incapacity, his/her restoration of mental capacity shall result in his or her immediate return as Trustee or Co-Trustee hereunder. If either original Trustee should cease to act as sole Trustee or a Co-Trustee with the other original Trustee due to his/her resignation, he/she may at any time subsequent, elect to act again as sole Trustee or a Co-Trustee with the other original Trustee. Said election shall be made by filing same with either of the then acting Trustee or by recording said election in the County of residence of said Trustee making such election.

In the event both (1)__________________ and (4)____________should die, refuse to act, or for any other reason be unable to act, then (25)________________________ shall act as (26)____Trustee_ hereunder (27) without bond. In the event he/she/they should die, decline to act, or for any other reason, be unable to act as Trustee then (28)___________________ shall act as Trustee hereunder (27) without bond.

Paragraph 4.02. Substitute Trustee. The Settlors jointly, or the surviving Settlor upon the death of the predeceased Settlor, may appoint a substitute or successor Trustee to act as Trustee of any trust or trusts created hereunder in the place and stead of, or as successor to, any Trustee named in Section 4.01 above. Such substitution shall be in writing.

Paragraph 4.04. Trustee Liability. No person named as Trustee in this instrument or appointed as Trustee in the manner specified herein shall be liable to any beneficiary or to any heir of either Settlor for the Trustee's acts or failure to act, except for willful misconduct or gross negligence. No such Trustee shall be liable or responsible for any act, omission or default of any other Trustee provided that they shall have had no knowledge of facts that might reasonably be expected to put the Trustee on notice of it.

Paragraph 4.05. Title to Trust Estate. The legal title to all property held in trust hereunder shall be, remain and become vested in the Trustee or successor Trustee from time to time acting hereunder, without any act of conveyance or transfer to or by or acceptance from, any succeeding, retiring or predecessor Trustee; however, any removed or resigning Trustee shall execute and deliver any and all conveyances and documents requested and reasonably necessary to transfer the trust estate and its assets to a successor Trustee. Each successor Trustee from time to time acting hereunder shall have all the rights, powers immunities and authorities, discretionary or otherwise and the duties and obligations herein granted to the original Trustee. No successor Trustee shall be obligated to inquire into or be in any way responsible for the previous administration of any trust created herein or of the trust estate or for any act or default of any predecessor Trustee.

Paragraph 4.06. Powers of Trustee. To carry out the purposes of any trust created under this Trust Declaration, and subject to any limitations stated elsewhere in this Trust Declaration, the Trustee is vested with the following powers with respect to the Trust Estate, and any part of it, in addition to those powers now or hereafter conferred by law.

A. Power to Invest. To invest and reinvest the Trust Estate in every kind of property, real, personal or mixed, and every kind of investment, specifically including but not by way of limitation, corporate obligations of every kind, stocks, preferred or common, shares of investment trusts, investment companies, mutual funds, market index funds and mortgage participations which individuals of prudence, discretion and intelligence acquire for their own account, and any common trust fund administered by any Trustee under this Trust Declaration.

B. Power to Retain Property. To retain any property which was an asset of the Trust Estate during the Settlor's lifetime or received without consideration by the Trustee as long as the Trustee deems advisable whether or not of the character permitted by law for the investment of trust funds. The trust properties and investment need not be diversified and the Trustee shall have no duty to dispose or convert any trust assets to effect diversification.

C. Power to Manage Securities. With respect to securities held in this Trust Declaration, to have all the rights, powers and privileges of an owner, including but not by way of limitation, the power to vote, give proxies and pay assessments, to participate in voting trusts, pooling agreements, foreclosures, reorganizations, consolidations, mergers, liquidations, sales and leases and, incident to such participation, to deposit securities with and transfer title to any protective or other committee on such terms as the Trustee may deem advisable, to exercise and sell stock subscription or conversion rights and to hold securities in "street name".

D. Power of Sale, Exchange, Repair. To manage, control, foreclose, repossess, grant options on, grant easements on, sell (for cash), convey, exchange, partition, divide, improve and repair trust property.

The power to sell, at the termination of the trust, any trust property if the Trustee feels said disposition would assist in the distribution of the trust property at termination.

E. Power to Lease. To lease trust property for terms within or beyond the term of the trust and for any purpose, including exploration for and removal of gas, oil and other minerals; and to enter into community oil leases, pooling and unitization agreements, operating agreements or otherwise, and to create restrictions, easements or other servitudes thereon, to assign, partition, divide, subdivide, transfer to a corporation in exchange for stock, improve, repair, loan, reloan, invest and reinvest the trust estate or any part thereof.

F. Power to Insure. To carry, at the expense of the Trust Estate, insurance of such kinds and in such amounts as the Trustee shall deem advisable to protect the Trust Estate and the Trustee against any hazard.

G. Power to Commence or Defend Litigation. To commence or defend such litigation with respect to the Trust or any property of the Trust Estate as the Trustee may deem advisable, at the expense of the Trust Declaration.

H. Power to Compromise Claim. To compromise or otherwise adjust any claims or litigation against or in favor of the Trust Declaration.

I. Power to Employ Consultants. To employ any custodian, investment advisor, attorney, accountant or other agents to assist the Trustee in administration of this Trust Declaration and to rely upon the advice given by these agents. Reasonable compensation shall be paid to these agents for all services performed.

J. Power to Adjust for Tax Consequences. To take any action and to make any election the Trustee shall deem advisable to minimize the tax liabilities of this trust and its beneficiaries, to allocate the benefits among the various beneficiaries and to make adjustments in the rights of any beneficiaries or group of beneficiaries or between principal and income accounts, to compensate for the consequences of any tax election or any investment decision or administrative decision that has the effect of preferring one beneficiary or group of beneficiaries over others, provided such discretion shall not be exercised in any manner which will cause a loss of or a decrease in any marital or charitable deduction otherwise allowable in computing the then deceased Settlor's federal estate tax.

K. Trust Bank and Securities Accounts. During the joint lives of the Settlors, if the Settlors are serving as co-Trustees hereunder, the signature of either Trustor shall be sufficient to create, negotiate or endorse trust checks or to deposit or withdraw trust funds from trust bank or securities accounts or to trade securities in said securities accounts.

ARTICLE V
MISCELLANEOUS

Paragraph 5.01. No Assignment. Each beneficiary hereunder is hereby prohibited from anticipating, encumbering, assigning or in any other manner, alienating her or his interest in either income or principal of any trust created under this Trust Declaration and is without power to do so nor shall such interest be subject to her or his liabilities or obligations nor to attachment, execution or other legal processes, bankruptcy proceedings or claims of creditors or others. The Trustee may require the personal receipt of a beneficiary as a condition precedent to payment, distribution or delivery of any amount, property or benefit hereunder. The Trustee may, however, deposit in any bank designated in writing, by a beneficiary, to her or his credit, income or principal payable to such beneficiary.

Paragraph 5.02. Principal and Income. Except as otherwise specifically provided in this Trust Declaration, the determination of all matters with respect to what shall constitute principal and income of each trust estate, gross income therefrom and net income distributable under the terms of the Trust Declaration, shall be governed by the provisions of the Revised Uniform Principal and Income Act as enacted in the State of (2a)__________________, from time to time existing. All taxes, assessments, fees, charges and other expenses incurred by the Trustee in the administration, protection and distribution of each trust, shall be a charge upon the trust estate and shall be paid out of the income and/or principal, in accordance with the aforesaid Act.

Paragraph 5.03. Savings Clause. Unless sooner terminated in accordance with other provisions of this Trust Declaration, any trust created hereunder shall terminate twenty-one (21) years after the death of the last surviving member of the group consisting of the Settlor and the issue of the Settlor who are living and in being at the date of death of the Settlor.

Paragraph 5.04. Payments to Minors and Incompetents. The Trustee, in the Trustee's discretion, may apply payments directly for the benefit of any beneficiary, rather than directly to such beneficiary and, in the case of a beneficiary who is a minor or who is under any other disability, make payment to the guardian, conservator of the person or estate of such beneficiary, custodian under the Uniform Transfers to Minors Act, parent or any other suitable adult with whom the beneficiary resides or by expending the same for the care, education, maintenance or other benefit of said beneficiary. In addition, the Trustee, in the Trustee's discretion, may make payments directly to a beneficiary who is a minor if, in the Trustee's judgment, the minor is of sufficient age and maturity to properly manage the money or property so paid. The Trustee shall not be required to see to the application of any such payment so made to any said persons, but his, her or their receipt therefor shall be a full discharge to the Trustee.

Paragraph 5.05. No Physical Segregation. There need be no physical segregation or division of the various trusts except as segregation or division may be required by the termination of any of the trusts or as specifically provided, but the Trustee shall keep separate accounts for the different undivided interests.

Paragraph 5.06. Distribution. In any case in which the Trustee is required, pursuant to the provisions of the Trust, to divide any parts or shares for the purposes of distribution or otherwise, except as the donee of any power of appointment affecting such property may have expressly provided otherwise in the instrument exercising such power, the Trustee is authorized, in the Trustee's absolute discretion, to make the division and distribution (pro rata or otherwise) in kind, including an undivided interest in any property or partly in kind and partly in money, and for this purpose, to make such sales of the trust property as the Trustee may deem necessary, on such terms and conditions as the Trustee shall see fit. Any asset which is encumbered shall be assigned subject thereto, and its value or amount shall be given effect less such indebtedness.

Paragraph 5.07. Non-Pro Rata Distributions. As to distribution or division of property in kind under and for the several trusts, excepting the initial establishment of any trust for a pecuniary amount, the Trustee shall be cognizant of the differences between the tax cost bases and current value and shall endeavor, insofar as is practicable to distribute or set aside to or for each beneficiary or distributee, assets or property carrying amount or portions of the total unrealized taxable gains or losses embodied in all the assets and properties involved commensurate with the share or portion of each beneficiary or distributee.

Paragraph 5.08. Distribution If All Beneficiaries Die Before Full Distribution. If at any time before full distribution of the Trust Estate, the Settlor is deceased and no disposition of the property is directed by this Trust Declaration, the Trust Estate or the portion of it not disposed of under the Trust Declaration, whichever the case may be, shall thereupon be distributed one-half to those persons who would be the legal heirs of Husband and one-half to the legal heirs of Wife their identities and respective shares to be determined as though the death of Husband and Wife had occurred immediately following the event requiring distribution and according to the laws of the State of (2a)__________________ then in effect relating to the succession of separate property not acquired from a parent, grandparent or previously deceased spouse.

Paragraph 5.09. Additional Property. With consent of the Trustee, additional property may be added at any time from any source to any trust held under this Trust Declaration. No person dealing with the Trustee in any manner shall be under any obligation to see to the application of any money paid to the Trustee or to inquire into the validity, expediency or propriety of any act of the Trustee or into any of the provisions of any trust hereunder.

Paragraph 5.10. Fiduciary Capacity. All of the powers of the Trustee provided in this Trust Declaration shall be exercisable by the Trustee in the Trustee's fiduciary capacity and only in such capacity.

Paragraph 5.11. Corporate Office. No person shall, by reason of acting as Trustee, be in any way restricted or prohibited from holding office in any corporation in which any trust under this Trust Declaration holds securities or from receiving compensation from any such corporation for services performed as a director, officer or employee of such corporation or from purchasing, selling or otherwise dealing with the stock of any such corporation for the individual account of such Trustee or from voting the stock of any such corporation held by such trust, including voting those shares in favor of the Settlor or any other person.

Paragraph 5.12. Disclaimer of Powers. The Trustee may disclaim, release or restrict the scope of any power held in connection with any trust created under this Trust Declaration, including any administrative power, whether such power is expressly granted in this Trust Declaration or implied by law, by a written instrument specifying the power to be disclaimed, released or restricted and the nature of any such restriction. Any power disclaimed or released by the Trustee shall be extinguished except to the extent this Trust Declaration expressly provides that such power pass to another. This power shall be personal to the Trustee only and may not be exercised by any other person acting on behalf of the Trustee, including, but not limited to, any Trustee (other than the Trustee), Conservator, agent or guardian.

Paragraph 5.13. Notice. Unless the Trustee has received written notice of the occurrence of an event affecting the beneficial interest in any trust held under this Trust Declaration, the Trustee shall not be liable to any beneficiary of such trust for any distributions made or other actions taken by the Trustee in good faith as though such event had not occurred.

Paragraph 5.14. Invalidity of Any Provision. Should any provision of this Trust Declaration be or become invalid or unenforceable, the remaining provisions of this Trust Declaration shall be and continue to be fully effective.

Paragraph 5.15. Gender and Number. Except as provided otherwise herein, the masculine, feminine and neuter gender, and the singular or plural number, shall each be deemed to include the others whenever the context so indicates.

Paragraph 5.16. Law of Construction of Trust. This Trust Declaration, its validity, the construction of and all rights under the Trusts provided for in this Trust Declaration shall be governed by the laws of the State of (2a) ________________.

Paragraph 5.17. No Contest. The Settlors have intentionally and with full knowledge omitted to provide for their issue, ancestors, relatives and heirs living at the time of their demise, except for such provisions as are made specifically herein.

If any person who is or claims under or through a beneficiary of this Trust, or if any person who would be entitled to share in the Settlors' estate if either or both of the Settlors died intestate, should in any manner whatsoever, directly or indirectly, attack, contest or seek to impair or invalidate in court any provision of the following:

A. This Trust or any Amendment to this Trust;

B. Any Will or Codicil to any Will executed by either Settlor;

C. Any beneficiary designation executed by either Settlor with respect to any insurance policy, any "Totten trust" account, any joint tenancy or tenancy by the entirety, any "transfer on death" account or any pension plan, or conspire or cooperate with anyone attempting to do any of the actions or things aforesaid, then each such person and any devise, share or interest in the Trust or either Settlor's Estate otherwise given to each such person under this Trust or either Settlor's Estate to which each such person might be entitled by law, is hereby revoked and shall pass and be distributed as though each such person had predeceased the both Settlors leaving no issue or heirs whatsoever.

Any and every individual who asserts, or conspires or cooperates with any person who asserts, any claim against this Trust or the Estate of either Settlor of this Trust based on:

D. "Quantum meruit" theory;

E. Common law marriage, Marvin v. Marvin, 18 Cal. 3d 660 (1976) type of agreement or similar theory;

F. Constructive trust theory; or,

G. Oral agreement or written agreement which is to be proved by parole evidence, claiming that Settlor agreed to gift or devise anything to such person or to pay such person or another for services rendered, regardless of whether a court may find that such agreement existed, then each such person is disinherited and any devise, share or interest in this Trust or either Settlor's Estate otherwise given to each such person under this Trust or either Settlor's Estate or to which each such person might be entitled by law, is hereby revoked and shall pass and be distributed as though each such person had predeceased both Settlors leaving no issue or heirs whatsoever.

The Trustee is specifically authorized to defend any such attack, contest, claim or other proceeding of any nature concerning this Trust or of any provision hereof, and to employ legal counsel therefor, all at the expense of the Trust.

Paragraph 5.18. Survival. If any person fails to survive a Settlor by thirty (30) days, for all purposes of this Trust Declaration the person shall be considered to have predeceased such Settlor.

Paragraph 5.19. All typed and handwritten "fill-ins" where directed above were made before the execution of this Declaration of Trust and are not initialed by the Settlors. All crossed through words and inter-lineations were made before the execution of this Trust and are initialed by the Settlors.

CERTIFICATION OF HUSBAND AND WIFE

We, and each of us, certify that:

A.We, and each of us, have read the foregoing Trust Declaration;

B. The foregoing Trust Declaration correctly states the terms and conditions under which the Trust Estate is to be held, managed, administered and disposed of by the Trustee;

C. As the Settlors named in such Trust Declaration, we, and each of us, approve such Trust Declaration in all particulars; and

D. As the Trustees named in such Trust Declaration, we, and each of us, approve and accept the Trust provided for in such Declaration.

Dated: (40)______________________________

(1)______________________________, Settlor, Trustee

(1b)______________________________

(4)______________________________, Settlor, Trustee

STATE OF (2a)________________________)
) ss.
COUNTY OF (2)________________________)

On________________, 200__ before me, the undersigned, a Notary Public in and for said county and state, personally appeared (1)____________ and (4)____________, personally known to me (or proved to me on the basis of satisfactory evidence) to be the person(s) whose name(s) is/are subscribed to the within instrument and acknowledged that he/she/they executed the same in his/her/their authorized capacity(ies), and that by his/her/their signature(s) on the instrument the person(s), or the entity upon behalf of which the person(s) acted, executed the instrument.

WITNESS my hand and official seal.

____

Notary Public in and for said County and State

EXHIBIT A

Property Declared to be assets of the (1a)____ TRUST dated (48)________________:

(55)
1.

INTER-VIVOS TRUST

THE (1a)__________________________ TRUST

The Settlors named below hereby declare as follows:

ARTICLE I
ESTABLISHMENT OF TRUST

Paragraph 1.01. Creation of Trust. This Trust Declaration has been entered into between (1)__________________and (4)___________________ as Settlors and themselves as the Trustees. The Settlors, of (2)______________________ County, (2a)____________, have transferred, or will transfer, to the Trustee of this Trust Declaration the property described in the attached Exhibit "A" which will constitute, together with any other property that may be added to this Trust Declaration, the Trust Estate of an express trust which shall be held, administered and distributed by the Trustee as provided in this Trust Declaration.

Paragraph 1.02. Trust Name. This Trust Declaration shall be known as the (1a)"________________________________ TRUST" dated (48)__________________________.

Paragraph 1.03. Definitions. As used in this Trust Declaration:

A. Husband: The term "Husband" shall mean (1)___________.

B. Wife: The term "Wife" shall mean (4)________________.

C. Settlors: The term "Settlors" shall refer collectively to Husband and Wife.

D. Deceased Settlor: The term "deceased Settlor" shall refer to the Settlor who is first to die. However, the term, "then deceased Settlor" shall refer to the Settlor then deceased and may thus refer to the otherwise surviving Settlor.

E. Surviving Settlor: The term "surviving Settlor" shall refer to the Settlor who is last to die.

F. Trustee: The term "Trustee" or "Trustees" shall refer to whoever is serving as Trustee or Trustees under this Trust Declaration.

G. Trust Estate: The term "Trust Estate" shall refer to the property subject to this Trust Declaration.

Paragraph 1.04. Property to Retain Status. All property now or hereafter transferred to the Trustee which was community property, quasi-community property or separate property at the time of such transfer, shall remain, respectively, community property, quasi-community property or the separate property of the spouse or spouses transferring such property to the Trustee.

ARTICLE II
OPERATION OF TRUST DURING THE LIFE OF HUSBAND AND WIFE

Paragraph 2.01. Net Income. During the life of Husband and/or Wife, the Trustee shall pay to or apply for the benefit of both Husband and Wife, or the survivor thereof, in monthly or more frequent intervals, all of the net income of the community Trust Estate and shall pay to or apply for the benefit of the contributing spouse, in monthly or more frequent intervals, all of the net income of the separate property contributed or owned by that spouse.

Paragraph 2.02. Withdrawal of Principal. During the life of Husband and/or Wife, the Trustee shall also pay to or apply for the benefit of both Husband and Wife, or either, or the survivor thereof, so much of the community principal of the Trust Estate, up to the whole thereof, as both Husband and Wife shall direct, and shall, at the discretion of a spouse, pay to or apply for the benefit of that spouse so much of the principal of the Trust Estate, up to the whole thereof, as is that spouse's separate property.

Paragraph 2.03. Incapacity of Husband or Wife. If, at any time either Husband or Wife has become physically or mentally incapacitated so as to be unable to manage his or her affairs, whether or not a court of competent jurisdiction has declared him or her incompetent, mentally ill, or in need of a conservator, the Trustee shall pay to the non-incapacitated spouse or apply for the benefit of either spouse such amounts of the principal and/or income of the community estate as may be necessary, in the Trustee's discretion, for the care, maintenance and support of both spouses in accordance with their accustomed manner of living. The Trustee shall also pay to or apply for the benefit of the incapacitated spouse such amounts of income or principal of the separate property contributed by the incapacitated spouse as may be necessary, in the Trustee's discretion, for the care, maintenance, and support of the incapacitated spouse in accordance with his or her accustomed manner of living, taking into account payments made by the Trustee from the community Trust Estate. If a conservator of the person or estate is appointed for the incapacitated spouse, the Trustee shall take into account any payments made for the incapacitated spouse's benefit by the conservator.

The payments specified in this Section shall be made until the incapacitated spouse is again able to manage his or her own affairs, or until the death of the first spouse to die, whichever event may occur earlier.

Paragraph 2.04. Revocation of Trust. At any time during their joint lives, either Husband or Wife as to community property, and either spouse as to his or her separate property, may, by serving written notice on the Trustee, revoke the Trust created by this Trust Declaration, in whole or in part. Any community property withdrawn from the Trust Estate by reason of any such revocation shall be delivered by the Trustee to both Husband and Wife and any separate property withdrawn from the Trust shall be delivered by the Trustee to the spouse revoking the Trust.

Paragraph 2.05. Amendment of Trust. At any time during their joint lives, Husband and Wife, jointly as to community property, and either spouse as to his or her separate property, may, by serving written notice on the Trustee, alter, modify or amend the Trust created by this Trust Declaration in any respect. After the death of the deceased Settlor the surviving Settlor may, by serving written notice on the Trustee, alter, modify or amend the Trust created by this Trust Declaration in any respect.

ARTICLE III
OPERATION OF TRUST AFTER DEATH OF DECEASED SETTLOR AND DEATH OF SURVIVING SETTLOR

Paragraph 3.01. Collection of Assets and Payment of Debts: On the death of each Settlor the Trustee shall collect all assets belonging to the Trust Estate. As soon as practicable after the death of each Settlor the Trustee, except as otherwise provided herein, shall pay from the Trust Estate the just debts of the then deceased Settlor, as the case may be, (excluding any debts barred by provisions of law or not yet due), funeral expenses of the then deceased Settlor, and any inheritance, estate, or other death taxes that shall, by reason of the death of the then deceased Settlor, be attributable to the Trust Estate. This is not and shall not constitute a direction to pay all inheritance, estate or other death taxes from or charge the same to, the Trust Estate without apportionment.

Upon the death of the deceased Settlor all assets subject to this Declaration of Trust shall be and are confirmed as the separate property of the surviving Settlor.

Paragraph 3.02. Distribution of Trust Estate. Upon the death of the surviving Settlor, and after payment of expenses as set forth in Paragraph 3.01, the Trustee shall hold, administer and distribute the Trust Estate as follows:

A. The Trustee shall distribute to the following persons the cash amount listed after their respective names:
(10)

B. The Trustee shall distribute to the following persons the real property described after their respective names. (12) Said real property is given free of all encumbrances or liens thereon.
(11)

C. The Trustee shall distribute to (13)_____________________ a life estate in the following property located at: (14)____________________________. After the death of (13)______________________ said property shall go, outright, to (15)________________________________ as the remainder person(s).

D. The Trustee shall distribute all of the rest, residue and remainder of the Trust Estate, real, personal and mixed, of whatsoever kind or character and wheresoever situated, to the following persons or entities (16) in the proportions listed after their names (17) in equal shares.
(18)

(19)_______ shares to the Trustee hereinafter named, to have and to hold for the benefit of (20)______________ upon the uses, trusts, purposes and conditions hereinafter provided.

1. If (20)_________________ should at any time or from time to time be in need, in the discretion of the Trustee, of funds due to illness, infirmity or other physical or mental disability or any emergency, the Trustee may relieve or contribute toward the relief of any such need or needs of (20)___________________by paying to him or her or using and applying for his or her benefit, such sum or sums out of the income and/or principal of his or her trust as the Trustee, in the Trustee's discretion, may deem necessary or advisable.

2. The Trustee shall pay (20)______________________ all of the net income, in monthly or other convenient installments, from the trust.

3. (20)_________________________shall have the right to require the Trustee to convert any non-income producing asset into an income producing asset.

4. Upon the death of (20)________________________ the Trustee shall distribute any accrued but undistributed income to my spouse's estate. The Trustee shall distribute, free of trust, the remaining trust properties to: (23)___________________________________.

E. Distribution of Trust Assets. With respect to the distribution of any trust estate upon termination of any trust, and partial distribution of any trust, the liquidation and distribution by the Trustee of the Trust Estate involved or the distributable portion shall commence immediately and be accomplished as rapidly as possible, and deliveries of the trust properties to the beneficiary or beneficiaries may be made in installments or series, retaining only reasonable reserves for final charges and expenses. In no event shall it be necessary for the Trustee to await an accounting to the Court, or any Court order, before releasing and distributing the majority of the Trust Estate to be distributed.

F. Undistributed Income. All the net income of the respective trusts or trust estates, not distributed, used or applied as otherwise provided herein, shall be accumulated and added to the principals of the respective trusts.

Upon the change or succession of any beneficiary, distribution of trust properties or any trust estate or any portion thereof, or upon setting aside, apportionment or division of any trust estate or upon the termination of a trust or any interest therein, the beneficial interest, properties or balance of trust estate at the applicable time and to be dealt with shall include any and all income accumulated, accrued, uncollected or held undistributed and all of such income shall likewise be distributed, set aside or apportioned to the next or succeeding beneficiaries, distributees, shares or trusts, retaining its character as income.

ARTICLE IV

TRUSTEES

Paragraph 4.01. Appointment of Trustees. Settlors, (1)____________________ and (4)____________________ are appointed and confirmed as the Trustees, without bond. In the event either original Trustee should resign, die or become mentally incapacitated, the remaining Trustee shall act as sole Trustee. If either original Trustee should cease to act as Trustee due to a mental incapacity, his/her restoration of mental capacity shall result in his or her immediate return as Trustee or Co-Trustee hereunder. If either original Trustee should cease to act as sole Trustee or a Co-Trustee with the other original Trustee due to his/her resignation, he/she may at any time subsequent, elect to act again as sole Trustee or a Co-Trustee with the other original Trustee. Said election shall be made by filing same with either of the then acting Trustee or by recording said election in the County of residence of said Trustee making such election.

In the event both (1)__________________ and (4)_____________should die, refuse to act, or for any other reason be unable to act, then (25)____________________ shall act as (26)____Trustee_ hereunder (27) without bond. In the event he/she/they should die, decline to act, or for any other reason, be unable to act as Trustee then (28)___________________________ shall act as Trustee hereunder (27) without bond.

Paragraph 4.02. Substitute Trustee. The Settlors jointly, or the surviving Settlor upon the death of the predeceased Settlor, may appoint a substitute or successor Trustee to act as Trustee of any trust or trusts created hereunder in the place and stead of, or as successor to, any Trustee named in Section 4.01 above. Such substitution shall be in writing.

Paragraph 4.03. Trustee Liability. No person named as Trustee in this instrument or appointed as Trustee in the manner specified herein shall be liable to any beneficiary or to any heir of either Settlor for the Trustee's acts or failure to act, except for willful misconduct or gross negligence. No such Trustee shall be liable or responsible for any act, omission or default of any other Trustee provided that they shall have had no knowledge of facts that might reasonably be expected to put the Trustee on notice of it.

Paragraph 4.04. Title to Trust Estate. The legal title to all property held in trust hereunder shall be, remain and become vested in the Trustee or successor Trustee from time to time acting hereunder, without any act of conveyance or transfer to or by or acceptance from, any succeeding, retiring or predecessor Trustee; however, any removed or resigning Trustee shall execute and deliver any and all conveyances and documents requested and reasonably necessary to transfer the trust estate and its assets to a successor Trustee. Each successor Trustee from time to time acting hereunder shall have all the rights, powers immunities and authorities, discretionary or otherwise and the duties and obligations herein granted to the original Trustee. No successor Trustee shall be obligated to inquire into or be in any way responsible for the previous administration of any trust created herein or of the trust estate or for any act or default of any predecessor Trustee.

Paragraph 4.05. Powers of Trustee. To carry out the purposes of any trust created under this Trust Declaration, and subject to any limitations stated elsewhere in this Trust Declaration, the Trustee is vested with the following powers with respect to the Trust Estate, and any part of it, in addition to those powers now or hereafter conferred by law.

A. Power to Invest. To invest and reinvest the Trust Estate in every kind of property, real, personal or mixed, and every kind of investment, specifically including but not by way of limitation, corporate obligations of every kind, stocks, preferred or common, shares of investment trusts, investment companies, mutual funds, market index funds and mortgage participations which individuals of prudence, discretion and intelligence acquire for their own account, and any common trust fund administered by any Trustee under this Trust Declaration.

B. Power to Retain Property. To retain any property which was an asset of the Trust Estate during the Settlor's lifetime or received without consideration by the Trustee as long as the Trustee deems advisable whether or not of the character permitted by law for the investment of trust funds. The trust properties and investment need not be diversified and the Trustee shall have no duty to dispose or convert any trust assets to effect diversification.

C. Power to Manage Securities. With respect to securities held in this Trust Declaration, to have all the rights, powers and privileges of an owner, including but not by way of limitation, the power to vote, give proxies and pay assessments, to participate in voting trusts, pooling agreements, foreclosures, reorganizations, consolidations, mergers, liquidations, sales and leases and, incident to such participation, to deposit securities with and transfer title to any protective or other committee on such terms as the Trustee may deem advisable, to exercise and sell stock subscription or conversion rights and to hold securities in "street name".

D. Power of Sale, Exchange, Repair. To manage, control, foreclose, repossess, grant options on, grant easements on, sell (for cash), convey, exchange, partition, divide, improve and repair trust property.

The power to sell, at the termination of the trust, any trust property if the Trustee feels said disposition would assist in the distribution of the trust property at termination.

E. Power to Lease. To lease trust property for terms within or beyond the term of the trust and for any purpose, including exploration for and removal of gas, oil and other minerals; and to enter into community oil leases, pooling and unitization agreements, operating agreements or otherwise, and to create restrictions, easements or other servitudes thereon, to assign, partition, divide, subdivide, transfer to a corporation in exchange for stock, improve, repair, loan, reloan, invest and reinvest the trust estate or any part thereof.

F. Power to Insure. To carry, at the expense of the Trust Estate, insurance of such kinds and in such amounts as the Trustee shall deem advisable to protect the Trust Estate and the Trustee against any hazard.

G. Power to Commence or Defend Litigation. To commence or defend such litigation with respect to the Trust or any property of the Trust Estate as the Trustee may deem advisable, at the expense of the Trust Declaration.

H. Power to Compromise Claim. To compromise or otherwise adjust any claims or litigation against or in favor of the Trust Declaration.

I. Power to Employ Consultants. To employ any custodian, investment advisor, attorney, accountant or other agents to assist the Trustee in administration of this Trust Declaration and to rely upon the advice given by these agents. Reasonable compensation shall be paid to these agents for all services performed.

J. Power to Adjust for Tax Consequences. To take any action and to make any election the Trustee shall deem advisable to minimize the tax liabilities of this trust and its beneficiaries, to allocate the benefits among the various beneficiaries and to make adjustments in the rights of any beneficiaries or group of beneficiaries or between principal and income accounts, to compensate for the consequences of any tax election or any investment decision or administrative decision that has the effect of preferring one beneficiary or group of beneficiaries over others, provided such discretion shall not be exercised in any manner which will cause a loss of or a decrease in any marital or charitable deduction otherwise allowable in computing the then deceased Settlor's federal estate tax.

K. Trust Bank and Securities Accounts. During the joint lives of the Settlors, if the Settlors are serving as co-Trustees hereunder, the signature of either Trustor shall be sufficient to create, negotiate or endorse trust checks or to deposit or withdraw trust funds from trust bank or securities accounts or to trade securities in said securities accounts.

ARTICLE V
MISCELLANEOUS

Paragraph 5.01. No Assignment. Each beneficiary hereunder is hereby prohibited from anticipating, encumbering, assigning or in any other manner, alienating her or his interest in either income or principal of any trust created under this Trust Declaration and is without power to do so nor shall such interest be subject to her or his liabilities or obligations nor to attachment, execution or other legal processes, bankruptcy proceedings or claims of creditors or others. The Trustee may require the personal receipt of a beneficiary as a condition precedent to payment, distribution or delivery of any amount, property or benefit hereunder. The Trustee may, however, deposit in any bank designated in writing, by a beneficiary, to her or his credit, income or principal payable to such beneficiary.

Paragraph 5.02. Principal and Income. Except as otherwise specifically provided in this Trust Declaration, the determination of all matters with respect to what shall constitute principal and income of each trust estate, gross income therefrom and net income distributable under the terms of the Trust Declaration, shall be governed by the provisions of the Revised Uniform Principal and Income Act as enacted in the State of (2a)____________________, from time to time existing. All taxes, assessments, fees, charges and other expenses incurred by the Trustee in the administration, protection and distribution of each trust, shall be a charge upon the trust estate and shall be paid out of the income and/or principal, in accordance with the aforesaid Act.

Paragraph 5.03. Savings Clause. Unless sooner terminated in accordance with other provisions of this Trust Declaration, any trust created hereunder shall terminate twenty-one (21) years after the death of the last surviving member of the group consisting of the Settlor and the issue of the Settlor who are living and in being at the date of death of the Settlor.

Paragraph 5.04. Payments to Minors and Incompetents. The Trustee, in the Trustee's discretion, may apply payments directly for the benefit of any beneficiary, rather than directly to such beneficiary and, in the case of a beneficiary who is a minor or who is under any other disability, make payment to the guardian, conservator of the person or estate of such beneficiary, custodian under the Uniform Transfers to Minors Act, parent or any other suitable adult with whom the beneficiary resides or by expending the same for the care, education, maintenance or other benefit of said beneficiary. In addition, the Trustee, in the Trustee's discretion, may make payments directly to a beneficiary who is a minor if, in the Trustee's judgment, the minor is of sufficient age and maturity to properly manage the money or property so paid. The Trustee shall not be required to see to the application of any such payment so made to any said persons, but his, her or their receipt therefor shall be a full discharge to the Trustee.

Paragraph 5.05. No Physical Segregation. There need be no physical segregation or division of the various trusts except as segregation or division may be required by the termination of any of the trusts or as specifically provided, but the Trustee shall keep separate accounts for the different undivided interests.

Paragraph 5.06. Distribution. In any case in which the Trustee is required, pursuant to the provisions of the Trust, to divide any parts or shares for the purposes of distribution or otherwise, except as the donee of any power of appointment affecting such property may have expressly provided otherwise in the instrument exercising such power, the Trustee is authorized, in the Trustee's absolute discretion, to make the division and distribution (pro rata or otherwise) in kind, including an undivided interest in any property or partly in kind and partly in money, and for this purpose, to make such sales of the trust property as the Trustee may deem necessary, on such terms and conditions as the Trustee shall see fit. Any asset which is encumbered shall be assigned subject thereto, and its value or amount shall be given effect less such indebtedness.

Paragraph 5.07. Non-Pro Rata Distributions. As to distribution or division of property in kind under and for the several trusts, excepting the initial establishment of any trust for a pecuniary amount, the Trustee shall be cognizant of the differences between the tax cost bases and current value and shall endeavor, insofar as is practicable to distribute or set aside to or for each beneficiary or distributee, assets or property carrying amount or portions of the total unrealized taxable gains or losses embodied in all the assets and properties involved commensurate with the share or portion of each beneficiary or distributee.

Paragraph 5.08. Distribution If All Beneficiaries Die Before Full Distribution. If at any time before full distribution of the Trust Estate, the Settlor is deceased and no disposition of the property is directed by this Trust Declaration, the Trust Estate or the portion of it not disposed of under the Trust Declaration, whichever the case may be, shall thereupon be distributed one-half to those persons who would be the legal heirs of Husband and one-half to the legal heirs of Wife their identities and respective shares to be determined as though the death of Husband and Wife had occurred immediately following the event requiring distribution and according to the laws of the State of (2a)__________________ then in effect relating to the succession of separate property not acquired from a parent, grandparent or previously deceased spouse.

Paragraph 5.09. Additional Property. With consent of the Trustee, additional property may be added at any time from any source to any trust held under this Trust Declaration. No person dealing with the Trustee in any manner shall be under any obligation to see to the application of any money paid to the Trustee or to inquire into the validity, expediency or propriety of any act of the Trustee or into any of the provisions of any trust hereunder.

Paragraph 5.10. Fiduciary Capacity. All of the powers of the Trustee provided in this Trust Declaration shall be exercisable by the Trustee in the Trustee's fiduciary capacity and only in such capacity.

Paragraph 5.11. Corporate Office. No person shall, by reason of acting as Trustee, be in any way restricted or prohibited from holding office in any corporation in which any trust under this Trust Declaration holds securities or from receiving compensation from any such corporation for services performed as a director, officer or employee of such corporation or from purchasing, selling or otherwise dealing with the stock of any such corporation for the individual account of such Trustee or from voting the stock of any such corporation held by such trust, including voting those shares in favor of the Settlor or any other person.

Paragraph 5.12. Disclaimer of Powers. The Trustee may disclaim, release or restrict the scope of any power held in connection with any trust created under this Trust Declaration, including any administrative power, whether such power is expressly granted in this Trust Declaration or implied by law, by a written instrument specifying the power to be disclaimed, released or restricted and the nature of any such restriction. Any power disclaimed or released by the Trustee shall be extinguished except to the extent this Trust Declaration expressly provides that such power pass to another. This power shall be personal to the Trustee only and may not be exercised by any other person acting on behalf of the Trustee, including, but not limited to, any Trustee (other than the Trustee), Conservator, agent or guardian.

Paragraph 5.13. Notice. Unless the Trustee has received written notice of the occurrence of an event affecting the beneficial interest in any trust held under this Trust Declaration, the Trustee shall not be liable to any beneficiary of such trust for any distributions made or other actions taken by the Trustee in good faith as though such event had not occurred.

Paragraph 5.14. Invalidity of Any Provision. Should any provision of this Trust Declaration be or become invalid or unenforceable, the remaining provisions of this Trust Declaration shall be and continue to be fully effective.

Paragraph 5.15. Gender and Number. Except as provided otherwise herein, the masculine, feminine and neuter gender, and the singular or plural number, shall each be deemed to include the others whenever the context so indicates.

Paragraph 5.16. Law of Construction of Trust. This Trust Declaration, its validity, the construction of and all rights under the Trusts provided for in this Trust Declaration shall be governed by the laws of the State of (2a)__________________.

Paragraph 5.17. No Contest. The Settlors have intentionally and with full knowledge omitted to provide for his/her issue, ancestors, relatives and heirs living at the time of his/her demise, except for such provisions as are made specifically herein.

If any person who is or claims under or through a beneficiary of this Trust, or if any person who would be entitled to share in either Settlor's estate if either or both Settlors died intestate, should in any manner whatsoever, directly or indirectly, attack, contest or seek to impair or invalidate in court any provision of the following:

A. This Trust or any Amendment to this Trust;

B. Any Will or Codicil to any Will executed by either Settlor;

C. Any beneficiary designation executed by either Settlor with respect to any insurance policy, any "Totten trust" account, any joint tenancy or tenancy by the entirety, any "transfer on death" account or any pension plan, or conspire or cooperate with anyone attempting to do any of the actions or things aforesaid, then each such person and any devise, share or interest in the Trust or either Settlor's Estate otherwise given to each such person under this Trust or either Settlor's Estate to which each such person might be entitled by law, is hereby revoked and shall pass and be distributed as though each such person had predeceased either Settlor leaving no issue or heirs whatsoever.

Any and every individual who asserts, or conspires or cooperates with any person who asserts, any claim against this Trust or the Estate of either Settlor of this Trust based on:

D. "Quantum meruit" theory;

E. Common law marriage, Marvin v. Marvin, 18 Cal. 3d 660 (1976) type of agreement or similar theory;

F. Constructive trust theory; or,

G. Oral agreement or written agreement which is to be proved by parole evidence, claiming that either Settlor agreed to gift or devise anything to such person or to pay such person or another for services rendered, regardless of whether a court may find that such agreement existed, then each such person is disinherited and any devise, share or interest in this Trust or either Settlor's Estate otherwise given to each such person under this Trust or either Settlor's Estate or to which each such person might be entitled by law, is hereby revoked and shall pass and be distributed as though each such person had predeceased both Settlors leaving no issue or heirs whatsoever.

The Trustee is specifically authorized to defend any such attack, contest, claim or other proceeding of any nature concerning this Trust or of any provision hereof, and to employ legal counsel therefor, all at the expense of the Trust.

Paragraph 5.18. Survival. If any person fails to survive a Settlor by thirty (30) days, for all purposes of this Trust Declaration the person shall be considered to have predeceased such Settlor.

Paragraph 5.19. All typed and handwritten "fill-ins" where directed above were made before the execution of this Declaration of Trust and are not initialed by the Settlors. All crossed through words and inter-lineations were made before the execution of this Will and are initialed by the Settlors.

CERTIFICATION OF HUSBAND AND WIFE

We, and each of us, certify that:

A. We, and each of us, have read the foregoing Trust Declaration;

B. The foregoing Trust Declaration correctly states the terms and conditions under which the Trust Estate is to be held, managed, administered and disposed of by the Trustee;

C. As the Settlors named in such Trust Declaration, we, and each of us, approve such Trust Declaration in all particulars; and

D. As the Trustees named in such Trust Declaration, we, and each of us, approve and accept the Trust provided for in such Declaration.

Dated: (40)______________________________

(1)________________________________,Settlor, Trustee

(1b)______________________________

(4)________________________________, Settlor, Trustee

STATE OF (2a)______________________)
) ss.
COUNTY OF (2)______________________)

On______________, 200__ before me, the undersigned, a Notary Public in and for said county and state, personally appeared (1)______________ and (4)_____________, personally known to me (or proved to me on the basis of satisfactory evidence) to be the person(s) whose name(s) is/are subscribed to the within instrument and acknowledged that he/she/they executed the same in his/her/their authorized capacity(ies), and that by his/her/their signature(s) on the instrument the person(s), or the entity upon behalf of which the person(s) acted, executed the instrument.

WITNESS my hand and official seal.

____

Notary Public in and for said County and State

EXHIBIT A

Property Declared to be assets of the (1a)________________________________ TRUST dated (48)________________:

(55)

1.

INTER-VIVOS TRUST

THE (1a) Holmes Family TRUST

The Settlors named below hereby declare as follows:

ARTICLE I
ESTABLISHMENT OF TRUST

Paragraph 1.01. Creation of Trust. This Trust Declaration has been entered into between (1) Leigh and (4) Sally as Settlors and themselves as the Trustees. The Settlors, of (2) Comanche County, (2a) Ok, have transferred, or will transfer, to the Trustee of this Trust Declaration the property described in the attached Exhibit "A" which will constitute, together with any other property that may be added to this Trust Declaration, the Trust Estate of an express trust which shall be held, administered and distributed by the Trustee as provided in this Trust Declaration.

Paragraph 1.02. Trust Name. This Trust Declaration shall be known as the (1a)"Holmes Family TRUST" dated (48) ?.

Paragraph 1.03. Definitions. As used in this Trust Declaration:

A. Husband: The term "Husband" shall mean (1) Leigh.

B. Wife: The term "Wife" shall mean (4) Sally.

C. Settlors: The term "Settlors" shall refer collectively to Husband and Wife.

D. Deceased Settlor: The term "deceased Settlor" shall refer to the Settlor who is first to die. However, the term, "then deceased Settlor" shall refer to the Settlor then deceased and may thus refer to the otherwise surviving Settlor.

E. Surviving Settlor: The term "surviving Settlor" shall refer to the Settlor who is last to die.

F. Trustee: The term "Trustee" or "Trustees" shall refer to whoever is serving as Trustee or Trustees under this Trust Declaration.

G. Trust Estate: The term "Trust Estate" shall refer to the property subject to this Trust Declaration.

Paragraph 1.04. Property to Retain Status. All property now or hereafter transferred to the Trustee which was community property, quasi-community property or separate property at the time of such transfer, shall remain, respectively, community property, quasi-community property or the separate property of the spouse or spouses transferring such property to the Trustee.

ARTICLE II
OPERATION OF TRUST DURING THE LIFE OF HUSBAND AND WIFE

Paragraph 2.01. Net Income. During the life of Husband and/or Wife, the Trustee shall pay to or apply for the benefit of both Husband and Wife, or the survivor thereof, in monthly or more frequent intervals, all of the net income of the community Trust Estate and shall pay to or apply for the benefit of the contributing spouse, in monthly or more frequent intervals, all of the net income of the separate property contributed or owned by that spouse.

Paragraph 2.02. Withdrawal of Principal. During the life of Husband and/or Wife, the Trustee shall also pay to or apply for the benefit of both Husband and Wife, or either, or the survivor thereof, so much of the community principal of the Trust Estate, up to the whole thereof, as both Husband and Wife shall direct, and shall, at the discretion of a spouse, pay to or apply for the benefit of that spouse so much of the principal of the Trust Estate, up to the whole thereof, as is that spouse's separate property.

Paragraph 2.03. Incapacity of Husband or Wife. If, at any time either Husband or Wife has become physically or mentally incapacitated so as to be unable to manage his or her affairs, whether or not a court of competent jurisdiction has declared him or her incompetent, mentally ill, or in need of a conservator, the Trustee shall pay to the non-incapacitated spouse or apply for the benefit of either spouse such amounts of the principal and/or income of the community estate as may be necessary, in the Trustee's discretion, for the care, maintenance and support of both spouses in accordance with their accustomed manner of living. The Trustee shall also pay to or apply for the benefit of the incapacitated spouse such amounts of income or principal of the separate property contributed by the incapacitated spouse as may be necessary, in the Trustee's discretion, for the care, maintenance, and support of the incapacitated spouse in accordance with his or her accustomed manner of living, taking into account payments made by the Trustee from the community Trust Estate. If a conservator of the person or estate is appointed for the incapacitated spouse, the Trustee shall take into account any payments made for the incapacitated spouse's benefit by the conservator.

The payments specified in this Section shall be made until the incapacitated spouse is again able to manage his or her own affairs, or until the death of the first spouse to die, whichever event may occur earlier.

Paragraph 2.04. Revocation of Trust. At any time during their joint lives, either Husband or Wife as to community property, and either spouse as to his or her separate property, may, by serving written notice on the Trustee, revoke the Trust created by this Trust Declaration, in whole or in part. Any community property withdrawn from the Trust Estate by reason of any such revocation shall be delivered by the Trustee to both Husband and Wife and any separate property withdrawn from the Trust shall be delivered by the Trustee to the spouse revoking the Trust.

Paragraph 2.05. Amendment of Trust. At any time during their joint lives, Husband and Wife, jointly as to community property, and either spouse as to his or her separate property, may, by serving written notice on the Trustee, alter, modify or amend the Trust created by this Trust Declaration in any respect.

ARTICLE III

OPERATION OF TRUST AFTER DEATH OF DECEASED SETTLOR

Paragraph 3.01. Collection of Assets and Payment of Deceased Settlor's Debts. On the death of the deceased Settlor the Trustee shall collect all assets belonging to the Trust Estate. As soon as practicable after the death of the deceased settlor, the Trustee, except as otherwise provided herein, shall pay from the deceased settlor's share of the Trust Estate the just debts of the deceased settlor (excluding any debts barred by provisions of law or not yet due), funeral expenses of the deceased Settlor, and any inheritance, estate, or other death taxes that shall, by reason of the death of the deceased Settlor, be attributable to the Trust Estate. This is not and shall not constitute a direction to pay all inheritance, estate or other death taxes from or charge the same to, the Trust Estate without apportionment.

Paragraph 3.02. Trust to Continue. On the death of the deceased settlor, the Trustee shall divide the Trust Estate into two separate trusts. Such trusts shall be designated as the *Decedent's Trust* and the *Survivor's Trust.*

A. Decedent's trust. The *Decedent's Trust* shall be created from the deceased Settlor's interest in community property and quasi-community property and the separate property of the deceased Settlor which is included in the Trust Estate.

1. Allocation to *Decedent's Trust.* The *Decedent's Trust* shall be a unified credit trust, the principal of which shall consist of a pecuniary amount equal to the unused unified credit available at the time of the death of the deceased settlor under IRC Section 2010, as amended, plus any property disclaimed by the surviving settlor after taking into account:

(i) All deductions taken in determining the estate tax payable by reason of the deceased Settlor's death;

(ii) The net value of all other property, whether or not it is disposed of under this Trust and whether it passes at the time of the deceased Settlor's death or has passed before the deceased Settlor's death to or in trust for the surviving Settlor, so that it is included in the deceased Settlor's gross estate and does not qualify for the federal estate tax marital deduction. In determining the amount of Trust, however, disclaimers by the surviving Settlor shall be disregarded; and

(iii) All credits allowed for federal estate tax purposes.

The Trustee shall satisfy the amount so determined in cash or in kind, or partly in each, and shall allocate to this Trust any assets of the deceased Settlor contributed or added to the trust that are not eligible for the federal estate tax marital deduction. Assets allocated in kind shall be considered to satisfy this amount on the basis of their net fair market values at the date or dates of allocation to this Trust.

The Trustee shall select and allocate the cash, securities and other property, including real estate and interests therein, which shall constitute the trust, employing for the purpose values current at the time or times of allocation.

2. Revocation and Modification of the *Decedent's Trust* After Death of Deceased Settlor. The *Decedent's Trust* shall be irrevocable and may not be amended or modified in any respect after the death of the deceased Settlor.

B. Survivor's Trust.

1. Allocation to Survivor's Trust. The *Survivor's Trust* shall consist of the balance of the Trust Estate.

2. Revocation and Modification of Survivor's Trust. The surviving Settlor shall have the power to amend, revoke or terminate the *Survivor's Trust* exercisable by delivery of written notice to the Trustee. The surviving Settlor shall have the power to amend, revoke or terminate the *Survivor's Trust* exercisable by delivery of written notice to the Trustee. On revocation or termination of the *Survivor's Trust,* the Trustee shall deliver all of the assets of the *Survivor's Trust* to the surviving Settlor. On the death of the surviving Settlor, the *Survivor's Trust* shall be irrevocable and may not be amended or modified in any respect.

C. Distribution of Trust Estate.

1. The Trustee shall pay to or apply for the benefit of the surviving Settlor all the net income of the *Decedent's Trust* and *Survivor's Trust,* in monthly or more frequent intervals, but at least annually, during the surviving Settlor's lifetime.

2. If at any time or from time to time the surviving Settlor should be in need of funds in excess of all income and other property and resources available in a practicable manner for his or her benefit from the *Survivor's Trust* and all other sources, for his or her proper care, support or maintenance in his or her accustomed manner of living, or as a result of illness, physical or mental disability or other health requirement or expense, then the Trustee may relieve or contribute toward the relief of any such need of needs of said surviving Settlor by paying to him or her or using and applying for his or her benefit, such sum or sums out of the principal of the *Decedent's Trust* as may be necessary or advisable.

ARTICLE IV
OPERATION OF TRUST ON DEATH OF SURVIVING SETTLOR

Paragraph 4.01. Payment of Surviving Settlor's Debts. On the death of the surviving Settlor, the Trustee shall pay out of the principal or income of the *Survivor's Trust,* unless otherwise paid or provided for, the just debts of the surviving Settlor (excluding any debts barred by provisions of law or not yet due), funeral expenses of the surviving Settlor and any inheritance, estate or other death taxes that shall, by reason of the death of the surviving Settlor, be attributable to the *Survivor's Trust.* This is not and shall not constitute a direction to pay all inheritance, estate or other death taxes from the *Survivor's Trust* without apportionment.

Paragraph 4.02. Distribution of Survivor's Trust. Upon the death of the surviving Settlor, and after payment of expenses as set forth in Paragraph 4.01, the Trustee shall hold, administer and distribute all or any part of the balance of the *Survivor's Trust* shall be distributed to or for the benefit of such one or more persons or entities, including the estate of the surviving Settlor, on the terms and conditions, either outright or in trust, as the surviving Settlor may appoint by a written instrument other than a Will which specifically refers to and exercises this general testamentary power of appointment. Any of the *Survivor's Trust* not effectively appointed by the surviving Settlor shall be added to the balance of the *Decedent's Trust* to be held, administered and distributed as set forth below in Paragraph 4.03 below.

Paragraph 4.03. Distribution of decedent's trust. The *Decedent's Trust,* along with any of the *Survivor's Trust* not effectively appointed by the surviving Settlor, shall be distributed as follows:

A. The Trustee shall distribute to the following persons the cash amount listed after their respective names:
(10)

B. The Trustee shall distribute to the following persons the real property described after their respective names. (12) Said real property is given free of all encumbrances or liens thereon.
(11)

? Special Needs Trust?

?

C. The Trustee shall distribute to (13) Brandon a life estate in the following property located at: (14) 2717 NW 40. After the death of (13) Brandon said property shall go, outright, to (15) 3 Sons or their heirs as the remainder person(s).

D. The Trustee shall distribute all of the rest, residue and remainder of the Trust Estate, real, personal and mixed, of whatsoever kind or character and wheresoever situated, to the following persons or entities (16) in the proportions listed after their names.

(18) Kenneth, David & Phillip &/or issue of all 4 sons.

(19) 1/4 shares to the Trustee hereinafter named, to have and to hold for the benefit of (20) Brandon upon the uses, trusts, purposes and conditions hereinafter provided.

1. If (20) Brandon should at any time or from time to time be in need, in the discretion of the Trustee, of funds due to illness, infirmity or other physical or mental disability or any emergency, the Trustee may relieve or contribute toward the relief of any such need or needs of (20) Brandon by paying to him or her or using and applying for his or her benefit, such sum or sums out of the income and/or principal of his or her trust as the Trustee, in the Trustee's discretion, may deem necessary or advisable.

2. The Trustee shall pay (20) Brandon or his landlord all of the net income, in monthly or other convenient installments, from the trust. Bimonthly Elec, Phone, Gas, etc. taxes

NO

3. (20) N/A shall have the right to require the Trustee to convert any non-income producing asset into an income producing asset.

4. Upon the death of (20) Brandon the Trustee shall distribute, free of trust, the remaining trust properties to: (23) Ben + Elijah.

E. Distribution of Trust Assets. With respect to the distribution of any trust estate upon termination of any trust, and partial distribution of any trust, the liquidation and distribution by the Trustee of the Trust Estate involved or the distributable portion shall commence immediately and be accomplished as rapidly as possible, and deliveries of the trust properties to the beneficiary or beneficiaries may be made in installments or series, retaining only reasonable reserves for final charges and expenses. In no event shall it be necessary for the Trustee to await an accounting to the Court, or any Court order, before releasing and distributing the majority of the Trust Estate to be distributed.

F. Undistributed Income. All the net income of the respective trusts or trust estates, not distributed, used or applied as otherwise provided herein, shall be accumulated and added to the principals of the respective trusts.

Upon the change or succession of any beneficiary, distribution of trust properties or any trust estate or any portion thereof, or upon setting aside, apportionment or division of any trust estate or upon the termination of a trust or any interest therein, the beneficial interest, properties or balance of trust estate at the applicable time and to be dealt with shall include any and all income accumulated, accrued, uncollected or held undistributed and all of such income shall likewise be distributed, set aside or apportioned to the next or succeeding beneficiaries, distributees, shares or trusts, retaining its character as income.

ARTICLE V
TRUSTEES

Paragraph 5.01. Appointment of Trustees. Settlors, (1)Leigh and (4)Sally are appointed and confirmed as the Trustees, without bond. In the event either original Trustee should resign, die or become mentally incapacitated, the remaining Trustee shall act as sole Trustee. If either original Trustee should cease to act as Trustee due to a mental incapacity, his/her restoration of mental capacity shall result in his or her immediate return as Trustee or Co-Trustee hereunder. If either original Trustee should cease to act as sole Trustee or a Co-Trustee with the other original Trustee due to his/her resignation, he/she may at any time subsequent, elect to act again as sole Trustee or a Co-Trustee with the other original Trustee. Said election shall be made by filing same with either of the then acting Trustee or by recording said election in the County of residence of said Trustee making such election.

In the event both (1)Leigh and (4)Sally should die, refuse to act, or for any other reason be unable to act, then (25)David + Ken shall act as (26)co Trustees hereunder (27) without bond. In the event he/she/they should die, decline to act, or for any other reason, be unable to act as Trustee then (28)Philip shall act as Trustee hereunder (27) without bond.

Notwithstanding the above, at now time shall the surviving Settlor act as Trustee of any life insurance policy allocated to the *Decedent's Trust*. In that event the surviving Settlor shall appoint a special Trustee to hold title to and administer such policy or policies. No Life ins.

Paragraph 5.02. Substitute Trustee. The Settlors jointly, or the surviving Settlor upon the death of the predeceased Settlor, may appoint a substitute or successor Trustee to act as Trustee of any trust or trusts created hereunder in the place and stead of, or as successor to, any Trustee named in Section 4.01 above. Such substitution shall be in writing.

Paragraph 5.04. Trustee Liability. No person named as Trustee in this instrument or appointed as Trustee in the manner specified herein shall be liable to any beneficiary or to any heir of either Settlor for the Trustee's acts or failure to act, except for willful misconduct or gross negligence. No such Trustee shall be liable or responsible for any act, omission or default of any other Trustee provided that they shall have had no knowledge of facts that might reasonably be expected to put the Trustee on notice of it.

Paragraph 5.05. Title to Trust Estate. The legal title to all property held in trust hereunder shall be, remain and become vested in the Trustee or successor Trustee from time to time acting hereunder, without any act of conveyance or transfer to or by or acceptance from, any succeeding, retiring or predecessor Trustee; however, any removed or resigning Trustee shall execute and deliver any and all conveyances and documents requested and reasonably necessary to transfer the trust estate and its assets to a successor Trustee. Each successor Trustee from time to time acting hereunder shall have all the rights, powers immunities and authorities, discretionary or otherwise and the duties and obligations herein granted to the original Trustee. No successor Trustee shall be obligated to inquire into or be in any way responsible for the previous administration of any trust created herein or of the trust estate or for any act or default of any predecessor Trustee.

Paragraph 5.06. Powers of Trustee. To carry out the purposes of any trust created under this Trust Declaration, and subject to any limitations stated elsewhere in this Trust Declaration, the Trustee is vested with the following powers with respect to the Trust Estate, and any part of it, in addition to those powers now or hereafter conferred by law.

A. Power to Invest. To invest and reinvest the Trust Estate in every kind of property, real, personal or mixed, and every kind of investment, specifically including but not by way of limitation, corporate obligations of every kind, stocks, preferred or common, shares of investment trusts, investment companies, mutual funds, market index funds and mortgage participations which individuals of prudence, discretion and intelligence acquire for their own account, and any common trust fund administered by any Trustee under this Trust Declaration.

B. Power to Retain Property. To retain any property which was an asset of the Trust Estate during the Settlor's lifetime or received without consideration by the Trustee as long as the Trustee deems advisable whether or not of the character permitted by law for the investment of trust funds. The trust properties and investment need not be diversified and the Trustee shall have no duty to dispose or convert any trust assets to effect diversification.

C. Power to Manage Securities. With respect to securities held in this Trust Declaration, to have all the rights, powers and privileges of an owner, including but not by way of limitation, the power to vote, give proxies and pay assessments, to participate in voting trusts, pooling agreements, foreclosures, reorganizations, consolidations, mergers, liquidations, sales and leases and, incident to such participation, to deposit securities with and transfer title to any protective or other committee on such terms as the Trustee may deem advisable, to exercise and sell stock subscription or conversion rights and to hold securities in "street name".

D. Power of Sale, Exchange, Repair. To manage, control, foreclose, repossess, grant options on, grant easements on, sell (for cash), convey, exchange, partition, divide, improve and repair trust property.

The power to sell, at the termination of the trust, any trust property if the Trustee feels said disposition would assist in the distribution of the trust property at termination.

E. Power to Lease. To lease trust property for terms within or beyond the term of the trust and for any purpose, including exploration for and removal of gas, oil and other minerals; and to enter into community oil leases, pooling and unitization agreements, operating agreements or otherwise, and to create restrictions, easements or other servitudes thereon, to assign, partition, divide, subdivide, transfer to a corporation in exchange for stock, improve, repair, loan, reloan, invest and reinvest the trust estate or any part thereof.

F. Power to Insure. To carry, at the expense of the Trust Estate, insurance of such kinds and in such amounts as the Trustee shall deem advisable to protect the Trust Estate and the Trustee against any hazard.

G. Power to Commence or Defend Litigation. To commence or defend such litigation with respect to the Trust or any property of the Trust Estate as the Trustee may deem advisable, at the expense of the Trust Declaration.

H. Power to Compromise Claim. To compromise or otherwise adjust any claims or litigation against or in favor of the Trust Declaration.

I. Power to Employ Consultants. To employ any custodian, investment advisor, attorney, accountant or other agents to assist the Trustee in administration of this Trust Declaration and to rely upon the advice given by these agents. Reasonable compensation shall be paid to these agents for all services performed.

J. Power to Adjust for Tax Consequences. To take any action and to make any election the Trustee shall deem advisable to minimize the tax liabilities of this trust and its beneficiaries, to allocate the benefits among the various beneficiaries and to make adjustments in the rights of any beneficiaries or group of beneficiaries or between principal and income accounts, to compensate for the consequences of any tax election or any investment decision or administrative decision that has the effect of preferring one beneficiary or group of beneficiaries over others, provided such discretion shall not be exercised in any manner which will cause a loss of or a decrease in any marital or charitable deduction otherwise allowable in computing the then deceased Settlor's federal estate tax.

K. Trust Bank and Securities Accounts. During the joint lives of the Settlors, if the Settlors are serving as co-Trustees hereunder, the signature of either Trustor shall be sufficient to create, negotiate or endorse trust checks or to deposit or withdraw trust funds from trust bank or securities accounts or to trade securities in said securities accounts.

ARTICLE VI
MISCELLANEOUS

Paragraph 6.01. No Assignment. Each beneficiary hereunder is hereby prohibited from anticipating, encumbering, assigning or in any other manner, alienating her or his interest in either income or principal of any trust created under this Trust Declaration and is without power to do so nor shall such interest be subject to her or his liabilities or obligations nor to attachment, execution or other legal processes, bankruptcy proceedings or claims of creditors or others. The Trustee may require the personal receipt of a beneficiary as a condition precedent to payment, distribution or delivery of any amount, property or benefit hereunder. The Trustee may, however, deposit in any bank designated in writing, by a beneficiary, to her or his credit, income or principal payable to such beneficiary.

Paragraph 6.02. Principal and Income. Except as otherwise specifically provided in this Trust Declaration, the determination of all matters with respect to what shall constitute principal and income of each trust estate, gross income therefrom and net income distributable under the terms of the Trust Declaration, shall be governed by the provisions of the Revised Uniform Principal and Income Act as enacted in the State of (2a) Oklahoma, from time to time existing. All taxes, assessments, fees, charges and other expenses incurred by the Trustee in the administration, protection and distribution of each trust, shall be a charge upon the trust estate and shall be paid out of the income and/or principal, in accordance with the aforesaid Act.

Paragraph 6.03. Savings Clause. Unless sooner terminated in accordance with other provisions of this Trust Declaration, any trust created hereunder shall terminate twenty-one (21) years after the death of the last surviving member of the group consisting of the Settlor and the issue of the Settlor who are living and in being at the date of death of the Settlor.

Paragraph 6.04. Payments to Minors and Incompetents. The Trustee, in the Trustee's discretion, may apply payments directly for the benefit of any beneficiary, rather than directly to such beneficiary and, in the case of a beneficiary who is a minor or who is under any other disability, make payment to the guardian, conservator of the person or estate of such beneficiary, custodian under the Uniform Transfers to Minors Act, parent or any other suitable adult with whom the beneficiary resides or by expending the same for the care, education, maintenance or other benefit of said beneficiary. In addition, the Trustee, in the Trustee's discretion, may make payments directly to a beneficiary who is a minor if, in the Trustee's judgment, the minor is of sufficient age and maturity to properly manage the money or property so paid. The Trustee shall not be required to see to the application of any such payment so made to any said persons, but his, her or their receipt therefor shall be a full discharge to the Trustee.

Paragraph 6.05. No Physical Segregation. There need be no physical segregation or division of the various trusts except as segregation or division may be required by the termination of any of the trusts or as specifically provided, but the Trustee shall keep separate accounts for the different undivided interests. ?

Paragraph 6.06. Distribution. In any case in which the Trustee is required, pursuant to the provisions of the Trust, to divide any parts or shares for the purposes of distribution or otherwise, except as the donee of any power of appointment affecting such property may have expressly provided otherwise in the instrument exercising such power, the Trustee is authorized, in the Trustee's absolute discretion, to make the division and distribution (pro rata or otherwise) in kind, including an undivided interest in any property or partly in kind and partly in money, and for this purpose, to make such sales of the trust property as the Trustee may deem necessary, on such terms and conditions as the Trustee shall see fit. Any asset which is encumbered shall be assigned subject thereto, and its value or amount shall be given effect less such indebtedness.

Paragraph 6.07. Non-Pro Rata Distributions. As to distribution or division of property in kind under and for the several trusts, excepting the initial establishment of any trust for a pecuniary amount, the Trustee shall be cognizant of the differences between the tax cost bases and current value and shall endeavor, insofar as is practicable to distribute or set aside to or for each beneficiary or distributee, assets or property carrying amount or portions of the total unrealized taxable gains or losses embodied in all the assets and properties involved commensurate with the share or portion of each beneficiary or distributee.

Paragraph 6.08. Distribution If All Beneficiaries Die Before Full Distribution. If at any time before full distribution of the Trust Estate, the Settlor is deceased and no disposition of the property is directed by this Trust Declaration, the Trust Estate or the portion of it not disposed of under the Trust Declaration, whichever the case may be, shall thereupon be distributed one-half to those persons who would be the legal heirs of Husband and one-half to the legal heirs of Wife their identities and respective shares to be determined as though the death of Husband and Wife had occurred immediately following the event requiring distribution and according to the laws of the State of (2a) Oklahoma then in effect relating to the succession of separate property not acquired from a parent, grandparent or previously deceased spouse.

Paragraph 6.09. Additional Property. With consent of the Trustee, additional property may be added at any time from any source to any trust held under this Trust Declaration. No person dealing with the Trustee in any manner shall be under any obligation to see to the application of any money paid to the Trustee or to inquire into the validity, expediency or propriety of any act of the Trustee or into any of the provisions of any trust hereunder.

Paragraph 6.10. Fiduciary Capacity. All of the powers of the Trustee provided in this Trust Declaration shall be exercisable by the Trustee in the Trustee's fiduciary capacity and only in such capacity.

Paragraph 6.11. Corporate Office. No person shall, by reason of acting as Trustee, be in any way restricted or prohibited from holding office in any corporation in which any trust under this Trust Declaration holds securities or from receiving compensation from any such corporation for services performed as a director, officer or employee of such corporation or from purchasing, selling or otherwise dealing with the stock of any such corporation for the individual account of such Trustee or from voting the stock of any such corporation held by such trust, including voting those shares in favor of the Settlor or any other person.

Paragraph 6.12. Disclaimer of Powers. The Trustee may disclaim, release or restrict the scope of any power held in connection with any trust created under this Trust Declaration, including any administrative power, whether such power is expressly granted in this Trust Declaration or implied by law, by a written instrument specifying the power to be disclaimed, released or restricted and the nature of any such restriction. Any power disclaimed or released by the Trustee shall be extinguished except to the extent this Trust Declaration expressly provides that such power pass to another. This power shall be personal to the Trustee only and may not be exercised by any other person acting on behalf of the Trustee, including, but not limited to, any Trustee (other than the Trustee), Conservator, agent or guardian.

Paragraph 6.13. Notice. Unless the Trustee has received written notice of the occurrence of an event affecting the beneficial interest in any trust held under this Trust Declaration, the Trustee shall not be liable to any beneficiary of such trust for any distributions made or other actions taken by the Trustee in good faith as though such event had not occurred.

Paragraph 6.14. Invalidity of Any Provision. Should any provision of this Trust Declaration be or become invalid or unenforceable, the remaining provisions of this Trust Declaration shall be and continue to be fully effective.

Paragraph 6.15. Gender and Number. Except as provided otherwise herein, the masculine, feminine and neuter gender, and the singular or plural number, shall each be deemed to include the others whenever the context so indicates.

Paragraph 6.16. Law of Construction of Trust. This Trust Declaration, its validity, the construction of and all rights under the Trusts provided for in this Trust Declaration shall be governed by the laws of the State of (2a) Oklahoma.

Paragraph 6.17. No Contest. The Settlors have intentionally and with full knowledge omitted to provide for his/her issue, ancestors, relatives and heirs living at the time of his/her demise, except for such provisions as are made specifically herein.

If any person who is or claims under or through a beneficiary of this Trust, or if any person who would be entitled to share in either Settlor's estate if either or both Settlors died intestate, should in any manner whatsoever, directly or indirectly, attack, contest or seek to impair or invalidate in court any provision of the following:

A. This Trust or any Amendment to this Trust;

B. Any Will or Codicil to any Will executed by either Settlor;

C. Any beneficiary designation executed by either Settlor with respect to any insurance policy, any "Totten trust" account, any joint tenancy or tenancy by the entirety, any "transfer on death" account or any pension plan, or conspire or cooperate with anyone attempting to do any of the actions or things aforesaid, then each such person and any devise, share or interest in the Trust or either Settlor's Estate otherwise given to each such person under this Trust or either Settlor's Estate to which each such person might be entitled by law, is hereby revoked and shall pass and be distributed as though each such person had predeceased either Settlor leaving no issue or heirs whatsoever.

Brandon due to mental illness will be excluded from this

Any and every individual who asserts, or conspires or cooperates with any person who asserts, any claim against this Trust or the Estate of either Settlor of this Trust based on:

D. "Quantum meruit" theory;

E. Common law marriage, Marvin v. Marvin, 18 Cal. 3d 660 (1976) type of agreement or similar theory;

F. Constructive trust theory; or,

G. Oral agreement or written agreement which is to be proved by parole evidence, claiming that either Settlor agreed to gift or devise anything to such person or to pay such person or another for services rendered, regardless of whether a court may find that such agreement existed, then each such person is disinherited and any devise, share or interest in this Trust or either Settlor's Estate otherwise given to each such person under this Trust or either Settlor's Estate or to which each such person might be entitled by law, is hereby revoked and shall pass and be distributed as though each such person had predeceased both Settlors leaving no issue or heirs whatsoever.

The Trustee is specifically authorized to defend any such attack, contest, claim or other proceeding of any nature concerning this Trust or of any provision hereof, and to employ legal counsel therefor, all at the expense of the Trust.

Paragraph 6.18. Survival. If any person fails to survive a Settlor by thirty (30) days, for all purposes of this Trust Declaration the person shall be considered to have predeceased such Settlor.

Paragraph 6.19. All typed and handwritten "fill-ins" where directed above were made before the execution of this Declaration of Trust and are not initialed by the Settlors. All crossed through words and inter-lineations were made before the execution of this Trust and are initialed by the Settlors.

CERTIFICATION OF HUSBAND AND WIFE

We, and each of us, certify that:

A. We, and each of us, have read the foregoing Trust Declaration;

B. The foregoing Trust Declaration correctly states the terms and conditions under which the Trust Estate is to be held, managed, administered and disposed of by the Trustee;

C. As the Settlors named in such Trust Declaration, we, and each of us, approve such Trust Declaration in all particulars; and

D. As the Trustees named in such Trust Declaration, we, and each of us, approve and accept the Trust provided for in such Declaration.

Dated: (40)______________________________

(1)____________________, Settlor, Trustee

(1b)____________________________

(4)____________________, Settlor, Trustee

STATE OF (2a)________________________)
) ss.
COUNTY OF (2)________________________)

On ________________, 200__ before me, the undersigned, a Notary Public in and for said county and state, personally appeared (1)____________ and (4)___________, personally known to me (or proved to me on the basis of satisfactory evidence) to be the person(s) whose name(s) is/are subscribed to the within instrument and acknowledged that he/she/they executed the same in his/her/their authorized capacity(ies), and that by his/her/their signature(s) on the instrument the person(s), or the entity upon behalf of which the person(s) acted, executed the instrument.

WITNESS my hand and official seal.

____
Notary Public in and for said County and State

EXHIBIT A

Property Declared to be assets of the (1a)______________________________ TRUST dated (48)_______________:

(55)

1. Sally's Edward Jones Acct.
T Rowe Price Acts
Janus Acts
Paul Revere Annuity ?

INTER-VIVOS TRUST

THE (1a)_________________________ TRUST

The Settlors named below hereby declare as follows:

ARTICLE I
ESTABLISHMENT OF TRUST

Paragraph 1.01. Creation of Trust. This Trust Declaration has been entered into between (1)___________________and (4)____________________ as Settlors and themselves as the Trustees. The Settlors, of (2)____________________ County, (2a)___________________, have transferred, or will transfer, to the Trustee of this Trust Declaration the property described in the attached Exhibit "A" which will constitute, together with any other property that may be added to this Trust Declaration, the Trust Estate of an express trust which shall be held, administered and distributed by the Trustee as provided in this Trust Declaration.

Paragraph 1.02. Trust Name. This Trust Declaration shall be known as the (1a)"_______________________________ TRUST" dated (48)________________________.

Paragraph 1.03. Definitions. As used in this Trust Declaration:

A.Husband: The term "Husband" shall mean (1)__________.

B. Wife: The term "Wife" shall mean (4)______________.

C. Settlors: The term "Settlors" shall refer collectively to Husband and Wife.

D. Deceased Settlor: The term "deceased Settlor" shall refer to the Settlor who is first to die. However, the term, "then deceased Settlor" shall refer to the Settlor then deceased and may thus refer to the otherwise surviving Settlor.

E. Surviving Settlor: The term "surviving Settlor" shall refer to the Settlor who is last to die.

F. Trustee: The term "Trustee" or "Trustees" shall refer to whoever is serving as Trustee or Trustees under this Trust Declaration.

G. Trust Estate: The term "Trust Estate" shall refer to the property subject to this Trust Declaration.

Paragraph 1.04. Property to Retain Status. All property now or hereafter transferred to the Trustee which was community property, quasi-community property or separate property at the time of such transfer, shall remain, respectively, community property, quasi-community property or the separate property of the spouse or spouses transferring such property to the Trustee.

ARTICLE II
OPERATION OF TRUST DURING THE LIFE OF HUSBAND AND WIFE

Paragraph 2.01. Net Income. During the life of Husband and/or Wife, the Trustee shall pay to or apply for the benefit of both Husband and Wife, or the survivor thereof, in monthly or more frequent intervals, all of the net income of the community Trust Estate and shall pay to or apply for the benefit of the contributing spouse, in monthly or more frequent intervals, all of the net income of the separate property contributed or owned by that spouse.

Paragraph 2.02. Withdrawal of Principal. During the life of Husband and/or Wife, the Trustee shall also pay to or apply for the benefit of both Husband and Wife, or either, or the survivor thereof, so much of the community principal of the Trust Estate, up to the whole thereof, as both Husband and Wife shall direct, and shall, at the discretion of a spouse, pay to or apply for the benefit of that spouse so much of the principal of the Trust Estate, up to the whole thereof, as is that spouse's separate property.

Paragraph 2.03. Incapacity of Husband or Wife. If, at any time either Husband or Wife has become physically or mentally incapacitated so as to be unable to manage his or her affairs, whether or not a court of competent jurisdiction has declared him or her incompetent, mentally ill, or in need of a conservator, the Trustee shall pay to the non-incapacitated spouse or apply for the benefit of either spouse such amounts of the principal and/or income of the community estate as may be necessary, in the Trustee's discretion, for the care, maintenance and support of both spouses in accordance with their accustomed manner of living. The Trustee shall also pay to or apply for the benefit of the incapacitated spouse such amounts of income or principal of the separate property contributed by the incapacitated spouse as may be necessary, in the Trustee's discretion, for the care, maintenance, and support of the incapacitated spouse in accordance with his or her accustomed manner of living, taking into account payments made by the Trustee from the community Trust Estate. If a conservator of the person or estate is appointed for the incapacitated spouse, the Trustee shall take into account any payments made for the incapacitated spouse's benefit by the conservator.

The payments specified in this Section shall be made until the incapacitated spouse is again able to manage his or her own affairs, or until the death of the first spouse to die, whichever event may occur earlier.

Paragraph 2.04. Revocation of Trust. At any time during their joint lives, either Husband or Wife as to community property, and either spouse as to his or her separate property, may, by serving written notice on the Trustee, revoke the Trust created by this Trust Declaration, in whole or in part. Any community property withdrawn from the Trust Estate by reason of any such revocation shall be delivered by the Trustee to both Husband and Wife and any separate property withdrawn from the Trust shall be delivered by the Trustee to the spouse revoking the Trust.

Paragraph 2.05. Amendment of Trust. At any time during their joint lives, Husband and Wife, jointly as to community property, and either spouse as to his or her separate property, may, by serving written notice on the Trustee, alter, modify or amend the Trust created by this Trust Declaration in any respect.

ARTICLE III
OPERATION OF TRUST AFTER DEATH OF DECEASED SETTLOR

Paragraph 3.01. Collection of Assets and Payment of Deceased Settlor's Debts. On the death of the deceased Settlor the Trustee shall collect all assets belonging to the Trust Estate. As soon as practicable after the death of the deceased Settlor, the Trustee, except as otherwise provided herein, shall pay from the deceased Settlor's share of the Trust Estate the just debts of the deceased Settlor (excluding any debts barred by provisions of law or not yet due), funeral expenses of the deceased Settlor, and any inheritance, estate, or other death taxes that shall, by reason of the death of the deceased Settlor, be attributable to the Trust Estate. This is not and shall not constitute a direction to pay all inheritance, estate or other death taxes from or charge the same to, the Trust Estate without apportionment.

Paragraph 3.02. Trust to Continue. On the death of the deceased Settlor, the Trustee shall divide the Trust Estate into as many as three separate trusts. Such trusts shall be designated as the *Decedent's Trust*, the *Marital Trust* and the *Survivor's Trust*.

A. Decedent's trust. The *Decedent's Trust* shall be created from the deceased Settlor's interest in community property and quasi-community property and the separate property of the deceased Settlor which is included in the Trust Estate.

1. Allocation to Decedent's Trust. The *Decedent's Trust* shall be a unified credit trust, the principal of which shall consist of a pecuniary amount equal to the unused unified credit available at the time of the death of the deceased Settlor under IRC Section 2010, as amended, plus any property disclaimed by the surviving Settlor after taking into account:

(i) All deductions taken in determining the estate tax payable by reason of the deceased Settlor's death;

(ii) The net value of all other property, whether or not it is disposed of under this Trust and whether it passes at the time of the deceased Settlor's death or has passed before the deceased Settlor's death to or in trust for the surviving Settlor, so that it is included in the deceased Settlor's gross estate and does not qualify for the federal estate tax marital deduction. In determining the amount of Trust, however, disclaimers by the surviving Settlor shall be disregarded; and

(iii) All credits allowed for federal estate tax purposes.

The Trustee shall satisfy the amount so determined in cash or in kind, or partly in each, and shall allocate to this Trust any assets of the deceased Settlor contributed or added to the trust that are not eligible for the federal estate tax marital deduction. Assets allocated in kind shall be considered to satisfy this amount on the basis of their net fair market values at the date or dates of allocation to this Trust.

The Trustee shall select and allocate the cash, securities and other property, including real estate and interests therein, which shall constitute the trust, employing for the purpose values current at the time or times of allocation.

2. Revocation and Modification of the Decedent's Trust After Death of Deceased Settlor. The *Decedent's Trust* shall be irrevocable and may not be amended or modified in any respect after the death of the deceased Settlor.

B. Marital Trust.

1. Allocation to Marital Trust. The *Marital Trust* shall be created from the deceased Settlor's remaining, if any, interest in community property and quasi-community property and the separate property of the deceased Settlor which is included in the Trust Estate and which qualify for the federal estate tax marital deduction.

Assets qualifying for the federal estate tax marital deduction shall be transferred to the *Marital Trust* only to the extent they reduce the federal estate tax otherwise payable. No assets for which a credit for foreign death taxes is allowed shall be includable in the *Marital Trust* unless that estate contains insufficient other property to fully fund the *Marital Trust.*

2. Revocation and Modification of the Marital Trust After Death of Deceased Settlor. The *Marital Trust* shall be irrevocable and may not be amended or modified in any respect after the death of the deceased Settlor.

C. Survivor's Trust.

1. Allocation to Survivor's Trust. The *Survivor's Trust* shall consist of the balance of the Trust Estate.

2. Revocation and Modification of Survivor's Trust. The surviving Settlor shall have the power to amend, revoke or terminate the *Survivor's Trust* exercisable by delivery of written notice to the Trustee. The surviving Settlor shall have the power to amend, revoke or terminate the *Survivor's Trust* exercisable by delivery of written notice to the Trustee. On revocation or termination of the *Survivor's Trust,* the Trustee shall deliver all of the assets of the *Survivor's Trust* to the surviving Settlor. On the death of the surviving Settlor, the *Survivor's Trust* shall be irrevocable and may not be amended or modified in any respect.

D. DISTRIBUTION OF TRUST ESTATE

1. The Trustee shall pay to or apply for the benefit of the surviving Settlor all the net income of the *Decedent's Trust, Marital Trust* and *Survivor's Trust,* in monthly or more frequent intervals, but at least annually, during the surviving Settlor's lifetime.

2. The surviving Settlor shall have the right to require the Trustee to convert any non-income producing asset held by the *Marital Trust* to an income producing asset.

3. In addition to any other payments to the surviving Settlor hereunder, the Trustee shall, upon the written request of the surviving Settlor in December of year calendar year, pay to the surviving Settlor amounts from principal that the surviving Settlor requests, not exceeding in any single calendar year the greater of the following amounts: $5,000.00 or 5 percent of the value of the principal of the *Marital Trust* (determined as of the end of the calendar year. This right of withdrawal is noncumulative, so that if the beneficiary does not withdraw the full amount permitted to be withdrawn during any calendar year, the right to withdraw the remaining amount will lapse at the end of the calendar year.

4. If at any time or from time to time the surviving Settlor should be in need of funds in excess of all income and other property and resources available in a practicable manner for his or her benefit from the *Survivor's Trust* and all other sources, for his or her proper care, support or maintenance in his or her accustomed manner of living, or as a result of illness, physical or mental disability or other health requirement or expense, then the Trustee may relieve or contribute toward the relief of any such need of needs of said surviving Settlor by paying to him or her or using and applying for his or her benefit, such sum or sums out of the principal of the *Marital Trust* or *Decedent's Trust* as may be necessary or advisable.

ARTICLE IV
OPERATION OF TRUST ON DEATH OF SURVIVING SETTLOR

Paragraph 4.01. Payment of Surviving Settlor's Debts. On the death of the surviving Settlor, the Trustee shall pay out of the principal or income of the *Survivor's Trust,* unless otherwise paid or provided for, the just debts of the surviving Settlor (excluding any debts barred by provisions of law or not yet due), funeral expenses of the surviving Settlor and any inheritance, estate or other death taxes that shall, by reason of the death of the surviving Settlor, be attributable to the *Survivor's Trust.* This is not and shall not constitute a direction to pay all inheritance, estate or other death taxes from the *Survivor's Trust* without apportionment.

Any accrued but unpaid income of the *Marital Trust* shall be paid to the estate of the surviving Settlor.

Paragraph 4.02. Distribution of Survivor's Trust. Upon the death of the surviving Settlor, and after payment of expenses as set forth in Paragraph 4.01, the Trustee shall hold, administer and distribute all or any part of the balance of the *Survivor's Trust* shall be distributed to or for the benefit of such one or more persons or entities, including the estate of the surviving Settlor, on the terms and conditions, either outright or in trust, as the surviving Settlor may appoint by a written instrument other than a Will which specifically refers to and exercises this general testamentary power of appointment. Any of the *Survivor's Trust* not effectively appointed by the surviving Settlor shall be added to the balance of the *Decedent's Trust* to be held, administered and distributed as set forth below in Paragraph 4.03 below.

Paragraph 4.03. Distribution of Decedent's Trust and Marital Trust. The *Marital Trust*, the *Decedent's Trust*, along with any of the *Survivor's Trust* not effectively appointed by the surviving Settlor, shall be distributed as follows:

A. The Trustee shall distribute to the following persons the cash amount listed after their respective names:
(10)

B. The Trustee shall distribute to the following persons the real property described after their respective names. (12) Said real property is given free of all encumbrances or liens thereon.
(11)

C. The Trustee shall distribute to (13)__________________ a life estate in the following property located at: (14)________________________. After the death of (13)____________________ said property shall go, outright, to (15)__________________________ as the remainder person(s).

D. The Trustee shall distribute all of the rest, residue and remainder of the Trust Estate, real, personal and mixed, of whatsoever kind or character and wheresoever situated, to the following persons or entities (16) in the proportions listed after their names (17) in equal shares.
(18)

E. Distribution of Trust Assets. With respect to the distribution of any trust estate upon termination of any trust, and partial distribution of any trust, the liquidation and distribution by the Trustee of the Trust Estate involved or the distributable portion shall commence immediately and be accomplished as rapidly as possible, and deliveries of the trust properties to the beneficiary or beneficiaries may be made in installments or series, retaining only reasonable reserves for final charges and expenses. In no event shall it be necessary for the Trustee to await an accounting to the Court, or any Court order, before releasing and distributing the majority of the Trust Estate to be distributed.

F. Undistributed Income. All the net income of the respective trusts or trust estates, not distributed, used or applied as otherwise provided herein, shall be accumulated and added to the principals of the respective trusts.

Upon the change or succession of any beneficiary, distribution of trust properties or any trust estate or any portion thereof, or upon setting aside, apportionment or division of any trust estate or upon the termination of a trust or any interest therein, the beneficial interest, properties or balance of trust estate at the applicable time and to be dealt with shall include any and all income accumulated, accrued, uncollected or held undistributed and all of such income shall likewise be distributed, set aside or apportioned to the next or succeeding beneficiaries, distributees, shares or trusts, retaining its character as income.

ARTICLE V
TRUSTEES

Paragraph 5.01. Appointment of Trustees. Settlors, (1)_____________________and (4)____________________ are appointed and confirmed as the Trustees, without bond. In the event either original Trustee should resign, die or become mentally incapacitated, the remaining Trustee shall act as sole Trustee. If either original Trustee should cease to act as Trustee due to a mental incapacity, his/her restoration of mental capacity shall result in his or her immediate return as Trustee or Co-Trustee hereunder. If either original Trustee should cease to act as sole Trustee or a Co-Trustee with the other original Trustee due to his/her resignation, he/she may at any time subsequent, elect to act again as sole Trustee or a Co-Trustee with the other original Trustee. Said election shall be made by filing same with either of the then acting Trustee or by recording said election in the County of residence of said Trustee making such election.

In the event both (1)__________________ and (4)______________should die, refuse to act, or for any other reason be unable to act, then (25)____________________ shall act as (26)_____Trustee_ hereunder (27) without bond. In the event he/she/they should die, decline to act, or for any other reason, be unable to act as Trustee then (28)___________________________ shall act as Trustee hereunder (27) without bond.

Notwithstanding the above, at now time shall the surviving Settlor act as Trustee of any life insurance policy allocated to the *Decedent's Trust*. In that event the surviving Settlor shall appoint a special Trustee to hold title to and administer such policy or policies.

Paragraph 5.02. Substitute Trustee. The Settlors jointly, or the surviving Settlor upon the death of the predeceased Settlor, may appoint a substitute or successor Trustee to act as Trustee of any trust or trusts created hereunder in the place and stead of, or as successor to, any Trustee named in Section 4.01 above. Such substitution shall be in writing.

Paragraph 5.04. Trustee Liability. No person named as Trustee in this instrument or appointed as Trustee in the manner specified herein shall be liable to any beneficiary or to any heir of either Settlor for the Trustee's acts or failure to act, except for willful misconduct or gross negligence. No such Trustee shall be liable or responsible for any act, omission or default of any other Trustee provided that they shall have had no knowledge of facts that might reasonably be expected to put the Trustee on notice of it.

Paragraph 5.05. Title to Trust Estate. The legal title to all property held in trust hereunder shall be, remain and become vested in the Trustee or successor Trustee from time to time acting hereunder, without any act of conveyance or transfer to or by or acceptance from, any succeeding, retiring or predecessor Trustee; however, any removed or resigning Trustee shall execute and deliver any and all conveyances and documents requested and reasonably necessary to transfer the trust estate and its assets to a successor Trustee. Each successor Trustee from time to time acting hereunder shall have all the rights, powers immunities and authorities, discretionary or otherwise and the duties and obligations herein granted to the original Trustee. No successor

Trustee shall be obligated to inquire into or be in any way responsible for the previous administration of any trust created herein or of the trust estate or for any act or default of any predecessor Trustee.

Paragraph 5.06. Powers of Trustee. To carry out the purposes of any trust created under this Trust Declaration, and subject to any limitations stated elsewhere in this Trust Declaration, the Trustee is vested with the following powers with respect to the Trust Estate, and any part of it, in addition to those powers now or hereafter conferred by law. The Trustee shall not exercise any power, right or discretion in a manner which will cause the loss of or a decrease in any marital or charitable deduction otherwise allowable in computing the federal estate tax of either Trustor.

A. Power to Invest. Subject to Paragraph 3.02 D. 2, to invest and reinvest the Trust Estate in every kind of property, real, personal or mixed, and every kind of investment, specifically including but not by way of limitation, corporate obligations of every kind, stocks, preferred or common, shares of investment trusts, investment companies, mutual funds, market index funds and mortgage participations which individuals of prudence, discretion and intelligence acquire for their own account, and any common trust fund administered by any Trustee under this Trust Declaration.

B. Power to Retain Property. To retain any property which was an asset of the Trust Estate during the Settlor's lifetime or received without consideration by the Trustee as long as the Trustee deems advisable whether or not of the character permitted by law for the investment of trust funds. The trust properties and investment need not be diversified and the Trustee shall have no duty to dispose or convert any trust assets to effect diversification.

C. Power to Manage Securities. With respect to securities held in this Trust Declaration, to have all the rights, powers and privileges of an owner, including but not by way of limitation, the power to vote, give proxies and pay assessments, to participate in voting trusts, pooling agreements, foreclosures, reorganizations, consolidations, mergers, liquidations, sales and leases and, incident to such participation, to deposit securities with and transfer title to any protective or other committee on such terms as the Trustee may deem advisable, to exercise and sell stock subscription or conversion rights and to hold securities in "street name".

D. Power of Sale, Exchange, Repair. To manage, control, foreclose, repossess, grant options on, grant easements on, sell (for cash), convey, exchange, partition, divide, improve and repair trust property.

The power to sell, at the termination of the trust, any trust property if the Trustee feels said disposition would assist in the distribution of the trust property at termination.

E. Power to Lease. To lease trust property for terms within or beyond the term of the trust and for any purpose, including exploration for and removal of gas, oil and other minerals; and to enter into community oil leases, pooling and unitization agreements, operating agreements or otherwise, and to create restrictions, easements or other servitudes thereon, to assign, partition, divide, subdivide, transfer to a corporation in exchange for stock, improve, repair, loan, reloan, invest and reinvest the trust estate or any part thereof.

F. Power to Insure. To carry, at the expense of the Trust Estate, insurance of such kinds and in such amounts as the Trustee shall deem advisable to protect the Trust Estate and the Trustee against any hazard.

G. Power to Commence or Defend Litigation. To commence or defend such litigation with respect to the Trust or any property of the Trust Estate as the Trustee may deem advisable, at the expense of the Trust Declaration.

H. Power to Compromise Claim. To compromise or otherwise adjust any claims or litigation against or in favor of the Trust Declaration.

I. Power to Employ Consultants. To employ any custodian, investment advisor, attorney, accountant or other agents to assist the Trustee in administration of this Trust Declaration and to rely upon the advice given by these agents. Reasonable compensation shall be paid to these agents for all services performed.

J. Power to Adjust for Tax Consequences. To take any action and to make any election the Trustee shall deem advisable to minimize the tax liabilities of this trust and its beneficiaries, to allocate the benefits among the various beneficiaries and to make adjustments in the rights of any beneficiaries or group of beneficiaries or between principal and income accounts, to compensate for the consequences of any tax election or any investment decision or administrative decision that has the effect of preferring one beneficiary or group of beneficiaries over others, provided such discretion shall not be exercised in any manner which will cause a loss of or a decrease in any marital or charitable deduction otherwise allowable in computing the then deceased Settlor's federal estate tax.

K. Trust Bank and Securities Accounts. During the joint lives of the Settlors, if the Settlors are serving as co-Trustees hereunder, the signature of either Trustor shall be sufficient to create, negotiate or endorse trust checks or to deposit or withdraw trust funds from trust bank or securities accounts or to trade securities in said securities accounts.

ARTICLE VI
MISCELLANEOUS

Paragraph 6.01. No Assignment. Each beneficiary hereunder is hereby prohibited from anticipating, encumbering, assigning or in any other manner, alienating her or his interest in either income or principal of any trust created under this Trust Declaration and is without power to do so nor shall such interest be subject to her or his liabilities or obligations nor to attachment, execution or other legal processes, bankruptcy proceedings or claims of creditors or others. The Trustee may require the personal receipt of a beneficiary as a condition precedent to payment, distribution or delivery of any amount, property or benefit hereunder. The Trustee may, however, deposit in any bank designated in writing, by a beneficiary, to her or his credit, income or principal payable to such beneficiary.

Paragraph 6.02. Principal and Income. Except as otherwise specifically provided in this Trust Declaration, the determination of all matters with respect to what shall constitute principal and income of each trust estate, gross income therefrom and net income distributable under the terms of the Trust Declaration, shall be governed by the provisions of the Revised Uniform Principal and Income Act as enacted in the State of (2a)________________, from time to time existing. All taxes, assessments, fees, charges and other expenses incurred by the Trustee in the administration, protection and distribution of each trust, shall be a charge upon the trust estate and shall be paid out of the income and/or principal, in accordance with the aforesaid Act.

Paragraph 6.03. Savings Clause. Unless sooner terminated in accordance with other provisions of this Trust Declaration, any trust created hereunder shall terminate twenty-one (21) years after the death of the last surviving member of the group consisting of the Settlor and the issue of the Settlor who are living and in being at the date of death of the Settlor.

Paragraph 6.04. Payments to Minors and Incompetents. The Trustee, in the Trustee's discretion, may apply payments directly for the benefit of any beneficiary, rather than directly to such beneficiary and, in the case of a beneficiary who is a minor or who is under any other disability, make payment to the guardian, conservator of the person or estate of such beneficiary, custodian under the Uniform Transfers to Minors Act, parent or any other suitable adult with whom the beneficiary resides or by expending the same for the care, education, maintenance or other benefit of said beneficiary. In addition, the Trustee, in the Trustee's discretion, may make payments directly to a beneficiary who is a minor if, in the Trustee's judgment, the minor is of sufficient age and maturity to properly manage the money or property so paid. The Trustee shall not be required to see to the application of any such payment so made to any said persons, but his, her or their receipt therefor shall be a full discharge to the Trustee.

Paragraph 6.05. No Physical Segregation. There need be no physical segregation or division of the various trusts except as segregation or division may be required by the termination of any of the trusts or as specifically provided, but the Trustee shall keep separate accounts for the different undivided interests.

Paragraph 6.06. Distribution. In any case in which the Trustee is required, pursuant to the provisions of the Trust, to divide any parts or shares for the purposes of distribution or otherwise, except as the donee of any power of appointment affecting such property may have expressly provided otherwise in the instrument exercising such power, the Trustee is authorized, in the Trustee's absolute discretion, to make the division and distribution (pro rata or otherwise) in kind, including an undivided interest in any property or partly in kind and partly in money, and for this purpose, to make such sales of the trust property as the Trustee may deem necessary, on such terms and conditions as the Trustee shall see fit. Any asset which is encumbered shall be assigned subject thereto, and its value or amount shall be given effect less such indebtedness.

Paragraph 6.07. Non-Pro Rata Distributions. As to distribution or division of property in kind under and for the several trusts, excepting the initial establishment of any trust for a pecuniary amount, the Trustee shall be cognizant of the differences between the tax cost bases and current value and shall endeavor, insofar as is practicable to distribute or set aside to or for each beneficiary or distributee, assets or property carrying amount or portions of the total unrealized taxable gains or losses embodied in all the assets and properties involved commensurate with the share or portion of each beneficiary or distributee.

Paragraph 6.08. Distribution If All Beneficiaries Die Before Full Distribution. If at any time before full distribution of the Trust Estate, the Settlor is deceased and no disposition of the property is directed by this Trust Declaration, the Trust Estate or the portion of it not disposed of under the Trust Declaration, whichever the case may be, shall thereupon be distributed one-half to those persons who would be the legal heirs of Husband and one-half to the legal heirs of Wife their identities and respective shares to be determined as though the death of Husband and Wife had occurred immediately following the event requiring distribution and according to the laws of the State of (2a)__________________ then in effect relating to the succession of separate property not acquired from a parent, grandparent or previously deceased spouse.

Paragraph 6.09. Additional Property. With consent of the Trustee, additional property may be added at any time from any source to any trust held under this Trust Declaration. No person dealing with the Trustee in any manner shall be under any obligation to see to the application of any money paid to the Trustee or to inquire into the validity, expediency or propriety of any act of the Trustee or into any of the provisions of any trust hereunder.

Paragraph 6.10. Fiduciary Capacity. All of the powers of the Trustee provided in this Trust Declaration shall be exercisable by the Trustee in the Trustee's fiduciary capacity and only in such capacity.

Paragraph 6.11. Corporate Office. No person shall, by reason of acting as Trustee, be in any way restricted or prohibited from holding office in any corporation in which any trust under this Trust Declaration holds securities or from receiving compensation from any such corporation for services performed as a director, officer or employee of such corporation or from purchasing, selling or otherwise dealing with the stock of any such corporation for the individual account of such Trustee or from voting the stock of any such corporation held by such trust, including voting those shares in favor of the Settlor or any other person.

Paragraph 6.12. Disclaimer of Powers. The Trustee may disclaim, release or restrict the scope of any power held in connection with any trust created under this Trust Declaration, including any administrative power, whether such power is expressly granted in this Trust Declaration or implied by law, by a written instrument specifying the power to be disclaimed, released or restricted and the nature of any such restriction. Any power disclaimed or released by the Trustee shall be extinguished except to the extent this Trust Declaration expressly provides that such power pass to another. This power shall be personal to the Trustee only and may not be exercised by any other person acting on behalf of the Trustee, including, but not limited to, any Trustee (other than the Trustee), Conservator, agent or guardian.

Paragraph 6.13. Notice. Unless the Trustee has received written notice of the occurrence of an event affecting the beneficial interest in any trust held under this Trust Declaration, the Trustee shall not be liable to any beneficiary of such trust for any distributions made or other actions taken by the Trustee in good faith as though such event had not occurred.

Paragraph 6.14. Invalidity of Any Provision. Should any provision of this Trust Declaration be or become invalid or unenforceable, the remaining provisions of this Trust Declaration shall be and continue to be fully effective.

Paragraph 6.15. Gender and Number. Except as provided otherwise herein, the masculine, feminine and neuter gender, and the singular or plural number, shall each be deemed to include the others whenever the context so indicates.

Paragraph 6.16. Law of Construction of Trust. This Trust Declaration, its validity, the construction of and all rights under the Trusts provided for in this Trust Declaration shall be governed by the laws of the State of (2a)____________________.

Paragraph 6.17. No Contest. The Settlors have intentionally and with full knowledge omitted to provide for his/her issue, ancestors, relatives and heirs living at the time of his/her demise, except for such provisions as are made specifically herein.

If any person who is or claims under or through a beneficiary of this Trust, or if any person who would be entitled to share in either Settlor's estate if either or both Settlors died intestate, should in any manner whatsoever, directly or indirectly, attack, contest or seek to impair or invalidate in court any provision of the following:

A. This Trust or any Amendment to this Trust;

B. Any Will or Codicil to any Will executed by either Settlor;

C. Any beneficiary designation executed by either Settlor with respect to any insurance policy, any "Totten trust" account, any joint tenancy or tenancy by the entirety, any "transfer on death" account or any pension plan, or conspire or cooperate with anyone attempting to do any of the actions or things aforesaid, then each such person and any devise, share or interest in the Trust or either Settlor's Estate otherwise given to each such person under this Trust or either Settlor's Estate to which each such person might be entitled by law, is hereby revoked and shall pass and be distributed as though each such person had predeceased either Settlor leaving no issue or heirs whatsoever.

Any and every individual who asserts, or conspires or cooperates with any person who asserts, any claim against this Trust or the Estate of either Settlor of this Trust based on:

D. "Quantum meruit" theory;

E. Common law marriage, Marvin v. Marvin, 18 Cal. 3d 660 (1976) type of agreement or similar theory;

F. Constructive trust theory; or,

G. Oral agreement or written agreement which is to be proved by parole evidence, claiming that either Settlor agreed to gift or devise anything to such person or to pay such person or another for services rendered, regardless of whether a court may find that such agreement existed, then each such person is disinherited and any devise, share or interest in this Trust or either Settlor's Estate otherwise given to each such person under this Trust or either Settlor's Estate or to which each such person might be entitled by law, is hereby revoked and shall pass and be distributed as though each such person had predeceased both Settlors leaving no issue or heirs whatsoever.

The Trustee is specifically authorized to defend any such attack, contest, claim or other proceeding of any nature concerning this Trust or of any provision hereof, and to employ legal counsel therefor, all at the expense of the Trust.

Paragraph 6.18. Survival. If any person fails to survive a Settlor by thirty (30) days, for all purposes of this Trust Declaration the person shall be considered to have predeceased such Settlor.

Paragraph 6.19. All typed and handwritten "fill-ins" where directed above were made before the execution of this Declaration of Trust and are not initialed by the Settlors. All crossed through words and inter-lineations were made before the execution of this Trust and are initialed by the Settlors.

CERTIFICATION OF HUSBAND AND WIFE

We, and each of us, certify that:

A.We, and each of us, have read the foregoing Trust Declaration;

B. The foregoing Trust Declaration correctly states the terms and conditions under which the Trust Estate is to be held, managed, administered and disposed of by the Trustee;

C. As the Settlors named in such Trust Declaration, we, and each of us, approve such Trust Declaration in all particulars; and

D. As the Trustees named in such Trust Declaration, we, and each of us, approve and accept the Trust provided for in such Declaration.

Dated: (40)______________________________

(1)____________________,Settlor, Trustee

(1b)_____________________________

(4)____________________, Settlor, Trustee

STATE OF (2a)______________________)
) ss.
COUNTY OF (2)______________________)

On _______________, 200__ before me, the undersigned, a Notary Public in and for said county and state, personally appeared (1)______________ and (4)______________, personally known to me (or proved to me on the basis of satisfactory evidence) to be the person(s) whose name(s) is/are subscribed to the within instrument and acknowledged that he/she/they executed the same in his/her/their authorized capacity(ies), and that by his/her/their signature(s) on the instrument the person(s), or the entity upon behalf of which the person(s) acted, executed the instrument.

WITNESS my hand and official seal.

____
Notary Public in and for said County and State

EXHIBIT A

Property Declared to be assets of the (1a)________________________________ TRUST dated (48)_______________:

(55)
1.

INTER-VIVOS TRUST

THE (1a)_____________________ TRUST

The Settlors named below hereby declare as follows:

ARTICLE I
ESTABLISHMENT OF TRUST

Paragraph 1.01. Creation of Trust. This Trust Declaration has been entered into between (1)________________and (4)__________________ as Settlors and themselves as the Trustees. The Settlors, of (2)________ County, (2a)___________, have transferred, or will transfer, to the Trustee of this Trust Declaration the property described in the attached Exhibit "A" which will constitute, together with any other property that may be added to this Trust Declaration, the Trust Estate of an express trust which shall be held, administered and distributed by the Trustee as provided in this Trust Declaration.

Paragraph 1.02. Trust Name. This Trust Declaration shall be known as the (1a)"_____________________________ TRUST" dated (48)_______________________.

Paragraph 1.03. Definitions. As used in this Trust Declaration:

A. Husband: The term "Husband" shall mean (1)__________.

B. Wife: The term "Wife" shall mean (4)______________.

C. Settlors: The term "Settlors" shall refer collectively to Husband and Wife.

D. Deceased Settlor: The term "deceased Settlor" shall refer to the Settlor who is first to die. However, the term, "then deceased Settlor" shall refer to the Settlor then deceased and may thus refer to the otherwise surviving Settlor.

E. Surviving Settlor: The term "surviving Settlor" shall refer to the Settlor who is last to die.

F. Trustee: The term "Trustee" or "Trustees" shall refer to whoever is serving as Trustee or Trustees under this Trust Declaration.

G. Trust Estate: The term "Trust Estate" shall refer to the property subject to this Trust Declaration.

H. Issue: The term "issue" shall refer only to a person who is a lineal descendant of any degree of either the Husband and the Wife and shall (59) not include adopted persons.

Paragraph 1.04. Property to Retain Status. All property now or hereafter transferred to the Trustee which was community property, quasi-community property or separate property at the time of such transfer, shall remain, respectively, community property, quasi-community property or the separate property of the spouse or spouses transferring such property to the Trustee.

ARTICLE II
OPERATION OF TRUST DURING THE LIFE OF HUSBAND AND WIFE

Paragraph 2.01. Net Income. During the life of Husband and/or Wife, the Trustee shall pay to or apply for the benefit of both Husband and Wife, or the survivor thereof, in monthly or more frequent intervals, all of the net income of the community Trust Estate and shall pay to or apply for the benefit of the contributing spouse, in monthly or more frequent intervals, all of the net income of the separate property contributed or owned by that spouse.

Paragraph 2.02. Withdrawal of Principal. During the life of Husband and/or Wife, the Trustee shall also pay to or apply for the benefit of both Husband and Wife, or either, or the survivor thereof, so much of the community principal of the Trust Estate, up to the whole thereof, as both Husband and Wife shall direct, and shall, at the discretion of a spouse, pay to or apply for the benefit of that spouse so much of the principal of the Trust Estate, up to the whole thereof, as is that spouse's separate property.

Paragraph 2.03. Incapacity of Husband or Wife. If, at any time either Husband or Wife has become physically or mentally incapacitated so as to be unable to manage his or her affairs, whether or not a court of competent jurisdiction has declared him or her incompetent, mentally ill, or in need of a conservator, the Trustee shall pay to the non-incapacitated spouse or apply for the benefit of either spouse such amounts of the principal and/or income of the community estate as may be necessary, in the Trustee's discretion, for the care, maintenance and support of both spouses in accordance with their accustomed manner of living. The Trustee shall also pay to or apply for the benefit of the incapacitated spouse such amounts of income or principal of the separate property contributed by the incapacitated spouse as may be necessary, in the Trustee's discretion, for the care, maintenance, and support of the incapacitated spouse in accordance with his or her accustomed manner of living, taking into account payments made by the Trustee from the community Trust Estate. If a conservator of the person or estate is appointed for the incapacitated spouse, the Trustee shall take into account any payments made for the incapacitated spouse's benefit by the conservator.

The payments specified in this Section shall be made until the incapacitated spouse is again able to manage his or her own affairs, or until the death of the first spouse to die, whichever event may occur earlier.

Paragraph 2.04. Revocation of Trust. At any time during their joint lives, either Husband or Wife as to community property, and either spouse as to his or her separate property, may, by serving written notice on the Trustee, revoke the Trust created by this Trust Declaration, in whole or in part. Any community property withdrawn from the Trust Estate by reason of any such revocation shall be delivered by the Trustee to both Husband and Wife and any separate property withdrawn from the Trust shall be delivered by the Trustee to the spouse revoking the Trust.

Paragraph 2.05. Amendment of Trust. At any time during their joint lives, Husband and Wife, jointly as to community property, and either spouse as to his or her separate property, may, by serving written notice on the Trustee, alter, modify or amend the Trust created by this Trust Declaration in any respect.

ARTICLE III

OPERATION OF TRUST AFTER DEATH OF DECEASED SETTLOR

Paragraph 3.01. Collection of Assets and Payment of Deceased Settlor's Debts. On the death of the deceased Settlor the Trustee shall collect all assets belonging to the Trust Estate. As soon as practicable after the death of the deceased settlor, the Trustee, except as otherwise provided herein, shall pay from the deceased settlor's share of the Trust Estate the just debts of the deceased settlor (excluding any debts barred by provisions of law or not yet due), funeral expenses of the deceased Settlor, and any inheritance, estate, or other death taxes that shall, by reason of the death of the deceased Settlor, be attributable to the Trust Estate. This is not and shall not constitute a direction to pay all inheritance, estate or other death taxes from or charge the same to, the Trust Estate without apportionment.

Paragraph 3.02. Trust to Continue. On the death of the deceased settlor, the Trustee shall divide the Trust Estate into as many as three separate trusts. Such trusts shall be designated as the *Decedent's Trust*, the *Marital Trust* and the *Survivor's Trust*.

A.Decedent's Trust. The *Decedent's Trust* shall be created from the deceased Settlor's interest in community property and quasi-community property and the separate property of the deceased Settlor which is included in the Trust Estate.

1.Allocation to Decedent's Trust. The *Decedent's Trust* shall be a unified credit trust, the principal of which shall consist of a pecuniary amount equal to the unused unified credit available at the time of the death of the deceased settlor under IRC Section 2010, as amended, plus any property disclaimed by the surviving settlor after taking into account:

(i) All deductions taken in determining the estate tax payable by reason of the deceased Settlor's death;

(ii) The net value of all other property, whether or not it is disposed of under this Trust and whether it passes at the time of the deceased Settlor's death or has passed before the deceased Settlor's death to or in trust for the surviving Settlor, so that it is included in the deceased Settlor's gross estate and does not qualify for the federal estate tax marital deduction. In determining the amount of Trust, however, disclaimers by the surviving Settlor shall be disregarded; and

(iii) All credits allowed for federal estate tax purposes.

The Trustee shall satisfy the amount so determined in cash or in kind, or partly in each, and shall allocate to this Trust any assets of the deceased Settlor contributed or added to the trust that are not eligible for the federal estate tax marital deduction. Assets allocated in kind shall be considered to satisfy this amount on the basis of their net fair market values at the date or dates of allocation to this Trust.

The Trustee shall select and allocate the cash, securities and other property, including real estate and interests therein, which shall constitute the trust, employing for the purpose values current at the time or times of allocation.

2. Revocation and Modification of the Decedent's Trust After Death of Deceased Settlor. The *Decedent's Trust* shall be irrevocable and may not be amended or modified in any respect after the death of the deceased Settlor.

B. Marital Trust.

1. Allocation to Marital Trust. The *Marital Trust* shall be created from the deceased Settlor's remaining, if any, interest in community property and quasi-community property and the separate property of the deceased Settlor which is included in the Trust Estate and which qualify for the federal estate tax marital deduction.

Assets qualifying for the federal estate tax marital deduction shall be transferred to the *Marital Trust* only to the extent they reduce the federal estate tax otherwise payable. No assets for which a credit for foreign death taxes is allowed shall be includable in the *Marital Trust* unless that estate contains insufficient other property to fully fund the *Marital Trust.*

2. Revocation and Modification of the Marital Trust After Death of Deceased Settlor. The *Marital Trust* shall be irrevocable and may not be amended or modified in any respect after the death of the deceased Settlor.

C. Survivor's Trust.

1. Allocation to Survivor's Trust. The *Survivor's Trust* shall consist of the balance of the Trust Estate.

2. Revocation and Modification of Survivor's Trust. The surviving Settlor shall have the power to amend, revoke or terminate the *Survivor's Trust* exercisable by delivery of written notice to the Trustee. The surviving Settlor shall have the power to amend, revoke or terminate the *Survivor's Trust* exercisable by delivery of written notice to the Trustee. On revocation or termination of the *Survivor's Trust*, the Trustee shall deliver all of the assets of the *Survivor's Trust* to the surviving Settlor. On the death of the surviving Settlor, the *Survivor's Trust* shall be irrevocable and may not be amended or modified in any respect.

D. Distribution of Trust Estate.

1. The Trustee shall pay to or apply for the benefit of the surviving Settlor all the net income of the *Decedent's Trust*, *Marital Trust* and *Survivor's Trust*, in monthly or more frequent intervals, but at least annually, during the surviving Settlor's lifetime.

2.The surviving Settlor shall have the right to require the Trustee to convert any non-income producing asset held by the *Marital Trust* to an income producing asset.

3. In addition to any other payments to the surviving Settlor hereunder, the Trustee shall, upon the written request of the surviving Settlor in December of year calendar year, pay to the surviving Settlor amounts from principal that the surviving Settlor requests, not exceeding in any single calendar year the greater of the following amounts: $5,000.00 or 5 percent of the value of the principal of the *Marital Trust* (determined as of the end of the calendar year. This right of withdrawal is noncumulative, so that if the beneficiary does not withdraw the full amount permitted to be withdrawn during any calendar year, the right to withdraw the remaining amount will lapse at the end of the calendar year.

4. If at any time or from time to time the surviving Settlor should be in need of funds in excess of all income and other property and resources available in a practicable manner for his or her benefit from the *Survivor's Trust* and all other sources, for his or her proper care, support or maintenance in his or her accustomed manner of living, or as a result of illness, physical or mental disability or other health requirement or expense, then the Trustee may relieve or contribute toward the relief of any such need of needs of said surviving Settlor by paying to him or her or using and applying for his or her benefit, such sum or sums out of the principal of the *Marital Trust* or *Decedent's Trust* as may be necessary or advisable.

ARTICLE IV
OPERATION OF TRUST ON DEATH OF SURVIVING SETTLOR

Paragraph 4.01. Payment of Surviving Settlor's Debts. On the death of the surviving Settlor, the Trustee shall pay out of the principal or income of the *Survivor's Trust*, unless otherwise paid or provided for, the just debts of the surviving Settlor (excluding any debts barred by provisions of law or not yet due), funeral expenses of the surviving Settlor and any inheritance, estate or other death taxes that shall, by reason of the death of the surviving Settlor, be attributable to the *Survivor's Trust*. This is not and shall not constitute a direction to pay all inheritance, estate or other death taxes from the *Survivor's Trust* without apportionment.

Any accrued but unpaid income of the *Marital Trust* shall be paid to the estate of the surviving Settlor.

Paragraph 4.02. Distribution of Survivor's Trust. Upon the death of the surviving Settlor, and after payment of expenses as set forth in Paragraph 4.01, the Trustee shall hold, administer and distribute all or any part of the balance of the *Survivor's Trust* shall be distributed to or for the benefit of such one or more persons or entities, including the estate of the surviving Settlor, on the terms and conditions, either outright or in trust, as the surviving Settlor may appoint by a written instrument other than a Will which specifically refers to and exercises this general testamentary power of appointment. Any of the *Survivor's Trust* not effectively appointed by the surviving Settlor shall be added to the balance of the *Decedent's Trust* to be held, administered and distributed as set forth below in Paragraph 4.03 below.

Paragraph 4.03. Distribution of Decedent's Trust and Marital Trust. The *Marital Trust*, the *Decedent's Trust*, along with any of the *Survivor's Trust* not effectively appointed by the surviving Settlor, shall be distributed as follows:

A. The Trustee shall distribute to the following persons the cash amount listed after their respective names:
(10)

B. The Trustee shall distribute to the following persons the real property described after their respective names. (12) Said real property is given free of all encumbrances or liens thereon.
(11)

C. The Trustee shall distribute to (13)____________________ a life estate in the following property located at: (14)__________________________. After the death of (13)______________________ said property shall go, outright, to (15)______________________________ as the remainder person(s).

D. The Trustee shall distribute all of the rest, residue and remainder of the Trust Estate, real, personal and mixed, of whatsoever kind or character and wheresoever situated, to the Trustee hereinafter named, to have and to hold upon the uses, trusts, purposes and conditions hereinafter provided.

The Trustee, shall allocate the trust properties into as many shares as there are children of the joint Settlors then living and children of the joint Settlors then deceased who left issue then living. One such equal share shall be set aside for each of the joint Settlors' children then living and one such equal share shall be set aside for the issue then living, by right of representation, of each of the joint Settlors' children who are then deceased but left issue then living. Said shares shall be held, administered, and distributed as provided in the following sections:

Each share set aside for a child of the joint Settlors shall be held, administered and delivered for and to such beneficiary as follows:

1. The net income from the trust while said beneficiary is under 19 years of age and not a high school graduate shall be added to principal, from which the Trustee shall pay to or for the benefit of such beneficiary such sums as in the Trustee's discretion the Trustee shall deem necessary for such beneficiary's proper care, comfort, maintenance, support or education.

In making payments for the benefit of any beneficiary pursuant to this section 1, the Trustee shall construe his or her authority liberally to permit payments reasonably necessary to ease the financial burden on the guardian of the person of such beneficiary or other suitable individual with whom they reside, and on his or her family, resulting from such beneficiary's presence in his or her household.

2. Upon the beneficiary reaching 19 years of age or finishing high school(whichever occurs first), the Trustee shall pay to or apply for his or her benefit, from his or her trust, as much of the trust principal as the Trustee, in the Trustee's discretion, considers appropriate pursuant to sections 3 and 4 following.

3. After the beneficiary attains 19 years of age or finishes high school (whichever occurs first), the Trustee may, in the Trustee's discretion, pay to or apply from his or her trust, such amounts necessary for his or her education. For purposes hereof, education shall mean enrollment, attendance, and satisfactory progression towards a degree as a student at a recognized and accredited college, university, or similar institution of higher learning, including any graduate, professional school or college or trade school. Such educational payments and benefits shall include tuition, books, all direct educational costs and fees, and all reasonable living and transportation expenses. Payments hereunder shall be made during vacation periods within the regular school term under which the beneficiary is attending school and during "summer vacation" or similar vacation period between the regular school terms.

The Trustee may invest any portion of a beneficiary's trust share in an IRC 529 college savings plan for the benefit of said beneficiary.

4. If the beneficiary, his or her spouse, or any of his or her children should at any time or from time to time be in need, in the discretion of the Trustee, of funds due to illness, infirmity or other physical or mental disability or any emergency, the Trustee may relieve or contribute toward the relief of any such need or needs of the beneficiary by paying to him or her or using and applying for his or her benefit, such sum or sums out of the income and/or principal of his or her trust as the Trustee, in the Trustee's discretion, may deem necessary or advisable.

5. Upon the beneficiary attaining the age of 21 years, the Trustee shall begin to pay the beneficiary all of the net income, in monthly or other convenient installments, from the trust.

6. Upon the beneficiary attaining the age of (21)_______years, the Trustee shall distribute and deliver to such beneficiary one-half of his or her trust estate. Upon each beneficiary attaining the age of (22)_______ years, the Trustee shall distribute and deliver to such beneficiary all of the remainder of his or her trust estate.

7. If, upon the attaining of the above ages, the Trustee suspects that said beneficiary may be abusing drugs, the Trustee may require the beneficiary to take a reasonable drug test. If the beneficiary fails said drug test, the Trustee shall defer said principal payment to the beneficiary until the beneficiary passes said drug test. After a failed drug test, subsequent drug tests shall be administered at six month intervals. In the event a beneficiary fails a drug test, the Trustee may use said beneficiary's trust estate to pay for a drug abuse rehabilitation program and may require the beneficiary to enroll and to complete said program as a condition precedent to the taking of a subsequent drug test.

8. In the event the beneficiary should die before complete distribution to him or her of his or her trust estate, his or her entire trust estate on hand at the time of his or her death shall thereupon be apportioned and distributed to his or her surviving issue, by right of representation. If such beneficiary should die before complete distribution to him or her of his or her trust estate and leave no surviving issue, then the balance of the trust estate then on hand shall go and be distributed one-half to those persons who would be the legal heirs of

Husband and one-half to the legal heirs of Wife their identities and respective shares to be determined as though the death of Husband and Wife had occurred immediately following the event requiring distribution and according to the laws of the State of (2a)_________________ then in effect relating to the succession of separate property not acquired from a parent, grandparent or previously deceased spouse.

9. If, at any time, a trust created hereunder shall, in the sole judgment of the Trustee, be of the aggregate principal value of Fifty Thousand Dollars ($50,000.00) or less, the Trustee may, but need not, terminate such trust and distribute the assets thereof in the Trustee's possession to the beneficiary or beneficiaries, at the time of the current income thereof, and if there is more than one beneficiary, in the proportion in which they are beneficiaries.

E. Distribution of Trust Assets. With respect to the distribution of any trust estate upon termination of any trust, and partial distribution of any trust, the liquidation and distribution by the Trustee of the Trust Estate involved or the distributable portion shall commence immediately and be accomplished as rapidly as possible, and deliveries of the trust properties to the beneficiary or beneficiaries may be made in installments or series, retaining only reasonable reserves for final charges and expenses. In no event shall it be necessary for the Trustee to await an accounting to the Court, or any Court order, before releasing and distributing the majority of the Trust Estate to be distributed.

F. Undistributed Income. All the net income of the respective trusts or trust estates, not distributed, used or applied as otherwise provided herein, shall be accumulated and added to the principals of the respective trusts.

Upon the change or succession of any beneficiary, distribution of trust properties or any trust estate or any portion thereof, or upon setting aside, apportionment or division of any trust estate or upon the termination of a trust or any interest therein, the beneficial interest, properties or balance of trust estate at the applicable time and to be dealt with shall include any and all income accumulated, accrued, uncollected or held undistributed and all of such income shall likewise be distributed, set aside or apportioned to the next or succeeding beneficiaries, distributees, shares or trusts, retaining its character as income.

ARTICLE V
TRUSTEES

Paragraph 5.01. Appointment of Trustees. Settlors, (1)____________________ and (4)____________________ are appointed and confirmed as the Trustees, without bond. In the event either original Trustee should resign, die or become mentally incapacitated, the remaining Trustee shall act as sole Trustee. If either original Trustee should cease to act as Trustee due to a mental incapacity, his/her restoration of mental capacity shall result in his immediate return as Trustee or Co-Trustee hereunder. If either original Trustee should cease to act as sole Trustee or a Co-Trustee with the other original Trustee due to his/her resignation, he/she may at any time subsequent, elect to act again as sole Trustee or a Co-Trustee with the other original Trustee. Said election shall be made by filing same with either of the then acting Trustee or by recording said election in the County of residence of said Trustee making such election.

In the event both (1)__________________ and (4)_____________should die, refuse to act, or for any other reason be unable to act, then (25)____________________ shall act as (26)____Trustee_ hereunder (27) without bond. In the event he/she/they should die, decline to act, or for any other reason, be unable to act as Trustee then (28)___________________________ shall act as Trustee hereunder (27) without bond.

Notwithstanding the above, at now time shall the surviving Settlor act as Trustee of any life insurance policy allocated to the *Decedent's Trust.* In that event the surviving Settlor shall appoint a special Trustee to hold title to and administer such policy or policies.

Paragraph 5.02. Substitute Trustee. The Settlors jointly, or the surviving Settlor upon the death of the predeceased Settlor, may appoint a substitute or successor Trustee to act as Trustee of any trust or trusts created hereunder in the place and stead of, or as successor to, any Trustee named in Section 4.01 above. Such substitution shall be in writing.

Paragraph 5.04. Trustee Liability. No person named as Trustee in this instrument or appointed as Trustee in the manner specified herein shall be liable to any beneficiary or to any heir of either Settlor for the Trustee's acts or failure to act, except for willful misconduct or gross negligence. No such Trustee shall be liable or responsible for any act, omission or default of any other Trustee provided that they shall have had no knowledge of facts that might reasonably be expected to put the Trustee on notice of it.

Paragraph 5.05. Title to Trust Estate. The legal title to all property held in trust hereunder shall be, remain and become vested in the Trustee or successor Trustee from time to time acting hereunder, without any act of conveyance or transfer to or by or acceptance from, any succeeding, retiring or predecessor Trustee; however, any removed or resigning Trustee shall execute and deliver any and all conveyances and documents requested and reasonably necessary to transfer the trust estate and its assets to a successor Trustee. Each successor Trustee from time to time acting hereunder shall have all the rights, powers immunities and authorities, discretionary or otherwise and the duties and obligations herein granted to the original Trustee. No successor Trustee shall be obligated to inquire into or be in any way responsible for the previous administration of any trust created herein or of the trust estate or for any act or default of any predecessor Trustee.

Paragraph 5.06. Powers of Trustee. To carry out the purposes of any trust created under this Trust Declaration, and subject to any limitations stated elsewhere in this Trust Declaration, the Trustee is vested with the following powers with respect to the Trust Estate, and any part of it, in addition to those powers now or hereafter conferred by law. The Trustee shall not exercise any power, right or discretion in a manner which will cause the loss of or a decrease in any marital or charitable deduction otherwise allowable in computing the federal estate tax of either Trustor.

A. Power to Invest. Subject to Paragraph 3.02 D. 2, to invest and reinvest the Trust Estate in every kind of property, real, personal or mixed, and every kind of investment, specifically including but not by way of limitation, corporate obligations of every kind, stocks, preferred or common, shares of investment trusts, investment companies, mutual funds, market index funds and mortgage participations which individuals of prudence, discretion and intelligence acquire for their own account, and any common trust fund administered by any Trustee under this Trust Declaration.

B. Power to Retain Property. To retain any property which was an asset of the Trust Estate during the Settlor's lifetime or received without consideration by the Trustee as long as the Trustee deems advisable whether or not of the character permitted by law for the investment of trust funds. The trust properties and investment need not be diversified and the Trustee shall have no duty to dispose or convert any trust assets to effect diversification.

C. Power to Manage Securities. With respect to securities held in this Trust Declaration, to have all the rights, powers and privileges of an owner, including but not by way of limitation, the power to vote, give proxies and pay assessments, to participate in voting trusts, pooling agreements, foreclosures, reorganizations, consolidations, mergers, liquidations, sales and leases and, incident to such participation, to deposit securities with and transfer title to any protective or other committee on such terms as the Trustee may deem advisable, to exercise and sell stock subscription or conversion rights and to hold securities in "street name".

D. Power of Sale, Exchange, Repair. To manage, control, foreclose, repossess, grant options on, grant easements on, sell (for cash), convey, exchange, partition, divide, improve and repair trust property.

The power to sell, at the termination of the trust, any trust property if the Trustee feels said disposition would assist in the distribution of the trust property at termination.

E. Power to Lease. To lease trust property for terms within or beyond the term of the trust and for any purpose, including exploration for and removal of gas, oil and other minerals; and to enter into community oil leases, pooling and unitization agreements, operating agreements or otherwise, and to create restrictions, easements or other servitudes thereon, to assign, partition, divide, subdivide, transfer to a corporation in exchange for stock, improve, repair, loan, reloan, invest and reinvest the trust estate or any part thereof.

F. Power to Insure. To carry, at the expense of the Trust Estate, insurance of such kinds and in such amounts as the Trustee shall deem advisable to protect the Trust Estate and the Trustee against any hazard.

G. Power to Commence or Defend Litigation. To commence or defend such litigation with respect to the Trust or any property of the Trust Estate as the Trustee may deem advisable, at the expense of the Trust Declaration.

H. Power to Compromise Claim. To compromise or otherwise adjust any claims or litigation against or in favor of the Trust Declaration.

I. Power to Employ Consultants. To employ any custodian, investment advisor, attorney, accountant or other agents to assist the Trustee in administration of this Trust Declaration and to rely upon the advice given by these agents. Reasonable compensation shall be paid to these agents for all services performed.

J. Power to Adjust for Tax Consequences. To take any action and to make any election the Trustee shall deem advisable to minimize the tax liabilities of this trust and its beneficiaries, to allocate the benefits among the various beneficiaries and to make adjustments in the rights of any beneficiaries or group of beneficiaries or between principal and income accounts, to compensate for the consequences of any tax election or any investment decision or administrative decision that has the effect of preferring one beneficiary or group of beneficiaries over others, provided such discretion shall not be exercised in any manner which will cause a loss of or a decrease in any marital or charitable deduction otherwise allowable in computing the then deceased Settlor's federal estate tax.

K. Trust Bank and Securities Accounts. During the joint lives of the Settlors, if the Settlors are serving as co-Trustees hereunder, the signature of either Trustor shall be sufficient to create, negotiate or endorse trust checks or to deposit or withdraw trust funds from trust bank or securities accounts or to trade securities in said securities accounts.

ARTICLE VI
MISCELLANEOUS

Paragraph 6.01. No Assignment. Each beneficiary hereunder is hereby prohibited from anticipating, encumbering, assigning or in any other manner, alienating her or his interest in either income or principal of any trust created under this Trust Declaration and is without power to do so nor shall such interest be subject to her or his liabilities or obligations nor to attachment, execution or other legal processes, bankruptcy proceedings or claims of creditors or others. The Trustee may require the personal receipt of a beneficiary as a condition precedent to payment, distribution or delivery of any amount, property or benefit hereunder. The Trustee may, however, deposit in any bank designated in writing, by a beneficiary, to her or his credit, income or principal payable to such beneficiary.

Paragraph 6.02. Principal and Income. Except as otherwise specifically provided in this Trust Declaration, the determination of all matters with respect to what shall constitute principal and income of each trust estate, gross income therefrom and net income distributable under the terms of the Trust Declaration, shall be governed by the provisions of the Revised Uniform Principal and Income Act as enacted in the State of (2a)_________________, from time to time existing. All taxes, assessments, fees, charges and other expenses incurred by the Trustee in the administration, protection and distribution of each trust, shall be a charge upon the trust estate and shall be paid out of the income and/or principal, in accordance with the aforesaid Act.

Paragraph 6.03. Savings Clause. Unless sooner terminated in accordance with other provisions of this Trust Declaration, any trust created hereunder shall terminate twenty-one (21) years after the death of the last surviving member of the group consisting of the Settlor and the issue of the Settlor who are living and in being at the date of death of the Settlor.

Paragraph 6.04. Payments to Minors and Incompetents. The Trustee, in the Trustee's discretion, may apply payments directly for the benefit of any beneficiary, rather than directly to such beneficiary and, in the case of a beneficiary who is a minor or who is under any other disability, make payment to the guardian, conservator of the person or estate of such beneficiary, custodian under the Uniform Transfers to Minors Act, parent or any other suitable adult with whom the beneficiary resides or by expending the same for the care, education, maintenance or other benefit of said beneficiary. In addition, the Trustee, in the Trustee's discretion, may make payments directly to a beneficiary who is a minor if, in the Trustee's judgment, the minor is of sufficient age and maturity to properly manage the money or property so paid. The Trustee shall not be required to see to the application of any such payment so made to any said persons, but his, her or their receipt therefor shall be a full discharge to the Trustee.

Paragraph 6.05. No Physical Segregation. There need be no physical segregation or division of the various trusts except as segregation or division may be required by the termination of any of the trusts or as specifically provided, but the Trustee shall keep separate accounts for the different undivided interests.

Paragraph 6.06. Distribution. In any case in which the Trustee is required, pursuant to the provisions of the Trust, to divide any parts or shares for the purposes of distribution or otherwise, except as the donee of any power of appointment affecting such property may have expressly provided otherwise in the instrument exercising such power, the Trustee is authorized, in the Trustee's absolute discretion, to make the division and distribution (pro rata or otherwise) in kind, including an undivided interest in any property or partly in kind and partly in money, and for this purpose, to make such sales of the trust property as the Trustee may deem necessary, on such terms and conditions as the Trustee shall see fit. Any asset which is encumbered shall be assigned subject thereto, and its value or amount shall be given effect less such indebtedness.

Paragraph 6.07. Non-Pro Rata Distributions. As to distribution or division of property in kind under and for the several trusts, excepting the initial establishment of any trust for a pecuniary amount, the Trustee shall be cognizant of the differences between the tax cost bases and current value and shall endeavor, insofar as is practicable to distribute or set aside to or for each beneficiary or distributee, assets or property carrying amount or portions of the total unrealized taxable gains or losses embodied in all the assets and properties involved commensurate with the share or portion of each beneficiary or distributee.

Paragraph 6.08. Distribution If All Beneficiaries Die Before Full Distribution. If at any time before full distribution of the Trust Estate, the Settlor is deceased and no disposition of the property is directed by this Trust Declaration, the Trust Estate or the portion of it not disposed of under the Trust Declaration, whichever the case may be, shall thereupon be distributed one-half to those persons who would be the legal heirs of Husband and one-half to the legal heirs of Wife their identities and respective shares to be determined as though the death of Husband and Wife had occurred immediately following the event requiring distribution and according to the laws of the State of (2a)__________________ then in effect relating to the succession of separate property not acquired from a parent, grandparent or previously deceased spouse.

Paragraph 6.09. Additional Property. With consent of the Trustee, additional property may be added at any time from any source to any trust held under this Trust Declaration. No person dealing with the Trustee in any manner shall be under any obligation to see to the application of any money paid to the Trustee or to inquire into the validity, expediency or propriety of any act of the Trustee or into any of the provisions of any trust hereunder.

Paragraph 6.10. Fiduciary Capacity. All of the powers of the Trustee provided in this Trust Declaration shall be exercisable by the Trustee in the Trustee's fiduciary capacity and only in such capacity.

Paragraph 6.11. Corporate Office. No person shall, by reason of acting as Trustee, be in any way restricted or prohibited from holding office in any corporation in which any trust under this Trust Declaration holds securities or from receiving compensation from any such corporation for services performed as a director, officer or employee of such corporation or from purchasing, selling or otherwise dealing with the stock of any such corporation for the individual account of such Trustee or from voting the stock of any such corporation held by such trust, including voting those shares in favor of the Settlor or any other person.

Paragraph 6.12. Disclaimer of Powers. The Trustee may disclaim, release or restrict the scope of any power held in connection with any trust created under this Trust Declaration, including any administrative power, whether such power is expressly granted in this Trust Declaration or implied by law, by a written instrument specifying the power to be disclaimed, released or restricted and the nature of any such restriction. Any power disclaimed or released by the Trustee shall be extinguished except to the extent this Trust Declaration expressly provides that such power pass to another. This power shall be personal to the Trustee only and may not be exercised by any other person acting on behalf of the Trustee, including, but not limited to, any Trustee (other than the Trustee), Conservator, agent or guardian.

Paragraph 6.13. Notice. Unless the Trustee has received written notice of the occurrence of an event affecting the beneficial interest in any trust held under this Trust Declaration, the Trustee shall not be liable to any beneficiary of such trust for any distributions made or other actions taken by the Trustee in good faith as though such event had not occurred.

Paragraph 6.14. Invalidity of Any Provision. Should any provision of this Trust Declaration be or become invalid or unenforceable, the remaining provisions of this Trust Declaration shall be and continue to be fully effective.

Paragraph 6.15. Gender and Number. Except as provided otherwise herein, the masculine, feminine and neuter gender, and the singular or plural number, shall each be deemed to include the others whenever the context so indicates.

Paragraph 6.16. Law of Construction of Trust. This Trust Declaration, its validity, the construction of and all rights under the Trusts provided for in this Trust Declaration shall be governed by the laws of the State of (2a)__________________.

Paragraph 6.17. No Contest. The Settlors have intentionally and with full knowledge omitted to provide for his/her issue, ancestors, relatives and heirs living at the time of his/her demise, except for such provisions as are made specifically herein.

If any person who is or claims under or through a beneficiary of this Trust, or if any person who would be entitled to share in either Settlor's estate if either or both Settlors died intestate, should in any manner whatsoever, directly or indirectly, attack, contest or seek to impair or invalidate in court any provision of the following:

A. This Trust or any Amendment to this Trust;

B. Any Will or Codicil to any Will executed by either Settlor;

C. Any beneficiary designation executed by either Settlor with respect to any insurance policy, any "Totten trust" account, any joint tenancy or tenancy by the entirety, any "transfer on death" account or any pension plan, or conspire or cooperate with anyone attempting to do any of the actions or things aforesaid, then each such person and any devise, share or interest in the Trust or either Settlor's Estate otherwise given to each such person under this Trust or either Settlor's Estate to which each such person might be entitled by law, is hereby revoked and shall pass and be distributed as though each such person had predeceased either Settlor leaving no issue or heirs whatsoever.

Any and every individual who asserts, or conspires or cooperates with any person who asserts, any claim against this Trust or the Estate of either Settlor of this Trust based on:

D. "Quantum meruit" theory;

E. Common law marriage, Marvin v. Marvin, 18 Cal. 3d 660 (1976) type of agreement or similar theory;

F. Constructive trust theory; or,

G. Oral agreement or written agreement which is to be proved by parole evidence, claiming that either Settlor agreed to gift or devise anything to such person or to pay such person or another for services rendered, regardless of whether a court may find that such agreement existed, then each such person is disinherited and any devise, share or interest in this Trust or either Settlor's Estate otherwise given to each such person under this Trust or either Settlor's Estate or to which each such person might be entitled by law, is hereby revoked and shall pass and be distributed as though each such person had predeceased both Settlors leaving no issue or heirs whatsoever.

The Trustee is specifically authorized to defend any such attack, contest, claim or other proceeding of any nature concerning this Trust or of any provision hereof, and to employ legal counsel therefor, all at the expense of the Trust.

Paragraph 6.18. Survival. If any person fails to survive a Settlor by thirty (30) days, for all purposes of this Trust Declaration the person shall be considered to have predeceased such Settlor.

Paragraph 6.19. All typed and handwritten "fill-ins" where directed above were made before the execution of this Declaration of Trust and are not initialed by the Settlors. All crossed through words and inter-lineations were made before the execution of this Trust and are initialed by the Settlors.

CERTIFICATION OF HUSBAND AND WIFE

We, and each of us, certify that:
A. We, and each of us, have read the foregoing Trust Declaration;
B. The foregoing Trust Declaration correctly states the terms and conditions under which the Trust Estate is to be held, managed, administered and disposed of by the Trustee;
C. As the Settlors named in such Trust Declaration, we, and each of us, approve such Trust Declaration in all particulars; and
D. As the Trustees named in such Trust Declaration, we, and each of us, approve and accept the Trust provided for in such Declaration.

Dated: (40)______________________________

(1)______________________________,Settlor, Trustee

(1b)______________________________

(4)______________________________, Settlor, Trustee

STATE OF (2a)________________)
) ss.
COUNTY OF (2)________________)

On ________________, 200__ before me, the undersigned, a Notary Public in and for said county and state, personally appeared (1)______________ and (4)______________, personally known to me (or proved to me on the basis of satisfactory evidence) to be the person(s) whose name(s) is/are subscribed to the within instrument and acknowledged that he/she/they executed the same in his/her/their authorized capacity(ies), and that by his/her/their signature(s) on the instrument the person(s), or the entity upon behalf of which the person(s) acted, executed the instrument.

WITNESS my hand and official seal.

____
Notary Public in and for said County and State

EXHIBIT A

Property Declared to be assets of the (1a)________________________________ TRUST dated (48)______________:

(55)
1.

INTER-VIVOS TRUST

THE (1a)______________________ TRUST

The Settlors named below hereby declare as follows:

ARTICLE I
ESTABLISHMENT OF TRUST

Paragraph 1.01. Creation of Trust. This Trust Declaration has been entered into between (1)__________________and (4)____________________ as Settlors and themselves as the Trustees. The Settlors, of (2)__________________ County, (2a)___________________, has transferred, or will transfer, to the Trustee of this Trust Declaration the property described in the attached Exhibit "A" which will constitute, together with any other property that may be added to this Trust Declaration, the Trust Estate of an express trust which shall be held, administered and distributed by the Trustee as provided in this Trust Declaration.

Paragraph 1.02. Trust Name. This Trust Declaration shall be known as the (1a)"_______________________________ TRUST" dated (48)__________________________.

Paragraph 1.03. Definitions. As used in this Trust Declaration:

A. Husband: The term "Husband" shall mean (1)___________.

B. Wife: The term "Wife" shall mean (4)_______________.

C. Settlors: The term "Settlors" shall refer collectively to Husband and Wife.

D. Deceased Settlor: The term "deceased Settlor" shall refer to the Settlor who is first to die. However, the term, "then deceased Settlor" shall refer to the Settlor then deceased and may thus refer to the otherwise surviving Settlor.

E. Surviving Settlor: The term "surviving Settlor" shall refer to the Settlor who is last to die.

F. Trustee: The term "Trustee" or "Trustees" shall refer to whoever is serving as Trustee or Trustees under this Trust Declaration.

G. Trust Estate: The term "Trust Estate" shall refer to the property subject to this Trust Declaration.

H. Issue: The term "issue" shall refer only to a person who is a lineal descendant of any degree of either the Husband and the Wife and shall (59) not include adopted persons.

Paragraph 1.04. Property to Retain Status. All property now or hereafter transferred to the Trustee which was community property, quasi-community property or separate property at the time of such transfer, shall remain, respectively, community property, quasi-community property or the separate property of the spouse or spouses transferring such property to the Trustee.

ARTICLE II
OPERATION OF TRUST DURING THE LIFE OF HUSBAND AND WIFE

Paragraph 2.01. Net Income. During the life of Husband and/or Wife, the Trustee shall pay to or apply for the benefit of both Husband and Wife, or the survivor thereof, in monthly or more frequent intervals, all of the net income of the community Trust Estate and shall pay to or apply for the benefit of the contributing spouse, in monthly or more frequent intervals, all of the net income of the separate property contributed or owned by that spouse.

Paragraph 2.02. Withdrawal of Principal. During the life of Husband and/or Wife, the Trustee shall also pay to or apply for the benefit of both Husband and Wife, or either, or the survivor thereof, so much of the community principal of the Trust Estate, up to the whole thereof, as both Husband and Wife shall direct, and shall, at the discretion of a spouse, pay to or apply for the benefit of that spouse so much of the principal of the Trust Estate, up to the whole thereof, as is that spouse's separate property.

Paragraph 2.03. Incapacity of Husband or Wife. If, at any time either Husband or Wife has become physically or mentally incapacitated so as to be unable to manage his or her affairs, whether or not a court of competent jurisdiction has declared him or her incompetent, mentally ill, or in need of a conservator, the Trustee shall pay to the non-incapacitated spouse or apply for the benefit of either spouse such amounts of the principal and/or income of the community estate as may be necessary, in the Trustee's discretion, for the care, maintenance and support of both spouses in accordance with their accustomed manner of living. The Trustee shall also pay to or apply for the benefit of the incapacitated spouse such amounts of income or principal of the separate property contributed by the incapacitated spouse as may be necessary, in the Trustee's discretion, for the care, maintenance, and support of the incapacitated spouse in accordance with his or her accustomed manner of living, taking into account payments made by the Trustee from the community Trust Estate. If a conservator of the person or estate is appointed for the incapacitated spouse, the Trustee shall take into account any payments made for the incapacitated spouse's benefit by the conservator.

The payments specified in this Section shall be made until the incapacitated spouse is again able to manage his or her own affairs, or until the death of the first spouse to die, whichever event may occur earlier.

Paragraph 2.04. Revocation of Trust. At any time during their joint lives, either Husband or Wife as to community property, and either spouse as to his or her separate property, may, by serving written notice on the Trustee, revoke the Trust created by this Trust Declaration, in whole or in part. Any community property withdrawn from the Trust Estate by reason of any such revocation shall be delivered by the Trustee to both Husband and Wife and any separate property withdrawn from the Trust shall be delivered by the Trustee to the spouse revoking the Trust.

Paragraph 2.05. Amendment of Trust. At any time during their joint lives, Husband and Wife, jointly as to community property, and either spouse as to his or her separate property, may, by serving written notice on the Trustee, alter, modify or amend the Trust created by this Trust Declaration in any respect.

ARTICLE III

OPERATION OF TRUST AFTER DEATH OF DECEASED SETTLOR

Paragraph 3.01. Collection of Assets and Payment of Deceased Settlor's Debts. On the death of the deceased Settlor the Trustee shall collect all assets belonging to the Trust Estate. As soon as practicable after the death of the deceased settlor, the Trustee, except as otherwise provided herein, shall pay from the deceased settlor's share of the Trust Estate the just debts of the deceased settlor (excluding any debts barred by provisions of law or not yet due), funeral expenses of the deceased spouse, and any inheritance, estate, or other death taxes that shall, by reason of the death of the deceased spouse, be attributable to the Trust Estate. This is not and shall not constitute a direction to pay all inheritance, estate or other death taxes from or charge the same to, the Trust Estate without apportionment.

Paragraph 3.02. Trust to Continue. On the death of the deceased settlor, the Trustee shall divide the Trust Estate into two separate trusts. Such trusts shall be designated as the *Decedent's Trust* and the *Survivor's Trust*.

A. Decedent's Trust.

1. Allocation to Decedent's Trust. The *Decedent's Trust* shall be a unified credit trust, the principal of which shall consist of a pecuniary amount equal to the unused unified credit available at the time of the death of the deceased settlor under IRC Section 2010, as amended, plus any property disclaimed by the surviving settlor after taking into account:

(i) All deductions taken in determining the estate tax payable by reason of the deceased spouse's death;

(ii) The net value of all other property, whether or not it is disposed of under this Trust and whether it passes at the time of the deceased spouse's death or has passed before the deceased spouse's death to or in trust for the surviving Settlor, so that it is included in the deceased spouse's gross estate and does not qualify for the federal estate tax marital deduction. In determining the amount of Trust, however, disclaimers by the surviving Settlor shall be disregarded; and

(iii) All credits allowed for federal estate tax purposes.

The Trustee shall satisfy the amount so determined in cash or in kind, or partly in each, and shall allocate to this Trust any assets of the predeceased spouse contributed or added to the trust that are not eligible for the federal estate tax marital deduction. Assets allocated in kind shall be considered to satisfy this amount on the basis of their net fair market values at the date or dates of allocation to this Trust.

The Trustee shall select and allocate the cash, securities and other property, including real estate and interests therein, which shall constitute the trust, employing for the purpose values current at the time or times of allocation.

2. Revocation and Modification of the Decedent's Trust After Death of Deceased Settlor. The *Decedent's Trust* shall be irrevocable and may not be amended or modified in any respect after the death of the deceased spouse.

B. Survivor's Trust.

1. Allocation to Survivor's Trust. The *Survivor's Trust* shall consist of the balance of the Trust Estate.

2. Revocation and Modification of *Survivor's Trust.* The surviving Settlor shall have the power to amend, revoke or terminate the *Survivor's Trust* exercisable by delivery of written notice to the Trustee. The surviving Settlor shall have the power to amend, revoke or terminate the *Survivor's Trust* exercisable by delivery of written notice to the Trustee. On revocation or termination of the *Survivor's Trust*, the Trustee shall deliver all of the assets of the *Survivor's Trust* to the surviving Settlor. On the death of the surviving Settlor, the *Survivor's Trust* shall be irrevocable and may not be amended or modified in any respect.

C. Distribution of Trust Estate.

1. The Trustee shall pay to or apply for the benefit of the surviving Settlor all the net income of the *Decedent's Trust* and *Survivor's Trust*, in monthly or more frequent intervals, but at least annually, during the surviving Settlor's lifetime.

2. If at any time or from time to time the surviving Settlor should be in need of funds in excess of all income and other property and resources available in a practicable manner for his or her benefit from the *Survivor's Trust* and all other sources, for his or her proper care, support or maintenance in his or her accustomed manner of living, or as a result of illness, physical or mental disability or other health requirement or expense, then the Trustee may relieve or contribute toward the relief of any such need of needs of said surviving Settlor by paying to him or her or using and applying for his or her benefit, such sum or sums out of the principal of the *Decedent's Trust* as may be necessary or advisable.

ARTICLE IV
OPERATION OF TRUST ON DEATH OF SURVIVING SETTLOR

Paragraph 4.01. Payment of Surviving Settlor's Debts. On the death of the surviving Settlor, the Trustee shall pay out of the principal or income of the *Survivor's Trust,* unless otherwise paid or provided for, the just debts of the surviving Settlor (excluding any debts barred by provisions of law or not yet due), funeral expenses of the surviving Settlor and any inheritance, estate or other death taxes that shall, by reason of the death of the surviving Settlor, be attributable to the *Survivor's Trust.* This is not and shall not constitute a direction to pay all inheritance, estate or other death taxes from the *Survivor's Trust* without apportionment.

Paragraph 4.02. Distribution of Survivor's Trust. Upon the death of the surviving Settlor, and after payment of expenses as set forth in Paragraph 4.01, the Trustee shall hold, administer and distribute all or any part of the balance of the *Survivor's Trust* shall be distributed to or for the benefit of such one or more persons or entities, including the estate of the surviving Settlor, on the terms and conditions, either outright or in trust, as the surviving Settlor may appoint by a written instrument other than a Will which specifically refers to and exercises this general testamentary power of appointment. Any of the *Survivor's Trust* not effectively appointed by the surviving Settlor shall be added to the balance of the *Decedent's Trust* to be held, administered and distributed as set forth below in Paragraph 4.03 below.

Paragraph 4.03. Distribution of Decedent's Trust. The *Decedent's Trust,* along with any of the *Survivor's Trust* not effectively appointed by the surviving Settlor, along with any other portion of the trust estate not in the *Survivor's Trust,* shall be distributed as follows:

A. The Trustee shall distribute to the following persons the cash amount listed after their respective names:
(10)

B The Trustee shall distribute to the following persons the real property described after their respective names. (12) Said real property is given free of all encumbrances or liens thereon.
(11)

C. The Trustee shall distribute to (13)__________________ a life estate in the following property located at: (14)________________________. After the death of (13)________________ said property shall go, outright, to (15)______________________________ as the remainder person(s).

D. The Trustee shall distribute all of the rest, residue and remainder of the Trust Estate, real, personal and mixed, of whatsoever kind or character and wheresoever situated, to the Trustee hereinafter named, to have and to hold upon the uses, trusts, purposes and conditions hereinafter provided.

The Trustee, shall allocate the trust properties into as many shares as there are children of the joint Settlors then living and children of the joint Settlors then deceased who left issue then living. One such equal share shall be set aside for each of the joint Settlors' children then living and one such equal share shall be set aside for the issue then living, by right of representation, of each of the joint Settlors' children who are then deceased but left issue then living. Said shares shall be held, administered, and distributed as provided in the following sections:

Each share set aside for a child of the joint Settlors shall be held, administered and delivered for and to such beneficiary as follows:

1. The net income from the trust while said beneficiary is under 19 years of age and not a high school graduate shall be added to principal, from which the Trustee shall pay to or for the benefit of such beneficiary such sums as in the Trustee's discretion the Trustee shall deem necessary for such beneficiary's proper care, comfort, maintenance, support or education.

In making payments for the benefit of any beneficiary pursuant to this section 1, the Trustee shall construe his or her authority liberally to permit payments reasonably necessary to ease the financial burden on the guardian of the person of such beneficiary or other suitable individual with whom they reside, and on his or her family, resulting from such beneficiary's presence in his or her household.

2. Upon the beneficiary reaching 19 years of age or finishing high school(whichever occurs first), the Trustee shall pay to or apply for his or her benefit, from his or her trust, as much of the trust principal as the Trustee, in the Trustee's discretion, considers appropriate pursuant to sections 3 and 4 following.

3. After the beneficiary attains 19 years of age or finishes high school (whichever occurs first), the Trustee may, in the Trustee's discretion, pay to or apply from his or her trust, such amounts necessary for his or her education. For purposes hereof, education shall mean enrollment, attendance, and satisfactory progression towards a degree as a student at a recognized and accredited college, university, or similar institution of higher learning, including any graduate, professional school or college or trade school. Such educational payments and benefits shall include tuition, books, all direct educational costs and fees, and all reasonable living and transportation expenses. Payments hereunder shall be made during vacation periods within the regular school term under which the beneficiary is attending school and during "summer vacation" or similar vacation period between the regular school terms.

The Trustee may invest any portion of a beneficiary's trust share in an IRC 529 college savings plan for the benefit of said beneficiary.

4. If the beneficiary, his or her spouse, or any of his or her children should at any time or from time to time be in need, in the discretion of the Trustee, of funds due to illness, infirmity or other physical or mental disability or any emergency, the Trustee may relieve or contribute toward the relief of any such need or needs of the beneficiary by paying to him or her or using and applying for his or her benefit, such sum or sums out of the income and/or principal of his or her trust as the Trustee, in the Trustee's discretion, may deem necessary or advisable.

5. Upon the beneficiary attaining the age of 21 years, the Trustee shall begin to pay the beneficiary all of the net income, in monthly or other convenient installments, from the trust.

6. Upon the beneficiary attaining the age of (21)_______ years, the Trustee shall distribute and deliver to such beneficiary one-half of his or her trust estate. Upon each beneficiary attaining the age of (22)_______ years, the Trustee shall distribute and deliver to such beneficiary all of the remainder of his or her trust estate.

7. If, upon the attaining of the above ages, the Trustee suspects that said beneficiary may be abusing drugs, the Trustee may require the beneficiary to take a reasonable drug test. If the beneficiary fails said drug test, the Trustee shall defer said principal payment to the beneficiary until the beneficiary passes said drug test. After a failed drug test, subsequent drug tests shall be administered at six month intervals. In the event a beneficiary fails a drug test, the Trustee may use said beneficiary's trust estate to pay for a drug abuse rehabilitation program and may require the beneficiary to enroll and to complete said program as a condition precedent to the taking of a subsequent drug test.

8. In the event the beneficiary should die before complete distribution to him or her of his or her trust estate, his or her entire trust estate on hand at the time of his or her death shall thereupon be apportioned and distributed to his or her surviving issue, by right of representation. If such beneficiary should die before complete distribution to him or her of his or her trust estate and leave no surviving issue, then the balance of the trust estate then on hand shall go and be distributed one-half to those persons who would be the legal heirs of Husband and one-half to the legal heirs of Wife their identities and respective shares to be determined as

though the death of Husband and Wife had occurred immediately following the event requiring distribution and according to the laws of the State of (2a)_________________ then in effect relating to the succession of separate property not acquired from a parent, grandparent or previously deceased spouse.

9. If, at any time, a trust created hereunder shall, in the sole judgment of the Trustee, be of the aggregate principal value of Fifty Thousand Dollars ($50,000.00) or less, the Trustee may, but need not, terminate such trust and distribute the assets thereof in the Trustee's possession to the beneficiary or beneficiaries, at the time of the current income thereof, and if there is more than one beneficiary, in the proportion in which they are beneficiaries.

E. Distribution of Trust Assets. With respect to the distribution of any trust estate upon termination of any trust, and partial distribution of any trust, the liquidation and distribution by the Trustee of the Trust Estate involved or the distributable portion shall commence immediately and be accomplished as rapidly as possible, and deliveries of the trust properties to the beneficiary or beneficiaries may be made in installments or series, retaining only reasonable reserves for final charges and expenses. In no event shall it be necessary for the Trustee to await an accounting to the Court, or any Court order, before releasing and distributing the majority of the Trust Estate to be distributed.

F .Undistributed Income. All the net income of the respective trusts or trust estates, not distributed, used or applied as otherwise provided herein, shall be accumulated and added to the principals of the respective trusts.

Upon the change or succession of any beneficiary, distribution of trust properties or any trust estate or any portion thereof, or upon setting aside, apportionment or division of any trust estate or upon the termination of a trust or any interest therein, the beneficial interest, properties or balance of trust estate at the applicable time and to be dealt with shall include any and all income accumulated, accrued, uncollected or held undistributed and all of such income shall likewise be distributed, set aside or apportioned to the next or succeeding beneficiaries, distributees, shares or trusts, retaining its character as income.

ARTICLE V
TRUSTEES

Paragraph 5.01. Appointment of Trustees. Settlors, (1)____________________ and (4)____________________ are appointed and confirmed as the Trustees, without bond. In the event either original Trustee should resign, die or become mentally incapacitated, the remaining Trustee shall act as sole Trustee. If either original Trustee should cease to act as Trustee due to a mental incapacity, his/her restoration of mental capacity shall result in his or her immediate return as Trustee or Co-Trustee hereunder. If either original Trustee should cease to act as sole Trustee or a Co-Trustee with the other original Trustee due to his/her resignation, he/she may at any time subsequent, elect to act again as sole Trustee or a Co-Trustee with the other original Trustee. Said election shall be made by filing same with either of the then acting Trustee or by recording said election in the County of residence of said Trustee making such election.

In the event both (1)__________________ and (4)_____________should die, refuse to act, or for any other reason be unable to act, then (25)____________________ shall act as (26)____Trustee_ hereunder (27) without bond. In the event he/she/they should die, decline to act, or for any other reason, be unable to act as Trustee then (28)__________________________ shall act as Trustee hereunder (27) without bond.

Notwithstanding the above, at now time shall the surviving Settlor act as Trustee of any life insurance policy allocated to the *Decedent's Trust*. In that event the surviving Settlor shall appoint a special Trustee to hold title to and administer such policy or policies.

Paragraph 5.02. Substitute Trustee. The Settlors jointly, or the surviving Settlor upon the death of the predeceased Settlor, may appoint a substitute or successor Trustee to act as Trustee of any trust or trusts created hereunder in the place and stead of, or as successor to, any Trustee named in Section 4.01 above. Such substitution shall be in writing.

Paragraph 5.04. Trustee Liability. No person named as Trustee in this instrument or appointed as Trustee in the manner specified herein shall be liable to any beneficiary or to any heir of either Settlor for the Trustee's acts or failure to act, except for willful misconduct or gross negligence. No such Trustee shall be liable or responsible for any act, omission or default of any other Trustee provided that they shall have had no knowledge of facts that might reasonably be expected to put the Trustee on notice of it.

Paragraph 5.05. Title to Trust Estate. The legal title to all property held in trust hereunder shall be, remain and become vested in the Trustee or successor Trustee from time to time acting hereunder, without any act of conveyance or transfer to or by or acceptance from, any succeeding, retiring or predecessor Trustee; however, any removed or resigning Trustee shall execute and deliver any and all conveyances and documents requested and reasonably necessary to transfer the trust estate and its assets to a successor Trustee. Each successor Trustee from time to time acting hereunder shall have all the rights, powers immunities and authorities, discretionary or otherwise and the duties and obligations herein granted to the original Trustee. No successor Trustee shall be obligated to inquire into or be in any way responsible for the previous administration of any trust created herein or of the trust estate or for any act or default of any predecessor Trustee.

Paragraph 5.06. Powers of Trustee. To carry out the purposes of any trust created under this Trust Declaration, and subject to any limitations stated elsewhere in this Trust Declaration, the Trustee is vested with the following powers with respect to the Trust Estate, and any part of it, in addition to those powers now or hereafter conferred by law.

A. Power to Invest. To invest and reinvest the Trust Estate in every kind of property, real, personal or mixed, and every kind of investment, specifically including but not by way of limitation, corporate obligations of every kind, stocks, preferred or common, shares of investment trusts, investment companies, mutual funds, market index funds and mortgage participations which individuals of prudence, discretion and intelligence acquire for their own account, and any common trust fund administered by any Trustee under this Trust Declaration.

B. Power to Retain Property. To retain any property which was an asset of the Trust Estate during the Settlor's lifetime or received without consideration by the Trustee as long as the Trustee deems advisable whether or not of the character permitted by law for the investment of trust funds. The trust properties and investment need not be diversified and the Trustee shall have no duty to dispose or convert any trust assets to effect diversification.

C. Power to Manage Securities. With respect to securities held in this Trust Declaration, to have all the rights, powers and privileges of an owner, including but not by way of limitation, the power to vote, give proxies and pay assessments, to participate in voting trusts, pooling agreements, foreclosures, reorganizations, consolidations, mergers, liquidations, sales and leases and, incident to such participation, to deposit securities with and transfer title to any protective or other committee on such terms as the Trustee may deem advisable, to exercise and sell stock subscription or conversion rights and to hold securities in "street name".

D. Power of Sale, Exchange, Repair. To manage, control, foreclose, repossess, grant options on, grant easements on, sell (for cash), convey, exchange, partition, divide, improve and repair trust property.

The power to sell, at the termination of the trust, any trust property if the Trustee feels said disposition would assist in the distribution of the trust property at termination.

E. Power to Lease. To lease trust property for terms within or beyond the term of the trust and for any purpose, including exploration for and removal of gas, oil and other minerals; and to enter into community oil leases, pooling and unitization agreements, operating agreements or otherwise, and to create restrictions, easements or other servitudes thereon, to assign, partition, divide, subdivide, transfer to a corporation in exchange for stock, improve, repair, loan, reloan, invest and reinvest the trust estate or any part thereof.

F. Power to Insure. To carry, at the expense of the Trust Estate, insurance of such kinds and in such amounts as the Trustee shall deem advisable to protect the Trust Estate and the Trustee against any hazard.

G. Power to Commence or Defend Litigation. To commence or defend such litigation with respect to the Trust or any property of the Trust Estate as the Trustee may deem advisable, at the expense of the Trust Declaration.

H. Power to Compromise Claim. To compromise or otherwise adjust any claims or litigation against or in favor of the Trust Declaration.

I. Power to Employ Consultants. To employ any custodian, investment advisor, attorney, accountant or other agents to assist the Trustee in administration of this Trust Declaration and to rely upon the advice given by these agents. Reasonable compensation shall be paid to these agents for all services performed.

J. Power to Adjust for Tax Consequences. To take any action and to make any election the Trustee shall deem advisable to minimize the tax liabilities of this trust and its beneficiaries, to allocate the benefits among the various beneficiaries and to make adjustments in the rights of any beneficiaries or group of beneficiaries or between principal and income accounts, to compensate for the consequences of any tax election or any investment decision or administrative decision that has the effect of preferring one beneficiary or group of beneficiaries over others, provided such discretion shall not be exercised in any manner which will cause a loss of or a decrease in any marital or charitable deduction otherwise allowable in computing the then deceased Settlor's federal estate tax.

K. Trust Bank and Securities Accounts. During the joint lives of the Settlors, if the Settlors are serving as co-Trustees hereunder, the signature of either Trustor shall be sufficient to create, negotiate or endorse trust checks or to deposit or withdraw trust funds from trust bank or securities accounts or to trade securities in said securities accounts.

ARTICLE VI
MISCELLANEOUS

Paragraph 6.01. No Assignment. Each beneficiary hereunder is hereby prohibited from anticipating, encumbering, assigning or in any other manner, alienating her or his interest in either income or principal of any trust created under this Trust Declaration and is without power to do so nor shall such interest be subject to her or his liabilities or obligations nor to attachment, execution or other legal processes, bankruptcy proceedings or claims of creditors or others. The Trustee may require the personal receipt of a beneficiary as a condition precedent to payment, distribution or delivery of any amount, property or benefit hereunder. The Trustee may, however, deposit in any bank designated in writing, by a beneficiary, to her or his credit, income or principal payable to such beneficiary.

Paragraph 6.02. Principal and Income. Except as otherwise specifically provided in this Trust Declaration, the determination of all matters with respect to what shall constitute principal and income of each trust estate, gross income therefrom and net income distributable under the terms of the Trust Declaration, shall be governed by the provisions of the Revised Uniform Principal and Income Act as enacted in the State of (2a)________________, from time to time existing. All taxes, assessments, fees, charges and other expenses incurred by the Trustee in the administration, protection and distribution of each trust, shall be a charge upon the trust estate and shall be paid out of the income and/or principal, in accordance with the aforesaid Act.

Paragraph 6.03. Savings Clause. Unless sooner terminated in accordance with other provisions of this Trust Declaration, any trust created hereunder shall terminate twenty-one (21) years after the death of the last surviving member of the group consisting of the Settlor and the issue of the Settlor who are living and in being at the date of death of the Settlor.

Paragraph 6.04. Payments to Minors and Incompetents. The Trustee, in the Trustee's discretion, may apply payments directly for the benefit of any beneficiary, rather than directly to such beneficiary and, in the case of a beneficiary who is a minor or who is under any other disability, make payment to the guardian, conservator of the person or estate of such beneficiary, custodian under the Uniform Transfers to Minors Act, parent or any other suitable adult with whom the beneficiary resides or by expending the same for the care, education, maintenance or other benefit of said beneficiary. In addition, the Trustee, in the Trustee's discretion, may make payments directly to a beneficiary who is a minor if, in the Trustee's judgment, the minor is of sufficient age and maturity to properly manage the money or property so paid. The Trustee shall not be required to see to the application of any such payment so made to any said persons, but his, her or their receipt therefor shall be a full discharge to the Trustee.

Paragraph 6.05. No Physical Segregation. There need be no physical segregation or division of the various trusts except as segregation or division may be required by the termination of any of the trusts or as specifically provided, but the Trustee shall keep separate accounts for the different undivided interests.

Paragraph 6.06. Distribution. In any case in which the Trustee is required, pursuant to the provisions of the Trust, to divide any parts or shares for the purposes of distribution or otherwise, except as the donee of any power of appointment affecting such property may have expressly provided otherwise in the instrument exercising such power, the Trustee is authorized, in the Trustee's absolute discretion, to make the division and distribution (pro rata or otherwise) in kind, including an undivided interest in any property or partly in kind and partly in money, and for this purpose, to make such sales of the trust property as the Trustee may deem necessary, on such terms and conditions as the Trustee shall see fit. Any asset which is encumbered shall be assigned subject thereto, and its value or amount shall be given effect less such indebtedness.

Paragraph 6.07. Non-Pro Rata Distributions. As to distribution or division of property in kind under and for the several trusts, excepting the initial establishment of any trust for a pecuniary amount, the Trustee shall be cognizant of the differences between the tax cost bases and current value and shall endeavor, insofar as is practicable to distribute or set aside to or for each beneficiary or distributee, assets or property carrying amount or portions of the total unrealized taxable gains or losses embodied in all the assets and properties involved commensurate with the share or portion of each beneficiary or distributee.

Paragraph 6.08. Distribution If All Beneficiaries Die Before Full Distribution. If at any time before full distribution of the Trust Estate, the Settlor is deceased and no disposition of the property is directed by this Trust Declaration, the Trust Estate or the portion of it not disposed of under the Trust Declaration, whichever the case may be, shall thereupon be distributed one-half to those persons who would be the legal heirs of Husband and one-half to the legal heirs of Wife their identities and respective shares to be determined as though the death of Husband and Wife had occurred immediately following the event requiring distribution and according to the laws of the State of (2a)________________ then in effect relating to the succession of separate property not acquired from a parent, grandparent or previously deceased spouse.

Paragraph 6.09. Additional Property. With consent of the Trustee, additional property may be added at any time from any source to any trust held under this Trust Declaration. No person dealing with the Trustee in any manner shall be under any obligation to see to the application of any money paid to the Trustee or to inquire into the validity, expediency or propriety of any act of the Trustee or into any of the provisions of any trust hereunder.

Paragraph 6.10. Fiduciary Capacity. All of the powers of the Trustee provided in this Trust Declaration shall be exercisable by the Trustee in the Trustee's fiduciary capacity and only in such capacity.

Paragraph 6.11. Corporate Office. No person shall, by reason of acting as Trustee, be in any way restricted or prohibited from holding office in any corporation in which any trust under this Trust Declaration holds securities or from receiving compensation from any such corporation for services performed as a director, officer or employee of such corporation or from purchasing, selling or otherwise dealing with the stock of any such corporation for the individual account of such Trustee or from voting the stock of any such corporation held by such trust, including voting those shares in favor of the Settlor or any other person.

Paragraph 6.12. Disclaimer of Powers. The Trustee may disclaim, release or restrict the scope of any power held in connection with any trust created under this Trust Declaration, including any administrative power, whether such power is expressly granted in this Trust Declaration or implied by law, by a written instrument specifying the power to be disclaimed, released or restricted and the nature of any such restriction. Any power disclaimed or released by the Trustee shall be extinguished except to the extent this Trust Declaration expressly provides that such power pass to another. This power shall be personal to the Trustee only and may not be exercised by any other person acting on behalf of the Trustee, including, but not limited to, any Trustee (other than the Trustee), Conservator, agent or guardian.

Paragraph 6.13. Notice. Unless the Trustee has received written notice of the occurrence of an event affecting the beneficial interest in any trust held under this Trust Declaration, the Trustee shall not be liable to any beneficiary of such trust for any distributions made or other actions taken by the Trustee in good faith as though such event had not occurred.

Paragraph 6.14. Invalidity of Any Provision. Should any provision of this Trust Declaration be or become invalid or unenforceable, the remaining provisions of this Trust Declaration shall be and continue to be fully effective.

Paragraph 6.15. Gender and Number. Except as provided otherwise herein, the masculine, feminine and neuter gender, and the singular or plural number, shall each be deemed to include the others whenever the context so indicates.

Paragraph 6.16. Law of Construction of Trust. This Trust Declaration, its validity, the construction of and all rights under the Trusts provided for in this Trust Declaration shall be governed by the laws of the State of (2a)__________________.

Paragraph 6.17. No Contest. The Settlors have intentionally and with full knowledge omitted to provide for his/her issue, ancestors, relatives and heirs living at the time of his/her demise, except for such provisions as are made specifically herein.

If any person who is or claims under or through a beneficiary of this Trust, or if any person who would be entitled to share in either Settlor's estate if either or both Settlors died intestate, should in any manner whatsoever, directly or indirectly, attack, contest or seek to impair or invalidate in court any provision of the following:

A. This Trust or any Amendment to this Trust;

B. Any Will or Codicil to any Will executed by either Settlor;

C. Any beneficiary designation executed by either Settlor with respect to any insurance policy, any "Totten trust" account, any joint tenancy or tenancy by the entirety, any "transfer on death" account or any pension plan, or conspire or cooperate with anyone attempting to do any of the actions or things aforesaid, then each such person and any devise, share or interest in the Trust or either Settlor's Estate otherwise given to each such person under this Trust or either Settlor's Estate to which each such person might be entitled by law, is hereby revoked and shall pass and be distributed as though each such person had predeceased either Settlor leaving no issue or heirs whatsoever.

Any and every individual who asserts, or conspires or cooperates with any person who asserts, any claim against this Trust or the Estate of either Settlor of this Trust based on:

D. "Quantum meruit" theory;

E. Common law marriage, Marvin v. Marvin, 18 Cal. 3d 660 (1976) type of agreement or similar theory;

F. Constructive trust theory; or,

G. Oral agreement or written agreement which is to be proved by parole evidence, claiming that either Settlor agreed to gift or devise anything to such person or to pay such person or another for services rendered, regardless of whether a court may find that such agreement existed, then each such person is disinherited and any devise, share or interest in this Trust or either Settlor's Estate otherwise given to each such person under this Trust or either Settlor's Estate or to which each such person might be entitled by law, is hereby revoked and shall pass and be distributed as though each such person had predeceased both Settlors leaving no issue or heirs whatsoever.

The Trustee is specifically authorized to defend any such attack, contest, claim or other proceeding of any nature concerning this Trust or of any provision hereof, and to employ legal counsel therefor, all at the expense of the Trust.

Paragraph 6.18. Survival. If any person fails to survive a Settlor by thirty (30) days, for all purposes of this Trust Declaration the person shall be considered to have predeceased such Settlor.

Paragraph 6.19. All typed and handwritten "fill-ins" where directed above were made before the execution of this Declaration of Trust and are not initialed by the Settlors. All crossed through words and inter-lineations were made before the execution of this Trust and are initialed by the Settlors.

CERTIFICATION OF HUSBAND AND WIFE

We, and each of us, certify that:

A. We, and each of us, have read the foregoing Trust Declaration;
B. The foregoing Trust Declaration correctly states the terms and conditions under which the Trust Estate is to be held, managed, administered and disposed of by the Trustee;
C. As the Settlors named in such Trust Declaration, we, and each of us, approve such Trust Declaration in all particulars; and
D. As the Trustees named in such Trust Declaration, we, and each of us, approve and accept the Trust provided for in such Declaration.

Dated: (40)______________________________

(1)________________________________, Settlor, Trustee

(1b)______________________________

(4)________________________________, Settlor, Trustee

STATE OF (2a)________________)
) ss.
COUNTY OF (2)________________)

On ________________, 200__ before me, the undersigned, a Notary Public in and for said county and state, personally appeared (1)______________ and (4)______________, personally known to me (or proved to me on the basis of satisfactory evidence) to be the person(s) whose name(s) is/are subscribed to the within instrument and acknowledged that he/she/they executed the same in his/her/their authorized capacity(ies), and that by his/her/their signature(s) on the instrument the person(s), or the entity upon behalf of which the person(s) acted, executed the instrument.

WITNESS my hand and official seal.

____
Notary Public in and for said County and State

EXHIBIT A

Property Declared to be assets of the (1a)________________________________ TRUST dated (48)________________:

(55)

1.

INTER-VIVOS TRUST

THE (1a)____________________________ TRUST

The Settlors named below hereby declare as follows:

ARTICLE I
ESTABLISHMENT OF TRUST

Paragraph 1.01. Creation of Trust. This Trust Declaration has been entered into between (1)__________________and (4)___________________ as Settlors and themselves as the Trustees. The Settlors, of (2)__________________ County, (2a)__________________, have transferred, or will transfer, to the Trustee of this Trust Declaration the property described in the attached Exhibit "A" which will constitute, together with any other property that may be added to this Trust Declaration, the Trust Estate of an express trust which shall be held, administered and distributed by the Trustee as provided in this Trust Declaration.

Paragraph 1.02. Trust Name. This Trust Declaration shall be known as the (1a)"_________________________________ TRUST" dated (48)__________________________.

Paragraph 1.03. Definitions. As used in this Trust Declaration:

A. Husband: The term "Husband" shall mean (1)___________.

B. Wife: The term "Wife" shall mean (4)_______________.

C. Settlors: The term "Settlors" shall refer collectively to Husband and Wife.

D. Deceased Settlor: The term "deceased Settlor" shall refer to the Settlor who is first to die. However, the term, "then deceased Settlor" shall refer to the Settlor then deceased and may thus refer to the otherwise surviving Settlor.

E. Surviving Settlor: The term "surviving Settlor" shall refer to the Settlor who is last to die.

F. Trustee: The term "Trustee" or "Trustees" shall refer to whoever is serving as Trustee or Trustees under this Trust Declaration.

G. Trust Estate: The term "Trust Estate" shall refer to the property subject to this Trust Declaration.

Paragraph 1.04. Property to Retain Status. All property now or hereafter transferred to the Trustee which was community property, quasi-community property or separate property at the time of such transfer, shall remain, respectively, community property, quasi-community property or the separate property of the spouse transferring such property to the Trustee.

ARTICLE II
OPERATION OF TRUST DURING THE LIFE OF HUSBAND AND WIFE

Paragraph 2.01. Net Income. During the life of Husband and/or Wife, the Trustee shall pay to or apply for the benefit of both Husband and Wife, or the survivor thereof, in monthly or more frequent intervals, all of the net income of the community Trust Estate and shall pay to or apply for the benefit of the contributing spouse, in monthly or more frequent intervals, all of the net income of the separate property contributed or owned by that spouse.

Paragraph 2.02. Withdrawal of Principal. During the life of Husband and/or Wife, the Trustee shall also pay to or apply for the benefit of both Husband and Wife, or either, or the survivor thereof, so much of the community principal of the Trust Estate, up to the whole thereof, as both Husband and Wife shall direct, and shall, at the discretion of a spouse, pay to or apply for the benefit of that spouse so much of the principal of the Trust Estate, up to the whole thereof, as is that spouse's separate property.

Paragraph 2.03. Incapacity of Husband or Wife. If, at any time either Husband or Wife has become physically or mentally incapacitated so as to be unable to manage his or her affairs, whether or not a court of competent jurisdiction has declared him or her incompetent, mentally ill, or in need of a conservator, the Trustee shall pay to the non-incapacitated spouse or apply for the benefit of either spouse such amounts of the principal and/or income of the community estate as may be necessary, in the Trustee's discretion, for the care, maintenance and support of both spouses in accordance with their accustomed manner of living. The Trustee shall also pay to or apply for the benefit of the incapacitated spouse such amounts of income or principal of the separate property contributed by the incapacitated spouse as may be necessary, in the Trustee's discretion, for the care, maintenance, and support of the incapacitated spouse in accordance with his or her accustomed manner of living, taking into account payments made by the Trustee from the community Trust Estate. If a conservator of the person or estate is appointed for the incapacitated spouse, the Trustee shall take into account any payments made for the incapacitated spouse's benefit by the conservator.

The payments specified in this Section shall be made until the incapacitated spouse is again able to manage his or her own affairs, or until the death of the first spouse to die, whichever event may occur earlier.

Paragraph 2.04. Revocation of Trust. At any time during their joint lives, either Husband or Wife as to community property, and either spouse as to his or her separate property, may, by serving written notice on the Trustee, revoke the Trust created by this Trust Declaration, in whole or in part. Any community property withdrawn from the Trust Estate by reason of any such revocation shall be delivered by the Trustee to both Husband and Wife and any separate property withdrawn from the Trust shall be delivered by the Trustee to the spouse revoking the Trust.

Paragraph 2.05. Amendment of Trust. At any time during their joint lives, Husband and Wife, jointly as to community property, and either spouse as to his or her separate property, may, by serving written notice on the Trustee, alter, modify or amend the Trust created by this Trust Declaration in any respect.

ARTICLE III

OPERATION OF TRUST AFTER DEATH OF DECEASED SETTLOR

Paragraph 3.01. Collection of Assets and Payment of Deceased Settlor's Debts. On the death of the deceased Settlor the Trustee shall collect all assets belonging to the Trust Estate. As soon as practicable after the death of the deceased Settlor, the Trustee, except as otherwise provided herein, shall pay from the deceased Settlor's share of the Trust Estate the just debts of the deceased Settlor (excluding any debts barred by provisions of law or not yet due), funeral expenses of the deceased Settlor, and any inheritance, estate, or other death taxes that shall, by reason of the death of the deceased Settlor, be attributable to the Trust Estate. This is not and shall not constitute a direction to pay all inheritance, estate or other death taxes from or charge the same to, the Trust Estate without apportionment.

Paragraph 3.02. Trust to Continue. On the death of the deceased Settlor, the Trustee shall divide the Trust Estate into as many as three separate trusts. Such trusts shall be designated as the *Decedent's Trust*, the *Marital Trust* and the *Survivor's Trust.*

A.Decedent's Trust. The *Decedent's Trust* shall be created from the deceased Settlor's interest in community property and quasi-community property and the separate property of the deceased Settlor which is included in the Trust Estate.

1. Allocation to Decedent's Trust. The *Decedent's Trust* shall be a unified credit trust, the principal of which shall consist of a pecuniary amount equal to the unused unified credit available at the time of the death of the deceased Settlor under IRC Section 2010, as amended, plus any property disclaimed by the surviving Settlor after taking into account:

(i) All deductions taken in determining the estate tax payable by reason of the deceased Settlor's death;

(ii) The net value of all other property, whether or not it is disposed of under this Trust and whether it passes at the time of the deceased Settlor's death or has passed before the deceased Settlor's death to or in trust for the surviving Settlor, so that it is included in the deceased Settlor's gross estate and does not qualify for the federal estate tax marital deduction. In determining the amount of Trust, however, disclaimers by the surviving Settlor shall be disregarded; and

(iii) All credits allowed for federal estate tax purposes.

The Trustee shall satisfy the amount so determined in cash or in kind, or partly in each, and shall allocate to this Trust any assets of the deceased Settlor contributed or added to the trust that are not eligible for the federal estate tax marital deduction. Assets allocated in kind shall be considered to satisfy this amount on the basis of their net fair market values at the date or dates of allocation to this Trust.

The Trustee shall select and allocate the cash, securities and other property, including real estate and interests therein, which shall constitute the trust, employing for the purpose values current at the time or times of allocation.

2. Revocation and Modification of the Decedent's Trust After Death of Deceased Settlor. The *Decedent's Trust* shall be irrevocable and may not be amended or modified in any respect after the death of the deceased Settlor.

B. Marital Trust.

1. Allocation to Marital Trust. The *Marital Trust* shall be created from the deceased Settlor's remaining, if any, interest in community property and quasi-community property and the separate property of the deceased Settlor which is included in the Trust Estate and which qualify for the federal estate tax marital deduction.

Assets qualifying for the federal estate tax marital deduction shall be transferred to the *Marital Trust* only to the extent they reduce the federal estate tax otherwise payable. No assets for which a credit for foreign death taxes is allowed shall be includable in the *Marital Trust* unless that estate contains insufficient other property to fully fund the *Marital Trust.*

2. Revocation and Modification of the Marital Trust After
Death of Deceased Settlor. The *Marital Trust* shall be irrevocable and may not be amended or modified in any respect after the death of the deceased Settlor.

C. Survivor's Trust.

1. Allocation to Survivor's Trust. The *Survivor's Trust* shall consist of the balance of the Trust Estate.

2. Revocation and Modification of Survivor's Trust. The surviving Settlor shall have the power to amend, revoke or terminate the *Survivor's Trust* exercisable by delivery of written notice to the Trustee. The surviving Settlor shall have the power to amend, revoke or terminate the *Survivor's Trust* exercisable by delivery of written notice to the Trustee. On revocation or termination of the *Survivor's Trust*, the Trustee shall deliver all of the assets of the *Survivor's Trust* to the surviving Settlor. On the death of the surviving Settlor, the *Survivor's Trust* shall be irrevocable and may not be amended or modified in any respect.

D. Distribution of Trust Estate.

1. The Trustee shall pay to or apply for the benefit of the surviving Settlor all the net income of the *Decedent's Trust, Marital Trust* and *Survivor's Trust*, in monthly or more frequent intervals, but at least annually, during the surviving Settlor's lifetime.

2. The surviving Settlor shall have the right to require the Trustee to convert any non-income producing asset held by the *Marital Trust* to an income producing asset.

3. In addition to any other payments to the surviving Settlor hereunder, the Trustee shall, upon the written request of the surviving Settlor in December of year calendar year, pay to the surviving Settlor amounts from principal that the surviving Settlor requests, not exceeding in any single calendar year the greater of the following amounts: $5,000.00 or 5 percent of the value of the principal of the *Marital Trust* (determined as of the end of the calendar year. This right of withdrawal is noncumulative, so that if the beneficiary does not withdraw the full amount permitted to be withdrawn during any calendar year, the right to withdraw the remaining amount will lapse at the end of the calendar year.
4. If at any time or from time to time the surviving Settlor should be in need of funds in excess of all income and other property and resources available in a practicable manner for his or her benefit from the *Survivor's Trust* and all other sources, for his or her proper care, support or maintenance in his or her accustomed manner of living, or as a result of illness, physical or mental disability or other health requirement or expense, then the Trustee may relieve or contribute toward the relief of any such need of needs of said surviving Settlor by paying to him or her or using and applying for his or her benefit, such sum or sums out of the principal of the *Marital Trust* or *Decedent's Trust* as may be necessary or advisable.

ARTICLE IV
OPERATION OF TRUST ON DEATH OF SURVIVING SETTLOR

Paragraph 4.01. Payment of Surviving Settlor's Debts. On the death of the surviving Settlor, the Trustee shall pay out of the principal or income of the *Survivor's Trust*, unless otherwise paid or provided for, the just debts of the surviving Settlor (excluding any debts barred by provisions of law or not yet due), funeral expenses of the surviving Settlor and any inheritance, estate or other death taxes that shall, by reason of the death of the surviving Settlor, be attributable to the *Survivor's Trust*. This is not and shall not constitute a direction to pay all inheritance, estate or other death taxes from the *Survivor's Trust* without apportionment.

Any accrued but unpaid income of the *Marital Trust* shall be paid to the estate of the surviving Settlor.

Paragraph 4.02. Distribution of Survivor's Trust. Upon the death of the surviving Settlor, and after payment of expenses as set forth in Paragraph 4.01, the Trustee shall hold, administer and distribute all or any part of the balance of the *Survivor's Trust* shall be distributed to or for the benefit of such one or more persons or entities, including the estate of the surviving Settlor, on the terms and conditions, either outright or in trust, as the surviving Settlor may appoint by a written instrument other than a Will which specifically refers to and exercises this general testamentary power of appointment. Any of the *Survivor's Trust* not effectively appointed by the surviving Settlor shall be added to the balance of the *Decedent's Trust* to be held, administered and distributed as set forth below in Paragraph 4.03 below.

Paragraph 4.03. Distribution of Decedent's Trust and Marital Trust. The *Marital Trust*, the *Decedent's Trust*, along with any of the *Survivor's Trust* not effectively appointed by the surviving Settlor, shall be distributed as follows:

A. The Trustee shall distribute to the following persons the cash amount listed after their respective names:
(10)

B. The Trustee shall distribute to the following persons the real property described after their respective names. (12) Said real property is given free of all encumbrances or liens thereon.
(11)

C. The Trustee shall distribute to (13)__________________ a life estate in the following property located at: (14)________________________. After the death of (13)___________________ said property shall go, outright, to (15)___________________________ as the remainder person(s).

(19)______ shares to the Trustee hereinafter named, to have and to hold for the benefit of (20)_____________ upon the uses, trusts, purposes and conditions hereinafter provided.
1. If (20)_______________ should at any time or from time to time be in need, in the discretion of the Trustee, of funds due to illness, infirmity or other physical or mental disability or any emergency, the Trustee may relieve or contribute toward the relief of any such need or needs of (20)_________________by paying to him or her or using and applying for his or her benefit, such sum or sums out of the income and/or principal of his or her trust as the Trustee, in the Trustee's discretion, may deem necessary or advisable.
2. The Trustee shall pay (20)___________________ all of the net income, in monthly or other convenient installments, from the trust.
3. (20)_____________________shall have the right to require the Trustee to convert any non-income producing asset into an income producing asset.
4. Upon the death of (20)___________________ the Trustee shall distribute, free of trust, the remaining trust properties to: (23)____________________________.

E. Distribution of Trust Assets. With respect to the distribution of any trust estate upon termination of any trust, and partial distribution of any trust, the liquidation and distribution by the Trustee of the Trust Estate involved or the distributable portion shall commence immediately and be accomplished as rapidly as possible, and deliveries of the trust properties to the beneficiary or beneficiaries may be made in installments or series, retaining only reasonable reserves for final charges and expenses. In no event shall it be necessary for the Trustee to await an accounting to the Court, or any Court order, before releasing and distributing the majority of the Trust Estate to be distributed.

F. Undistributed Income. All the net income of the respective trusts or trust estates, not distributed, used or applied as otherwise provided herein, shall be accumulated and added to the principals of the respective trusts.

Upon the change or succession of any beneficiary, distribution of trust properties or any trust estate or any portion thereof, or upon setting aside, apportionment or division of any trust estate or upon the termination of a trust or any interest therein, the beneficial interest, properties or balance of trust estate at the applicable time and to be dealt with shall include any and all income accumulated, accrued, uncollected or held undistributed and all of such income shall likewise be distributed, set aside or apportioned to the next or succeeding beneficiaries, distributees, shares or trusts, retaining its character as income.

ARTICLE V
TRUSTEES

Paragraph 5.01. Appointment of Trustees. Settlors, (1a)___________________ and (4)___________________ are appointed and confirmed as the Trustees, without bond. In the event either original Trustee should resign, die or become mentally incapacitated, the remaining Trustee shall act as sole Trustee. If either original Trustee should cease to act as Trustee due to a mental incapacity, his/her restoration of mental capacity shall result in his or her immediate return as Trustee or Co-Trustee hereunder. If either original Trustee should cease to act as sole Trustee or a Co-Trustee with the other original Trustee due to his/her resignation, he/she may at any time subsequent, elect to act again as sole Trustee or a Co-Trustee with the other original Trustee. Said election shall be made by filing same with either of the then acting Trustee or by recording said election in the County of residence of said Trustee making such election.

In the event both (1a)__________________ and (4)_____________should die, refuse to act, or for any other reason be unable to act, then (25)____________________ shall act as (26)____Trustee_ hereunder (27) without bond. In the event he/she/they should die, decline to act, or for any other reason, be unable to act as Trustee then (28)__________________________ shall act as Trustee hereunder (27) without bond.

Notwithstanding the above, at now time shall the surviving Settlor act as Trustee of any life insurance policy allocated to the *Decedent's Trust*. In that event the surviving Settlor shall appoint a special Trustee to hold title to and administer such policy or policies.

Paragraph 5.02. Substitute Trustee. The Settlors jointly, or the surviving Settlor upon the death of the predeceased Settlor, may appoint a substitute or successor Trustee to act as Trustee of any trust or trusts created hereunder in the place and stead of, or as successor to, any Trustee named in Section 4.01 above. Such substitution shall be in writing.

Paragraph 5.04. Trustee Liability. No person named as Trustee in this instrument or appointed as Trustee in the manner specified herein shall be liable to any beneficiary or to any heir of either Settlor for the Trustee's acts or failure to act, except for willful misconduct or gross negligence. No such Trustee shall be liable or responsible for any act, omission or default of any other Trustee provided that they shall have had no knowledge of facts that might reasonably be expected to put the Trustee on notice of it.

Paragraph 5.05. Title to Trust Estate. The legal title to all property held in trust hereunder shall be, remain and become vested in the Trustee or successor Trustee from time to time acting hereunder, without any act of conveyance or transfer to or by or acceptance from, any succeeding, retiring or predecessor Trustee; however, any removed or resigning Trustee shall execute and deliver any and all conveyances and documents requested and reasonably necessary to transfer the trust estate and its assets to a successor Trustee. Each successor Trustee from time to time acting hereunder shall have all the rights, powers immunities and authorities, discretionary or otherwise and the duties and obligations herein granted to the original Trustee. No successor Trustee shall be obligated to inquire into or be in any way responsible for the previous administration of any trust created herein or of the trust estate or for any act or default of any predecessor Trustee.

Paragraph 5.06. Powers of Trustee. To carry out the purposes of any trust created under this Trust Declaration, and subject to any limitations stated elsewhere in this Trust Declaration, the Trustee is vested with the following powers with respect to the Trust Estate, and any part of it, in addition to those powers now or hereafter conferred by law. The Trustee shall not exercise any power, right or discretion in a manner which will cause the loss of or a decrease in any marital or charitable deduction otherwise allowable in computing the federal estate tax of either Trustor.

A. Power to Invest. Subject to Paragraph 3.02 D. 2, to invest and reinvest the Trust Estate in every kind of property, real, personal or mixed, and every kind of investment, specifically including but not by way of limitation, corporate obligations of every kind, stocks, preferred or common, shares of investment trusts, investment companies, mutual funds, market index funds and mortgage participations which individuals of prudence, discretion and intelligence acquire for their own account, and any common trust fund administered by any Trustee under this Trust Declaration.

B. Power to Retain Property. To retain any property which was an asset of the Trust Estate during the Settlor's lifetime or received without consideration by the Trustee as long as the Trustee deems advisable whether or not of the character permitted by law for the investment of trust funds. The trust properties and investment need not be diversified and the Trustee shall have no duty to dispose or convert any trust assets to effect diversification.

C. Power to Manage Securities. With respect to securities held in this Trust Declaration, to have all the rights, powers and privileges of an owner, including but not by way of limitation, the power to vote, give proxies and pay assessments, to participate in voting trusts, pooling agreements, foreclosures, reorganizations, consolidations, mergers, liquidations, sales and leases and, incident to such participation, to deposit securities with and transfer title to any protective or other committee on such terms as the Trustee may deem advisable, to exercise and sell stock subscription or conversion rights and to hold securities in "street name".

D. Power of Sale, Exchange, Repair. To manage, control, foreclose, repossess, grant options on, grant easements on, sell (for cash), convey, exchange, partition, divide, improve and repair trust property.

The power to sell, at the termination of the trust, any trust property if the Trustee feels said disposition would assist in the distribution of the trust property at termination.

E. Power to Lease. To lease trust property for terms within or beyond the term of the trust and for any purpose, including exploration for and removal of gas, oil and other minerals; and to enter into community oil leases, pooling and unitization agreements, operating agreements or otherwise, and to create restrictions, easements or other servitudes thereon, to assign, partition, divide, subdivide, transfer to a corporation in exchange for stock, improve, repair, loan, reloan, invest and reinvest the trust estate or any part thereof.

F. Power to Insure. To carry, at the expense of the Trust Estate, insurance of such kinds and in such amounts as the Trustee shall deem advisable to protect the Trust Estate and the Trustee against any hazard.

G. Power to Commence or Defend Litigation. To commence or defend such litigation with respect to the Trust or any property of the Trust Estate as the Trustee may deem advisable, at the expense of the Trust Declaration.

H. Power to Compromise Claim. To compromise or otherwise adjust any claims or litigation against or in favor of the Trust Declaration.

I. Power to Employ Consultants. To employ any custodian, investment advisor, attorney, accountant or other agents to assist the Trustee in administration of this Trust Declaration and to rely upon the advice given by these agents. Reasonable compensation shall be paid to these agents for all services performed.

J. Power to Adjust for Tax Consequences. To take any action and to make any election the Trustee shall deem advisable to minimize the tax liabilities of this trust and its beneficiaries, to allocate the benefits among the various beneficiaries and to make adjustments in the rights of any beneficiaries or group of beneficiaries or between principal and income accounts, to compensate for the consequences of any tax election or any investment decision or administrative decision that has the effect of preferring one beneficiary or group of beneficiaries over others, provided such discretion shall not be exercised in any manner which will cause a loss of or a decrease in any marital or charitable deduction otherwise allowable in computing the then deceased Settlor's federal estate tax.

K. Trust Bank and Securities Accounts. During the joint lives of the Settlors, if the Settlors are serving as co-Trustees hereunder, the signature of either Trustor shall be sufficient to create, negotiate or endorse trust checks or to deposit or withdraw trust funds from trust bank or securities accounts or to trade securities in said securities accounts.

ARTICLE VI
MISCELLANEOUS

Paragraph 6.01. No Assignment. Each beneficiary hereunder is hereby prohibited from anticipating, encumbering, assigning or in any other manner, alienating her or his interest in either income or principal of any trust created under this Trust Declaration and is without power to do so nor shall such interest be subject to her or his liabilities or obligations nor to attachment, execution or other legal processes, bankruptcy proceedings or claims of creditors or others. The Trustee may require the personal receipt of a beneficiary as a condition precedent to payment, distribution or delivery of any amount, property or benefit hereunder. The Trustee may, however, deposit in any bank designated in writing, by a beneficiary, to her or his credit, income or principal payable to such beneficiary.

Paragraph 6.02. Principal and Income. Except as otherwise specifically provided in this Trust Declaration, the determination of all matters with respect to what shall constitute principal and income of each trust estate, gross income therefrom and net income distributable under the terms of the Trust Declaration, shall be governed by the provisions of the Revised Uniform Principal and Income Act as enacted in the State of (2a)__________________, from time to time existing. All taxes, assessments, fees, charges and other expenses incurred by the Trustee in the administration, protection and distribution of each trust, shall be a charge upon the trust estate and shall be paid out of the income and/or principal, in accordance with the aforesaid Act.

Paragraph 6.03. Savings Clause. Unless sooner terminated in accordance with other provisions of this Trust Declaration, any trust created hereunder shall terminate twenty-one (21) years after the death of the last surviving member of the group consisting of the Settlor and the issue of the Settlor who are living and in being at the date of death of the Settlor.

Paragraph 6.04. Payments to Minors and Incompetents. The Trustee, in the Trustee's discretion, may apply payments directly for the benefit of any beneficiary, rather than directly to such beneficiary and, in the case of a beneficiary who is a minor or who is under any other disability, make payment to the guardian, conservator of the person or estate of such beneficiary, custodian under the Uniform Transfers to Minors Act, parent or any other suitable adult with whom the beneficiary resides or by expending the same for the care, education, maintenance or other benefit of said beneficiary. In addition, the Trustee, in the Trustee's discretion, may make payments directly to a beneficiary who is a minor if, in the Trustee's judgment, the minor is of sufficient age and maturity to properly manage the money or property so paid. The Trustee shall not be required to see to the application of any such payment so made to any said persons, but his, her or their receipt therefor shall be a full discharge to the Trustee.

Paragraph 6.05. No Physical Segregation. There need be no physical segregation or division of the various trusts except as segregation or division may be required by the termination of any of the trusts or as specifically provided, but the Trustee shall keep separate accounts for the different undivided interests.

Paragraph 6.06. Distribution. In any case in which the Trustee is required, pursuant to the provisions of the Trust, to divide any parts or shares for the purposes of distribution or otherwise, except as the donee of any power of appointment affecting such property may have expressly provided otherwise in the instrument exercising such power, the Trustee is authorized, in the Trustee's absolute discretion, to make the division and distribution (pro rata or otherwise) in kind, including an undivided interest in any property or partly in kind and partly in money, and for this purpose, to make such sales of the trust property as the Trustee may deem necessary, on such terms and conditions as the Trustee shall see fit. Any asset which is encumbered shall be assigned subject thereto, and its value or amount shall be given effect less such indebtedness.

Paragraph 6.07. Non-Pro rata Distributions. As to distribution or division of property in kind under and for the several trusts, excepting the initial establishment of any trust for a pecuniary amount, the Trustee shall be cognizant of the differences between the tax cost bases and current value and shall endeavor, insofar as is practicable to distribute or set aside to or for each beneficiary or distributee, assets or property carrying amount or portions of the total unrealized taxable gains or losses embodied in all the assets and properties involved commensurate with the share or portion of each beneficiary or distributee.

Paragraph 6.08. Distribution If All Beneficiaries Die Before Full Distribution. If at any time before full distribution of the Trust Estate, the Settlor is deceased and no disposition of the property is directed by this Trust Declaration, the Trust Estate or the portion of it not disposed of under the Trust Declaration, whichever the case may be, shall thereupon be distributed one-half to those persons who would be the legal heirs of Husband and one-half to the legal heirs of Wife their identities and respective shares to be determined as though the death of Husband and Wife had occurred immediately following the event requiring distribution and according to the laws of the State of (2a)_________________ then in effect relating to the succession of separate property not acquired from a parent, grandparent or previously deceased spouse.

Paragraph 6.09. Additional Property. With consent of the Trustee, additional property may be added at any time from any source to any trust held under this Trust Declaration. No person dealing with the Trustee in any manner shall be under any obligation to see to the application of any money paid to the Trustee or to inquire into the validity, expediency or propriety of any act of the Trustee or into any of the provisions of any trust hereunder.

Paragraph 6.10. Fiduciary Capacity. All of the powers of the Trustee provided in this Trust Declaration shall be exercisable by the Trustee in the Trustee's fiduciary capacity and only in such capacity.

Paragraph 6.11. Corporate Office. No person shall, by reason of acting as Trustee, be in any way restricted or prohibited from holding office in any corporation in which any trust under this Trust Declaration holds securities or from receiving compensation from any such corporation for services performed as a director, officer or employee of such corporation or from purchasing, selling or otherwise dealing with the stock of any such corporation for the individual account of such Trustee or from voting the stock of any such corporation held by such trust, including voting those shares in favor of the Settlor or any other person.

Paragraph 6.12. Disclaimer of Powers. The Trustee may disclaim, release or restrict the scope of any power held in connection with any trust created under this Trust Declaration, including any administrative power, whether such power is expressly granted in this Trust Declaration or implied by law, by a written instrument specifying the power to be disclaimed, released or restricted and the nature of any such restriction. Any power disclaimed or released by the Trustee shall be extinguished except to the extent this Trust Declaration expressly provides that such power pass to another. This power shall be personal to the Trustee only and may not be exercised by any other person acting on behalf of the Trustee, including, but not limited to, any Trustee (other than the Trustee), Conservator, agent or guardian.

Paragraph 6.13. Notice. Unless the Trustee has received written notice of the occurrence of an event affecting the beneficial interest in any trust held under this Trust Declaration, the Trustee shall not be liable to any beneficiary of such trust for any distributions made or other actions taken by the Trustee in good faith as though such event had not occurred.

Paragraph 6.14. Invalidity of Any Provision. Should any provision of this Trust Declaration be or become invalid or unenforceable, the remaining provisions of this Trust Declaration shall be and continue to be fully effective.

Paragraph 6.15. Gender and Number. Except as provided otherwise herein, the masculine, feminine and neuter gender, and the singular or plural number, shall each be deemed to include the others whenever the context so indicates.

Paragraph 6.16. Law of Construction of Trust. This Trust Declaration, its validity, the construction of and all rights under the Trusts provided for in this Trust Declaration shall be governed by the laws of the State of (2a)___________________.

Paragraph 6.17. No Contest. The Settlors have intentionally and with full knowledge omitted to provide for his/her issue, ancestors, relatives and heirs living at the time of his/her demise, except for such provisions as are made specifically herein.

If any person who is or claims under or through a beneficiary of this Trust, or if any person who would be entitled to share in either Settlor's estate if either or both Settlors died intestate, should in any manner whatsoever, directly or indirectly, attack, contest or seek to impair or invalidate in court any provision of the following:

A. This Trust or any Amendment to this Trust;

B. Any Will or Codicil to any Will executed by either Settlor;

C. Any beneficiary designation executed by either Settlor with respect to any insurance policy, any "Totten trust" account, any joint tenancy or tenancy by the entirety, any "transfer on death" account or any pension plan, or conspire or cooperate with anyone attempting to do any of the actions or things aforesaid, then each such person and any devise, share or interest in the Trust or either Settlor's Estate otherwise given to each such person under this Trust or either Settlor's Estate to which each such person might be entitled by law, is hereby revoked and shall pass and be distributed as though each such person had predeceased either Settlor leaving no issue or heirs whatsoever.

Any and every individual who asserts, or conspires or cooperates with any person who asserts, any claim against this Trust or the Estate of either Settlor of this Trust based on:

D. "Quantum meruit" theory;

E. Common law marriage, Marvin v. Marvin, 18 Cal. 3d 660 (1976) type of agreement or similar theory;

F. Constructive trust theory; or,

G. Oral agreement or written agreement which is to be proved by parole evidence, claiming that either Settlor agreed to gift or devise anything to such person or to pay such person or another for services rendered, regardless of whether a court may find that such agreement existed, then each such person is disinherited and any devise, share or interest in this Trust or either Settlor's Estate otherwise given to each such person under this Trust or either Settlor's Estate or to which each such person might be entitled by law, is hereby revoked and shall pass and be distributed as though each such person had predeceased both Settlors leaving no issue or heirs whatsoever.

The Trustee is specifically authorized to defend any such attack, contest, claim or other proceeding of any nature concerning this Trust or of any provision hereof, and to employ legal counsel therefor, all at the expense of the Trust.

Paragraph 6.18. Survival. If any person fails to survive a Settlor by thirty (30) days, for all purposes of this Trust Declaration the person shall be considered to have predeceased such Settlor.

Paragraph 6.19. All typed and handwritten "fill-ins" where directed above were made before the execution of this Declaration of Trust and are not initialed by the Settlors. All crossed through words and inter-lineations were made before the execution of this Trust and are initialed by the Settlors.

CERTIFICATION OF HUSBAND AND WIFE

We, and each of us, certify that:
A. We, and each of us, have read the foregoing Trust Declaration;
B. The foregoing Trust Declaration correctly states the terms and conditions under which the Trust Estate is to be held, managed, administered and disposed of by the Trustee;
C. As the Settlors named in such Trust Declaration, we, and each of us, approve such Trust Declaration in all particulars; and,
D. As the Trustees named in such Trust Declaration, we, and each of us, approve and accept the Trust provided for in such Declaration.

Dated: (40)______________________________

(1)________________________________, Settlor, Trustee

(1b)______________________________

(4)________________________________, Settlor, Trustee

STATE OF (2a)________________)
) ss.
COUNTY OF (2)________________)

On ________________, 200__ before me, the undersigned, a Notary Public in and for said county and state, personally appeared (1)______________ and (4)_____________, personally known to me (or proved to me on the basis of satisfactory evidence) to be the person(s) whose name(s) is/are subscribed to the within instrument and acknowledged that he/she/they executed the same in his/her/their authorized capacity(ies), and that by his/her/their signature(s) on the instrument the person(s), or the entity upon behalf of which the person(s) acted, executed the instrument.

WITNESS my hand and official seal.

____
Notary Public in and for said County and State

EXHIBIT A

Property Declared to be assets of the (1a)______________________________ TRUST dated (48)______________:

(55)

1.

INTER-VIVOS TRUST

THE (1a)________________________ TRUST

The Settlors named below hereby declare as follows:

ARTICLE I
ESTABLISHMENT OF TRUST

Paragraph 1.01. Creation of Trust. This Trust Declaration has been entered into between (1)________________and (4)__________________ as Settlors and themselves as the Trustees. The Settlors, of (2)_____________ County, (2a)_______________, have transferred, or will transfer, to the Trustee of this Trust Declaration the property described in the attached Exhibit "A" which will constitute, together with any other property that may be added to this Trust Declaration, the Trust Estate of an express trust which shall be held, administered and distributed by the Trustee as provided in this Trust Declaration.

Paragraph 1.02. Trust Name. This Trust Declaration shall be known as the (1a)"____________________________ TRUST" dated (48)______________________.

Paragraph 1.03. Definitions. As used in this Trust Declaration:

A. Husband: The term "Husband" shall mean (1)__________.

B. Wife: The term "Wife" shall mean (4)______________.

C. Settlors: The term "Settlors" shall refer collectively to Husband and Wife.

D. Deceased Settlor: The term "deceased Settlor" shall refer to the Settlor who is first to die. However, the term, "then deceased Settlor" shall refer to the Settlor then deceased and may thus refer to the otherwise surviving Settlor.

E. Surviving Settlor: The term "surviving Settlor" shall refer to the Settlor who is last to die.

F. Trustee: The term "Trustee" or "Trustees" shall refer to whoever is serving as Trustee or Trustees under this Trust Declaration.

G. Trust Estate: The term "Trust Estate" shall refer to the property subject to this Trust Declaration.

Paragraph 1.04. Property to Retain Status. All property now or hereafter transferred to the Trustee which was community property, quasi-community property or separate property at the time of such transfer, shall remain, respectively, community property, quasi-community property or the separate property of the spouse or spouses transferring such property to the Trustee.

ARTICLE II
OPERATION OF TRUST DURING THE LIFE OF HUSBAND AND WIFE

Paragraph 2.01. Net Income. During the life of Husband and Wife, the Trustee shall pay to or apply for the benefit of both Husband and Wife, or the survivor thereof, in monthly or more frequent intervals, all of the net income of the community Trust Estate and shall pay to or apply for the benefit of the contributing spouse, in monthly or more frequent intervals, all of the net income of the separate property contributed or owned by that spouse.

Paragraph 2.02. Withdrawal of Principal. During the life of Husband and Wife, the Trustee shall also pay to or apply for the benefit of both Husband and Wife, or either, or the survivor thereof, so much of the community principal of the Trust Estate, up to the whole thereof, as both Husband and Wife shall direct, and shall, at the discretion of a spouse, pay to or apply for the benefit of that spouse so much of the principal of the Trust Estate, up to the whole thereof, as is that spouse's separate property.

Paragraph 2.03. Incapacity of Husband or Wife. If, at any time either Husband or Wife has become physically or mentally incapacitated so as to be unable to manage his or her affairs, whether or not a court of competent jurisdiction has declared him or her incompetent, mentally ill, or in need of a conservator, the Trustee shall pay to the non-incapacitated spouse or apply for the benefit of either spouse such amounts of the principal and/or income of the community estate as may be necessary, in the Trustee's discretion, for the care, maintenance and support of both spouses in accordance with their accustomed manner of living. The Trustee shall also pay to or apply for the benefit of the incapacitated spouse such amounts of income or principal of the separate property contributed by the incapacitated spouse as may be necessary, in the Trustee's discretion, for the care, maintenance, and support of the incapacitated spouse in accordance with his or her accustomed manner of living, taking into account payments made by the Trustee from the community Trust Estate. If a conservator of the person or estate is appointed for the incapacitated spouse, the Trustee shall take into account any payments made for the incapacitated spouse's benefit by the conservator.

The payments specified in this Paragraph shall be made until the incapacitated spouse is again able to manage his or her own affairs.

Paragraph 2.04. Revocation of Trust. At any time during their joint lives, either Husband or Wife as to community property, and either spouse as to his or her separate property, may, by serving written notice on the Trustee, revoke the Trust created by this Trust Declaration, in whole or in part. Any community property withdrawn from the Trust Estate by reason of any such revocation shall be delivered by the Trustee to both Husband and Wife and any separate property withdrawn from the Trust shall be delivered by the Trustee to the spouse revoking the Trust.

Paragraph 2.05. Amendment of Trust. At any time during their joint lives, Husband and Wife, jointly as to community property, and either spouse as to his or her separate property, may, by serving written notice on the Trustee, alter, modify or amend the Trust created by this Trust Declaration in any respect.

ARTICLE III

OPERATION OF TRUST AFTER DEATH OF DECEASED SETTLOR

Paragraph 3.01. Collection of Assets and Payment of Deceased Settlor's Debts. On the death of the deceased Settlor the Trustee shall collect all assets belonging to the Trust Estate. As soon as practicable after the death of the deceased settlor, the Trustee, except as otherwise provided herein, shall pay from the deceased settlor's share of the Trust Estate the just debts of the deceased settlor (excluding any debts barred by provisions of law or not yet due), funeral expenses of the deceased Settlor, and any inheritance, estate, or other death taxes that shall, by reason of the death of the deceased Settlor, be attributable to the Trust Estate. This is not and shall not constitute a direction to pay all inheritance, estate or other death taxes from or charge the same to, the Trust Estate without apportionment.

Paragraph 3.02. Trust to Continue. On the death of the deceased settlor, the Trustee shall divide the Trust Estate into two separate trusts. Such trusts shall be designated as the *Decedent's Trust* and the *Survivor's Trust.*

A. Decedent's Trust. The *Decedent's Trust* shall be created from the deceased Settlor's interest in community property and quasi-community property and the separate property of the deceased Settlor which is included in the Trust Estate.

1. Allocation to Decedent's Trust. The *Decedent's Trust* shall be a unified credit trust, the principal of which shall consist of a pecuniary amount equal to the unused unified credit available at the time of the death of the deceased settlor under IRC Section 2010, as amended, plus any property disclaimed by the surviving settlor after taking into account:

(i) All deductions taken in determining the estate tax payable by reason of the deceased Settlor's death;

(ii) The net value of all other property, whether or not it is disposed of under this Trust and whether it passes at the time of the deceased Settlor's death or has passed before the deceased Settlor's death to or in trust for the surviving Settlor, so that it is included in the deceased Settlor's gross estate and does not qualify for the federal estate tax marital deduction. In determining the amount of Trust, however, disclaimers by the surviving Settlor shall be disregarded; and

(iii) All credits allowed for federal estate tax purposes.

The Trustee shall satisfy the amount so determined in cash or in kind, or partly in each, and shall allocate to this Trust any assets of the deceased Settlor contributed or added to the trust that are not eligible for the federal estate tax marital deduction. Assets allocated in kind shall be considered to satisfy this amount on the basis of their net fair market values at the date or dates of allocation to this Trust.

The Trustee shall select and allocate the cash, securities and other property, including real estate and interests therein, which shall constitute the trust, employing for the purpose values current at the time or times of allocation.

2. Revocation and Modification of the Decedent's Trust. After Death of Deceased Settlor. The *Decedent's Trust* shall be irrevocable and may not be amended or modified in any respect after the death of the deceased Settlor.

B. Survivor's Trust.

1. Allocation to Survivor's Trust. The *Survivor's Trust* shall consist of the balance of the Trust Estate.

2. Revocation and Modification of *Survivor's Trust*. The surviving Settlor shall have the power to amend, revoke or terminate the *Survivor's Trust* exercisable by delivery of written notice to the Trustee. The surviving Settlor shall have the power to amend, revoke or terminate the *Survivor's Trust* exercisable by delivery of written notice to the Trustee. On revocation or termination of the *Survivor's Trust*, the Trustee shall deliver all of the assets of the *Survivor's Trust* to the surviving Settlor. On the death of the surviving Settlor, the *Survivor's Trust* shall be irrevocable and may not be amended or modified in any respect.

C. Distribution of Trust Estate.

1. The Trustee shall pay to or apply for the benefit of the surviving Settlor all the net income of the *Decedent's Trust* and *Survivor's Trust*, in monthly or more frequent intervals, but at least annually, during the surviving Settlor's lifetime. In addition, the Trustee shall pay to or for the benefit of the surviving Settlor all of the principal of the *Survivor's Trust* as may be requested by the surviving Settlor.

2. If at any time or from time to time the surviving Settlor should be in need of funds in excess of all income and other property and resources available in a practicable manner for his or her benefit from the *Survivor's Trust* and all other sources, for his or her proper care, support or maintenance in his or her accustomed manner of living, or as a result of illness, physical or mental disability or other health requirement or expense, then the Trustee may relieve or contribute toward the relief of any such need of needs of said surviving Settlor by paying to him or her or using and applying for his or her benefit, such sum or sums out of the principal of the *Decedent's Trust* as may be necessary or advisable.

ARTICLE IV
OPERATION OF TRUST ON DEATH OF SURVIVING SETTLOR.

Paragraph 4.01. Payment of Surviving Settlor's Debts. On the death of the surviving Settlor, the Trustee shall pay out of the principal or income of the *Survivor's Trust*, unless otherwise paid or provided for, the just debts of the surviving Settlor (excluding any debts barred by provisions of law or not yet due), funeral expenses of the surviving Settlor and any inheritance, estate or other death taxes that shall, by reason of the death of the surviving Settlor, be attributable to the *Survivor's Trust.* This is not and shall not constitute a direction to pay all inheritance, estate or other death taxes from the *Survivor's Trust* without apportionment.

Paragraph 4.02. Distribution of Survivor's Trust. Upon the death of the surviving Settlor, and after payment of expenses as set forth in Paragraph 3.01, the Trustee shall hold, administer and distribute all or any part of the balance of the *Survivor's Trust* shall be distributed to or for the benefit of such one or more persons or entities, including the estate of the surviving Settlor, on the terms and conditions, either outright or in trust, as the surviving Settlor may appoint by a written instrument other than a Will which specifically refers to and exercises this general testamentary power of appointment. Any of the *Survivor's Trust* not effectively appointed by the surviving Settlor shall be added to the balance of the *Decedent's Trust* to be held, administered and distributed as set forth below in Paragraph 4.03 below.

Paragraph 4.03. Distribution of Decedent's Trust. The *Decedent's Trust,* along with any of the *Survivor's Trust* not effectively appointed by the surviving Settlor, shall be distributed as follows:

A. The Trustee shall distribute to the following persons the cash amount listed after their respective names:

(10)

B. The Trustee shall distribute to the following persons the real property described after their respective names. (12) Said real property is given free of all encumbrances or liens thereon.

(11)

C. The Trustee shall distribute to (13)____________________ a life estate in the following property located at: (14)____________________________. After the death of (13)______________________ said property shall go, outright, to (15)_______________________________ as the remainder person(s).

D. The Trustee shall distribute all of the rest, residue and remainder of the Trust Estate, real, personal and mixed, of whatsoever kind or character and wheresoever situated, to the following persons or entities (16) in the proportions listed after their names.

(18)

E. Distribution of Trust Assets. With respect to the distribution of any trust estate upon termination of any trust, and partial distribution of any trust, the liquidation and distribution by the Trustee of the Trust Estate involved or the distributable portion shall commence immediately and be accomplished as rapidly as possible, and deliveries of the trust properties to the beneficiary or beneficiaries may be made in installments or series, retaining only reasonable reserves for final charges and expenses. In no event shall it be necessary for the Trustee to await an accounting to the Court, or any Court order, before releasing and distributing the majority of the Trust Estate to be distributed.

F. Undistributed Income. All the net income of the respective trusts or trust estates, not distributed, used or applied as otherwise provided herein, shall be accumulated and added to the principals of the respective trusts.

Upon the change or succession of any beneficiary, distribution of trust properties or any trust estate or any portion thereof, or upon setting aside, apportionment or division of any trust estate or upon the termination of a trust or any interest therein, the beneficial interest, properties or balance of trust estate at the applicable time and to be dealt with shall include any and all income accumulated, accrued, uncollected or held undistributed and all of such income shall likewise be distributed, set aside or apportioned to the next or succeeding beneficiaries, distributees, shares or trusts, retaining its character as income.

ARTICLE V
TRUSTEES

Paragraph 5.01. Appointment of Trustees. Settlors, (1)____________________ and (4)____________________ are appointed and confirmed as the Trustees, without bond. In the event either original Trustee should resign, die or become mentally incapacitated, the remaining Trustee shall act as sole Trustee. If either original Trustee should cease to act as Trustee due to a mental incapacity, his/her restoration of mental capacity shall result in his or her immediate return as Trustee or Co-Trustee hereunder. If either original Trustee should cease to act as sole Trustee or a Co-Trustee with the other original Trustee due to his/her resignation, he/she may at any time subsequent, elect to act again as sole Trustee or a Co-Trustee with the other original Trustee. Said election shall be made by filing same with either of the then acting Trustee or by recording said election in the County of residence of said Trustee making such election.

In the event both (1)__________________ and (4)______________should die, refuse to act, or for any other reason be unable to act, then (25)____________________ shall act as (26)____Trustee_ hereunder (27) without bond. In the event he/she/they should die, decline to act, or for any other reason, be unable to act as Trustee then (28)____________________________ shall act as Trustee hereunder (27) without bond.

Notwithstanding the above, at now time shall the surviving Settlor act as Trustee of any life insurance policy allocated to the *Decedent's Trust*. In that event the surviving Settlor shall appoint a special Trustee to hold title to and administer such policy or policies.

Paragraph 5.02. Substitute Trustee. The Settlors jointly, or the surviving Settlor upon the death of the predeceased Settlor, may appoint a substitute or successor Trustee to act as Trustee of any trust or trusts created hereunder in the place and stead of, or as successor to, any Trustee named in Section 4.01 above. Such substitution shall be in writing.

Paragraph 5.04. Trustee Liability. No person named as Trustee in this instrument or appointed as Trustee in the manner specified herein shall be liable to any beneficiary or to any heir of either Settlor for the Trustee's acts or failure to act, except for willful misconduct or gross negligence. No such Trustee shall be liable or responsible for any act, omission or default of any other Trustee provided that they shall have had no knowledge of facts that might reasonably be expected to put the Trustee on notice of it.

Paragraph 5.05. Title to Trust Estate. The legal title to all property held in trust hereunder shall be, remain and become vested in the Trustee or successor Trustee from time to time acting hereunder, without any act of conveyance or transfer to or by or acceptance from, any succeeding, retiring or predecessor Trustee; however, any removed or resigning Trustee shall execute and deliver any and all conveyances and documents requested and reasonably necessary to transfer the trust estate and its assets to a successor Trustee. Each successor Trustee from time to time acting hereunder shall have all the rights, powers immunities and authorities, discretionary or otherwise and the duties and obligations herein granted to the original Trustee. No successor Trustee shall be obligated to inquire into or be in any way responsible for the previous administration of any trust created herein or of the trust estate or for any act or default of any predecessor Trustee.

Paragraph 5.06. Powers of Trustee. To carry out the purposes of any trust created under this Trust Declaration, and subject to any limitations stated elsewhere in this Trust Declaration, the Trustee is vested with the following powers with respect to the Trust Estate, and any part of it, in addition to those powers now or hereafter conferred by law.

A. Power to Invest. To invest and reinvest the Trust Estate in every kind of property, real, personal or mixed, and every kind of investment, specifically including but not by way of limitation, corporate obligations of every kind, stocks, preferred or common, shares of investment trusts, investment companies, mutual funds, market index funds and mortgage participations which individuals of prudence, discretion and intelligence acquire for their own account, and any common trust fund administered by any Trustee under this Trust Declaration.

B. Power to Retain Property. To retain any property which was an asset of the Trust Estate during the Settlor's lifetime or received without consideration by the Trustee as long as the Trustee deems advisable whether or not of the character permitted by law for the investment of trust funds. The trust properties and investment need not be diversified and the Trustee shall have no duty to dispose or convert any trust assets to effect diversification.

C. Power to Manage Securities. With respect to securities held in this Trust Declaration, to have all the rights, powers and privileges of an owner, including but not by way of limitation, the power to vote, give proxies and pay assessments, to participate in voting trusts, pooling agreements, foreclosures, reorganizations, consolidations, mergers, liquidations, sales and leases and, incident to such participation, to deposit securities with and transfer title to any protective or other committee on such terms as the Trustee may deem advisable, to exercise and sell stock subscription or conversion rights and to hold securities in "street name".

D. Power of Sale, Exchange, Repair. To manage, control, foreclose, repossess, grant options on, grant easements on, sell (for cash), convey, exchange, partition, divide, improve and repair trust property.

The power to sell, at the termination of the trust, any trust property if the Trustee feels said disposition would assist in the distribution of the trust property at termination.

E. Power to Lease. To lease trust property for terms within or beyond the term of the trust and for any purpose, including exploration for and removal of gas, oil and other minerals; and to enter into community oil leases, pooling and unitization agreements, operating agreements or otherwise, and to create restrictions, easements or other servitudes thereon, to assign, partition, divide, subdivide, transfer to a corporation in exchange for stock, improve, repair, loan, reloan, invest and reinvest the trust estate or any part thereof.

F. Power to Insure. To carry, at the expense of the Trust Estate, insurance of such kinds and in such amounts as the Trustee shall deem advisable to protect the Trust Estate and the Trustee against any hazard.

G. Power to Commence or Defend Litigation. To commence or defend such litigation with respect to the Trust or any property of the Trust Estate as the Trustee may deem advisable, at the expense of the Trust Declaration.

H. Power to Compromise Claim. To compromise or otherwise adjust any claims or litigation against or in favor of the Trust Declaration.

I. Power to Employ Consultants. To employ any custodian, investment advisor, attorney, accountant or other agents to assist the Trustee in administration of this Trust Declaration and to rely upon the advice given by these agents. Reasonable compensation shall be paid to these agents for all services performed.

J. Power to Adjust for Tax Consequences. To take any action and to make any election the Trustee shall deem advisable to minimize the tax liabilities of this trust and its beneficiaries, to allocate the benefits among the various beneficiaries and to make adjustments in the rights of any beneficiaries or group of beneficiaries or between principal and income accounts, to compensate for the consequences of any tax election or any investment decision or administrative decision that has the effect of preferring one beneficiary or group of beneficiaries over others, provided such discretion shall not be exercised in any manner which will cause a loss of or a decrease in any marital or charitable deduction otherwise allowable in computing the then deceased Settlor's federal estate tax.

K. Trust Bank and Securities Accounts. During the joint lives of the Settlors, if the Settlors are serving as co-Trustees hereunder, the signature of either Settlor shall be sufficient to create, negotiate or endorse trust checks or to deposit or withdraw trust funds from trust bank or securities accounts or to trade securities in said securities accounts.

ARTICLE VI
MISCELLANEOUS

Paragraph 6.01. No Assignment. Each beneficiary hereunder is hereby prohibited from anticipating, encumbering, assigning or in any other manner, alienating her or his interest in either income or principal of any trust created under this Trust Declaration and is without power to do so nor shall such interest be subject to her or his liabilities or obligations nor to attachment, execution or other legal processes, bankruptcy proceedings or claims of creditors or others. The Trustee may require the personal receipt of a beneficiary as a condition precedent to payment, distribution or delivery of any amount, property or benefit hereunder. The Trustee may, however, deposit in any bank designated in writing, by a beneficiary, to her or his credit, income or principal payable to such beneficiary.

Paragraph 6.02. Principal and Income. Except as otherwise specifically provided in this Trust Declaration, the determination of all matters with respect to what shall constitute principal and income of each trust estate, gross income therefrom and net income distributable under the terms of the Trust Declaration, shall be governed by the provisions of the Revised Uniform Principal and Income Act as enacted in the State of (2a)________________, from time to time existing. All taxes, assessments, fees, charges and other expenses incurred by the Trustee in the administration, protection and distribution of each trust, shall be a charge upon the trust estate and shall be paid out of the income and/or principal, in accordance with the aforesaid Act.

Paragraph 6.03. Savings Clause. Unless sooner terminated in accordance with other provisions of this Trust Declaration, any trust created hereunder shall terminate twenty-one (21) years after the death of the last surviving member of the group consisting of the Settlor and the issue of the Settlor who are living and in being at the date of death of the Settlor.

Paragraph 6.04. Payments to Minors and Incompetents. The Trustee, in the Trustee's discretion, may apply payments directly for the benefit of any beneficiary, rather than directly to such beneficiary and, in the case of a beneficiary who is a minor or who is under any other disability, make payment to the guardian, conservator of the person or estate of such beneficiary, custodian under the Uniform Transfers to Minors Act, parent or any other suitable adult with whom the beneficiary resides or by expending the same for the care, education, maintenance or other benefit of said beneficiary. In addition, the Trustee, in the Trustee's discretion, may make payments directly to a beneficiary who is a minor if, in the Trustee's judgment, the minor is of sufficient age and maturity to properly manage the money or property so paid. The Trustee shall not be required to see to the application of any such payment so made to any said persons, but his, her or their receipt therefor shall be a full discharge to the Trustee.

Paragraph 6.05. No Physical Segregation. There need be no physical segregation or division of the various trusts except as segregation or division may be required by the termination of any of the trusts or as specifically provided, but the Trustee shall keep separate accounts for the different undivided interests.

Paragraph 6.06. Distribution. In any case in which the Trustee is required, pursuant to the provisions of the Trust, to divide any parts or shares for the purposes of distribution or otherwise, except as the donee of any power of appointment affecting such property may have expressly provided otherwise in the instrument exercising such power, the Trustee is authorized, in the Trustee's absolute discretion, to make the division and distribution (pro rata or otherwise) in kind, including an undivided interest in any property or partly in kind and partly in money, and for this purpose, to make such sales of the trust property as the Trustee may deem necessary, on such terms and conditions as the Trustee shall see fit. Any asset which is encumbered shall be assigned subject thereto, and its value or amount shall be given effect less such indebtedness.

Paragraph 6.07. Non-Pro Rata Distributions. As to distribution or division of property in kind under and for the several trusts, excepting the initial establishment of any trust for a pecuniary amount, the Trustee shall be cognizant of the differences between the tax cost bases and current value and shall endeavor, insofar as is practicable to distribute or set aside to or for each beneficiary or distributee, assets or property carrying amount or portions of the total unrealized taxable gains or losses embodied in all the assets and properties involved commensurate with the share or portion of each beneficiary or distributee.

Paragraph 6.08. Distribution If All Beneficiaries Die Before Full Distribution. If at any time before full distribution of the Trust Estate, the Settlor is deceased and no disposition of the property is directed by this Trust Declaration, the Trust Estate or the portion of it not disposed of under the Trust Declaration, whichever the case may be, shall thereupon be distributed one-half to those persons who would be the legal heirs of Husband and one-half to the legal heirs of Wife their identities and respective shares to be determined as though the death of Husband and Wife had occurred immediately following the event requiring distribution and according to the laws of the State of (2a)________________ then in effect relating to the succession of separate property not acquired from a parent, grandparent or previously deceased spouse.

Paragraph 6.09. Additional Property. With consent of the Trustee, additional property may be added at any time from any source to any trust held under this Trust Declaration. No person dealing with the Trustee in any manner shall be under any obligation to see to the application of any money paid to the Trustee or to inquire into the validity, expediency or propriety of any act of the Trustee or into any of the provisions of any trust hereunder.

Paragraph 6.10. Fiduciary Capacity. All of the powers of the Trustee provided in this Trust Declaration shall be exercisable by the Trustee in the Trustee's fiduciary capacity and only in such capacity.

Paragraph 6.11. Corporate Office. No person shall, by reason of acting as Trustee, be in any way restricted or prohibited from holding office in any corporation in which any trust under this Trust Declaration holds securities or from receiving compensation from any such corporation for services performed as a director, officer or employee of such corporation or from purchasing, selling or otherwise dealing with the stock of any such corporation for the individual account of such Trustee or from voting the stock of any such corporation held by such trust, including voting those shares in favor of the Settlor or any other person.

Paragraph 6.12. Disclaimer of Powers. The Trustee may disclaim, release or restrict the scope of any power held in connection with any trust created under this Trust Declaration, including any administrative power, whether such power is expressly granted in this Trust Declaration or implied by law, by a written instrument specifying the power to be disclaimed, released or restricted and the nature of any such restriction. Any power disclaimed or released by the Trustee shall be extinguished except to the extent this Trust Declaration expressly provides that such power pass to another. This power shall be personal to the Trustee only and may not be exercised by any other person acting on behalf of the Trustee, including, but not limited to, any Trustee (other than the Trustee), Conservator, agent or guardian.

Paragraph 6.13. Notice. Unless the Trustee has received written notice of the occurrence of an event affecting the beneficial interest in any trust held under this Trust Declaration, the Trustee shall not be liable to any beneficiary of such trust for any distributions made or other actions taken by the Trustee in good faith as though such event had not occurred.

Paragraph 6.14. Invalidity of Any Provision. Should any provision of this Trust Declaration be or become invalid or unenforceable, the remaining provisions of this Trust Declaration shall be and continue to be fully effective.

Paragraph 6.15. Gender and Number. Except as provided otherwise herein, the masculine, feminine and neuter gender, and the singular or plural number, shall each be deemed to include the others whenever the context so indicates.

Paragraph 6.16. Law of Construction of Trust. This Trust Declaration, its validity, the construction of and all rights under the Trusts provided for in this Trust Declaration shall be governed by the laws of the State of (2a)___________________.

Paragraph 6.17. No Contest. The Settlors have intentionally and with full knowledge omitted to provide for his/her issue, ancestors, relatives and heirs living at the time of his/her demise, except for such provisions as are made specifically herein.

If any person who is or claims under or through a beneficiary of this Trust, or if any person who would be entitled to share in either Settlor's estate if either or both Settlors died intestate, should in any manner whatsoever, directly or indirectly, attack, contest or seek to impair or invalidate in court any provision of the following:

A. This Trust or any Amendment to this Trust;

B. Any Will or Codicil to any Will executed by either Settlor;

C. Any beneficiary designation executed by either Settlor with respect to any insurance policy, any "Totten trust" account, any joint tenancy or tenancy by the entirety, any "transfer on death" account or any pension plan, or conspire or cooperate with anyone attempting to do any of the actions or things aforesaid, then each such person and any devise, share or interest in the Trust or either Settlor's Estate otherwise given to each such person under this Trust or either Settlor's Estate to which each such person might be entitled by law, is hereby revoked and shall pass and be distributed as though each such person had predeceased either Settlor leaving no issue or heirs whatsoever.

Any and every individual who asserts, or conspires or cooperates with any person who asserts, any claim against this Trust or the Estate of either Settlor of this Trust based on:

D. "Quantum meruit" theory;

E. Common law marriage, Marvin v. Marvin, 18 Cal. 3d 660 (1976) type of agreement or similar theory;

F. Constructive trust theory; or,

G. Oral agreement or written agreement which is to be proved by parole evidence, claiming that either Settlor agreed to gift or devise anything to such person or to pay such person or another for services rendered, regardless of whether a court may find that such agreement existed, then each such person is disinherited and any devise, share or interest in this Trust or either Settlor's Estate otherwise given to each such person under this Trust or either Settlor's Estate or to which each such person might be entitled by law, is hereby revoked and shall pass and be distributed as though each such person had predeceased both Settlors leaving no issue or heirs whatsoever.

The Trustee is specifically authorized to defend any such attack, contest, claim or other proceeding of any nature concerning this Trust or of any provision hereof, and to employ legal counsel therefor, all at the expense of the Trust.

Paragraph 6.18. Survival. If any person fails to survive a Settlor by thirty (30) days, for all purposes of this Trust Declaration the person shall be considered to have predeceased such Settlor.

Paragraph 6.19. All typed and handwritten "fill-ins" where directed above were made before the execution of this Declaration of Trust and are not initialed by the Settlors. All crossed through words and inter-lineations were made before the execution of this Trust and are initialed by the Settlors.

CERTIFICATION OF HUSBAND AND WIFE

We, and each of us, certify that:
A. We, and each of us, have read the foregoing Trust Declaration;
B. The foregoing Trust Declaration correctly states the terms and conditions under which the Trust Estate is to be held, managed, administered and disposed of by the Trustee;
C. As the Settlors named in such Trust Declaration, we, and each of us, approve such Trust Declaration in all particulars; and
D. As the Trustees named in such Trust Declaration, we, and each of us, approve and accept the Trust provided for in such Declaration.

Dated: (40)____________________

(1)____________________, Settlor, Trustee

(1b)____________________

(4)____________________, Settlor, Trustee

STATE OF (2a)_______________)
) ss.
COUNTY OF (2)_______________)

On _______________. 200__ before me, the undersigned, a Notary Public in and for said county and state, personally appeared (1)__________ and (4)__________, personally known to me (or proved to me on the basis of satisfactory evidence) to be the person(s) whose name(s) is/are subscribed to the within instrument and acknowledged that he/she/they executed the same in his/her/their authorized capacity(ies), and that by his/her/their signature(s) on the instrument the person(s), or the entity upon behalf of which the person(s) acted, executed the instrument.

WITNESS my hand and official seal.

____
Notary Public in and for said County and State

EXHIBIT A

Property Declared to be assets of the (1a)____________________________________ TRUST dated (48)_________________:

(55)
1.

AMENDMENT TO THE (1a)__________TRUST

THE (1a)____________________ TRUST was created (48)______________, by Declaration of Trust of (1)__________________, in his/her capacity as Settlor with (56)__________________ in his/her/their capacity as Trustee(s). Said Trust has (57) not been previously amended.

In accordance with the enabling provisions of the Trust instrument, THE (1a)________________ TRUST dated (48)__________________, is (58) further amended and modified as hereinafter set forth.

1. Article _____ , Section _________ is hereby amended to read in full as follows:

CERTIFICATION OF TRUSTOR and TRUSTEE

I, (1)_____________________, certify that:

A. I have read the foregoing amendment to my Declaration of Trust;

B. The foregoing amendment to my Declaration of Trust correctly states the terms and conditions under which the Trust is to be held, managed, administered, and disposed of by the Trustee; and,

C. As the Settlor approve such Declaration of Trust, as amended herein, in all particulars.

I, (48)__________________________, certify that:

As Trustee I approve and accept such Declaration of Trust, as amended herein, in all particulars.

Executed on (38)_______________

(40)____________________________ (48)____________________________

(1)___________________, Settlor (54)______________, Trustee

STATE OF (2a)________________)

) ss.

COUNTY OF (2)_________________)

On ________________. 200__ before me, the undersigned, a Notary Public in and for said county and state, personally appeared (1)______________________, personally known to me (or proved to me on the basis of satisfactory evidence) to be the person(s) whose name(s) is/are subscribed to the within instrument and acknowledged that he/she/they executed the same in his/her/their authorized capacity(ies), and that by his/her/their signature(s) on the instrument the person(s), or the entity upon behalf of which the person(s) acted, executed the instrument.

WITNESS my hand and official seal.

____

Notary Public in and for said County and State

AMENDMENT TO THE (1a)____________ TRUST

THE (1a)__________________ TRUST was created (48)____________, by Declaration of Trust of (1)________________, in his/her capacity as Settlor with (56)_______________ in his/her/their capacity as Trustee(s). Said Trust has (57) not been previously amended.

In accordance with the enabling provisions of the Trust instrument, THE (1a)______________ TRUST dated (48)________________, is (58) further amended and modified via a restatement, to read in full as stated in Attachment "A" hereto:

CERTIFICATION OF TRUSTOR and TRUSTEE

I, (1)___________________, certify that:

A. I have read the foregoing amendment (Restatement) to my Declaration of Trust;
B. The foregoing amendment to my Declaration of Trust correctly states the terms and conditions under which the Trust is to be held, managed, administered, and disposed of by the Trustee; and,
C. As the Settlor approve such Declaration of Trust, as amended herein, in all particulars.

I, (48)_______________________, certify that:

As Trustee I approve and accept such Declaration of Trust, as amended herein, in all particulars.

Executed on (38)_____________

(40)________________________ (48)________________________

(1)__________________, Settlor (54)_____________, Trustee

STATE OF (2a)________________)
) ss.
COUNTY OF (2)________________)

On ________________, 200__ before me, the undersigned, a Notary Public in and for said county and state, personally appeared (1)_____________________, personally known to me (or proved to me on the basis of satisfactory evidence) to be the person(s) whose name(s) is/are subscribed to the within instrument and acknowledged that he/she/they executed the same in his/her/their authorized capacity(ies), and that by his/her/their signature(s) on the instrument the person(s), or the entity upon behalf of which the person(s) acted, executed the instrument.
WITNESS my hand and official seal.

____
Notary Public in and for said County and State

AMENDMENT TO THE (1a)____________ TRUST

THE (1a)____________________ TRUST was created (48)______________, by Declaration of Trust of (1)__________________and (4)______________________, in their capacity as Settlors with (49)___________________ in his/her/their capacity as Trustee(s). Said Trust has (57) not been previously amended.

In accordance with the enabling provisions of the Trust instrument, THE (1a)________________ TRUST dated (48)__________________, is (58) further amended and modified as hereinafter set forth.

1. Article _____ , Section _________ is hereby amended to read in full as follows:

CERTIFICATION OF TRUSTORS and TRUSTEE(S)

We, (1)______________and (4)________________, each certify that:

A. We have read the foregoing amendment to our Declaration of Trust;

B. The foregoing amendment to our Declaration of Trust correctly states the terms and conditions under which the Trust is to be held, managed, administered, and disposed of by the Trustee; and,

C. As the Settlors we approve such Declaration of Trust, as amended herein, in all particulars.

I, (49)____________________________, certify that:

As Trustee I approve and accept such Declaration of Trust, as amended herein, in all particulars.

Executed on (38)________________

(40)_____________________________

(1) ___________________,Settlor

(1b)_____________________

(4)_____________________, Settlor

(48)____________________________

(54)_____________________, Trustee

STATE OF (2a)__________________)
) ss.
COUNTY OF (2)____________________)

On __________________, 200__ before me, the undersigned, a Notary Public in and for said county and state, personally appeared (1)________________________and (4)________________________ and (54)______________________, personally known to me (or proved to me on the basis of satisfactory evidence) to be the person(s) whose name(s) is/are subscribed to the within instrument and acknowledged that he/she/they executed the same in his/her/their authorized capacity(ies), and that by his/her/their signature(s) on the instrument the person(s), or the entity upon behalf of which the person(s) acted, executed the instrument.

WITNESS my hand and official seal.

____

Notary Public in and for said County and State

AMENDMENT TO THE (1a)____________ TRUST

THE (1a)____________________ TRUST was created (48)______________, by Declaration of Trust of (1)____________________and (4)____________________, in their capacity as Settlors with (56)__________________ in his/her/their capacity as Trustee(s). Said Trust has (57) not been previously amended.

In accordance with the enabling provisions of the Trust instrument, THE (1a)________________ TRUST dated (48)__________________, is (58) further amended and modified via a restatement, to read in full as stated in Attachment "A" hereto:

CERTIFICATION OF TRUSTORS and TRUSTEE(S)

We, (1)______________and (4)________________, each certify that:

A. We have read the foregoing amendment (Restatement) to our Declaration of Trust;

B. The foregoing amendment to our Declaration of Trust correctly states the terms and conditions under which the Trust is to be held, managed, administered, and disposed of by the Trustee; and,

C. As the Settlors we approve such Declaration of Trust, as amended herein, in all particulars.

I, (48)____________________________, certify that:

As Trustee(s) I approve and accept such Declaration of Trust, as amended herein, in all particulars.

Executed on (38)_______________

(40)____________________________	(48)____________________________
(1) __________________, Settlor	(54)__________________, Trustee
(1b)______________________	(48)____________________________
(4)__________________, Settlor	(54)__________________, Trustee

STATE OF (2a)__________________)

) ss.

COUNTY OF (2)__________________)

On __________________, 200__ before me, the undersigned, a Notary Public in and for said county and state, personally appeared (1)______________________and (4)__________________________ and (54)________________ , 200__ personally known to me (or proved to me on the basis of satisfactory evidence) to be the person(s) whose name(s) is/are subscribed to the within instrument and acknowledged that he/she/they executed the same in his/her/their authorized capacity(ies), and that by his/her/their signature(s) on the instrument the person(s), or the entity upon behalf of which the person(s) acted, executed the instrument.

WITNESS my hand and official seal.

____

Notary Public in and for said County and State

TRUST CERTIFICATION

1. EXISTENCE OF TRUST AND DATE OF EXECUTION: The (1a)_______________
TRUST created (48)_______________ is in existence and was executed on (48)_______________
2. IDENTITY OF SETTLORS: (1)_______________ and (4)_______________
3. IDENTITY OF CURRENTLY ACTING TRUSTEE(S): (49)_______________
4. IDENTITY OF SUCCESSOR TRUSTEE(S): In the event (49)_______________ should decline, become unable or, for any reason, cease to serve as a Trustee then (51)_______________ shall act as Trustee(s).
5. REVOCABILITY OF TRUST: Said Trust is revocable and said power is held by the Settlors.
6. TRUST TAX IDENTIFICATION NUMBER: The trust uses the social security number of the Settlor:
7. TITLE TO TRUST ASSETS: Title to trust assets should be (49) "_______________, Trustee of the (1a)_______________Trust dated (48)_______________."
8. MATERIAL AMENDMENT OR REVOCATION OF TRUST: Said Trust has not been amended or revoked in any manner which would cause a representation made herein to be incorrect.
9. POWERS OF THE TRUSTEES: To carry out the purposes of any trust created under this Declaration of Trust, and subject to any limitations stated elsewhere in this Declaration, the Trustee is vested with the following powers with respect to the Trust Estate, and any part of it, in addition to those powers now or hereafter conferred by law.
See Attached Powers
(Paragraph 4.6 or Paragraph 5.6)
(53)

CERTIFICATION OF TRUSTEE(S)

I, certify that I have read the foregoing Trust Certification and that the foregoing Trust Certification is correct as to matters stated therein.

Dated: (54)_______________ (54)_______________

(49)_______________Trustee (49)_______________Trustee

STATE OF (2a)_______________)
) ss.
COUNTY OF (2)_______________)

On _______________, 200__ before me, the undersigned, a Notary Public in and for said county and state, personally appeared (49)_______________, personally known to me (or proved to me on the basis of satisfactory evidence) to be the person(s) whose name(s) is/are subscribed to the within instrument and acknowledged that he/she/they executed the same in his/her/their authorized capacity(ies), and that by his/her/their signature(s) on the instrument the person(s), or the entity upon behalf of which the person(s) acted, executed the instrument.
WITNESS my hand and official seal.

____
Notary Public in and for said County and State

TRUST CERTIFICATION

1. EXISTENCE OF TRUST AND DATE OF EXECUTION: The (1a)____________________ TRUST created (48)______________ is in existence and was executed on (48)______________
2. IDENTITY OF SETTLORS: (1)____________ and (4)____________
3. IDENTITY OF CURRENTLY ACTING TRUSTEE(S): (49)____________
4. IDENTITY OF SUCCESSOR TRUSTEE(S): In the event (49)__________________should decline, become unable or, for any reason, cease to serve as a Trustee then (51)__________________ shall act as Trustee(s).
5. REVOCABILITY OF TRUST: Said Trust is revocable and said power is held by the Settlors.
6. TRUST TAX IDENTIFICATION NUMBER: The trust uses the social security number of either of the Settlors:
7. TITLE TO TRUST ASSETS: Title to trust assets should be (49) "__________________, Trustee of the (1a)__________________Trust dated (48)__________."
8. MATERIAL AMENDMENT OR REVOCATION OF TRUST: Said Trust has not been amended or revoked in any manner which would cause a representation made herein to be incorrect.
9. POWERS OF THE TRUSTEES: To carry out the purposes of any trust created under this Declaration of Trust, and subject to any limitations stated elsewhere in this Declaration, the Trustee is vested with the following powers with respect to the Trust Estate, and any part of it, in addition to those powers now or hereafter conferred by law.

See Attached Powers
(Paragraph 4.6 or Paragraph 5.6)
(53)

CERTIFICATION OF TRUSTEE(S)

I, certify that I have read the foregoing Trust Certification and that the foregoing Trust Certification is correct as to matters stated therein.

Dated: (54)______________ (54)__________________

(49)______________Trustee (49)______ Trustee

STATE OF)
) ss.
COUNTY OF)

On ____________, 200__ before me, the undersigned, a Notary Public in and for said county and state, personally appeared (49)____________________, personally known to me (or proved to me on the basis of satisfactory evidence) to be the person(s) whose name(s) is/are subscribed to the within instrument and acknowledged that he/she/they executed the same in his/her/their authorized capacity(ies), and that by his/her/their signature(s) on the instrument the person(s), or the entity upon behalf of which the person(s) acted, executed the instrument.

WITNESS my hand and official seal.

____
Notary Public in and for said County and State

REVOCATION OF THE (1a)__________________ TRUST

Recitals: The (1a)________________________TRUST was created (48)______________________, by Declaration of Trust by (1)____________________ in his or her capacity as Settlor with himself/herself in his or her capacity as Trustee. Said Settlor now wishes to revoke said Trust in full.
REVOCATION: In accordance with the enabling provisions of the trust instrument, the (1a)__________________________, is hereby revoked in full.

IN WITNESS WHEREOF, the Settlor has duly executed this Revocation of the (1a)__________________________and made the same fully effective this date.

Dated:
(40)________________________

(1)________________, Settlor

STATE OF (2a)_______________)
) ss.
COUNTY OF (2)________________)

On ________________, 200__ before me, the undersigned, a Notary Public in and for said county and state, personally appeared (1)____________________ personally known to me (or proved to me on the basis of satisfactory evidence) to be the person(s) whose name(s) is/are subscribed to the within instrument and acknowledged that he/she/they executed the same in his/her/their authorized capacity(ies), and that by his/her/their signature(s) on the instrument the person(s), or the entity upon behalf of which the person(s) acted, executed the instrument.

WITNESS my hand and official seal.

____
Notary Public in and for said County and State

REVOCATION OF THE (1a)__________________ TRUST

Recitals: The (1a)__________________________TRUST was created (48)_______________________, by Declaration of Trust by (1)_______________________ and (4)___________________________ in their capacity as Settlors with themselves in their capacity as Trustees. Said Settlors now wish to revoke said Trust in full.

REVOCATION: In accordance with the enabling provisions of the trust instrument, the (1a)_______________________________, is hereby revoked in full.

IN WITNESS WHEREOF, the Settlors have duly executed this Revocation of the (1a)_______________________________ and made the same fully effective this date.

Dated:

(40)____________________________ (1b)____________________________

(1)__________________, Settlor (4)__________________, Settlor

STATE OF (2a)__________________)
) ss.
COUNTY OF (2)__________________)

On __________________, 200__ before me, the undersigned, a Notary Public in and for said county and state, personally appeared (1)______________________ and (4)__________________ , personally known to me (or proved to me on the basis of satisfactory evidence) to be the person(s) whose name(s) is/are subscribed to the within instrument and acknowledged that he/she/they executed the same in his/her/their authorized capacity(ies), and that by his/her/their signature(s) on the instrument the person(s), or the entity upon behalf of which the person(s) acted, executed the instrument.

WITNESS my hand and official seal.

____
Notary Public in and for said County and State

Date:

Name/Address of Addressee:

Re: Change of Title to Account #________________

Dear Sirs:

Please change the vesting on the undersigned's (name of addressee)________________________ Account #__________________ from (current title vesting)__________________ to (name of Trustee and Trust, e.g., "Bob Smith, Trustee of the Bob Smith Trust dated 4/1/03")
(Do not change the vesting on the IRA portion of said account.)
Enclosed for your records is a Trust Certification.

Dated: ________________________

(Sender)

ASSIGNMENT

The undersigned, (1)____________________, owner of the (complete description of asset):

hereby Assigns same to (49)____________________ and (if applicable)(58)____________________ Trustee(s) of the (1a)____________________________ dated (48)________________. The undersigned, as Trustee(s) of said Trust hereby accepts said Assignment.

Date:
(40)____________________

(1)____________________

(1b)____________________

(4)____________________

(Optional)
STATE OF __________________________)
) ss.
COUNTY OF __________________________)

On ________________, 200__ before me, the undersigned, a Notary Public in and for said county and state, personally appeared (1)______________ and (4)______________, personally known to me (or proved to me on the basis of satisfactory evidence) to be the person(s) whose name(s) is/are subscribed to the within instrument and acknowledged that he/she/they executed the same in his/her/their authorized capacity(ies), and that by his/her/their signature(s) on the instrument the person(s), or the entity upon behalf of which the person(s) acted, executed the instrument.

WITNESS my hand and official seal.

____
Notary Public in and for said County and State

INDEX

F

G

H

I

J

L

M

N

P

Q

R

S

T

U

V

W

Your #1 Source for Real World Legal Information...

SPHINX® PUBLISHING

An Imprint of Sourcebooks, Inc.®

- Written by lawyers
- Simple English explanation of the law
- Forms and instructions included

SOCIAL SECURITY Q&A

Learn more about Social Security through the questions asked by people around the country. Includes information on child, spousal, survivor, and retirement benefits.

192 pages; $12.95;
ISBN 1-57248-216-8

THE 529 COLLEGE SAVINGS PLAN

Demonstrates how everyone can save for college—tax free. Explains the 529 Plan state requirements for all participating states and clarifies beneficiary issues.

248 pages; $16.95;
ISBN 1-57248-238-9

THE MOST VALUABLE PERSONAL LEGAL FORMS YOU'LL EVER NEED, 2E

This book contains more than 100 ready-to-use forms. It includes such forms as mortages, employment applications, sales contracts, and change of adddress.

288 pages; $26.95;
ISBN 1-57248-360-1

See the following order form for books written specifically for California, the District of Columbia, Florida, Georgia, Illinois, Maryland, Massachusetts, Michigan, Minnesota, New Jersey, New York, North Carolina, Ohio, Pennsylvania, Texas, and Virginia!

What our customers say about our books:

"It couldn't be more clear for the lay person." —R.D.

"I want you to know I really appreciate your book. It has saved me a lot of time and money." —L.T.

"Your real estate contracts book has saved me nearly $12,000.00 in closing costs over the past year." —A.B.

"...many of the legal questions that I have had over the years were answered clearly and concisely through your plain English interpretation of the law." —C.E.H.

"If there weren't people out there like you I'd be lost. You have the best books of this type out there." —S.B.

"...your forms and directions are easy to follow." —C.V.M.

Sphinx Publishing's Legal Survival Guides
are directly available from Sourcebooks, Inc., or from your local bookstores.

For credit card orders call 1–800–432–7444, write P.O. Box 4410, Naperville, IL 60567-4410, or fax 630-961-2168

Find more legal information at: **www.SphinxLegal.com**

Sphinx® Publishing's National Titles

Valid in All 50 States

Legal Survival in Business

The Complete Book of Corporate Forms	$24.95
The Complete Patent Book	$26.95
The Entrepreneur's Internet Handbook	$21.95
How to Form a Limited Liability Company (2E)	$24.95
Incorporate in Delaware from Any State	$24.95
Incorporate in Nevada from Any State	$24.95
How to Form a Nonprofit Corporation (2E)	$24.95
How to Form Your Own Corporation (4E)	$26.95
How to Form Your Own Partnership (2E)	$24.95
How to Register Your Own Copyright (4E)	$24.95
How to Register Your Own Trademark (3E)	$21.95
Most Valuable Business Legal Forms You'll Ever Need (3E)	$21.95
Profit from Intellectual Property	$28.95
Protect Your Patent	$24.95
The Small Business Owner's Guide to Bankruptcy	$21.95

Legal Survival in Court

Crime Victim's Guide to Justice (2E)	$21.95
Grandparents' Rights (3E)	$24.95
Help Your Lawyer Win Your Case (2E)	$14.95
Jurors' Rights (2E)	$12.95
Legal Research Made Easy (3E)	$21.95
Winning Your Personal Injury Claim (2E)	$24.95
Your Rights When You Owe Too Much	$16.95

Legal Survival in Real Estate

Essential Guide to Real Estate Contracts (2E)	$18.95
Essential Guide to Real Estate Leases	$18.95
How to Buy a Condominium or Townhome (2E)	$19.95
How to Buy Your First Home	$18.95
Working with Your Homeowners Association	$19.95

Legal Survival in Personal Affairs

The 529 College Savings Plan	$16.95
The Antique and Art Collector's Legal Guide	$24.95
Cómo Hacer su Propio Testamento	$16.95
Cómo Restablecer su propio Crédito y Renegociar sus Deudas	$21.95
Cómo Solicitar su Propio Divorcio	$24.95
The Complete Legal Guide to Senior Care	$21.95
Family Limited Partnership	$26.95
Gay & Lesbian Rights	$26.95
Guía de Inmigración a Estados Unidos (3E)	$24.95
Guía de Justicia para Víctimas del Crimen	$21.95
How to File Your Own Bankruptcy (5E)	$21.95
How to File Your Own Divorce (5E)	$26.95
How to Make Your Own Simple Will (3E)	$18.95
How to Write Your Own Living Will (3E)	$18.95
How to Write Your Own Premarital Agreement (3E)	$24.95
Inmigración a los EE. UU. Paso a Paso	$22.95
Living Trusts and Other Ways to Avoid Probate (3E)	$24.95
Manual de Beneficios para el Seguro Social	$18.95
Mastering the MBE	$16.95
Most Valuable Personal Legal Forms You'll Ever Need	$24.95
Neighbor v. Neighbor (2E)	$16.95
The Nanny and Domestic Help Legal Kit	$22.95
The Power of Attorney Handbook (4E)	$19.95
Repair Your Own Credit and Deal with Debt (2E)	$18.95
El Seguro Social Preguntas y Respuestas	$14.95
Sexual Harassment:Your Guide to Legal Action	$18.95
The Social Security Benefits Handbook (3E)	$18.95
Social Security Q&A	$12.95
Teen Rights	$22.95
Unmarried Parents' Rights (2E)	$19.95
U.S. Immigration Step by Step	$21.95
U.S.A. Immigration Guide (4E)	$24.95
The Visitation Handbook	$18.95
The Wills, Estate Planning and Trusts Legal Kit	&26.95
Win Your Unemployment Compensation Claim (2E)	$21.95
Your Right to Child Custody, Visitation and Support (2E)	$24.95

Legal Survival Guides are directly available from Sourcebooks, Inc., or from your local bookstores.

SPHINX® PUBLISHING ORDER FORM

BILL TO:		SHIP TO:	
Phone #	Terms	F.O.B. Chicago, IL	Ship Date

Charge my: ☐ VISA ☐ MasterCard ☐ American Express

☐ Money Order or Personal Check

Credit Card Number

Expiration Date

SPHINX PUBLISHING NATIONAL TITLES

Qty	ISBN	Title	Retail	Ext.
	1-57248-238-9	The 529 College Savings Plan	$16.95	
	1-57248-349-0	The Antique and Art Collector's Legal Guide	$24.95	
	1-57248-148-X	Cómo Hacer su Propio Testamento	$16.95	
	1-57248-226-5	Cómo Restablecer su propio Crédito y Renegociar sus Deudas	$21.95	
	1-57248-147-1	Cómo Solicitar su Propio Divorcio	$24.95	
	1-57248-166-8	The Complete Book of Corporate Forms	$24.95	
	1-57248-229-X	The Complete Legal Guide to Senior Care	$21.95	
	1-57248-201-X	The Complete Patent Book	$26.95	
	1-57248-163-3	Crime Victim's Guide to Justice (2E)	$21.95	
	1-57248-251-6	The Entrepreneur's Internet Handbook	$21.95	
	1-57248-346-6	Essential Guide to Real Estate Contracts (2E)	$18.95	
	1-57248-160-9	Essential Guide to Real Estate Leases	$18.95	
	1-57248-254-0	Family Limited Partnership	$26.95	
	1-57248-331-8	Gay & Lesbian Rights	$26.95	
	1-57248-139-0	Grandparents' Rights (3E)	$24.95	
	1-57248-188-9	Guía de Inmigración a Estados Unidos (3E)	$24.95	
	1-57248-187-0	Guía de Justicia para Víctimas del Crimen	$21.95	
	1-57248-103-X	Help Your Lawyer Win Your Case (2E)	$14.95	
	1-57248-164-1	How to Buy a Condominium or Townhome (2E)	$19.95	
	1-57248-328-8	How to Buy Your First Home	$18.95	
	1-57248-191-9	How to File Your Own Bankruptcy (5E)	$21.95	
	1-57248-343-1	How to File Your Own Divorce (5E)	$26.95	
	1-57248-222-2	How to Form a Limited Liability Company (2E)	$24.95	
	1-57248-231-1	How to Form a Nonprofit Corporation (2E)	$24.95	
	1-57248-345-8	How to Form Your Own Corporation (4E)	$26.95	
	1-57248-224-9	How to Form Your Own Partnership (2E)	$24.95	
	1-57248-232-X	How to Make Your Own Simple Will (3E)	$18.95	
	1-57248-200-1	How to Register Your Own Copyright (4E)	$24.95	
	1-57248-104-8	How to Register Your Own Trademark (3E)	$21.95	
	1-57248-233-8	How to Write Your Own Living Will (3E)	$18.95	
	1-57248-156-0	How to Write Your Own Premarital Agreement (3E)	$24.95	
	1-57248-230-3	Incorporate in Delaware from Any State	$24.95	
	1-57248-158-7	Incorporate in Nevada from Any State	$24.95	
	1-57248-250-8	Inmigración a los EE.UU. Paso a Paso	$22.95	
	1-57071-333-2	Jurors' Rights (2E)	$12.95	
	1-57248-223-0	Legal Research Made Easy (3E)	$21.95	
	1-57248-165-X	Living Trusts and Other Ways to Avoid Probate (3E)	$24.95	
	1-57248-186-2	Manual de Beneficios para el Seguro Social	$18.95	
	1-57248-220-6	Mastering the MBE	$16.95	
	1-57248-167-6	Most Valuable Bus. Legal Forms You'll Ever Need (3E)	$21.95	
	1-57248-130-7	Most Valuable Personal Legal Forms You'll Ever Need	$24.95	
	1-57248-098-X	The Nanny and Domestic Help Legal Kit	$22.95	
	1-57248-089-0	Neighbor v. Neighbor (2E)	$16.95	
	1-57248-169-2	The Power of Attorney Handbook (4E)	$19.95	
	1-57248-332-6	Profit from Intellectual Property	$28.95	
	1-57248-329-6	Protect Your Patent	$24.95	
	1-57248-344-X	Repair Your Own Credit and Deal with Debt (2E)	$18.95	
	1-57248-350-4	El Seguro Social Preguntas y Respuestas	$14.95	
	1-57248-217-6	Sexual Harassment: Your Guide to Legal Action	$18.95	
	1-57248-219-2	The Small Business Owner's Guide to Bankruptcy	$21.95	
	1-57248-168-4	The Social Security Benefits Handbook (3E)	$18.95	
	1-57248-216-8	Social Security Q&A	$12.95	
	1-57248-221-4	Teen Rights	$22.95	
	1-57248-236-2	Unmarried Parents' Rights (2E)	$19.95	
	1-57248-218-4	U.S. Immigration Step by Step	$21.95	
	1-57248-161-7	U.S.A. Immigration Guide (4E)	$24.95	
	1-57248-192-7	The Visitation Handbook	$18.95	
	1-57248-225-7	Win Your Unemployment Compensation Claim (2E)	$21.95	
	1-57248-330-X	The Wills, Estate Planning and Trusts Legal Kit	&26.95	
	1-57248-138-2	Winning Your Personal Injury Claim (2E)	$24.95	
	1-57248-333-4	Working with Your Homeowners Association	$19.95	
	1-57248-162-5	Your Right to Child Custody, Visitation and Support (2E)	$24.95	
	1-57248-157-9	Your Rights When You Owe Too Much	$16.95	

CALIFORNIA TITLES

Qty	ISBN	Title	Retail	Ext.
	1-57248-150-1	CA Power of Attorney Handbook (2E)	$18.95	
	1-57248-337-7	How to File for Divorce in CA (4E)	$26.95	
	1-57248-145-5	How to Probate and Settle an Estate in CA	$26.95	
	1-57248-146-3	How to Start a Business in CA	$18.95	
	1-57248-194-3	How to Win in Small Claims Court in CA (2E)	$18.95	
	1-57248-246-X	Make Your Own CA Will	$18.95	
	1-57248-196-X	The Landlord's Legal Guide in CA	$24.95	
	1-57248-241-9	Tenants' Rights in CA	$21.95	

FLORIDA TITLES

Qty	ISBN	Title	Retail	Ext.
	1-57071-363-4	Florida Power of Attorney Handbook (2E)	$16.95	
	1-57248-176-5	How to File for Divorce in FL (7E)	$26.95	
	1-57248-177-3	How to Form a Corporation in FL (5E)	$24.95	
	1-57248-203-6	How to Form a Limited Liability Co. in FL (2E)	$24.95	
	1-57071-401-0	How to Form a Partnership in FL	$22.95	
	1-57248-113-7	How to Make a FL Will (6E)	$16.95	
	1-57248-088-2	How to Modify Your FL Divorce Judgment (4E)	$24.95	
	1-57248-144-7	How to Probate and Settle an Estate in FL (4E)	$26.95	
	1-57248-339-3	How to Start a Business in FL (7E)	$21.95	
	1-57248-204-4	How to Win in Small Claims Court in FL (7E)	$18.95	
	1-57248-202-8	Land Trusts in Florida (6E)	$29.95	
	1-57248-338-5	Landlords' Rights and Duties in FL (9E)	$22.95	

Form Continued on Following Page **SUBTOTAL** ______

To order, call Sourcebooks at 1-800-432-7444 or FAX (630) 961-2168 (Bookstores, libraries, wholesalers—please call for discount)

Prices are subject to change without notice.

Find more legal information at: **www.SphinxLegal.com**

SPHINX® PUBLISHING ORDER FORM

Qty	ISBN	Title	Retail	Ext.
		GEORGIA TITLES		
____	1-57248-340-7	How to File for Divorce in GA (5E)	$21.95	____
____	1-57248-180-3	How to Make a GA Will (4E)	$21.95	____
____	1-57248-341-5	How to Start a Business in Georgia (3E)	$21.95	____
		ILLINOIS TITLES		
____	1-57248-244-3	Child Custody, Visitation, and Support in IL	$24.95	____
____	1-57248-206-0	How to File for Divorce in IL (3E)	$24.95	____
____	1-57248-170-6	How to Make an IL Will (3E)	$16.95	____
____	1-57248-247-8	How to Start a Business in IL (3E)	$21.95	____
____	1-57248-252-4	The Landlord's Legal Guide in IL	$24.95	____
		MARYLAND, VIRGINIA AND THE DISTRICT OF COLUMBIA		
____	1-57248-240-0	How to File for Divorce in MD, VA and DC	$28.95	____
		MASSACHUSETTS TITLES		
____	1-57248-128-5	How to File for Divorce in MA (3E)	$24.95	____
____	1-57248-115-3	How to Form a Corporation in MA	$24.95	____
____	1-57248-108-0	How to Make a MA Will (2E)	$16.95	____
____	1-57248-248-6	How to Start a Business in MA (3E)	$21.95	____
____	1-57248-209-5	The Landlord's Legal Guide in MA	$24.95	____
		MICHIGAN TITLES		
____	1-57248-215-X	How to File for Divorce in MI (3E)	$24.95	____
____	1-57248-182-X	How to Make a MI Will (3E)	$16.95	____
____	1-57248-183-8	How to Start a Business in MI (3E)	$18.95	____
		MINNESOTA TITLES		
____	1-57248-142-0	How to File for Divorce in MN	$21.95	____
____	1-57248-179-X	How to Form a Corporation in MN	$24.95	____
____	1-57248-178-1	How to Make a MN Will (2E)	$16.95	____
		NEW JERSEY TITLES		
____	1-57248-239-7	How to File for Divorce in NJ	$24.95	____
		NEW YORK TITLES		
____	1-57248-193-5	Child Custody, Visitation and Support in NY	$26.95	____
____	1-57248-351-2	File for Divorce in NY	$26.95	____
____	1-57248-249-4	How to Form a Corporation in NY (2E)	$24.95	____
____	1-57248-095-5	How to Make a NY Will (2E)	$16.95	____
____	1-57248-199-4	How to Start a Business in NY (2E)	$18.95	____
____	1-57248-198-6	How to Win in Small Claims Court in NY (2E)	$18.95	____
____	1-57248-197-8	Landlords' Legal Guide in NY	$24.95	____
____	1-57071-188-7	New York Power of Attorney Handbook	$19.95	____
____	1-57248-122-6	Tenants' Rights in NY	$21.95	____

Qty	ISBN	Title	Retail	Ext.
		NORTH CAROLINA TITLES		
____	1-57248-185-4	How to File for Divorce in NC (3E)	$22.95	____
____	1-57248-129-3	How to Make a NC Will (3E)	$16.95	____
____	1-57248-184-6	How to Start a Business in NC (3E)	$18.95	____
____	1-57248-091-2	Landlords' Rights & Duties in NC	$21.95	____
		OHIO TITLES		
____	1-57248-190-0	How to File for Divorce in OH (2E)	$24.95	____
____	1-57248-174-9	How to Form a Corporation in OH	$24.95	____
____	1-57248-173-0	How to Make an OH Will	$16.95	____
		PENNSYLVANIA TITLES		
____	1-57248-242-7	Child Custody, Visitation and Support in PA	$26.95	____
____	1-57248-211-7	How to File for Divorce in PA (3E)	$26.95	____
____	1-57248-094-7	How to Make a PA Will (2E)	$16.95	____
____	1-57248-112-9	How to Start a Business in PA (2E)	$18.95	____
____	1-57248-245-1	The Landlord's Legal Guide in PA	$24.95	____
		TEXAS TITLES		
____	1-57248-171-4	Child Custody, Visitation, and Support in TX	$22.95	____
____	1-57248-172-2	How to File for Divorce in TX (3E)	$24.95	____
____	1-57248-114-5	How to Form a Corporation in TX (2E)	$24.95	____
____	1-57248-255-9	How to Make a TX Will (3E)	$16.95	____
____	1-57248-214-1	How to Probate and Settle an Estate in TX (3E)	$26.95	____
____	1-57248-228-1	How to Start a Business in TX (3E)	$18.95	____
____	1-57248-111-0	How to Win in Small Claims Court in TX (2E)	$16.95	____
____	1-57248-110-2	Landlords' Rights and Duties in TX (2E)	$21.95	____

SUBTOTAL THIS PAGE ______

SUBTOTAL PREVIOUS PAGE ______

Shipping— $5.00 for 1st book, $1.00 each additional ______

Illinois residents add 6.75% sales tax ______

Connecticut residents add 6.00% sales tax ______

TOTAL ______

To order, call Sourcebooks at 1-800-432-7444 or FAX (630) 961-2168 (Bookstores, libraries, wholesalers—please call for discount)

Prices are subject to change without notice.

Find more legal information at: **www.SphinxLegal.com**